Rachel,

I am forever endebted to you for your excellent strengths-based needs assessment of Yonkers. I learned a lot from that article (Chapter 3 pp 62-66) which reflects your optimistic attitude toward life!

Thanks!

Mike

Handbook of Program Evaluation for Social Work and Health Professionals

Handbook of Program Evaluation for Social Work and Health Professionals

MICHAEL J. SMITH

OXFORD
UNIVERSITY PRESS

2010

OXFORD
UNIVERSITY PRESS

Oxford University Press, Inc., publishes works that further
Oxford University's objective of excellence
in research, scholarship, and education.

Oxford   New York
Auckland   Cape Town   Dar es Salaam   Hong Kong   Karachi
Kuala Lumpur   Madrid   Melbourne   Mexico City   Nairobi
New Delhi   Shanghai   Taipei   Toronto

With offices in
Argentina   Austria   Brazil   Chile   Czech Republic   France   Greece
Guatemala   Hungary   Italy   Japan   Poland   Portugal   Singapore
South Korea   Switzerland   Thailand   Turkey   Ukraine   Vietnam

Published by Oxford University Press, Inc.
198 Madison Avenue, New York, New York 10016

www.oup.com

Oxford is a registered trademark of Oxford University Press.

Library of Congress Cataloging-in-Publication Data
Smith, Michael J.
Handbook of program evaluation for social work and health professionals / Michael J. Smith.
p.   cm.
Includes bibliographical references and index.
ISBN 978-0-19-515843-4
1. Human services—Evaluation.   I. Title.
HV40.S6152 2010
361.2—dc22
2009017439

9   8   7   6   5   4   3   2   1

Printed in the United States of America
on acid-free paper

Acknowledgments

I want to acknowledge the support that Hunter College gave me by granting me a sabbatical that made it possible to complete this book. I extend my thanks to the administration of the College, Jennifer J. Raab, President, and Vita Rabinowitz, Provost and Vice-President for Academic Affairs.

Special thanks go to Jacqueline B. Mondros, Dean of the Hunter College School of Social Work, for supporting my work in the sabbatical year and since she has been dean. Darrell P. Wheeler, Associate Dean for Research, provided an excellent exemplar article on the place of logic modeling in evaluation. Professors Roberta Graziano and Barbara Rinehart were generous in providing their data on a pilot evaluation of the Hunter College MSW Program in Health and Aging as a way to develop goals along the lines of the KBASS model.

My colleagues at the Hunter College Employee Assistance Program and I participated in the development of a model of accountability for that program which helped in discussions of program monitoring. This includes Florence Vigilante, Paul Kurzman, Pat McDonald, Cristina Ramirez, and Roberta Graziano.

Michael Fabricant, Executive Officer of the Ph.D. Program in Social Welfare at Hunter College and the CUNY Graduate Center, and I collaborated on the mental health evaluation used in the qualitative data analysis section of the chapter on data analysis.

His leadership on the PSC-CUNY faculty union also helped establish more generous sabbaticals so that I could finally take one. Contributions from the many colleagues who were doctoral students at Hunter and who developed exhibits for this book include Benjamin Shepard, Brande Maury, Danielle Strauss, and Susan McConnaughy.

Master's students Gina Arnone and Katie Mc Kaskie had important points to make about resilience and program implementation, respectively.

Esther Rohatiner of the School of Social Work did a splendid job on typing major parts of the manuscript.

Tony Tripodi, who was the Moses Professor at the Hunter College School of Social Work, was supportive of this work and generous in providing insight on how to stay on track and complete this project.

My many years of teaching an evaluation course in the Master's program in Health Advocacy at Sarah Lawrence College as an adjunct faculty member were extremely rewarding and provided the health portion of this book. The administrators in the program there were especially supportive, and their students produced many excellent beginning evaluations. Susan Guma, Dean of Graduate Studies, Rachel Grob, Associate Dean for Graduate Studies, and Laura Weil, the current Director of the Master's Program in Health Advocacy program have all been friends and colleagues throughout my time there. Marsha Hurst, former Director of Health Advocacy and currently Director of the MS Program in Narrative Medicine at Columbia University set up excellent internships for most of the students who had example evaluations in this book. Examples of different types of evaluation were generously provided by students in the Health Advocacy program: Gail Garrick, Deborah Guiffre, Eleanor Scarcella, Sherisse Webb, Shawna Irish, and Nike Whittemore. Marleise Brosnan, Stephanie Krieg, and Adrienne Wilbrect provided insights on program description, discussed in Chapter 4 from their work in my course. Likewise, Melvin Finkelstein provided excellent intensive case data on the evaluation of a senior outreach program.

Caroline Lieber, Director of the Human Genetics Graduate Program, let me teach research related to students' Master's theses. Peggy Cottrell's thesis in the Master's Program in Human Genetics provided an excellent example of a pre–post evaluation study.

Oxford University Press provided great support, especially from Maura Roessner, Senior Editor for Social Work at Oxford, who showed great patience in waiting for the manuscript. Mallory Jensen and Nicholas Liu were always there to help in any way. Lynda Crawford, senior production editor, and Jerri Hurlbutt, copy editor, and Suwathiga Velayutham, project manager, put in excellent work in the production of the book.

Professor Albert Roberts, whose passing was a great shock, provided encouragement throughout this process and was instrumental in collaborations with Oxford University Press.

Francis G. Caro, Professor Emeritus of the Gerontology Program at the University of Massachusetts Boston and an expert in evaluation, provided excellent support throughout my career and shared with me his passion for and research on home care for developmentally disabled children. He was an extremely valuable reviewer for the manuscript and provided solid guidance on changes that needed to be made.

Last and most important are my family: Rosemarie Rerisi Smith, who has always been loving and supportive and, in this case, patient; my daughters Elizabeth Smith Thielemann and Suzanne Smith, who are now experienced educators completing their doctorates; my grandchildren Matthew Robert Thielemann and Ryan Michael Thielemann, who love their "ga-ga" and "pa-pa," and my son-in-law Robert Thielemann and future son-in-law Philip Carlucci, who are great additions to our family.

Michael J. Smith
New York

Contents

List of Exhibits

Handbook of Program Evaluation for Social Work and Health Professionals

1

Introduction to Program Evaluation

Purpose of the Book

The primary audience for this book is social work and health professionals employed in social agencies and health care settings. This includes direct-service staff, program managers, program executives and administrators, and planners in health and social service organizations. The book aims to provide a quick and simple overview of program evaluation by outlining the process of conducting an evaluation study. The purpose is to provide one resource where health and social work professionals could access evaluation basics *and* research methods, as well as current trends in evaluation. For most professionals much time has passed between their graduate and undergraduate research courses, so a review of research methods is needed. If research methods can be integrated with program evaluation, so much the better.

Likewise, the book can be used as a primary or secondary text in a program evaluation course in social work and health. In this book, research methodology is presented so that the student will not have to review a basic research methods text but can study basic research methods in the context of program evaluation in an integrated way. Also, if only one evaluation research course is part of a graduate program, the book has even more relevance. Integrating evaluation and research methods should work both for professionals in the field and for students in social work and health programs.

This book stresses important reasons why social work and health professionals need to know more about evaluation:

1. Program evaluation is integral to the work of a social work or health professional. Program evaluation flows from the self-reflection and self-evaluation of professionals providing the service and is crucial for people who care about the consumers they serve and the services they provide.

2. Increasingly, administrators and direct-service staff have been called upon to engage in program evaluation activities. As administrators and staff play increasing roles in evaluation research and evaluation processes, more knowledge is needed.

3. Professionals may be asked to do small scale program evaluations, especially when there are limited resources for evaluation. In fact, limited resources for evaluation have been the rule rather then the exception, Organizations are less likely to have or hire their own evaluation staff, or the evaluation consultants that have been hired are contracted for fewer hours. Yet, programs need to be evaluated. The simple concepts and examples in this book can help professionals conduct a small scale evaluation.

4. If the organization hires a consultant to conduct an evaluation or has evaluators on staff, someone needs to supervise, manage, and oversee the evaluator's work. Social work and health professionals need to learn how to supervise and relate to program evaluators and appreciate the mindset of an evaluator in determining how the program is working and if it is successful. Likewise, professionals need to see that evaluators appreciate the difficulties in planning and implementing a quality program so that the evaluators provide a fair assessment of the program.

5. As funding pressures persist, both direct-service and administrative staff have been asked to develop proposals for outside funds. Part of the process of developing a program grant for funding includes the development of a methodology for evaluating the program. In a way, evaluation can be the path to increased funding.

6. While most programs have hardly enough money to provide the service to consumers, social and health organizations need a commitment to evaluation that translates into at least 5% and maybe as much as 15% of the program budget for evaluation. This represents a commitment to the consumers who are served as well as the staff who provide services, the organization providing the program, and the larger community served.

7. Professionals need to know how to read and understand evaluation reports. They need to know how to digest the program evaluation literature in a field to assess how a particular practice or program is delivered, and to assess if the program is reaching its goals and outcomes.

8. Evaluations help elucidate and describe how programs and interventions work, which strategies they are using, which goals they are pursuing, and how the program was monitored and assessed.

9. As the evaluation field continues to stress participatory evaluations and empowerment evaluations in which stakeholders are involved with planning and carrying out the evaluation (see Chapter 3), more knowledge of evaluation will be needed so that professionals can participate in this process of participatory and collaborative evaluation as an equal partner representing their own professional voice and the voices of consumers in this process.

10. By emphasizing the strengths and assets of a program in evaluation (see the strengths-based perspective Chapter 3), professionals can appreciate the value of programs, communities, and the consumers that programs serve.

11. If evidence-based practice (Chapter 3) continues to play a role in the development of programs and practice methods from evidence based primarily on research findings from experimental studies, why not consider all evaluation research findings, not just those from experimental studies in the development of how professionals practice.

We hope the reader will appreciate the themes developed in this book. One primary, simple theme is the importance of *describing* the program before evaluating it. A description of the program informs everyone and can aid in uncovering program processes and elucidating how the program is operating. Another theme is the value of formative evaluations such as program monitoring and process evaluations and the use of qualitative data. One should not shy away from formative evaluations for fear that these evaluations are not impact assessments with experimental designs and do not "prove" the causal connection between program and outcomes. This fear may become more prevalent now if the trend toward evidence-based practice continues, and only practice methods that have been validated through experimental designs are allowed as acceptable professional practice.

An Introduction to Program Evaluation

In this book, *program evaluation* is defined as the use of research methods to assess the planning, implementation, and outcomes of social work, health, and other human service programs. Human service professionals in social work, health, psychology, counseling, education, and other human service professions need to know about the techniques and trends in program evaluation. Program evaluation operates in the real world of social and health programs. Evaluation is part and parcel of the work of a human service or health professionals. Program evaluation is not some dreary laboratory-type of research; it is research involving real people, real programs, and real life experiences.

Program evaluation can be used to help answer the following types of questions about social, health, and human service programs:

- Are the consumers who are referred to a job-training program actually attending? Is the program preparing people for the job market? Are they finding jobs?
- Are people with substance abuse problems achieving short- and long-term success in the treatment program they are attending? Are they helped by the groups, the individual treatment, or the additional services they receive?
- Which types of preventative services are provided to parents of children who are in danger of being placed in foster care, and which services are the parents using more often?
- Is a women's health outreach and breast cancer screening program for Latina women reaching the intended groups of women?
- Is a hospital-based program for children with chronic illness improving their self-image or helping them feel less depressed and more integrated into life at home and in school?
- Is a caregiver group for the relatives of patients with Alzheimer's helping clients find services and lowering their stress levels and the overall impact of caregiving?
- Are health-care advocates providing effective interventions when they meet with groups of seniors to provide information about Medicare and Medicare Part D on prescription drug coverage?
- Are clients in a homeless shelter being successfully referred to short-and longer-term housing, along with supportive services?
- Is the work of a patient representative in a hospital in connecting with families of patients resulting in the patient feeling more positive about health care services?

- Are children with attention deficit hyperactivity disorder (ADHD) being treated in such a way that their lives have improved and their symptoms have been reduced?

Through program evaluation these very basic questions about health and human service programs can be answered. Everyone involved with social work, health, and human service programs needs to be involved in program evaluation and needs a deep commitment to evaluation. **Very concretely, at least a modest amount, around 15% of a program budget, should be allocated to evaluate a program.**

An Ethical Responsibility to Evaluate

Program evaluation is serious business because professionals have an ethical responsibility to evaluate their practice with patients or clients, and an ethical commitment to see that the programs where they are working are successful. Professional interventions must also be held accountable. Thus ethical professionals need to know about program evaluation and how it is conducted so that they can know what is working and what is not working. Program evaluation can be used to provide these answers and show if the whole program is on the right or wrong track and whether parts of the program are working or not. Ultimately, programs need to commit to some level or standard below which they should not be operating, be that high consumer satisfaction, decreased hospitalizations, increased longevity, or reduced social isolation.

Also, regardless of whether public or private program funds are being spent, someone needs to be held accountable for expenditures. The financial commitment to program evaluation must be clear, consistent, and permanent.

Accountability extends to all the departments of professionals employed in health and human service organizations. Organizations and by extension their employees need to provide quality services. In so doing, these professionals have a responsibility for evaluation which extends to the following parties:

A. The consumers and clients served
B. The community in which the program is located
C. Their professional organizations and licensing agencies
D. The larger organization that sponsors and runs the program

E. The organizations and branches of government and the voluntary sector that have funded the program and are charged with monitoring the program

F. Themselves, the professionals providing the service.

In sum, program evaluation will *always* be needed because the accountability question will never go away. In organizations that do not conduct routine program evaluation, accountability is much more difficult to resolve. The following example illustrates this.

One agency had a volunteer program in which college students volunteered to assist the agency in helping the elderly with home visits, companionship, shopping, etc. The agency believed that the volunteers and the elderly benefited greatly from this program. In addition to the help given to the seniors, the agency "thought" that many of the volunteers went into human service professions when they graduated from college. The board of directors wanted to know if this program was working. When the question of the program's effectiveness came up, the executive director always recounted one or two success stories about what the companionship meant to the elderly and the one or two college students who were pursuing careers in human services in college. No one ever surveyed the seniors in the program to determine what the service meant to them. Also, no one followed up with the volunteers to see whether they were personally fulfilled by providing the assistance and whether this experience influenced their choice of a career path in human services. Every year, the program faced possible reduction of funds or elimination, and there were no solid data to argue for or against support for the program. Every year, administrators squirmed in their chairs as the board looked for indicators of the success of the program. Every year, the accountability question was raised; it never went away.

Professionals who do not take program evaluation seriously appear to not care about the program, the results of the program, or the results of their practice. They appear to not care about their clients and consumers, the community they serve, the organization providing the program, the government agencies and foundations providing the funding, their own professions, or themselves. While there are difficult issues in program evaluation such as determining the means of measuring results and whether all the variables involved in one program can be measured, a professional who takes the stance that no evaluation is possible takes an untenable position. There is no alternative to program evaluation, and agencies and organizations that do not take evaluation seriously are not being accountable and are not acting responsibly.

Practice to Program Level

A health or human service professional must constantly be searching for the most efficient and effective methods to use. A human service professional needs to know if the patients, clients, students, etc., are making progress. A social worker doing group work or interventions in groups wants to know that members of the group are better off after the group sessions. A hospital or program administrator wants to know if patients and clients are satisfied with the health service they received. A community planner wants to know if there is a need for a youth center in their community. All these are questions are central to the day-to-day activities of a human service professional, and these questions can be answered through the type of research known as program evaluation.

Social and health professionals learn self-evaluation as they reflect on their practice using critical thinking skills to assess the methods they are using and the outcomes achieved or not achieved by those methods (Gambrill, 2006). Self-reflection is needed as well as a connection to the evaluation literature in a particular program field to help assess which types of methods work best in different program settings.

Fetterman describes how evaluation is innately linked to practice by professional processes of *self-evaluation*, which leads to the evaluation of whole programs.

> Employees often collaborate with both their supervisors and clients to establish goals, strategies for achieving these goals and documenting progress, and realistic timelines . . . . This individual self-evaluation process is easily transferable to the group or program level.
> (Fetterman, 1996, p. 13)

The professional assesses the program interventions given and whether or not a case achieved certain goals or outcomes. The following examples indicate how program evaluation proceeds from questions about the effects of practice to questions about the effects of practice on groups of cases or consumers.

Example of the Connection Between Practice Evaluation
and Program Evaluation

As members of a treatment team, a social worker, psychologist, psychiatrist, case manager, and other mental-health professionals are treating one person with chronic mental illness. The person with mental illness has received psychiatric treatment, medication, and supportive group and individual counseling. The professionals assess whether or not this treatment protocol is working for this client. In a process similar to program evaluation, the treatment team assesses the client against some standards of goal achievement such as symptom reduction, increased social functioning, reduced hospitalization, improved family life, and fewer periods of unemployment.

Program evaluation methods come into play when practitioners and administrators want to assess the whole program and whether it is working for groups of clients or every client in the program. An evaluation study can help determine which types of clients have had the most successful outcomes when measured against standards such as reducing symptoms and improving social functioning. An evaluation study will also reveal which intervention protocols seem to be associated with greater success or failure.

Example of Group Practice Where Program Evaluation Can be Applied Directly

A health-care educator or social worker is conducting a psychoeducational group for the relatives of persons with serious mental illness. The purpose of the program is to help relatives obtain services for the family member with mental illness and to increase their knowledge of diagnosis and treatment in the mental health field, as well as learn techniques to help with the illness. Since the health care worker is assessing how the program is affecting groups of clients, a small scale program evaluation can be conducted with all the relatives attending this one group. If a number of health-care workers are running these groups in the same setting, the program evaluation can study the performance of all the groups and would be even more reflective of the relative success of the program.

The evaluation could help determine whether the relatives' knowledge of the diagnosis and treatment of mental illness had increased at the conclusion of the program, whether they were more aware of services at the end of the program, and whether they learned the techniques to help the family member with their illness. The evaluation could also help determine if the relatives' attitudes toward the family member with mental illness improved once they learned more about mental illness.

There should be an ethical priority to conduct such program evaluations. In this example, evaluation can be used to determine if the relatives' attitudes toward the mentally ill relative improved, worsened, or remained unchanged. Also, data from program evaluation can be analyzed to see if there is a relationship between attitudes and knowledge. Did understanding more about mental illness improve their attitudes about their relative? Did they have even more concerns and stress once they learned about the seriousness of the diagnosis? While families may learn more about mental illness, this knowledge could make them more pessimistic about the relative with serious mental illness. They might then need more help in relating to that family member.

An ethical practitioner needs to know about the effect of his or her interventions on the families being served. Whether this is labeled "critical thinking" or "evidence-based practice", self-assessment and self-reflection are always the professional activities of an ethical practitioner.

Professionals' Roles in Program Evaluation

In either a direct service or an administrative capacity, all professionals in a health or human service field have roles as evaluators. They all have responsibilities that involve the planning, creating, and administering of programs, and evaluation is a key part of those activities. Involvement in program evaluation can take a number of forms:

- Involvement in program development and writing program proposals for funding often include developing a plan on how the program will be evaluated.
- The professional administering a new program may be responsible for conducting a program evaluation and may be charged with supervising a staff person or a consultant hired to evaluate the program.
- There may be limited funds for doing an evaluation and the health or human service professional may have to carry out a small scale evaluation on their own.
- Sometimes a government agency will be coming in to evaluate the program. The job is then to determine if the evaluation is conducted in a proper manner.
- The professional may be part of a working group conducting an evaluation and will need knowledge of evaluation methods, techniques, and issues to participate in the process of program evaluation even if a consultant is conducting the evaluation. Empowerment evaluations (see Chapter 3) focus on the participation of all parties in the planning and implementation of the evaluation at every step in the process.

If an outside organization is conducting an evaluation of a program, the professional needs to know what the evaluators are doing and how they are doing it. Is the program being described correctly? Is it being studied correctly?

Does the evaluation seem to be fair and impartial? Does the evaluation adhere to the basic principles of program evaluation? Knowledge about the research methods used to conduct the study is essential. Knowledge about the new trends in evaluation is also important. For example, did the evaluation address any of the new trends in evaluation, such as a strengths-based perspective on evaluation (see Chapter 3)?

Professionals as Consumers of Program Evaluation

Professionals are consumers of evaluation studies when they engage in either reflective practice or program planning and program development. Assessment of the research literature on evaluations of programs and practice techniques is important in planning new programs and in examining current programs. In planning new programs and interventions, human service professionals need to commit to the concept of evidence-based practice and need to understand and examine the evaluation literature in a particular field to determine the level of success that people have had using similar types of programs or interventions. Review of the evaluation literature is an essential part of needs assessment (see Chapter 5). As program evaluations are conducted, a review of the literature and assessment of the rates of success in an area of practice (see Chapter 4) establish a broader context for the one program being evaluated and provide a comparative database for the program being evaluated. Knowledge of evaluation issues and techniques is needed to properly review and assess the literature.

Assessment of the evaluation literature helps give direction to the types of programs that are proposed. For example, a social worker takes a new job in a social agency that has a program treating people with agoraphobia. The main intervention used by the agency is supportive, psychosocial counseling. The social worker has just graduated from a master's program and has reviewed the literature on evaluations of programs for people with agoraphobia, which showed that a set of behavioral interventions such as desensitization were the most successful interventions. The social worker encourages the agency to get consultation and expertise in the use of behavioral techniques.

Definition of a Program

What is a program? In its most simple form, a *program* is a strategy or intervention that has been planned and conducted on a group of people to achieve some desirable consequence. Sometimes programs are very broad in scope. For example, a Child Health Plus Program providing health services to a state population of children not covered by medical insurance is a program, as is a national program such as Head Start, which provides preschool services for lower-income groups. Programs can be also be very narrow and delimited, for example, a food pantry serving homeless people in a community within a 25-block radius.

To help define programs, it may be easier and more valuable to describe services we clearly know are programs.

- A job-training program teaches skills to people to make them more employable.
- A substance abuse program attempts to get people off drugs and alcohol.
- A preventive-service program tries to assist parents in keeping their families together and prevent foster care placement.
- A Head Start program tries to accelerate the intellectual development of preschoolers.
- A senior citizens' center provides mid-day lunches, discussion groups, trips, exercise, social activities, and access to home care and other social services.
- An advocacy program for parents of developmentally disabled children that helps them obtain in-home services.
- An outpatient health program for patients on dialysis that tries to help these patients see the value of regulating their diets and fluid intake.
- An outpatient drug treatment program for adolescents that tries to help them stay off drugs.
- Employee Assistance Programs that promote health and wellness among employees, treat substance abuse problems, and provide psychological counseling for employees and referral to community services.
- Violence prevention programs in high schools attempt to reduce violence and the potential for violence in the student population.
- An Alcoholics Anonymous program helps people with alcohol problems maintain short- and long-term sobriety.

The intent behind all of these programs is to do something productive, to achieve a desirable consequence, to achieve goals or outcomes. Note that a consequence, goal, or outcome is in the definition of a program and is central to what a program does.

Program Evaluation: An Exciting and Dynamic Field

Programs are diverse and complex phenomena. This makes program evaluation exciting! Program evaluation is a very dynamic and sophisticated activity.
Here are a number of reasons why the field is so exciting:

- Human relationships and personalities go into the planning,
  implementing, and evaluation of programs. People often run the
  program within the context of their own personality quirks or traits,
  their own orientations to practice, and their day-to-day manner of
  operating. Many human relationships are involved in one program.
- Since programs cost money, there is always money involved. There will
  be winners and losers. Internal politics are a very large part of program
  evaluation. People naturally have a stake in their own professional
  advancement. At times, evaluation and evaluation findings can take a
  back seat to one's person's professional career and organizational
  advancement.
- Evaluations also involve concepts and theories upon which the
  programs are based. There are many theories about how programs
  should operate. Program evaluation overlaps with program planning
  and conceptualizing and developing interventions that work, thus it is a
  very dynamic and exciting activity that involves translating ideas into
  practice. In one context behavior modification might be the theory being
  used in the program, and in another context psychosocial support may
  be the intervention being used.
- Programs operate in organizations where some professionals are being
  promoted and others are not. These decisions are not necessarily based
  on the findings from evaluation studies. Politics and power are at stake
  and determine whose views and values may be implemented.
- There is also political pressure from outside the organization that
  helps determine the programs of the organization and how they
  should be run.

Evaluation Provides Increased Knowledge-Building
About Programs

In program evaluation, a research methodology is used to generate knowledge
about programs, program interventions, program theories, and program practices. Programs can be in the fields of health, education, social services,

employment programs, services for the elderly, health outreach, probation and parole, drug and alcohol treatment and prevention, and mental health, to name a few. In all these fields of service, there is a literature of program evaluation that describes the programs and measures their levels of success. As a consumer of evaluation studies, professionals need to use the literature and knowledge about different types of programs, their distinctive features, and their relative levels of success.

In addition to being a consumer of evaluation studies, participation in evaluation provides hands-on knowledge about which types of interventions work the best. What are the positive aspects and outcomes in programs? What worked? What outreach methods were used? Were they effective? What professional interventions were employed? What was done to consumers, patients, or clients once they came in for service? Were the methods effective? What parts of the program and program activities did not work?

Maybe the outreach methods were good and people came for service but did not like the type of service provided. Perhaps there were problems in implementing the program, hiring staff, or securing office space. Perhaps the service was set up in a location that was too remote and people did not engage in the program. Maybe the cost of service was too high and a larger group of people could not be accommodated. Maybe people dropped out of service after a short time. Why was the program not successful, or, which parts of the program worked and which did not work?

A knowledge base of program interventions exists in the literature, and that knowledge base should be used when a program is being planned. Through program evaluation the program strategies and their impact can be determined. Good professionals and program planners stay attentive to service delivery and the variables involved in the program intervention; they do not treat the program as a "black or unknown box." They show concern about program processes (see Chapter 4). Human service professionals and program planners need to generate this knowledge of program interventions through evaluation studies.

Because programs often promise too much "bang for the buck," it is important to be grounded in the literature. Too many times programs do not have the intensity or strength to produce the intended effect. For instance, think of programs that try to treat alcoholism or drug abuse with 10 contacts with a social worker or health professional. Or consider a program that provides four group sessions on independent living with 18-year-olds who have lived for 10 years in foster care, with the intent that they will be gainfully employed and self-sufficient by the end of the four sessions. Consider whether or not there are unrealistic expectations in the program being planned or implemented. Is there a program logic? Does what is planned make sense?

The following example shows how expecting too much from an intervention can create false expectations. An urban program used computer matching of the characteristics of senior citizens who needed housing with the housing that was available for rentals in the same city. The program planners assumed this would be a successful program and would match 80% to 100% of the seniors with the housing vacancies. In evaluating the program, the agency found that matches where seniors actually found housing represented only 10% of the total cases. At that point, the program planners reviewed the literature and examined the knowledge base of other programs that employed computer matching to find seniors housing. They found that most of these programs achieved only a 15% to 20% rate of successful matches, so their experience was not a unique one. If they had consulted the knowledge base of programs when planning the program, they might have come up with a different program with a more intense and powerful intervention such as providing housing specialists and case managers to become more involved with the seniors and the housing program and landlords. In this way, they would have increased the level of program or intervention to achieve more successful housing placements.

Likewise, when planning an employee assistance program in a university setting the knowledge base of employee assistance programs in both university and other settings should be consulted. Program descriptions of other employee assistance programs exist in the literature, as well as program evaluations that assess the success of different models in attracting employees to the program and their success rates.

In the literature on employee assistance programs there are broad-brush models that provide a variety of counseling and advocacy services to employees, such as help with personal problems, assistance with finances and consumer debt, help finding day care for employees' children, and assistance with home care and nursing home placement for elderly parents. These broad-brush models appeal to a wider variety of employees and attract more clients.

There are also employee assistance programs that focus on a drug or alcohol program model. These models are used to help the organization or university assist employees with substantial drug or alcohol problems. These programs are not aimed at the average employee but rather serve a much narrower population of employees. Likewise, their success rates resemble the lower rates of success of substance programs in general. The knowledge base for employees with substance abuse problems is more clearly grounded in the literature of success rates in the more general field of substance abuse.

In addition to these pure types, there are hybrid or mixed program models of broad-brush and substance abuse programs. Those planning the university-based employee assistance program need to consult the knowledge base of employee assistance programs to determine which model should be used and understand the implications of choosing a particular program model.

A commitment to program evaluation helps the program planning process. Before the program becomes operational, a needs assessment study should be conducted to determine the needs of employees. As the program becomes operational, a program monitoring study should be conducted to determine how the program is doing with the first employees served. Ultimately, an outcome-oriented evaluation should be conducted to determine the rate of success of the program. Needs assessment, program monitoring, and outcome-oriented evaluations are all part of the field of program evaluation, which will be described in the Chapter 2.

Enhancing Belief Systems in Practice: Developing a Critical Mindset

Professionals in health and human services believe in what they do. For example, a health professional treating clients with agoraphobia has a system of desensitization techniques that he teaches clients to use if they see a panic attack coming on. The professional needs to be fully trained in these techniques, and needs to believe that they will work. Enthusiasm and commitment are needed to learn the skills, believe in their value, and use them in practice. In fact, research shows that hopefulness in practice improves the results of practice (Polansky & Kent, 1978).

However, belief, enthusiasm, and commitment are not enough. Regardless of whether a professional is working in health settings, child welfare programs, schools, or counseling agencies, it is not sufficient to simply believe in what one is doing. Professionals must also think critically about their practice and the program and try to determine what is being done and whether or not the practice is achieving its goals. Program evaluation can help in assessing both the processes and outcomes of practice. Program monitoring and evaluation are crucial to enhancing the beliefs that support the practice.

Belief in yourself as a professional must be combined with a critical mindset of questioning some of your own techniques and improving your practice. Professionals need to incorporate some of the questioning attitudes of program evaluation and review their cases to see which ones were successful and which were not. In addition, they need to study other factors that need to be present for a program to be successful. Programs have structural and organizational components that affect success or failure. For example, the most skilled professionals could be hired for a job-training program, but if the program only allows for six sessions of job training when 6 months of training is needed, all the belief and skill in the world will not make the program successful. Through program evaluation the structural components that affect practice can be examined. Evaluation of the program is the best way to look intensively at the program and enhance the confidence of all involved in the program.

Improved Program Planning

There is no doubt that program evaluation leads to better, more specific program planning. When programs are examined through the eyes of a research methodology, good things happen. In program evaluation clear and comprehensive descriptions of programs are written if that program is going to be researched and evaluated, thus giving everyone a clearer picture of how the program works. Having clarity about the program means it could be replicated if found to be successful. Comprehensive program descriptions include the theories on which the program is based, the intervention methods that are being used, the outreach methods used to get people in to the program, and the types of clients to be served (see Chapter 4).

Program evaluation contributes to more specific, targeted program planning. For example, in program evaluation, we develop measures of program and practice goals. This process produces a more specific statement and development of possible program goals. In program evaluation, data collection techniques such as questionnaires are developed to ask consumers, patients, and clients about the services they received. Developing questionnaires helps in conceptualizing the program and its objectives and goals more clearly. Once the data are in and the evaluation report is written, program planners, administrators, and direct-service staff can meet to discuss specific findings that have specific implications for improving the program. The discussion is often much more pointed than the usual program-planning meeting, and specific results are fed back to make specific improvements in the program.

Promoting the Consumer Perspective

Program evaluation can be a methodology for ensuring consumer empowerment. At a very beginning level of this process, consumers have a greater voice in organizations that conduct formal interviews to ask the recipients of service about their experiences in the program. The voice of the consumer can add balance to the more powerful voices of the administrators and direct-service professionals who are employed in the program. By understanding what the consumer received and did not receive from the program in their own words, we have a greater understanding of what the program achieved and what it did not achieve.

Involvement of consumers in program evaluation takes many forms. It might be based on a mailed or handed-out questionnaire in which the consumer can rate the service, or on a more in-depth personal interview in which the consumer describes their experience of the program. Consumers might also be involved in the planning and implementation of the program evaluation. Involvement of the consumer in evaluation can help prevent an attitude of "blaming the victim," which occurs when we attribute our failures in program planning and design to the clients or patients because of some personal defects or limitations (Ryan, 1971). Consumer empowerment is such an important topic in program evaluation that it will be discussed separately in Chapter 3.

Evaluation

What is an evaluation? *Evaluation* implies some type of judgment, assessment, or appraisal. Judgments are a part of everyday life and are a basis for decision-making. What time should I get up? Should I take that job or not? Whom should I choose for a mate? In which school should I enroll my children? Based on their appraisals, people decide to act or not to act and how to act. Assessments and judgments are sometimes made quickly and instinctively. For example:

- I see it's a nice day, so I'll go for a walk on the beach.
- There is no food for dinner, so I'll go out to the supermarket.
- I will skip a day of work because the U.S. Open Tennis Championships is being held at Flushing Meadows.

At other times, we put more time and effort into our assessments. Sometimes we go and collect data as part of our assessment and measurement process, and parts of a research methodology are employed. For example:

- If I am not sure where to eat in New York City, I will use the Zagat restaurant guide and use their reviews to help me make my decision.

- If you are not sure if you should marry Charlie or not, you might do a number of things. First, you might pray a lot. But you can also employ informal research methodologies. You can observe and collect data on Charlie in social situations to see if he has the personal and interpersonal characteristics you enjoy. You can observe and collect data on your close interactions with Charlie. You can talk to friends about their perceptions about Charlie. You can go for a weekend with Charlie to visit his relatives. You could see how Charlie interacts with any children that are around in these family visits. You can have discussions with him to see if you want the same things in life in terms of where to live and whether to have children or not. After collecting all this information, you can analyze it to make the decision of whether you will marry Charlie or not. While this shows how you can collect and analyze data to help in your evaluation and appraisal of whom to marry, do not take this too far. Do not tell Charlie you are collecting data to help you make a more objective decision. I can tell you from experience that my wife does not like it when we are involved in an important life decision and I say this would make for an interesting research study.

The Charlie example shows how we could collect and analyze data to help us in evaluating a situation in our personal lives. In program evaluation, we go even further and conduct a formal study to collect data as the basis for our decision-making about a program. Program evaluation refers to a process in which research methods are used to assess programs. Social science research methods are used to assess programs.

Most professionals work in organizations where employees are evaluated. Personnel evaluations are used to determine how well an employee is performing in his or her job. The decision-making context can be determining whether the employee should be promoted, remain in the same position, or be dismissed. Often research-type instruments are used in this process. For example, simple rating scales might ask a supervisor to assess an employee's "overall performance" or "work attendance" as "excellent," "very good," "good," "fair," or "poor." However, these are evaluations of employees or personnel evaluations, not program evaluations, since they do not conform to the characteristics of a research methodology and their purpose is not to generate knowledge about a program.

In many of our personal and professional evaluations we make use of data. We do this when we rate a course we are taking on a 10-point scale. Or, if we are rating employees on a scale from "excellent (5)" to "poor (1)," we can assign them a number or amount. So some *quantitative* number could be used. For example, if we wanted to evaluate a movie based on the reviews on TV, we might see if it got two thumbs up, one thumb up, or no thumbs up, so the possible ratings are 2, 1, or 0.

Likewise, we could use *qualitative* data to assess or evaluate. A supervisor might write some descriptive paragraphs about how well or poorly a particular employee is performing as part of the assessment. We could also read the actual movie review to find out what the reviewer liked or did not like about the movie.

Both quantitative and qualitative data are used in program evaluation. *Quantitative data* are structured data that can be analyzed using statistics. For example, if we ask clients or patients to rate the program and we present the categories of "excellent," "very good," "good," "fair," and "poor, we might find that 75% rated the program as "excellent." Or, if they are simply asked, "Did you like the program? Yes or No," we might find that 80% liked the program.

Qualitative data are more descriptive, less structured data that are analyzed with the intent of looking for trends and patterns. We might ask an open-ended question: "What did you like about the program?" From the answers to this question we would get descriptive data in the client's or patient's own words, and we would analyze the data by reporting trends of the major ways in which the program helped.

Studies usually have both quantitative and qualitative data in them. What makes a study quantitative or qualitative is the major type of data collected. So, if we conduct a survey of patients or clients with mostly closed-ended questions answered by "yes or no," or "strongly agree, agree, uncertain, disagree, or strongly disagree," we have a quantitative study. If a group of clients is asked mostly open-ended questions about the benefits of the program, the approach, called a *focus group*, produces mostly qualitative data and the study would be a qualitative study.

Use of a Research Methodology

In program evaluation, a research methodology is used according to the standards of social science research with formality and rigor (Weiss, 1998, p. 4). Research questions such as "Is the program achieving its goals?" or "Is the program reaching the intended audience?" are formulated. Because program evaluation is research, the principles of social science research are applied, and the systematic, standardized methods of social science are used to assess social, health, and educational interventions and programs. These methods are used to help formulate evaluative research questions, provide a guide for observing and collecting data that will help answer the research questions, and provide principles on how to analyze the data collected.

Program Evaluation as a Research Method

How are the criteria of formality and rigor in research fulfilled? There are a number of characteristics of research methods that need to be present for evaluation to be considered research.

First, there is problem formulation, in which the research focuses on certain questions. In program evaluation, the research questions and hypotheses are more fixed than they are in basic research. For example, basic research may focus on the way in which aggressive advocacy works, as a way to get people needed services. In program evaluation, however, aggressive advocacy might be one piece of a program designed to provide case management services and get services to people.

In program evaluation, the research questions revolve around the program. Is there is a need for the program? Is the program being implemented properly? Are the clients or patients satisfied with the program? Is the program achieving its goals and objectives? Problem formulation involves the program and is focused on either planning issues in the program and needs assessment, or observation and monitoring of the program in operation, or determining whether the program is achieving significant outcomes.

The second feature of research in program evaluation is the research design, or the plan of how the study will be carried out. Design is the logic or plan of the study. Will a survey design be used to produce correlational knowledge—whether certain program activities are correlated with certain program outcomes? Will an experimental or quasi-experimental design be employed to contrast two different forms of the program to see which is better?

The third characteristic involves sampling issues. How will cases be selected to evaluate the program? How will clients or professionals be selected for interviews? Will the sample be representative of the population of clients or workers? Has an unbiased sample been selected? Did we select the best cases or the worst cases?

The fourth feature is measurement. Measurement must be consistent and substantive, meaning it must be reliable and valid. *Reliability* refers to the consistency of measurement, so in measuring the client's sense of efficacy, a person's efficacy or empowerment score this week should be about the same as the score we get 3 weeks from now, given no major changes in the clients' life. Likewise, we want to have a valid measure of efficacy, that is, we want to have items in the measure that are conceptual and substantive in relation to empowerment. For example, clients might be asked how powerful they feel, if they think it makes a difference when they express their opinion, or if they think they can affect the types of services they can get.

The fifth characteristic of a research method is that there are principles of data collection. In constructing a questionnaire, clear and simple questions must be asked so that are not misunderstood. In conducting personal interviews, interactional effects that can influence the data need to be minimized. If data are collected through direct observation of the program, a clear method for collecting the data needs to be planned.

Finally, there are principles of data analysis. In quantitative research, accepted statistics exist to determine if there are statistically significant relationships between program intervention and program outcome. For qualitative data, acceptable qualitative-analysis techniques need to be used to determine if the trends in the data are valid. A thorough examination of the qualitative data can elicit the possible reasons and mechanisms for the program working or not working.

Program Evaluation as a Practice Method

In addition to being a research methodology, program evaluation is also a practice method. Program evaluators provide a service to funding agencies, service organizations, program administrators, direct-service staff, and clients or consumers.

What activities are involved in the practice of program evaluation? The program evaluator helps everyone keep their commitment to the overall mission of the organization and to the goals and objectives of the program. The evaluator helps the organization sort out program planning and implementation issues to assist in program development. The evaluator helps develop richer descriptions of the program and the intervention and practice methods. The evaluator helps identify the larger context of the program by reviewing literature related to the program and identifying the local, state, and national policy and program issues. The evaluator participates in discussions about the program goals and objectives, and identifies which goals may be more achievable given the level of program intervention. The evaluator helps direct-service staff uncover the practice principles that are used in the program. In that sense, the evaluator empowers consumers and staff (see Chapter 3).

Those who practice program evaluation need to overcome resistance and have excellent human-relations skills. People often feel threatened. Decisions are being made about the program. Jobs and funding might be lost. All parties involved need to be reminded that all have the same overall goal: better services to consumers and improvements in program quality. The evaluator is deeply involved in a participatory process and needs to care about the organization and the program, the organization's mission, the staff at all levels, the clients served, the larger community served, and the sponsors of the program.

In Chapter 2, some of the characteristics of the practice of ethical program evaluation will be discussed.

Program Evaluation as a Political Process

The practice of program evaluation means involvement in a political process. Weiss defines evaluation as a rational (research) process that takes place in a political environment (Weiss, 1998, p. 47). The decision to create the program involved a political process through which funds were allocated. Then there were decisions about how to implement the program and whom to hire to run the program. Since judgments about the program are the result of evaluation studies, there may be winners and losers, and changes in program funding.

The political process, based on power and consensus, carries more weight than evaluation based on research methods. However, in the long run, research on the program will help us to make better decisions and improve the political process. Patton has stated the issue clearly and eloquently.

> The evaluation gamble in an imperfect world is that data can make a difference; that some scientific logic and attention to empirical reality is better than none; and that some . . . grounding and concern for empirically derived judgments is better than a world of pure unadulterated politics based entirely on might. (Patton, 1987, p. 103)

As part of evaluation practice, Rossi, Freeman, and Lipsey (2004) discuss "tailoring the evaluation" to the political and organizational environment of the sponsoring agency. As the evaluator interacts with program funders, administrators, direct-service staff, and consumers of the program, the personal, professional, and political views of participants will be revealed.

People involved with the program have their own views about what should be done to improve the program. Often their views are personal and depend on who they are in the system. The administrators might say, "The real problem is that the direct-service workers do not really understand the program concepts." The direct-service staff might say, "The problem is the administrators. There is no leadership. They will not give us enough resources to provide adequate service." What does the evaluator do? The evaluator engages people in a relationship and moves people to consider the more substantive issues in the program and its implementation. The evaluator moves toward developing a plan for the evaluation, which becomes the evaluator's contract with the organization.

> Somewhat different perspectives from these various groups are to be expected and, in most instances, the evaluator will attempt to develop an evaluation plan that reflects all significant views and concerns, or at least is compatible with the prevailing views among the major parties. (Rossi et al., 1999, p. 47)

The evaluation plan must be a written document that sets out the purpose and scope of the evaluation, the questions about the program that will be answered, the research design specifying what type of study will be conducted (qualitative–quantitative, experimental study, survey, direct observation) and how the data will be collected and analyzed, and the budget needed to implement the evaluation and write the final report.

Summary

1. Learning the techniques and methods of program evaluation is essential for the human service professional. Program evaluation can help answer questions that are central to professional tasks in social work, health, psychology, counseling, education, and other forms of human services.
2. The commitment of human service professionals to the people they serve includes an ethical responsibility to evaluate. The need for program evaluation is essential and will never go away. Therefore, the commitment to evaluation needs to be clear, consistent, and permanent.
3. Human service professionals have direct roles to play in evaluation and are also consumers of evaluation studies.
4. Social, health, and educational programs are interventions planned to achieve desirable consequences or outcomes.
5. Program evaluation helps increase knowledge about social, health, and human service programs. Evaluation assists in developing and planning new programs and in documenting current programs.

6. Through program evaluation, human service professionals fulfill their accountability to the consumers served, to the community, to professional organizations and licensing agencies, to program funders, and, of course, to themselves.

7. Program evaluation enhances the belief systems underlying practice and helps develop a critical mindset. Belief in and commitment to practice is important; however, belief systems need to be supplemented with the documentation of program successes and failures. Also needed is documentation of how programs were implemented and whether or not certain goals were achieved.

8. Program evaluation leads to improved program planning, better program descriptions, increased specification of the program goals and objectives, and improved program development.

9. Program evaluation can be used to promote the consumers' perspective and as a method for achieving consumer or client empowerment.

10. An evaluation is a judgment, and the end product of evaluation is a series of judgments made about the program. This fact can make everyone involved nervous about evaluation outcomes.

11. Program evaluation is a research method that includes formulating research questions, planning a type of study to answer those questions, collecting and analyzing data, and formulating conclusions about the program.

12. Program evaluation is also a practice method in which the evaluator interacts with administrative and program staff to identify what the program is about, how it is being implemented, what the program goals are, and how well it is achieving those goals.

13. Program evaluation takes place in action settings where political decisions are made. Program evaluation is part of that political decision-making process and can improve the process of program development by providing data on the program.

REFERENCES

Fetterman, D.M. (1996). Empowerment evaluation: An introduction to theory and practice. In Fetterman, D.M., Kaftarian, S.J., & Wandersman, A. (eds.) *Empowerment Evaluation: Knowledge and Tools for Self Assessment and Accountability.* Thousand Oaks, CA: Sage Publications, pp. 3–46.

Gambrill, E.D. (2006) *Social Work Practice: A Critical Thinker's Guide.* New York: Oxford University Press.

Polansky, N.A., & Kent, M.L. (1978). Troubled people. In Maas, H. (ed.) *Social Service Research: Reviews of Studies.* Washington, DC: National Association of Social Workers.

Rossi, P.H., Lipsey, M.W., & Freeman H.E. (2004). *Evaluation: A Systematic Approach.* Thousand Oaks, CA: Sage Publications.

Ryan, W. (1971). *Blaming the Victim.* New York: Pantheon Books.

Weiss, C.H. (1998) *Evaluation: Methods for Studying Programs and Policies.* Upper Saddle River, NJ: Prentice-Hall.

2

Types of Program Evaluation Studies

The Formative–Summative Typology

One of the major concepts in the field of program evaluation is the *formative–summative* typology. These terms were first introduced by Scriven in 1967. Since then they have taken on a life of their own and have become key concepts and orientations in the evaluation field. Scriven originally meant to classify evaluations by what was done with the end product of evaluation. *Formative evaluations* are more preliminary evaluations in which results and data are fed back into the program in order to improve the intervention. *Summative evaluations* are outcome-oriented evaluations that assess the effectiveness of programs in more final terms—for example, should the program be funded or not, should the approach taken be abandoned, and should the program be started from scratch, with a totally new intervention. Scriven originally referred to the end product of evaluation and the decision-making context, which can be formative or summative.

Today the formative–summative typology extends beyond the ways in which evaluation results are used to a series of dimensions associated with formative or summative evaluations. *Formative–summative* can refer to types of evaluation studies or types of program goals, and can focus on program activities or outcomes, the stage of program development, who is sponsoring the evaluation, and the underlying values of those sponsoring the evaluation.

1. Types of studies can be formative or summative. Formative evaluations are associated with initial evaluations of new programs and are most helpful during the design and pre-testing of programs to guide the design process (Rossi et al., 2004, p. 34). Studies examining the need for the program, needs-assessment studies, studies of program process and operations, and program-monitoring studies tend to be formative. Summative evaluations are more likely associated with goal- or outcome-oriented studies. Some studies focusing on outcome have experimental types of designs that aim to establish cause-and-effect relationships between the program and its outcomes. These are often referred to as "impact assessment" studies, which are definitely classified as summative studies.

2. The goals that programs measure can be formative or summative. Formative studies tend to examine proximate, short-term goals, so-called soft goals or indicators. For example, the following questions might be asked: "How many people are coming to the program?" "How satisfied are they with the services?" "Do they have a sense of connectedness to the program?" Summative studies tend to examine more ultimate goals or outcomes, the very specific measurement of "hard" goals, and how well the program is achieving these outcomes. In these studies the following questions might be asked: "Did those in the group experience increases in knowledge?" "Did those attending an alcoholism treatment program maintain sobriety?" "Did the child's IQ score improve?" "Did the health of the patient improve?"

3. Formative evaluations focus more on program activities, and summative evaluations focus more on goals and outcomes. Those interested in program development would more likely take a formative stance to evaluation. An incremental approach to programs is implied. The resources of summative evaluators are more clearly directed at studying the goals and outcomes of programs rather than program activities.

4. Formative–summative evaluation is also correlated with the stage of program development. Formative evaluations are more likely conducted in the initial stages of program development when feedback of results to improve the program can be especially useful. Formative studies reflect the reality of program planning and development. For example, often it is useful to initiate a pilot program or a pretest program on a small sample of clients and assess the results with a formative evaluation. Summative evaluations are more appropriate when the program has reached a stable state and has had some time to develop when program goals and outcomes can be fully assessed.

5. Formative or summative strategies can be indicative of who is sponsoring the evaluation. Evaluators within the agency who are funded by the agency where the program is located are more likely to be doing formative evaluations when results are feedback for program development. Inside evaluators are more likely to interact with administrators and staff, and it is easier for them to implement the "feedback loop" when staff and administrators can meet to discuss improving the program. Outside evaluators who are sponsored by funding agencies are more likely to engage in summative studies to assess the ultimate value of spending money on the current interventions or programs.

6. The formative–summative typology often represents the underlying values of those sponsoring the evaluation. Those in favor of formative evaluations are frequently those committed to furthering program development. They support improving the approaches taken to improve the social, educational, or health problems that the program is designed to solve. Summative evaluations are more often used by fiscal conservatives who may be leery of the amount of funding spent or they may question the value of the particular programs being evaluated even before the evaluation has been conducted and before the tabulation and reporting of results.

Which type is better—formative program evaluations or summative evaluations? The ultimate value of the typology is to gain an appreciation of the values of both approaches. Formative evaluations focus on directing and improving the program. Summative evaluations focus on the public trust and funding and the need for all programs to truly achieve their goals. Overall, a holistic outlook and some type of balance between the formative and summative approaches may be the best. For example, if you are doing a formative evaluation in which the major focus is on describing program activities, the types of goals to be achieved should also be described. Likewise, in a summative study focusing on outcomes, attention should be paid to how the service is being delivered and is viewed subjectively by those attending the program.

For instance, in evaluating a Head Start program, a "summative" approach could be used to look at "hard" outcome indicators such as the child's improvement in IQ or other standardized tests to indicate the child's level of learning. However, on the more "formative" side of things, "softer" outcomes such as the child's attitude toward school and the parent's feelings about the program could be studied. Or, formative evaluations could include direct observations of the

Head Start classrooms to examine how the educational program was taught and whether or not children seemed to be connecting to the program.

All program evaluations can be located within the formative–summative typology. Generally, when doing evaluations, it may be more productive to stay on the formative side of evaluation. Formative evaluations that improve and develop the program are especially productive. Formative studies are more concerned with the types of program changes that are needed. For example, a formative study can show problems with outreach and suggest better ways to do outreach into the community. Formative evaluations reflect practice more. Practitioners, supervisors, and administrators know that programs are always changing, with modified results, and formative evaluations can help document those changes. One of the values of science is replication, and formative studies are better at describing the program activities so that a program can be replicated if we want to implement the program in another community. Even in summative studies that emphasize program outcomes, the program and its implementation, program activities, and program processes need to be addressed. On the other hand, a focus on program activities without program goals or outcomes violates the very nature of a social, health, or educational program.

Types of Evaluation Studies

We can take the formative–summative typology and deepen it by examining different types of evaluation studies to see what exciting possibilities exist for using program evaluation in program planning, development, and assessment. In describing different types of evaluation studies, be aware that *the categories of types of evaluation studies are not mutually exclusive.* There is overlap and parts of one type of study will appear in other types of studies. What determines the primary type of study is the major focus of the evaluation—is the focus on program need, program implementation, or program outcome? In the initial stages of planning an evaluation, it may be more important to think broadly about the different types that are possible, rather than worrying about which type of study you have.

There are many types of evaluation studies, depending on the focus of the investigation and the developmental stages of the program (Table 2.1). Questions may focus on the need for the program, program operations, or the achievement of proximate program goals or ultimate program outcomes and assessment of overall program impact.

One whole field of program evaluation consists of studies that focus on the need for the program. *Needs assessment studies* usually take place in the initial

TABLE 2.1. Types of Program Evaluations

Formative Evaluations for Program Planning and Development

1. Needs assessment studies
2. Program-monitoring studies
3. Process evaluations

Summative Evaluations for Program Development and Assessment

1. Goal or outcome evaluations
2. Impact assessment studies with experimental and quasi-experimental designs

planning stages of the intervention or program. Once program operations have begun, *program-monitoring studies* would be initiated to get some initial feedback on how the program is developing. Evaluations focusing more on in-depth descriptions of how the program or intervention is being delivered are *process evaluations*. *Goal or outcome studies* are conducted if the program has had some time to mature and achieve its goals. Finally, *impact assessment studies* consist of experimental and quasi-experimental studies to determine more finalized outcomes and cause-and-effect relationships between the program and its goals or outcomes.

Needs Assessment Studies

Needs assessment is the systematic appraisal of the type, depth, and scope of a problem that a program might ultimately address (Rossi et al., 2004, p. 102). Needs assessment studies are part of a program planning and development process which will ultimately result in planning the type of intervention which will meet those needs.

Needs assessment studies determine who the targets of the intervention or program should be and what the program should do to meet their needs. For example, a hospital was planning a resource center for cancer patients and their families, and a needs assessment study was conducted. Groups of patients and families were asked which types of medical information they needed and how they would likely obtain and use the information about the disease, for example, whether they would attend workshops, read articles, or use the Internet.

To determine the possible interventions that might be used, a literature search is often conducted to address the following questions: What are the needs for a particular target group that are found in the literature? What is the documentation in the literature about the program, its design, and success rates in meeting those needs? Which types of programs have met with success?

Which types of outreach are usually employed in these programs? These reviews of the literature and reviews of descriptions of similar programs are very useful in needs assessment and in *all* evaluations to determine the program models that have been used and how successful they have been.

Terms that Rossi, Lipsey, and Freeman (2004) use with needs assessment studies are "diagnosing" or "forecasting" need (p. 103). *Need* can be a very subjective term. What is thought to be a need in one historical era might be suspect in another time frame when different values exist. For example, the need to provide poor families with long-term economic support from the federal government seems to have disappeared as families were given a 5-year time limit through the Temporary Assistance to Needy Families (TANF or TANIF) program. In the disabilities field, the federal government provides economic support in Social Security Income (SSI) payments to parents of disabled children with moderate incomes. However, the need for practical in-home help for parents raising disabled children is not an established need in this country (Smith, Caro, & McKaig, 1987). When the tasks of projecting, diagnosing, and forecasting are added to the concept of need, needs assessment becomes a very imprecise science that is not always completely accurate.

Program-Monitoring Studies

Once the program starts, program-monitoring studies and process evaluations are the first types of evaluations that should be selected. In *program monitoring* the focus is on what is happening in the program and on assessing program operations. Was the projected need for the program substantiated by people who showed up to use the service? Is there a need for the program? Is there a program design? What is the design? Is it a good one? Is the design appropriate for those served? The purposes of monitoring includes determining if the program is being implemented as planned, which outreach methods are being used to get people into the program, how many clients are being seen, and if people are connecting to the program and receiving services.

Weiss (1998, pp. 50–51) sees program monitoring as a systematic process "generally undertaken by the funding agency that provides the financial support for the program or the oversight agency responsible for program standards." Program monitoring is achieved through a number of informal methods that might include, for example, making use of agency data about the program and determining if the program reached its intended audience or target population. Did the program serve those it was supposed to serve? What are the patterns of program use and utilization? What changes have taken place since the program was implemented? A monitoring study often examines data from the organization's management information system to help determine how many in the target population is the program reaching and what treatment is being given. Program-monitoring studies are extremely important; they should be routine if program planning and program development are truly taking place.

Process Evaluations

Process evaluation studies are related to identifying targets, determining if the program conforms to its design, examining issues of program implementation in the initial design, and "testing out" programs.

Process evaluations are characterized by more informal types of research, qualitative data on the program while it is in progress, use of agency reports, informal types of data collection, and other ways of examining what goes on inside the program. Process evaluations are more *descriptive* about the program than predictive about the program achievement of its goals and outcomes. The descriptive areas of the program can address how many people are attending or participating, the interventions or activities of the program, planning and implementation of the program, staff activities and practices, and client response to the initial program efforts. Weiss (1998, p. 51) indicates that a "process evaluation study gathers systematic data over a period of time about the implementation of program activities."

Process evaluations seem to be essential to a quality program planning process. Since evaluation is not always tied to the early stages of program development, one might assume that many program planning and development processes are flawed and could benefit from a process evaluation.

Goal or Outcome Evaluations

Goal or outcome evaluations focus on what happens to clients or patients after their participation in the program (Weiss, 1998, p. 33). These studies focus on assessing program goals or outcomes, the program's level of success, and its usefulness and failures. What are the goals and outcomes the program is trying to achieve? Were there unanticipated consequences of the program? The data for these studies could come from surveys where clients or consumers rate the level to which they thought certain goals or outcomes were achieved. Since the goals of many programs are to increase knowledge, improve attitudes and behavior, increase skill, or change a condition in a person, goal-outcome studies often make use of pre–post data and conceptualize goals and outcomes at a high level, which leads to sophisticated measurement and data collection and analysis of those goals and outcomes. For example, in a program serving seniors, measures of social isolation and social support are measured before and after the program to try and determine if the program reduced social isolation.

Impact Assessment Studies

When the program is more well-established, the major focus of study shifts to determining if it was the program that "caused" the outcome. This is an impact assessment study. *Impact assessments* are more formal research designs intended to show that it was the intervention and not some other factors that caused the effect or outcome. Impact assessments usually compare information for participants and non-participants to assess the "net effects" of the program. Impact assessments typically use pre-tests and posttests with program participants to determine if the program is achieving its goals. In impact assessments experimental and quasi-experimental designs are used to help fulfill this criterion. Experimental designs are those in which people are randomly assigned to a program group or a control group or to different forms of treatment. In quasi-experimental designs the group in the program is studied and compared to a sample of similar clients who are not in the program. Impact assessments are the most rigorous types of designs and the most summative studies. Their purpose is to uncover the true or net effects of the program that were caused directly by the program.

Example of Different Types of Studies in Evaluation of a Preventative Program for the Elderly

These different types of evaluation studies will now be described for the evaluation of a program of comprehensive services to the elderly in a large cooperative housing program. The program provided social, health, and senior services to the elderly residents of the cooperative housing. The goal of the program was to help seniors live independently and prevent nursing home placement. The program was located in cooperative apartments called "naturally occurring retirement communities," or NORCs—communities where there are high concentrations of the elderly. (See Chapter 4 for a full description of a NORC program.) In planning the evaluation, the evaluators had to determine which type of program evaluation would be conducted.

Since this was the program's first evaluation, a formative approach was selected rather than a summative approach. The purpose of the evaluation was to describe the program and how it worked in greater detail rather than to test the achievement of program goals in a more summative study.

Within the general category of formative studies, a needs assessment study was not appropriate because the program was beyond the planning stage and was already in operation, and some needs assessment had already been done in planning the program. Furthermore, agency administrators wanted initial feedback on how the program was progressing. It was decided that the study would look more like a process evaluation. A process evaluation was appropriate because the purpose of the study was to develop thorough, qualitative descriptions of the program model and its components, assess program implementation, and identify program and outcome variables that could be used in later outcome-oriented evaluations. So, for example, the evaluation questions became the following: How did the social-work practice part of the program work? What program interventions were provided by the home care workers, project nurses, psychiatric interns, and lawyers involved to assist the elderly in their own homes?

The major source of information was in-depth, qualitative interviews with staff, who were asked primarily open-ended questions to generate descriptions of the program's philosophy and interventions. Some qualitative interviews were also conducted with seniors who had used program services to get a client perspective on services, how they worked, and the possible advantages and disadvantages of those services.

Because the primary type of data collected was qualitative, the study described the process of how the program was implemented, how the service was delivered, and how the service progressed in different types of cases. If the primary type of descriptive data were more structured, for example, structured data from case records on what percentages of seniors got which services, hours of service given, length and duration of the services, length of time not in an institutional setting, the study would have been more clearly a program-monitoring study. The monitoring study would also have used structured surveys of seniors in which they would have rated the value of the services received and the value of their direct interaction with program staff, as well as structured surveys of staff with ratings of the services that more clearly seemed to help in promoting community care of the elderly.

The process evaluation conducted also made use of structured data from the program's management information system on how many seniors were served and the types and amounts of services received, but this was a secondary source in a process evaluation. It would be a primary data source in a program-monitoring study.

The process evaluation was especially useful in documenting program philosophy and goals and the subtle factors that could make a program like this one a success. For example, researchers asked staff about the program's philosophy and goals. Analysis of the qualitative data revealed a strong commitment to the program goals and philosophy and their enthusiasm in working to prevent nursing home placement.

> Working together to keep the clients at home, safe, in a livable manner. We're not big on nursing homes.... We pool our heads.... We keep the elderly in their own homes.
>
> To keep clients at home is our main goal and we are all committed to that. To keep them safe and at home.
>
> People stay in their own homes as long as possible. Homebound people can stay here and not be placed in nursing homes. It's great, especially for people whose families live far away.

Staff provided good descriptions of the comprehensive nature of the services provided:

> We offer case management, case assistance, advocacy; we'll get people Pampers, assist with writing a will.... We've got nurses here. We can get people physical or occupational therapists. We can get them home care or assistance with daily living. We make sure they have enough food. If they can't go out, we make sure the housekeeper gets food or we get volunteers to get food. On two or three occasions, I've gone out and bought food myself.

Qualitative descriptions were also provided about the advantages of providing services on site, in the cooperative apartment complex.

> We have doctors' offices in the housing complex and the hospitals have outpatient departments within a few blocks. Our services are all in one spot. As a tenant, you have lived all your life here. You are used to one geographic area and you don't have to move.

Likewise, workers provided excellent descriptions of each of the service provided—case management services, security service at the co-op, home care, financial management, discharge planning, day treatment, medical services, nursing care, psychiatric services, casework counseling services, bill paying and legal services. Thorough descriptions of the services and how they were used added greatly to the documentation of the program model and its components in this process evaluation.

If the program had had more time to mature and achieve its goals and we had already conducted process evaluations or program monitoring studies, goal or outcome evaluations might be the next studies done. The data for outcome studies could be the ratings by clients and workers on whether or not certain goals were achieved, given the services that were provided. Beginning measures of outcome could be achieved through consumer satisfaction surveys. Given the large variety of senior services provided in the program, seniors could be involved in rating overall and individual services and their effects. Average ratings for different service could be compared. The analysis could also examine the amount of services given by the functional abilities of the elderly to see if more services were directed at seniors with less functional abilities and in danger of being placed in a nursing home. The seniors could also rate the degree to which they thought certain goals of the program were achieved.

Another type of outcome study is a pre–post design. Here elderly clients are surveyed before service are received, and then at a later date when substantial service is in place. Pre- and post-measures can be taken on a variety of standardized scales and indices. For example, evaluators could study feelings of isolation, anxiety over the increased frailties of old age, feeling safe and secure at home, depression, and worries about the future to see if there were reductions in isolation, anxiety, depression, and worries about the future, and increases in safety and security. For example, results could show if, on a 20-point scale, feelings of isolation had a score of 15.52 before services but one that decreased to 9.50 after services, and a statistically significant reduction in isolation was achieved. One could look at service increases to see if increases in services were a factor in reducing isolation or if some other factor, for example, a family member moving closer to the elderly relative, was more related to reduced isolation.

The degree to which we can determine that it was the services provided and not other factors determines whether we are moving from an outcome evaluation to an impact assessment study. For example, we could conduct a quasi-experimental pre–post study on the elderly in the co-op housing program providing services and then select a co-op housing program with similar characteristics of elderly persons where no services or more traditional services are provided. An impact assessment study would measure both groups over a period of time to determine if, for example, the nursing home placement rate was lower for those who received comprehensive services. The two groups would be tested to show that they were similar in their functional abilities on an activities of daily living scale. Their demographic characteristics, dementia rates, number of family members involved, level of depression, and so on, would also be studied to see if they were similar. If no differences were found in the characteristics of seniors on these variables, and the seniors in the group that received comprehensive services showed a reduction in nursing home placements and reduced feelings of isolation, anxiety, and depression, then we could have more confidence in the finding that it was the program services that created a reduction in nursing home placement.

Both formative studies such as needs assessment, process evaluations, and program monitoring studies, and summative studies such as outcome evaluations and impact assessment studies produce data for more effective program planning and improved, more creative program development. Further examples of these different types of studies will be provided throughout the chapters of this book.

While there are different types of evaluation studies available, it is important to note that all evaluation studies proceed through nine steps, outlined below.

The Nine Steps in Program Evaluation

When we break down the program evaluation process, we find nine steps involved. The first six steps comprise planning of the study, and the last three steps involve implementation of the study.

Planning the Study

1. Describe the program (or the need to be assessed if conducting a needs assessment study).
2. Define the program activities and/or the goals of the program (or the needs if a needs assessment study).
3. Design or plan the study by selecting a type of study (e.g., an experimental study comparing different forms of the program, a survey of consumers, or a qualitative–formulative study involving personal interviews with a small number of consumers).
4. Choose a method of data collection (e.g., handed-out or mailed questionnaire, personal interview, direct observation, focus group, data from case records).
5. Decide on the type of sample you will have (e.g., a convenience sample of consumers who are available to you, a random sample from the population of consumers).
6. Construct the data collection instrument (e.g., the questionnaire or personal interview guide).

Implementing the Study

7. Implement the study by collecting the data.
8. Analyze the data using the techniques of quantitative or qualitative data analysis.
9. Report the results of your study: the findings, conclusions, implications, and limitations of your study.

These nine steps in program evaluation will be presented with examples, beginning with Chapter 4, Describing the Program.

Ethics in Program Evaluation

Ethics and ethical behavior are important in the field of program evaluation in three ways. First and foremost is the ethical imperative to evaluate practice and programs in social work and health, discussed in Chapter 1. Professionals need to engage in critical self-evaluation of their practice on a case-by-case basis as well as of their whole practice. They also need to evaluate themselves and in relation to all consumers who are given service in a program. As professionals determine the effect of their practice, they look for evidence of success, failure, and everything in between. This can be thought of as evidence-based practice. They can also examine evidence from the literature on which practice techniques have been validated through research (see Chapter 3). Professional practice should be based on "reflective practice" in which professionals think about their work and the outcomes it achieves (Gambrill, 2006). Program evaluation is part of that ethical imperative. Programs or practices affecting larger numbers of consumers need to be evaluated using program evaluation techniques to help ensure ethical practice and to make programs accountable.

The second way in which ethics is important to program evaluation is that research needs to conducted in an ethical manner, and human subjects who are participating in the research need to be protected. In program evaluation people are interviewed, sent questionnaires, or directly observed, or data from their cases are used. All research must go before institutional review boards (IRBs) to make sure that the rights of people are being protected and not violated as they participate in the evaluation study.

The final ethical issue is that the evaluator or evaluation team must maintain ethical behavior in conducting the evaluation. Principles and guidelines of how evaluators need to engage in ethical evaluation practice will be reviewed in this chapter.

The Protection of Human Subjects and Institutional Review Boards

Program evaluation and ethics go hand in hand. Evaluation research needs to adhere to ethical standards in protecting the human rights of research subjects, and evaluations should promote ethical behavior by making programs accountable. As a research methodology, evaluations, like other types of research, need to be examined by institutional review boards to ensure that the rights of research subjects are not being violated. The current federal standards for the protection of human subjects were developed because of previous violations of people's rights in some research studies and experiments, highlighting humankind's inhumanity to other humans in graphic ways.

In 2002, Oakes noted that the field of program evaluation has been slow to come to grips with IRB issues and the ethical treatment of human subjects. He also noted that most social scientists have poor training in this area and experience an inconsistent IRB process. Evaluators clearly need to protect human subjects and be able to estimate the risks of being a research subject.

During World War II, Nazi physicians conducted horrific experiments on prisoners who, among other things, were injected with live viruses to test vaccines and injected with poisons to study the effects of the poisons and how long it would take people to die from them (Annas & Gordon, 1992). After the war, these physicians were tried in a court of law at Nuremberg. The Nuremberg Code of Ethics was created as a standard for the ethical treatment of human subjects in research and to prevent other atrocities like these from occurring. The code established principles such as voluntary consent and the need to anticipate the risks to people as research subjects, and that these risks should not exceed the study's benefits.

In the United States in 1932, the U.S. Public Health Service sponsored the infamous Tuskegee Study, in which 399 poor African-American men with syphilis were denied treatment over a period of 40 years. During this time their spouses and children could also have been infected (Jones, 1981). The subjects were not even told that they had syphilis but were told they had "bad blood," a local term used for nonspecific diseases. Although they were told that they were being given treatment they received none, even though treatments were available to help their symptoms and even cure the disease, when penicillin was found to treat syphilis. Only in 1972 was the study stopped due to media coverage and public outrage.

There have been many other studies in this country, particularly in prisons and institutions, in which people were denied their rights and/or were coerced to participate in a study. Prisoners have been injected with diseases, injected with live cancer cells, and volunteered to receive open wounds on their bodies to test wound dressings (Hornblum, 1998).

In 1966, the National Institutes of Health (NIH) established institutional review boards as a formal and necessary component of all NIH research grants. In 1974, the National Commission for Protection of Human Subjects was established. In 1979 the Commission issued the Belmont Report, which spelled out the fundamental principles of ethical research and further established IRBs as a fundamental mechanism for the protection of human subjects (Oakes, 2002, p. 448). An IRB is a committee of five or more people who review protocols (e.g., research procedures, recruitment strategies, data collection instruments, etc.) and monitor ongoing studies to see if they meet ethical standards. The IRB committee is composed of people knowledgeable about research in different substantive areas and at least one lay citizen.

Principles for Protection of Human Subjects—Vulnerable Groups and Levels of Review

Vulnerable research subjects are groups that have been judged to be especially at risk for unethical research or have been exposed to excessive risks in the past. Certain groups have been officially designated as vulnerable groups (Oakes, 2002, p. 456). They are prisoners who are especially susceptible to coercion or affected by financial incentives, minors under 18 years of age, who must have their parents' informed consent, pregnant women and/or their fetuses, and cognitively or mentally impaired persons. Unofficial vulnerable groups would include students in a class or clients in a program in which the staff person is doing the recruitment, or professionals in a study where the supervisor is doing the recruitment. In both cases, the possibility of subjects feeling or being coerced to participate is high.

Research involving vulnerable groups always requires a full committee review. However, for other groups and studies that do not involve deception (i.e., giving people false beliefs in order to see how they will react), the study could be exempt or receive an expedited review. An *exempt study* is one that the IRB judges as not needing to follow federal policies for the protection of human subjects. Authors of such a study still need to apply to the IRB to see if it meets the criteria for exemption. Examples of an exempt study are evaluations of "normal" educational practices and settings. "New" educational practices are not exempt. Also, publicly available data are exempt if stripped of any identifying information. Evaluations of publicly funded public social programs (Medicaid, Unemployment Insurance, Social Security, etc.) that test the delivery of already proven interventions are also exempt. Experiments and new approaches are not exempt, nor are evaluations of nonpublic, private programs.

Expedited reviews are studies for which the IRB judges that minimal risk is involved. In expedited reviews, only one or two researchers from the IRB can review the proposal. If research has more than minimal risk to human subjects it goes to a full committee review, as do studies on vulnerable subjects. In all cases, however, the research needs to follow certain principles for the protection of human subjects. These principles are discussed below.

Denial of Treatment in Impact Assessment Studies

The most problematic designs with the largest risks in program evaluation are impact assessment studies using experimental designs. A risk in experimental research is the use of a control group who will not receive services in the study. Thought to be an essential part of experimental research, the withholding of services from a control group, especially if a known treatment they might benefit from could be provided, is usually unethical. There are, however, ethical ways in which a control group can be set up. For example, a waiting list of consumers can be studied for the period of time before they receive services. A patient on a waiting list could be included in the study as part of the control group. Then as they come off the waitlist they could continue to be studied and even become part of the experimental group as they receive the service being evaluated.

Another part of experimental studies that can be problematic is the use of a placebo group to correct for a placebo effect, in which a person's "just thinking" they are getting treatment might improve their situation. A placebo or "sugar pill" type treatment would look like a treatment but would not be expected to create the best outcomes. Placebo treatments are often hard to create in programs; however, if a placebo group were used, "real" treatment, which is thought to be the best treatment, would be denied to some people.

Denial of typical treatment in a control group or a placebo group can be problematic in the protection of human subjects. Furthermore, control and placebo groups can create tensions between practice staff, who are trained to advocate for services, and evaluation staff, who are trained in implementing experimental designs. If possible, the use of contrast or comparison groups of different forms of treatment can be used so that no consumer is denied current services. Of course, there must be clear-cut evidence in the research literature that one form of treatment or program is clearly more beneficial; this is where evidence-based practice (Chapter 3) comes in. What evidence is there in the literature to indicate that treatment X is an effective treatment?

Another problematic feature of experimental studies is the use of random assignment: consumers are placed randomly into different treatment groups or into control or placebo groups for the purpose of creating equivalent groups. Professionals are trained in making diagnosis about which type of consumer should get which type of service and to advocate for a certain service. In fact, consumers might do better with a certain type of service, so that random assignment could pose a risk. Also, assigning consumers randomly might not generalize to the typical way services are provided when practitioner decision-making is used to assign a consumer to a particular treatment or program. A quasi-experimental design in which different treatments are studied but consumers are not randomly assigned to those treatments can overcome this problem. However, the groups themselves might have different characteristics, so the outcomes might be caused by the characteristics of those who were in the different treatment groups rather than by the treatment or program itself.

Risks and Benefits

One of the ethical principles in the protection of human subjects is a risk–benefit ratio in which the risks involved in the research should not outweigh the benefits of the research. Research subjects need to be informed about risks, and researchers need to try and estimate those risks and probably even overestimate possible risks so that the public is protected.

The risks that IRBs should look for are subjects being obviously or subtly coerced into participation, threats to confidentiality and procedures for keeping data confidential, the psychological effects of sensitive questions (drug or alcohol use, personal problems), embarrassment or stigma from certain problems, or questions that might trigger flashbacks or other psychological reactions.

Sometimes risks are minimal—for instance, the risks ordinarily encountered in daily life for a normal healthy adult person—and there is the possibility of an expedited review. For studies with more than minimal risk, the IRB needs to be shown that the benefits clearly outweigh the risks, such as stress, physical, psychological or interpersonal hazards, and the possibility of pain, injury, discomfort, embarrassment, worry, or anxiety.

Generally researchers should be very conservative in estimating the benefits of participating in research. It is unethical to promise research subjects a benefit from participation in the research when there are no immediate benefits for them. Only benefits that can be reasonably expected should be included. In program evaluation, the researcher cannot guarantee that the subject will benefit from service they have or are going to receive if they choose to participate in the study. The IRB is given a presentation of possible risks and a risk–benefit ratio. The risks and benefits are then included in the informed-consent form given to the research subjects before the study.

Voluntary Participation, Informed Consent, Confidentiality

Obviously, prisoners in Nazi prisoner of war camps were not voluntary participants in their medical experiments. Participation in research must be voluntary and the participant must have given informed consent. This means that subjects need to know about the risks involved in the research. For example, a participant in experimental medical research testing a new drug would have to agree to participate in the research after being told that they would not know whether or not they were taking the new drug or a placebo. They would have to sign an informed-consent form stating that they understood that they could be receiving a placebo. They also need to be told that even if they get the drug, there might not be benefits from the new drug and there could be risks, which should be described as fully as possible. Needless to say, participation in medical research has slowed since potential subjects have been given full information.

An informed-consent form must be used for all research participants and it must clearly explain what is involved in the participation. There should be no possibility of coercion in the person's participation. The subjects need to be told about the risks and benefits. Also, if subjects are receiving service in a program, they need to be informed that there would be no loss of benefits or disruption of service if they do not participate in the evaluation study. They also need to know that they may discontinue participation in the study at any time. They can drop out of the study as it proceeds or choose not to answer particular questions if they find them too personal or a cause of anxiety or stress. If the study has the potential to cause more then minimal risk and anxiety or stress, subjects should be given some referrals to agencies and counselors where they can go to discuss those issues. Some referrals can be in the program or agency itself but others must be outside the agency. The participants would also receive the researcher's contact information if they had questions about the study, and the IRB's contact information to make future inquiries about their rights as research subjects and ways the research could have affected them.

Informed-consent forms also need to have an explanation about confidentiality and how confidentiality will be protected. IRBs prefer that participants be anonymous. For example, if a questionnaire is mailed out to a list of participants and needs to be mailed back, it should be done in such a way that the researcher has no way of knowing who participated. However, in most studies with a personal contact, the researcher needs to say that the person's participation is confidential, not anonymous, and an informed-consent form would need to be signed. In situations where having a signed consent form could put the participant at risk (e.g., for an undocumented worker), signing the informed-consent form could be waived. Forms with the subject's name on them need to be kept in a secure location, and the interview form itself and the data files created should not have any identifying information such as the subject's name. An ID number should be placed on the interview form itself in the data files and a list of names and their ID numbers kept under lock and key. Signed consent forms must also be kept under lock and key in a secure location.

When the research data are collected in group formats, such as in a study using focus groups to evaluate a program, there are has some special care provisions. The participants must know that they cannot discuss what is said in the group outside of the group. A special statement on the consent form should state the following: "To protect the privacy of group members, please refrain from speaking to others about what is said within the group." Also, since group members will know what each other said in the group, there needs to be a statement that confidentiality cannot be guaranteed.

The informed-consent form is reviewed by the IRB, who weighs the information given to subjects and determines if it conforms to standards (see Exhibit 1, p. 49). If personal interviews are used in the study, the researcher gives the participant the informed-consent form to read and two copies of the form are signed by both the respondent and the interviewer. The subject keeps one copy and the interviewer keeps the other copy. If audio or video tapes are used, special forms must be completed that describe how the tapes will be used and state that identifying names or ID numbers will not be kept on the tapes.

If the study uses individually identifiable protected health data or mental health information covered under the Health Insurance Portability and Accountability Act (HIPPA), HIPPA informed consent and procedures are needed for proper access to case record data. Data from HIPPA settings such as hospitals, physician's case records, health plans, health maintenance organizations (HMOs), mental health agencies, social agencies, and private-practice case files are subject to HIPPA regulations. HIPPA forms need to be filled out to obtain each person's informed consent to use their data, or a waiver from a HIPPA officer at the setting needs to be obtained, stating that the data are de-identified and no identifying information is included in the data to be analyzed. HIPPA forms must be completed and submitted to the IRB along with the IRB application.

The writing style and content of the informed-consent form must be clear and understandable. Oakes (2002, p. 464) has noted that consent forms are often impenetrable even by other social scientists, yet they need to be understood by subjects, or lay people. Informed-consent forms should be written at an eighth-grade level of reading and should be short and succinct.

Recruitment and Selection

The IRB also needs to know how subjects for research will be recruited. Selection criteria must be equitable and fit the study criteria. For example, if you are evaluating a program, consumers need to be told if all consumers were asked to participate in the study, if they were selected through random sampling, or if some subgroup was selected and, if so, what criteria were used for selection (e.g., equal numbers of males and females). This helps subjects know that they are not being singled out and that selection is equitable. The researcher also needs to establish that the study participant meets study criteria; for example, "First, does you daughter attend the Madison after-school program?"

Fliers and recruitment letters, e-mails, brochures, advertisements, and verbal exchanges can be used for recruiting subjects; however, IRBs prefer impersonal letters and fliers to verbal recruitment, as it can be unclear what those soliciting the subjects may say. If subjects are recruited in person, oral scripts need to be submitted to the IRB to ensure that coercion is not being employed and that unrealistic benefits are not being promised in exchange for study participation. When monetary compensation is given, the amount of money should not be high enough that it would be viewed as coercive. This can be a problem, for there are no federal guidelines on how much compensation is coercive (Oakes, 2002). If students in a class are asked to participate, the coercion rate could be high. If participation is a class requirement, an alternate assignment of equal effort should be given. Fliers, letters, and other recruiting materials also need to be reviewed by the IRB. These statements need to include the purpose of the study, what is involved in participation, any interventions that are experimental, where the study is being conducted and by whom, as well as the affiliation of the researcher(s) and contact information so potential subjects may contact them.

Special Provisions for Different Types of Vulnerable Subjects

There are special rules for children who are under 18, cognitively or mentally impaired persons, and prisoners, and their participation in a study always gets full

IRB committee review (Hunter College, 2009). For children under 18 or minors, the informed-consent form gets completed by the parent or guardian and the children sign an "informed assent" form. On the parental consent form there is a statement similar to the following: "My child will also be asked to participate. He/she does not have to participate even if I give my permission to participate." On the child assent form there should be the following statement: "You do not have to participate even if your parent gave permission for you to do so."

Cognitively or mentally impaired persons are presumed to be competent unless there is evidence that their disability impairs their judgment (Hunter College, 2009, p. 6). If there is evidence of impaired judgment, the proxy or guardian of the impaired person completes the inform consent. The impaired person participates voluntarily, does not have to participate, and can withdraw at any time even if the proxy has given permission to participate. For studies of people who might be mentally impaired, the researcher needs to specify criteria for judging whether a subject would be incompetent or not, so that competence or incompetence is not merely assumed and a case is made for whether or not a proxy would need to give consent.

Studies with prisoners can only be carried out if there is minimal risk, and must focus on research examining the treatment of prisoners as a class, such as research to help improve the health and well-being of prisoners (Hunter College, p. 7). The incentives or advantages given to the prisoner for participating must be compared to prison living conditions so that the prisoner is not coerced to do the study. Also, the risks taken by the prisoner should be the same as risks permitted for non-prison populations. Within the prison, there needs to be a fair selection process. Parole boards are not allowed to take participation in research into account when assessing the prisoner's possibility for parole.

Exhibit 1: Example of an Informed Consent Form

PURPOSE

The Madison Community Center is conducting a parent's satisfaction survey to determine how satisfied parents are with our after-school program. The survey is about your perceptions of the program as a whole and about specific parts of the program, such as homework help, the recreation program, and the self-esteem workshops that your child may be participating in. The results will be used to help us improve the program and to determine the strengths and weaknesses of the program. We will write a report of our findings and share them with the parents' advisory group and the Youth Services Administration that funds our program.

This questionnaire has been sent out to all parents whose children attend the after-school program.

Exhibit 1 (Continued)

VOLUNTARY PARTICIPATION

You are being asked to fill out this questionnaire, which should take you about 15 minutes. Your participation in this study is purely voluntary. If you choose not to complete the questionnaire it will in no way affect the services you or your child receives. You may skip questions if you feel they are too personal or you do not wish to answer them.

BENEFITS AND RISKS

There are no direct benefits to you if you choose to participate in this study. However, completing the questionnaire may help you assess parts of the program that your child benefits from and those that do not meet your expectations. Some of the questions may cause you discomfort, for example, questions about areas in which you feel the program does not serve your child well. However, our social workers (212-452-7029) are willing to discuss these issues with you, or you may want to talk to someone at another agency, the Day Care Council, which helps parents find after-school programs for their children. Their phone number is 212-395-7000.

CONFIDENTIALITY

After you have completed the questionnaire, please return it to room 203 in the secure box with the sign "Research" on it. The information you provide us is anonymous and confidential. No one will know how you responded to these questions. Please do not put your name or any identifying information on this questionnaire, to ensure anonymity.

CONTACT INFORMATION

If you have any questions about the study you may contact the researcher Thomas Jones at 212-325-7575. If you have any questions regarding your rights as a research subject you may call the City Youth Service IRB office at 212-887-7700.

INFORMED ASSENT

By completing and returning this questionnaire, you are giving your consent to participate in this study.

For a signed consent form see below:

I have read the contents of this consent form and have been encouraged to ask questions. I have received answers to my questions. I give me consent to participate in this study. I have received a copy of this form for my records and for future reference.

| _____ | _____ | _____ |
| Participant's Name | Signature | Date |

| _____ | _____ | _____ |
| Researcher's Name | Signature | Date |

Ethical Evaluation Practice

The evaluator and the evaluation team need to behave in an ethical and professional manner. A good resource for those interested in looking at the depth and breadth of evaluation activities is the American Evaluation Association. Their Web site lists the "Guiding Principles for Evaluators," which describe the standards that evaluators need to use for conducting ethical practice (American Evaluation Association, 2009). These principles and standards will be paraphrased here, with some pointed additions for clarity.

A number of the principles have to do with evaluators providing competent service to all the stakeholders—administrators, staff, clients and consumers, funding organizations, the community, and the public at large. Evaluators need to have the training and skills and further professional development to undertake various types of evaluation. Evaluators also need cultural competence to understand the backgrounds, values, and views of all the stakeholders and members of the evaluation team.

Many of the principles address good communication with stakeholders. Evaluation always involves complex relationships with administrators, staff, and consumers. The evaluator needs to explore with the organization the reasons for conducting the evaluation, the various methods that may be used. The evaluator also needs to clearly communicate the study results within the limitations of the methodology used.

Evaluators need to communicate with integrity and honesty. The research and evaluation plan is critical. The evaluation plan needs to be clear and honest, and should be negotiated with the client or party paying for the evaluation as well as other relevant stakeholders. The evaluation plan becomes the contract and spells out the purpose of the evaluation, the tasks to be done, the methodology and its limitations, the types of results that might be found, how these results might be used, and the cost of the evaluation. Changes in this plan or contract can be negotiated at the beginning and then as the evaluation proceeds and as changes are needed.

An evaluator's integrity and honesty require him or her to not distort the evaluation data that come from the study. The American Evaluation Association's principles link honesty and integrity in presenting evaluation findings to the concept of freedom of information in a democracy. People involved in planning and carrying out a program generally want to see that their efforts and the outcomes of their efforts are being achieved. The evaluator needs to report negative findings as well as positive findings and needs to maintain objectivity and see that all stakeholders understand the results. This usually involves complex ethical stands, especially if the evaluator is an employee of the organization or is hired as a consultant and paid directly by them. Evaluators hired by a third party outside the organization or a publicly funded body may identify less with the organization and may need more sensitivity to workers on the front lines and to the complex problems that consumers have.

The evaluator must have a real commitment to respecting the *consumer's* interest in having the service fairly evaluated. Evaluators also need to respect the security, dignity, and self-worth of consumers, clients, and all other stake-holders. Part of this respect is achieved by informed consent and implementing the principles on the protection of human subjects in the evaluation study. Beyond this, however, the American Evaluation Association notes that evalua-tors can sometimes harm stakeholders by their findings. For example, consu-mers may want a program to continue with all its flaws and shortcomings if it is the only service available to them. Likewise, a program administrator or execu-tive may have staked his or her fame and fortunes on a new and creative program and have a lot to lose when negative findings are reported. Thus evaluators need to be alert to what all the parties in the evaluation stand to gain and lose as a result of study data; the concerns of the "full range" of stakeholders need to be respected. The concerns of consumers or clients cannot be left out due to power inequities with program professionals and administrators. Evaluators should be committed to the public interest and public good, which is larger than the interests and good of any one stakeholder in the evaluation, especially if they are paying the evaluator's salary. Clearly the evaluator's role is full of complex relationships and negotiations, which makes evaluation challenging, but an ethical evaluator takes great pride in living up to those standards.

Summary

1. The formative–summative typology provides a perspective for examining different types of evaluations. Formative evaluations are more preliminary evaluations, focusing on program processes and

activities, while summative evaluations focus more on goals and outcomes.

2. Goals and outcomes can be formative or summative. Formative goals are more proximate goals related to initial questions about the program, for example: How many people are receiving service? How satisfied are they with the services received? Summative goals are more ultimate goals related to longer-range evaluative questions, for example: Was knowledge increased? Was health improved? Was drug use curtailed and eliminated?

3. There are three types of formative evaluations: needs assessment studies, program-monitoring studies, and process evaluations.

4. Needs assessment studies examine the extent of the social, health, or educational problems that a proposed program could correct. Needs assessment could include a local survey to see how many people are affected by the problem and to determine the extent of their needs.

5. Program-monitoring studies focus on program activities and operations. These studies answer questions such as the following: How many clients or patients are using the service? Does the program design seem to be working? Is the program being implemented as planned? Did the program reach the target population?

6. Process evaluations focus more on rich, descriptive data of the program in operation as well as data on who is using the program and internal program operations.

7. Summative evaluations include goal or outcome evaluations and impact assessment studies employing experimental and quasi-experimental designs.

8. Outcome evaluations focus more on what happened to people who attended the program. These studies include surveys of people who received the program intervention and pre–post studies to determine if there were changes in knowledge, attitude, behavior, skills, or health or status.

9. Impact assessment studies use more formal and sophisticated experimental or quasi-experimental designs with a control or comparison group to compare the achievement of program goals for those who used the program with outcomes for those who did not use the program or used a different form of the program. Impact assessment studies address whether it was the program and the program only and not some other factors that caused the achievement of program goals and outcomes.

10. There are nine steps involved in conducting all types of evaluation studies: *(1)* describing the program or the need the program is to

address; *(2)* defining program activities and goals; *(3)* designing or selecting a type of program evaluation; *(4)* choosing a method of data collection; *(5)* selecting a type of sample; *(6)* constructing the data collection instrument; *(7)* collecting the data; *(8)* analyzing the data; and *(9)* reporting the results of the study.

11. Ethics plays three important roles in program evaluation. First is the ethical imperative to evaluate programs and practices and establish a tradition of accountability in programs and the goals they strive to achieve. Second, since evaluation employs a research methodology, ethical standards for the treatment of human subjects in research need to be implemented through a review by the institutional review board. Third, evaluators and members of the evaluation team need to engage in ethical evaluation practice in implementing the evaluation, maintaining professional and interpersonal relationships, and reporting results with objectivity and integrity.

12. To protect human subjects participating in research, an evaluator needs a commitment to the principles of informed consent, voluntary participation, and confidentiality, all of which are implemented with the oversight of institutional review boards.

REFERENCES

American Evaluation Association (2009). Guiding principles for evaluators. http://www.eval.org/publications/GuidingPrinciplesPrintable.asp.

Annas, G.J. & Gordin, M.A. (1992). *The Nazi Doctors and the Nuremberg Code: Human Rights in Human Experimentation.* New York: Oxford University Press.

Gambrill, E.D. (2006). *Social Work Practice: A Critical Thinker's Guide.* New York: Oxford University Press.

Hornblum, A.M. (1998). *Acres of Skin: Human Experimentation at Holmesberg Prison.* New York: Routledge.

Hunter College (2009). Institutional Review Board for the Protection of Human Subjects, IRB protocol coversheet. http://hunter.cuny.edu/IRB.

Jones, J.H. (1981). *Bad Blood: The Tuskegee Syphilis Experiment.* New York: The Free Press.

Oakes, J.M. (2002). Rights and wrongs in social science research: An evaluator's guide to the IRB. *Evaluation Review* 26(5):444–479.

Rossi, P.H., Lipsey, M.W., & Freeman H.E. (2004). *Evaluation: A Systematic Approach.* Thousand Oaks, CA: Sage Publications.

Scriven, M. (1967). The methodology of evaluation. In Taylor, R.W., Gagne, R.M., & Scriven, M. (eds.) *Perspectives of Curriculum Evaluation.* AERA Monograph Series on Curriculum Evaluation, Vol. 1. Chicago: Rand McNally, pp. 39–83.

Smith, M.J., Caro, F., & McKaig, K. (1987). *Caring for the Developmentally Disabled Child at Home: The Experiences of Low Income Families.* New York: Community Service Society.

Weiss, C.H. (1998). *Evaluation: Methods for Studying Programs and Policies.* Englewood Cliffs, NJ: Prentice-Hall.

3

New Trends and Issues in Program Evaluation

The Strengths Perspective, Consumer Empowerment, Empowerment Evaluation, and Evidence-Based Practice

A number of cutting-edge trends have developed in program evaluation over the past few years. These new trends and important perspectives provide focus both in terms of practice in the human services field and in terms of program evaluation. One overarching theme in practice and programmatic research in the human services is the *strengths perspective* – to emphasize the positives in both the people that are served and the programs that are developed. It is a simple but important perspective.

Following from a strengths perspective, we need to focus on *consumer, patient,* or *client empowerment* in evaluation and consider the recently developing field of *empowerment evaluation*, which emphasizes the collaboration and participation of all those involved in the program.

Finally, while not central to program evaluation, current trends in evidence-based practice (EBP) are having a profound impact on programs and interventions in mental health, social work, health, and other human service fields. Professionals are encouraged to use evidence-based practice or practice that has been validated through experimental studies, and some funding sources, for example, a state department of mental health, are requiring EBP as a method for choosing interventions based on their success rates. In theory, the choice of intervention or program would be based on evaluation studies of practice, especially experimental studies and impact assessment evaluations.

The Strengths Perspective

Within the many human service professions, a strengths perspective has been developed. A strengths-based model is important in both practice and program evaluation. In direct practice, concentrating on the strengths of the people and the communities served, and not on their pathologies, means developing from the assets that already exist. In program evaluation, the whole concept of "programs that work" means that we locate positive programs and emphasize the parts of programs that are working. Just as strengths in people and communities should be emphasized in practice, the strengths and positive characteristics of people and communities and the strengths of programs should be emphasized in program evaluation.

Strengths in People and Communities

In practice, the strengths perspective is a relatively simple concept—build on client, consumer, or patient strengths.

> Practicing from a strengths orientation means this—everything you do . . . will be predicated in some way on helping to embellish, explore and exploit clients' strengths and resources in the service of assisting them to achieve their goals, realize their dreams, and shed the irons of their inhibitions and misgivings and society's domination . . . . When you adopt the strengths approach to practice, you can expect exciting changes in the character of your work and in the tenor of your relationships with your clients. (Saleeby, 2002, p. 1)

Saleeby (2002) notes that there are a number of human service fields currently employ similar positive perspectives, such as "developmental resilience, healing and wellness, solution-focused therapy, assets-based community development, and narrative and story" (p. 2). Part of the rationale for focusing on strengths is that a preoccupation with pathology may hinder clients from growing, developing, and changing direction (pp. 7–8). The philosophy of the strengths perspective is one of liberation and hope. The perspective recognizes the abilities of people to transcend their circumstances and emancipate their own internal powers.

Program evaluators, like practitioners, should recognize the strengths in the people that programs are designed to serve. A number of concepts and principles from the strengths perspective are more important for program evaluation:

1. *Empowerment* — discovering the power within people and communities to help solve their own problems (Saleeby, 2002, p. 9). Every individual, group family, and community has strengths. Assume that everyone has the capacity to grow and change. Collaborating with clients, patients, and consumers may be the best way to serve them. Every environment and person has resources.
2. *Resilience* — people and communities and institutions have the ability to rebound from adversity or the wrong way of doing things.

As Arnone (2002, p. 1) notes,

It is the reason we do our jobs . . . . When society has given up on the potential of individuals or a population, we jump in. When we cannot believe the history of life experiences in their sequence, and we cannot fathom the possibility of any person overcoming the sour grapes that they have been served, we push those doubts aside. We believe in our clients, in their human spirit, and hold onto the hope that they will succeed. At the end of the day, I would like my clients, particularly the little ones, to believe it too.

Strengths in Programs

Just as people's strengths are emphasized in this perspective, so too should the specific strong points in the programs. Some programs may be very efficient at outreach and making sure that the groups needing the service most are those who are recruited. Other programs may be more successful in providing quality interventions by skilled practitioners once the client or patient is enrolled in the program. In conducting evaluations, the specific strengths of the particular program need to be considered.

Based on criteria of success, some programs will show better results in terms of outcomes and in their orientation to practice and their methods of practice. Within the population of programs within a particular field, programs that work and best practices can be discovered through program evaluation.

A number of programs have had a substantial, positive impact on the lives of the people they have served and have benefited society as a whole. These programs are not miraculous. They do not completely solve any social problem. They do not help all of the people they serve or anything close to 100 percent. But they do substantially reduce the rates and severity of particular social problems among participants. (Crane, 1998, p. 1)

In his book *Social Programs that Work*, Crane (1998) has outlined the following criteria of success that could be used to judge successful programs:

1. There should be significant gains and benefits to those who participated.
2. There should be reasonable costs associated with the program or the cost–benefit ratio should be reasonable.
3. The benefit should be achieved in a reasonable amount of time.
4. The program should have been evaluated using a sound methodology.
5. The program should be described clearly enough so that it could be replicated in additional settings and locations.

Saleeby (2002) has detailed the program characteristics of successful programs from the work of Schorr (1997) on programs that work in the educational, family, and child welfare fields of practice. The characteristics of successful programs are as follows:

1. They are community based, involving residents and professionals in solving problems together.
2. They have a long-term commitment to the client problems being addressed.
3. They have an organizational structure committed to experimentation, collaboration, and innovation.
4. They have common beliefs and goals.
5. They are flexible in terms of strategies to achieve goals, for example, staff are willing to play many roles and are committed to the urgency of the problems the programs were designed to solve.

The elements of a successful program can be seen in data from the evaluation of a community-based program serving elderly clients with the aim of preventing nursing home placements (see end of Chapter 2). In this program, services were provided in a naturally occurring retirement community (NORC) where extensive services were provided in a neighborhood with large concentrations of the elderly. The program was community based, and the staff was heavily involved in the day-to-day lives of the elderly residents of the local community. The program strategies were flexible, and the staff had an urgency about providing community care and preventing the elderly from being placed in institutions. These program characteristics can be seen in some of the quotes from staff:

> [Our goal was] to help the elderly function in the community and give them community supports. We educate the elderly about services. We give then a lot of service. We are involved with nurses, lawyers, their relatives. We quiet down our clients. We make phone calls to reassure them.
>
> We have great communication between the staff and the seniors. Accessible services. A genuine concern. We have a tight community here. Everyone watches out for each other. There's an openness and innovation. "Let's try this or that." Seniors are actively involved in doing things, planning, helping set up the programs.

Limits of the Strengths Perspective

While a strengths perspective can be used in evaluation, one of the reasons evaluations are conducted is to find deficits in programs so that they can be improved. Although program strengths should be emphasized, the deficit side cannot be ignored. For example, from a strengths perspective, both client and program strengths can be seen if people have started attending the program. However, from a deficits perspective, they may not be able to use the program because they did not understand its value or what was being offered. This may reflect more the deficits in the program rather than deficits in the people attending the program.

It is important to examine first the strengths in both the clients and the program; then deficits should be considered. In examining deficits, program deficits should be examined first and client deficits second. From the standpoint of a strengths perspective, when a program is found to not work, rather than "blaming the victim" or the consumer who did not make use of the "excellent program," it is better to make sure that the program design has not contributed to the program's failures. The program may have been offered at a time of the day when consumers could not attend, or parents may have needed child care in order to attend. Programmatic shortcomings to be considered, rather than just the deficits of those clients or patients who were served. The following case study shows the value of a strengths perspective in a needs assessment study of community assets.

Case Study on the Strengths Perspective: Assessing Community Assets in Yonkers, New York

RACHEL GROB, PH.D.

ASSOCIATE DEAN FOR GRADUATE STUDIES,

SARAH LAWRENCE COLLEGE

[Other people] are amazed at the cooperation they see among the community-based organizations in Yonkers.

—Yonkers, NY resident (2000)

This quote from a Yonkers resident appears near the very front of the Yonkers Early Childhood Data Book 2000 (Grob, Harmon, LaGreca, & Mitchell, 2000; Data Book), a publication detailing the results of a 2-year community needs assessment process undertaken by the Yonkers Early Childhood Initiative (ECI). This quote appears in boldface in a prominent box on the page, for several reasons. First, the declaration of good things afoot in Yonkers indicates that the authors of this needs assessment looked for and found significant strengths in the community. This is an important perspective to declare from the outset, given that this city has been best known in the last 15 years for not only the host of economic and social problems endemic to many postindustrial eastern seaboard cities but also its particularly troubled racial politics.[1] Second, the quote uses the words of a resident rather than those of a professional or evaluator, letting the reader know from the outset that the assessment relied heavily on direct input from community members. Finally, the quote acknowledges hard work already accomplished by community institutions, and challenges each one to continue living up to this valued standard.

The messages implicit in this quote also illustrate critical aspects of the strengths-based approach to community needs assessment adopted by the Yonkers ECI as we designed our process and produced our award-winning Data Book (Grob et al., 2000).

IDENTIFYING STRENGTHS

As noted in the Data Book's introduction, the ECI made a conscious decision to focus throughout the needs assessment on balancing Yonkers' strengths and

---

1. In the 1980s, the NAACP took legal action against the city, arguing that persistent school segregation was intimately linked to housing segregation. The NAACP won in federal court, and the city was ordered to build public housing in scatter-site locations outside the narrow area where it had been confined and condensed in the past. Under pressure from white, middle class neighborhood groups, elected officials defied the federal court order, eventually bankrupting the city.

challenges, "looking for data that shows what is working well in Yonkers, along with data that will increase our understanding of unmet needs" (p. 3). In some cases, quantitative data had a hopeful story to tell—for example, serious crime data indicated a decline in murders, manslaughter, assault, and robbery. However, we knew from the outset that most quantitative indicators would do more to highlight remaining problems in Yonkers than to showcase accomplishments. We wanted to deliberately move away from what Kretzman and McKnight (1993) have dubbed the "needs map" model of community assessment because we agreed with their conclusion that

> Once accepted as the whole truth about troubled neighborhoods, this "needs" map determines how problems are to be addressed, through deficiency-oriented policies and programs. Public, private and non-profit human service systems, often supported by university research and foundation funding, translate the programs into local activities that teach people the nature and extent of their problems, and the value of services as the answer to their problems. (p. 2)

While we felt it was imperative to be candid and concrete about the very real challenges facing young children and their families in Yonkers, we also looked for qualitative data, case examples, and personal insights that would help us map our community's assets. Once these data were collected, we worked with a talented team of writers and designers to showcase them prominently throughout the Data Book. For example:

- *"Spotlight On . . ."* features—18 in the book in total—highlight block initiatives and "programs that work" in Yonkers. Data illustrating positive impact are included for each, as are lively photographs illustrating the initiative or program, narrative descriptions, and testimony from residents, staff, and/or community leaders about what was working well and why. For example, the "Spotlight On . . . Getting Closer to Victory on Elliott Avenue" includes a photograph of children in a play area recently made safer and more family friendly, a description of the group of agencies working together to improve the block, and a quote from a community police officer who has worked closely with residents to "develop mutual respect and cooperation."
- Descriptive text discussing both strengths and needs consistently highlights the former before turning to the latter. The book's subtitle. "Building on Our Strengths, Meeting Our Challenges," illustrates this commitment, as do the introductions to most chapters.

Case Study on the Strengths Perspective (Continued)

- Each of the Data Book's five chapters concludes with a *list of strengths* ("We can be proud that . . ."), followed by a *list of challenges* ("We must continue trying to . . ."). These summaries of things that Yonkers can be proud of—more than 40 of them—range from public-sector initiatives (e.g., "We can be proud that Yonkers has successfully implemented universal pre-kindergarten service city-wide [p. 69]), to improvements in measurable outcomes (e.g., "We can be proud that hospitalizations for asthma management are vastly decreased because of the school/hospital partnership" [p. 116]), to generalizations about what the people in the city are trying accomplish (e.g., "We can be proud that the Yonkers ECI is working hard to assure that families living in conditions of poverty have access to services and supports that can help young children overcome the impact of poverty" [p. 51]).

MAKING ROOM AT THE TABLE FOR COMMUNITY RESIDENTS

Community residents played a crucial role in Yonkers' needs assessment in several ways.

First, the ECI strove from the outset to make city residents, particularly parents of young children, integral to all its work. Like other community collaborative efforts started by city officials and/or service providers, we soon discovered that this was no easy task: bridging the gap between professionals and those who stake their claim on the basis of residency is a complex, delicate, and work-intensive process. However, the needs assessment helped us begin to build mechanisms for ongoing and meaningful participation of "community representatives." In contrast to much of the more purely conceptual groundwork that community collaborative efforts must undertake in their early days, the needs assessment process involved concrete tasks that community representatives could sink their teeth into, like gathering data, advising on layout and presentation, and obtaining and selecting photographs to include in the book. It also resulted in something very tangible–the Data Book itself. Once it was complete, the Data Book immediately became a recruiting tool for soliciting the commitment and participation of new community representatives.

Another way that residents contributed significantly to the assessment was that, as noted prominently in the Data Book's introduction, more than 200 city residents generously shared thoughts and opinions about the status of their children and community by participating in personal interviews and focus group discussions. Their distinctive stories and perspectives gave our needs assessment data the vitality and meaning of real lives (Data Book, p. 7). In order to bring their voices directly to Data Book readers, we published a large number of direct quotes, presenting each in an eye-catching, boldfaced, pull-out format entitled "A Parent Speaks" or "Yonkers Parents Speak." The quotes reflect the following issues:

- Candid advice to service providers (e.g., "All new parents need the reassurance that they're doing the right thing." [p. 125])
- Concrete suggestions for making the city more hospitable for families with children (e.g., "It sure would be helpful if voting polls were made kid friendly. . . and if grocery stores had those shopping carts that accommodate two children." [p. 22])
- Observations about what parents know works for kids (e.g., "I know I'm doing the best for my child when I make time to read, sing, and dance with him. His face lights up every time we read the nursery rhymes he heard at the library." [p. 53])
- Testimony about what is difficult about parenting in Yonkers (e.g., "I keep my kids inside. There are too many undesirables in the neighborhood." [p. 20]) and what should be done about it (e.g., "There needs to be more policing in the parks, especially after dark because that's where the drugs are being sold." [p. 20])

Reaching out to so many residents for interviews and focus groups also began creating momentum for the kinds of grassroots involvement in community building that the needs assessment process was hoping to find and inspire.

BUILDING ON COMMUNITY ASSETS

Good needs assessments do not set out to capture a static moment in the life of a community. Rather, they develop a dynamic picture of a community's complexity, while at the same time catalyzing change through the very process of examining the present state. By mapping assets as well as tenacious problems in Yonkers, the ECI helped those inside and outside Yonkers to see the city in a more favorable light and to build on the city's assets.

For example, community institutions and programs featured in the Data Book, as well as the ECI itself, have very successfully used the book to leverage more public and private funding for their work. Organizations also use it for their own strategic planning, working with their own boards of directors as well as with each other to carve out service niches that can meet real needs while minimizing destructive interagency competition or duplication of services. Indeed, the Data Book was an important catalyst in the ECI's efforts to spend

Case Study on the Strengths Perspective (Continued)

less collective energy competing over the proverbial funding pie, focusing instead on making "more pie" for all of us by building our credibility for outside funders, coordinating our efforts, and thinking together about what roles each can play in shoring up the service net. We have been able to share the Data Book and our experience developing it with community collaboratives in other cities, giving Yonkers the opportunity to be known for something positive and inspiring us to continue building on the good work that outsiders have come to recognize.

Kretzman and McKnight's (1993) generalization about the power of "asset mapping" summarizes our experience in Yonkers beautifully: "Once [a] guide to capacities has replaced the old one containing only needs and deficiencies, the regenerating community can begin to assemble its strengths into new combinations, [and] new structures of opportunity . . ." (p. 6). Does this sound like too much to ask from an evaluation process? Just give it a try!

REFERENCES

Grob, R., Harmon, M., LaGreca, K., & Mitchell, T. (2000). *Yonkers Early Childhood Data Book Building on Our Strengths, Meeting Our Challenges.* Yonkers: Yonkers Early Childhood Initiative. To obtain a copy of the Data Book, contact the Yonkers Early Childhood Initiative at the Andrus Children's Center in Yonkers, NY, or the author.

Kretzman, J., & McKnight, J. (1993). *Building Communities from the Inside Out: A Path Towards Finding and Mobilizing a Community's Assets.* Chicago: ACTA Publications.

Participation and Collaboration with Stakeholders

Many parties hold an interest in programs and their development. The term *stakeholder* is used widely in the field of program evaluation and is useful in helping focus on the interests of all parties involved with the program.

In the health field, stakeholders include doctors, nurses, health-care workers, politicians, administrators, managers, and researchers, pharmaceutical, insurance, and health maintenance enterprises, and finally, patients and potential service users. Each has a different perspective from which they view effective health-care strategies. They also have different stakes or interests in the system: some depend on it not only to resolve their health problems but also for their livelihood. (White, 2001, p. 466)

Evaluators' personal perspectives on the importance and value of certain stakeholders are extremely important.

[S]ome evaluators believe that evaluations should be directed toward helping program managers to improve their programs. . . . Others hold that the purpose of evaluations should be to help program beneficiaries (targets) to become empowered . . . engaging targets in a collaborative effort to define programs . . . which leads to an increased sense of personal efficacy . . . [A]t the other extreme are evaluators who believe that evaluations should mainly serve stakeholders who fund the evaluation. (Rossi et al., 2004, p. 398–399)

Weiss (1998) notes the importance of the current trend of enlisting stake-holders in the definition and conduct of the evaluation with hopes of "empow-ering" all those involved. The terms *participatory evaluation, collaborative evaluation,* and *empowerment evaluation* all refer to including multiple stake-holders in the process of conducting program evaluation.

Involving stakeholders is no easy task, because each party represents different interests.

[S]takeholders may hold competing and sometimes combative views on the appropriateness of the evaluation work and whose interest will be affected by the outcome. To conduct their work effectively and contribute to the resolution of the issues at hand, evaluators must understand their relationships with the stakeholders involved as well as the relationships between stakeholders. (Rossi et al., 2004, p. 374)

Conflict among stakeholders is very common.

Within stakeholder groups, various stakeholders typically have different perspectives on the meaning and importance of the evaluation's findings. These disparate views are a source of potential conflict not only between the stakeholders themselves but also between these persons and the evaluator. No matter how an evaluation turns out, there are some to whom the findings are good news and some to whom they are bad news. (Rossi et al., 2004, p. 374)

The starting point for involving stakeholders is to develop a list of all possible stakeholders and determine what their role in the evaluation would be. In developing an all-inclusive list of all stakeholders, we could separate groups into major and minor stakeholders.

Primary Group of Major Stakeholders

1. Agency administrators and program administrators
2. Practitioners and direct-service staff
3. Consumers, clients, and patients

Secondary Group of Major Stakeholders

1. Governmental agencies funding the program
2. Local private agencies and foundations involved with the program

Minor Stakeholders

1. The general public
2. National and local agencies affiliated with area of service
3. Experts and scholars in the programmatic area

The above groupings would be a template to use in developing a list of stakeholders. Stakeholders can be involved at all points of the evaluation process—in planning the evaluation, in describing the program and the theories on which the program is based, in conducting the evaluation, and in reporting and interpreting the results.

Among the stakeholders, the primary constituency should be consumers, since they are affected most by the program. A consumer-empowerment perspective should be primary. After consumers, all other parties or stakeholders in the evaluation process can participate.

Consumer, Patient, and Client Empowerment

Empowerment is now a major concept in health and the human services. In direct service or clinical work, the goal is to increase the power of the client or community so that action can be taken to change and prevent the problems that clients are facing. In the community-organizing and policy fields, the goal is to build stronger, more empowered community coalitions, and to develop client and community *ownership* of programs (Secret, Jordan, and Ford, 1999, p. 120).

As professionals, we have a commitment to the rights of consumers, patients, and clients we serve. Patients, consumers, and clients deserve quality service, not inferior service. Program evaluation can be used as a method to improve and maintain the quality of programs.

Program evaluation can also be used as a method to promote consumer participation and input into programs. Evaluators themselves should join with service professionals and administrators in an effort to achieve true consumer participation and empowerment.

> [E]valuators and social scientists could give voice to the people they work with and bring their concerns to policy brokers . . . . [T]he evaluator advocates for groups that have no control over their own fates. (Fetterman 1996, pp. 6, 9)

Consumer input can start with more *passive approaches* such as consumer feedback—for example, interviewing patients or clients with a consumer satisfaction questionnaire. Consumer input can then advance to more *active approaches* such as personal interviews with clients in which they can respond in-depth to the effects of the service on them. The most active approaches and true empowerment involve consumers as active participants in the planning, implementation, and evaluation of programs. A total consumer empowerment evaluation approach involves consumers in the design and implementation of social programs and in the planning and implementation of evaluation studies.

While any level of consumer participation is valued, the extent of consumer participation in the decision-making process determines whether this is a true empowerment approach. To establish what level of participation is being achieved in a particular situation, those involved should ask the following questions:

> Do consumers or communities gain access to core decision-making circles, entailing at least a partial transfer of power from those who already have control over that arena? Or is participation reduced to a data-collecting exercise, a one-way transfer of information from users to administrators, which further empowers core actors by increasing their knowledge base? (White, 2001, p. 469)

Interviewing consumers about the quality of program services through a formal evaluation is better than operating without any consumer feedback. Consumer opinions and feelings about the program should be an important part of program planning. However, a total or true empowerment approach requires commitment, work, and persistence. When it comes to consumer involvement, true empowerment is usually a goal to be achieved.

> Because not all social groups are equally well organized and do not all represent or express themselves in similar ways, not all are on equal footing. Certain participants (or groups of participants) are more likely than others to have their agendas prevail. In this light, the view of participation as the democratic expression of the "public will" is an overly abstract notion that is inadequate to capture the diversity of participants, and the asymmetry of participation in real world situations. (White, 2001, p. 466)

The definition of *consumer* is an important consideration. In some instances, a consumer is merely an interested community member who resides in the community that the program serves. At other times, the consumer is a recipient of services or a family member of that recipient. Furthermore, studies of lay members of Canadian health-care boards where interested and motivated citizens participated indicated that the professional staff had far greater stakes in maintaining control over services and were in a position to "handle" their boards in such a way as to limit their ability to influence the organization (Godbout, 1981). When consumers represent organized community interests and are accountable to their own constituencies, consumer participation is more likely to continue to exist (White, 2001, p. 472).

Consumer Participation Through Surveys

Royse, Thyer, Padgett, and Logan (2001, p. 191) have observed that most human service agencies would likely begin thinking about surveying clients if they were designing a program evaluation. As health, mental health, and social-service standards continue to emphasize consumer satisfaction, more organizations will initiate consumer surveys. Of course, once these surveys are completed, there are not assurances that the opinions of consumers will be heard by program planners.

In the health field, consumer feedback has been a requirement of the Joint Commission on the Accreditation of Healthcare Organizations (JCAHO). To fulfill this requirement, private hospitals have had to collect data from consumers on both the needs and satisfaction of patients whom they have served (JCAHO). Revealingly, public hospitals in New York City, described as "the health care provider of last resort for many of the poorest New Yorkers," reported their first system-wide patient satisfaction survey in 1999, at least 9 years later than the private hospitals (Kennedy, 1999, B1, B8).

> The survey was based on face-to-face interviews, in five languages with more than 16,000 patients in every part of the 11-hospital system—clinics, emergency rooms, inpatient wards, outpatient surgery departments, nursing homes, and other areas . . . [A] preliminary look at the overall results showed a fairly consistent pattern. . . . While 89 percent of 7,000 clinic patients interviewed said they were likely to return for their care to the clinics, almost 40 percent were dissatisfied with the doctors' manners, and with getting advice from them on how to stay healthy and instructions on how to stay healthy and instructions about medication and follow-up care . . . . In city emergency rooms, where slightly more than 4,000 people were interviewed, about 17 percent said they thought the doctors were discourteous and 20 percent said the same of nurses. At inpatient wards, interviewers found a 22 percent dissatisfaction rate with the doctors' courtesy and a 29 percent dissatisfaction rate with that of nurses. (Kennedy, 1999, B1)

While the above survey was a passive client feedback strategy, it "empowers" consumers by presenting their complaints with the public health-care system. The data speak for consumers who use the system, and show a lower rate of satisfaction than that for private systems of care. Of course, consumer empowerment only goes as far as the city's responsibility for improving the system of care, by improving bedside manner, warmth and communication with patients, and, most importantly, the medical advice and information given to patients.

A more active approach of consumer empowerment is provided in a study involving focus group interviews with parents whose children were in foster care. Kapp and Propp (2002) present the need for "moving the clients to center stage and adopting a more client-centered approach and philosophy of service delivery." They note that in the child welfare field, the viewpoints of parents whose children were placed in foster care have been routinely neglected. The findings indicate a lack of responsiveness to parents by both the state and private agencies and a severe lack of communication between parents and agencies. As one parent commented:

> No one knows what's going on. You talk to three different people and get three different answers. The state doesn't know what they are supposed to be doing . . . . [N]o one communicates with us anymore. Now I have two different agencies, the state agency and the private agency, that don't communicate with me.
>
> When you make probably 15 calls in one week and you don't get a call back, what are you going to do?

Another finding was the effect of frequent worker turnover had on these parents.

> I just get attached and feel good about working with someone, and then they are gone. It's hard for me to take the risk and doing that all over again, thinking that they are going to be out the door in six months.
>
> Every month or every two months they are changing your case manager. You never know who it is. They don't get in contact with you. First you have this person, then that person. By the time you are through a year, you've got eight different case managers, and none of them knows what's going on.

These comments clearly show the value of surveying patients, consumers, and clients as a means to achieve client empowerment. However, as Fetterman (1996) states, "The evaluator empowers no one. People empower themselves in an open forum" (p. 5). Consumers need access to organizational structures to make sure that empowerment takes place, and formal program evaluations can be one forum for participation.

In social work and the field of health advocacy, macro-practice consists of community organization activities to ensure consumer or client participation and participation by the communities where consumers live. Involvement of consumers in the program-planning process and in the evaluation itself would help. Consumers need to be organized into a constituency by professionals interested in true consumer participation. Connecting the organization firmly to the community would give professionals more potential consumers who can voice their concerns.

In this sense, evaluators need assistance from organizing professionals and administrators and staff within the organization where the evaluation is being conducted and where the consumer group needs to be empowered. Fetterman looks to people to empower themselves:

> An evaluator does not or cannot empower anyone; people empower themselves often with assistance and coaching. This process is fundamentally democratic. It invites (if not demands) participation, examining issues of concern to the community in an open form. (Fetterman 1996, p. 6)

Fetterman's concept of change seems somewhat naïve for the most powerless groups of consumers, those groups whom he says have been part of empowerment evaluations, such as parents in educational settings, American Indian tribes, patients with AIDS, the homeless, and populations who routinely drop out of social and health programs. In empowering consumers, a differential approach is needed. An excellent suggestion is to assess the consumers' level of oppression or disenfranchisement. More attention to empowerment of consumers is needed for programs that serve people who are most oppressed on the basis of race or ethnicity, gender, income, health, and disability status (Secret, Jordan, and Ford, 1999).

Evaluators also have "a moral responsibility to serve as (consumer) advocates, after the evaluation has been conducted." The final step of empowerment is often liberation:

> Liberation is the act of being freed or freeing oneself from pre-existing roles and constraints. It often involves new conceptualizations of oneself and others. (Fetterman, 1996, p. 16)

Fetterman discusses new health initiatives to minority populations of South Africa in spite of the disenfranchisement and high rates of disease and unemployment. In the United States, the higher death rates from less access to medical and preventative care for minority groups have resulted in outreach programs designed to improve access to health care. Consumer groups who are affected can be liberated as access to health care is improved.

Empowerment Evaluation

Empowerment evaluation, as described by Fetterman (1996), emphasizes the involvement of *all* program stakeholders, program funders, administrators, direct-service staff, and clients or consumers in collaborative and participatory processes. With greater participation of the parties involved, the hope is that program evaluation will then become ongoing and internalized in the system.

> Empowerment evaluation is not a research methodology, but a vehicle for participation. All types of evaluation designs as well as both qualitative and quantitative research approaches are included. Evaluators teach people to conduct their own evaluations and this is thought to make evaluation an integral part of program planning. Self-evaluation is emphasized—to help program participants evaluate themselves and their program to improve practice and foster self-determination. (Fetterman, 1996, p. 4)

In program evaluation, the goal is to develop empowerment and "stakeholder ownership" in evaluation products and processes.

> Empowerment evaluations have been applied to the following settings: conflict resolution, the drop-out problem in education, environmental health and safety, homelessness, educational reform, AIDS, Native American concerns, and the education of gifted children . . . . In an empowerment setting, advocate evaluators allow participants to shape the direction of the evaluation, suggest ideal solutions to their problems, and then take an active role in making social change happen. (Fetterman, 1996, pp. 6, 13)

Empowerment evaluation is a collaborative group activity in which all in the group get involved in evaluation discussions. Group work using participatory group techniques can encourage program involvement. Stakeholders are involved in the need to be engaged in the process of designing, implementing, and monitoring evaluation activities. The participants assess program components, establish program goals and strategies to achieve goals, and discuss how to document progress toward those goals.

One of the first steps in an empowerment evaluation is "taking stock" of the program's strengths and weaknesses (Secret, Jordan, & Ford, 2002, p. 120). The group then develops an evaluation research design or plan. As the evaluation develops, all involved have a stake in the program's improvement. Those involved in the evaluation explore successful program strategies to share lessons learned and enhance programming. Empowerment evaluation is clearly related to a strengths perspective in program evaluation.

While empowerment evaluation is strengths-based and the hope is that all groups will be empowered, Weiss (1998) notes that "the main players seem to be the professionals who run the projects and community members who take leadership roles in the projects are sometimes participants" (p. 99). Empowerment evaluation is fine as long as the empowerment needs of consumers come first, and this is not assured in the model.

Empowerment evaluation runs against top-down models of evaluation with heavy administrative authority or evaluations that do not ensure all stakeholders' participation, especially those evaluations done by outside evaluators with little knowledge of the internal workings of the program. By contrast, empowerment evaluation highlights the value of consumer participation, which may be underemphasized in evaluations done in the past. Although many evaluators have achieved relatively full participation in past evaluation studies, use of *empowerment evaluation* can help ensure that the evaluator emphasizes collaboration and participation throughout the process of conducting the evaluation study.

Evidence-Based Practice

Evidence-based practice (EBP) is not directly connected to program evaluation in the same way that a strengths perspective, consumer empowerment, and empowerment evaluation are. However, EBP is having such a profound effect on the practice techniques used by professionals that it must be considered important in program evaluation, because EBP has a strong effect on the interventions delivered in programs. Evidence-based practice was first developed in the field of medicine and health practice. Now EBP is having a profound effect on health and human service professionals, especially in mental health treatment, social work, education, and other areas in human services and health.

EBP has a simple premise: review the literature in an area of treatment and see what seems to work. In EBP, practitioners use interventions that have been shown to be effective in research studies with empirical data indicating that the treatment was linked to positive outcomes. Evidence-based treatments (EBTs) are "any practices that have been established as effective through scientific research according to a set of criteria" (Institute for the Advancement of Social Work Research [IASWR], 2008, p. 2). The criteria are based on the type of research design employed, with experimental studies using randomly assigned control or contrast groups considered the best studies or the gold standard for proving effectiveness of the intervention.

Randomized control studies are at the top of the hierarchy of study designs. The highest value is placed on experimental studies with random assignment to different forms of treatment (contrast groups) or no treatment (control or placebo groups). The next-best study for EBT has a quasi-experimental design, in which subjects are not randomly assigned but groups with different types of treatment are compared. Studies of treatment over time or cohort studies of a particular treatment are valued less, as are surveys of people in treatment. Finally, qualitative in-depth studies of interventions or individual case studies that do not have quantitative measures of outcome are low on the hierarchy of study designs assessing EBT.

In EBP and EBT, systematic reviews of the literature are conducted to establish the treatments that have had the most success for the problems that the intervention or program is addressing. Meta-analyses or analyses of outcome data across many studies are valued, particularly if those studies employed experimental designs.

This hierarchy of designs mirrors the types of evaluation studies presented in Chapter 2. In EBP, more summative designs are valued, such as impact assessment studies having experimental designs with random assignment to different forms of practice. Formative studies such as process evaluations of programs or program monitoring and program implementation studies are less valued because experimental designs are not used and quantitative outcome measures are not studied. The field of program evaluation focuses more on program development and the implementation phase that programs go through. EBP looks at more finalized conclusions about the outcome of practice.

Problems in the Use of Evidence-Based Practice

The use of EBP can be limited because in some practice areas the research evidence is either not clear or there is a lack of evidence as to which treatment or intervention is the best. Many times, the evidence does not fit the criteria of data from an experimental study with a randomized control group because assigning subjects to no treatment or a placebo treatment has serious ethical issues. Randomly assigning subjects to certain treatments in the contrast group also raises ethical concerns, as practitioners may feel that certain people should be assigned to certain treatments based on the unique qualities of the case. Quantitative outcome measures may also be limited or have measurement issues that make measuring change or success difficult.

For the field of program evaluation, there are unique problems in using EBP. EBT fits more narrowly defined clinical practice with consumers, for example, one-on-one counseling in mental health. Also, therapies such as cognitive-behavioral treatment (CBT), which have been studied more using experimental designs, are generally valued more. In program evaluation, the EBT is delivered in a broader program context or an organization-based context. In that context, variables such as program resources may affect how the EBT is delivered. Qualitative research, which is undervalued in EBP, may be especially useful in uncovering how initial program strategies are working. The local context and the cultural aspects of the program and clients may be given less focus in EBP but can be key in a program reaching a certain group of consumers and thus in being effective.

In Chapter 4, qualitative and in-depth descriptions of the program itself will be presented as scientific, even if the descriptions do not achieve the same type of scientific criteria as those of randomized controlled treatments. Program evaluation as a field of research may be regarded with suspicion by those who demand evidence from experimental studies. Program descriptions can also be scientific in terms of exploration and description; science is not based solely on impact assessment studies using experimental designs and quantitative outcome measures.

In fairness, this broader context is now used in EBP when EBP is defined as "a process in which the practitioner *combines* well-researched interventions with practice experience, ethics, client and community preferences and culture to inform the delivery of treatments and services that can be applied at the individual, family, group, or policy level" (IASWR, 2008, p. 1). Whether this broader premise is used is up to those examining how services are planned or allocated. They need to remember that this strict, narrow vision of the use of experimental designs is not the absolute criterion of EBP and EBT treatments and practitioners.

A number of Web sites are helpful in describing the field of evidence-based practice. These include the Campbell Collaborative (www.campbellcollaboration.org), Evidence-Based Behavioral Practice (www.ebbp.org), and Gibbs' Evidence-Based Practice for the Helping Professions (www.evidence.brookscole.com).

Summary

1. The strengths perspective, consumer empowerment, and empowerment evaluation are three very important trends in program evaluation.

2. The strengths perspective is applied to both direct practice and program evaluation. Practitioners and evaluators should emphasize the strengths and resilience *in people and communities* and the strengths *in programs and parts of programs* that work.

3. The identification and participation of *stakeholders* is an important part of the evaluation process.

4. Consumer, patient, and client empowerment can give a voice to the consumers of the program. Both passive approaches such as consumer surveys and especially more active approaches such as in-depth personal interviews can help represent consumers in the planning, implementation, and evaluation of human service programs.

5. Empowerment evaluation focuses on the involvement of all program stakeholders in collaborative and participatory processes. Administrators and direct-service staff need to participate in the evaluation if it is to have an impact on the program.

6. Programs and interventions will continue to be influenced by evidence-based practice (EBP) or the use of practice methods that have been shown to be effective through experimental studies. In EBP, more summative evaluations are valued, while formative evaluation studies and qualitative research may be undervalued.

REFERENCES

Arnone, G.M. (2002). *The Risk and Protective Factors of Resilience and the Implications for Social Work Practice.* New York: Hunter College School of Social Work.

Crane, J. (1998) Building on success. In Crane, J. (ed.) *Social Programs That Work.* New York: Russell Sage Foundation.

Fetterman, D.M. (1996). Empowerment evaluation: An introduction to theory and practice. In Fetterman, D.M., Kaftarian, S.J., & Wandersman, A. (eds.) *Empowerment Evaluation: Knowledge and Tools for Self Assessment and Accountability.* Thousand Oaks, CA: Sage Publications, pp. 3–46.

Godbout, J. (1981). Is consumer control possible in health care services? *International Journal of Health Care Services* 11:151–167.

Institute for the Advancement of Social Work Research (IASWR). (2008). Evidence-based practice: A brief from the Institute for the Advancement of Social Work Research. http://www.socialworkers.org/research/default.asp.

JACHO, Joint Commission on Accreditation in Healthcare Organizations, www.jcaho.org.

Kapp, S.A., & Propp, J. (2002). Client satisfaction methods: Input from parents and children in foster care. *Child and Adolescent Social Work Journal* 19(3):227–245.

Kennedy, R. (1999). City hospitals' first survey of satisfaction among customers finds it unexpectedly high. *The New York Times*, July 20, B1, B8.

Rossi, P.H., Lipsey, M.W., & Freeman H.E. (2004). *Evaluation: A Systematic Approach*. Thousand Oaks, CA: Sage Publications.

Royse, D., Thyer, B.A., Padgett, D.K., & Logan, T.K. (2001). *Program Evaluation: An Introduction*. Belmont, CA: Wadsworth/Thomson Learning.

Saleeby, D. (2002). *The Strengths Perspective in Social Work Practice*. Boston, MA: Allyn and Bacon.

Schorr, L. (1997). *Common Purpose: Strengthening Families and Neighborhoods to Rebuild America*. New York: Doubleday Anchor Books.

Secret, M., Jordan, A., & Ford, J. (1999). Empowerment evaluation as a social work strategy. *Health and Social Work* 45(2):120–127.

Weiss, C.H. (1998). Evaluation: *Methods for Studying Programs and Policies*. Upper Saddle River, NJ: Prentice-Hall.

White, D. (2001). Consumer and community participation: A reassessment of process, impact, and value. In Albrecht, G., Fitzpatrick, S., & Scrimshaw, S. (eds.) *Handbook of Social Studies in Health and Medicine*. Thousand Oaks, CA: Sage Publications, pp. 465–480.

4

Describing the Program

Describing the program may be the most important and valuable part of program evaluation. Sadly, program description has been de-valued in the field of program evaluation and in most evaluation texts program description has been implied but not directly proposed. This is not right.

Programs are complex and amorphous phenomena. In a somewhat whimsical vein, Weiss has defined a *program* as "an amalgam of dreams, personalities, theories and assumptions, rooms, paper clips, organizational structures, clients and activities, photo copies, budgets and great intentions" (Weiss, 1998, p. 48). Since programs are complex, they need to be described and defined clearly.

Programs have the characteristics of Pandora's box, in the sense that so many things are included in the program and need to be described. This makes presenting and describing the program to someone a real challenge, but, when the challenge is accepted, the resulting program description is totally gratifying.

Program description is the best way to prevent the "black-box" or "unknown-box" phenomenon where many evaluators can actually ignore the program and its idiosyncrasies. The black-box phenomenon happens in many evaluations, but occurs most in impact assessment and experimental studies in which more resources are spent allocating consumers to different programs or treatments and in defining outcome measures and less on describing the intervention. Perhaps the fact that there is so much to describe leads to a feeling that program descriptions are too difficult to write, so the evaluator ignores the details of the program. Or the organization doing the evaluation might not want to assign the resources needed to write a comprehensive program description in the first place.

Describing the program takes more time and effort than one might realize, but it is a rewarding and thankful process that makes everyone feel more secure about the professional work and the commitment to the program. This process is so important that the inability to develop an accurate and comprehensive description of the program has been cited as one of the major obstacles to program evaluation (Chapel, 2004, p. 636).

The development of program descriptions can be a method for operationalizing consumer empowerment, empowerment evaluation, a strengths perspective, and evidence-based practice, discussed in the previous chapter. Consumers and staff involved in the evaluation can play a role in describing the program and thus be empowered by participating in this process, through planning meetings for the evaluation and taking part in interviews that further document the program model. This involvement of consumers and staff can be an indication that all are dedicated to the program and its mission.

The program description can be written from a strengths perspective of emphasizing the positives in the program design and the strengths in the consumers served. At the same time, deficits should be examined. In spelling out these deficits improvements in the program and in the way consumers approach the program can be developed. Also, the more that is known about the program, the more evidence-based practice exists, thus the ways in which the practice worked or did not work can be substantiated.

While program description is a crucial step in formulating an evaluation study, surprisingly, program evaluation theorists do not directly emphasize this step. Weiss (1998, p. 3) uses the term "understanding the program," which may be one of the results of describing the program, but an evaluator needs first to describe the program to eventually understand it.

Rossi, Lipsey, and Freemen (2004, p. 93) emphasize one part of program description, "program theory description." This is one small part of describing the program. Likewise, a lot of recent attention has been given to the concept of logic modeling, where program inputs are placed in the expected sequence of steps to achieve program goals and outcomes. A comprehensive presentation of the sequence of inputs and outcomes is called a "full logic model," but this, too, is only one part of describing the program. Programs are not merely an accumulation of boxes and arrows which those who favor logic models might lead you to believe.

Evaluability assessment is a process that can be used to help describe the program. Evaluability assessment studies were used by evaluators at the Urban

Institute in Washington, D.C., to determine whether or not a program can be evaluated in its current state of implementation (Wholey, Hatry, & Newcomer, 1994). Evaluability assessment involves description of the program model, an assessment of how well defined and "evaluable" the program model is, and discussion of stakeholder interest in evaluation and the use of findings (Rossi et al., 2004, p. 136). It is the first part of evaluability assessment that is most useful—describing the program through collecting descriptive data on the program. The methods used in evaluability assessment show how data can be collected and used for developing a program description.

Thus understanding the program, program theory description, logic modeling, and evaluability assessment are all important parts the crucial process of describing the program. Overall, the concept of describing the program is the best way to think of all these activities together and program description should be our overriding concern and challenge. Describing the program is a process that is much more descriptive, qualitative, and in-depth than each of these activities alone. The whole program needs to be described, with the goal of developing a comprehensive program description or at least a description satisfying enough so that all have a clear idea of the program and the program evaluation can proceed within a more scientific framework.

The Black or Unknown Box

Describing the program helps prevent the black-box phenomenon in which the evaluator puts the bulk of the effort into measuring program goals and objectives and little effort into program description. This would be treating the program as a "black box," which might be more appropriately called the "unknown box."

Although Weiss described this phenomenon back in 1972, she still feels that some evaluators treat the program as the black or unknown box.

> A few evaluators still see the program as a black box, the contents of which do not concern them; they are charged with discovering effects. But if the evaluator has no idea of what the program really is, she may fail to use the right questions. Perhaps she believes the inflated barrage of program propaganda and expects mountain-moving outcomes from what are really puny efforts. More likely, she looks for the wrong order of effects. She looks for the attainment of the types of outcomes that have been verbalized, when the main resources of the operating program have been invested in a different course of action. (Weiss, 1998, p. 49)

If the evaluator treats the program as an unknown box, what happens if the program is totally successful and all the program goals and objectives are achieved? If the program is highly successful, but there is no comprehensive program description, it will not be clear how or why the program goals and objectives were achieved. Was it the outreach methods that succeeded in recruiting the target population of consumers? Was it the training provided to staff giving the service? Was it the theory on which the interventions were based? If the administrators are unclear about what the program is, how do they know how to replicate the program successfully in another setting?

The black- or unknown-box phenomenon has been associated most frequently with summative research including outcome studies and impact assessment studies using experimental and quasi-experimental designs. In these studies, people are randomly assigned to different forms of the intervention and very specific outcome variables are studied in an effort to determine which form of intervention "caused" the effect. Typically in these studies, more effort is directed at seeing that the groups of consumers are similar and in measuring the achievement of program goals, and less effort is put into describing the program.

Formative research, such as process evaluations and program-monitoring studies, specializes in describing the program. Formative research focuses more on program implementation and early program efforts and is more descriptive in nature. However, *all* evaluations should be suspect if they do not have comprehensive program descriptions and people do not understand what was offered. Thus describing programs is a first step in evaluation. Good program descriptions lay out the program rationale and can be an indicator of the logic associated with the program fulfilling its goals.

> [E]valuators (need to) pay close attention to the program. They should be familiar with the general field (of the program) very early in the game, and they should learn a good deal about the specific happenings of the program under study as the evaluation moves along. They should also understand exactly how the program expects to bring about required change. (Weiss, 1998, p. 46)

Evaluators who do evaluability assessments use the term "scouting the program," when they collecting data through reconnaissance work. The data collected can be used to develop a comprehensive description of the program. The comprehensive description needs to encompass the intervention, the outreach methods, and the program theory being used, among other things. All programs could merit from comprehensive descriptions that address each of the program areas in the program grid (see p. 90). For example, program descriptions usually emphasize program activities such as outreach strategies that called people's attention to the program, the interventions or what was done after the person came in for service, and the program theory on which the program was based.

A beginning evaluator might wonder why so much fuss is being made of describing the program. Since the program is in operation, someone must have written a program description. On what basis did the program go forward and get funded? Usually there is some description of the program; however, the program description is often not in-depth and the evaluator might have trouble using a thin description in developing an evaluation plan.

Other immediate and concrete reasons for the evaluator needing to describe the program include the following:

1. Sometimes no program description has been written. Some limited program documents are available but no real description or at least no thorough description has been written.
2. More often, a very cursory description of the program has been written and it needs to be improved before evaluation can proceed.
3. The program description may have been written during the program planning stage, but the program has changed as it became operational. There are usually differences between the planned program and the operational program. For example, in logic modeling of programs, Chapel (2004, p. 637) notes that the program model most often reflects what was intended; however, the program model changes as the program changes over time.
4. Programs always change over time, so we need an updated program description, since we are evaluating the program in its current state.
5. Program interventions differ from program to program and from worker to worker. There may not just be one program that is operating.

Describing the program is central to the purposes of research, which include exploration, description, replication, and knowledge building. These are the scientific reasons why program description is important:

1. One of the main purposes of social science research is *exploration*, to gain insight into and familiarity with a social phenomenon (Rubin & Babbie, 2005, p. 123). Each program is unique; an exploration of this particular program is needed if program evaluation is to proceed.

2. Another purpose of social science research is *description*, in which the researcher observes and describes what was observed. Research includes the description of situations and events through careful and deliberate observation that is more precise than casual descriptions (Rubin & Babbie, 2005, p. 124). Careful and exacting descriptions of the social phenomenon known as the program are important.
3. *Replication* is another value of social science methods. We need to have a comprehensive program description before we can ever reproduce the program at other sites and locations.
4. Research also produces *knowledge*. Comprehensive program descriptions increase our knowledge about how best to serve people and implement programs.

Descriptive processes in program evaluation have a scientific basis and can lead to explanations and predictions as well as causal inferences about the program and its effects. Weiss infers that describing one part of the program, for example, the unfolding of program theory, can help us infer some type of causal process.

> This is a big issue in evaluation; whether the program is responsible for whatever outcomes are observed . . . . [T]he usual way to tell whether the program was responsible is to compare units (people) that received the program with equivalent units (people) that did not. In many programs . . . it is not feasible to use comparison units; similar neighborhoods are too few and too different from each other to provide sensible comparisons. In order to get any purchase on the question of whether the program was the responsible agent, the tracing of program theory can help. A careful tracking of the unfolding program provides indications of how well the theories explain what happens and therefore how implicated the program was in events and outcomes. (Weiss, 1998, pp. 60–61)

Weiss's statements about program theory apply to the whole process of program description. Both quantitative and qualitative data are used to describe programs, with more emphasis on the qualitative, descriptive data. In achieving comprehensive descriptions of programs, there are parts of programs that can be described with quantitative data and parts that can be described with qualitative methods. The sociodemographic characteristics of clients, their presenting problems, how much service was given, the costs of the program, the number of employees and their professional backgrounds are all elements that can be described quantitatively. The program philosophy and rationale, its mission, the beliefs of the direct service staff, and the program environment and setting are the types of program components described better with qualitative methods.

PROGRAM ──────────────▶ GOALS

FIGURE 4.1. Usual model of program evaluation.

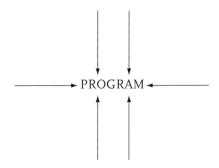

FIGURE 4.2. Model for program description.

Two simple diagrams can represent two ways of viewing processes in
program evaluation. The first diagram (Fig. 4.1) is a traditional way of viewing
program evaluation, especially in a summative view. It is based on purposes of
explanation and prediction in social science research. The aim is to determine
the degree to which the program can achieve its goals. The second diagram
(Fig. 4.2) is a model for describing the program in the initial stages of program
evaluation and in more formative studies such as program monitoring and
process evaluations. It is based on the use of social science research methods for
description. Effort is directed at the process of describing the program through
a number of activities conducted by the evaluator. In the next section, five
groups of activities that can help describe the program will be presented.

Evaluability Assessment

In describing the program, the evaluator might be involved in a number of
activities aimed at creating a comprehensive program description. These activities have been described in the field of evaluability assessment and are carried
out by evaluators to determine if the program has been defined sufficiently so
that it can be evaluated.

> Evaluability assessment is a process of negotiation and investigation
> undertaken jointly by the evaluator, the evaluation sponsor, and
> possibly other stakeholders to determine if a program meets the
> preconditions for evaluation and, if so, how the evaluation should be
> designed to ensure maximum utility (Rossi et al., 2004, p. 426)

Wholey (1994) developed evaluability assessment to determine if a particular program is worthy of evaluation. As for the activities of evaluability assessment, Rossi, Freeman, and Lipsey (2004) have identified three primary activities of evaluability assessment (p. 136):

1. Description of the program model with particular attention to defining program goals and objectives
2. Assessment of how well defined and evaluable the program model is
3. Identification of stakeholder interest in evaluation and the likely use of findings

Evaluability assessment studies can be done to determine if the program should be evaluated. However, the outcomes of evaluability assessment may be less desirable than the process itself. Few organizations will be interested in a complete study to determine if a program can be evaluated. However, a good evaluator can use the techniques suggested in evaluability assessment studies to create a comprehensive program description. The following techniques from evaluability assessment can be used to develop a comprehensive program description:

1. Examine and analyze all program documents and descriptions, such as annual reports, program proposals, administrative manuals, grant applications, contract documents, pamphlets describing the program, committee reports, minutes of meetings, staff lists, lists of agencies the program collaborates with, annual financial reports, audits and monitoring documents, previous evaluations of the program, needs assessment studies related to the program, news articles, and statements of program objectives, that describe the program and its activities. These program documents come under the rubric of "available data." Use whatever is available to assist in developing the program description.
2. Observe the program and program activities and functions in operation.
3. Have meetings in small groups with selected groups of staff, administrators, and clients to discuss the program and how it operates. Use a qualitative, flexible, approach to create in-depth program descriptions.
4. Conduct a pilot study in which you interview administrators, direct service staff, and clients, asking open-ended questions about the program, how it operates, its goals and philosophy, and issues in implementing the program, as well as the other content areas listed below.

5. Examine the literature in this program area to see what works and does not work and what other people have tried. Examine both descriptions of similar programs in the literature as well as evaluative reports that indicate the type of success that has been achieved.

Developing a full program description can be a daunting task. This could result in a whole descriptive study about the program that resembles studies of program processes called "process evaluations." However, usually evaluators do the best they can, given the limited resources in the initial stages of conducting the evaluation study, because the complete evaluation study still needs to be planned and implemented. It is probably easiest to use the available data about the program and do some observation of the program and a few interviews or focus groups with key groups so that the evaluator can meet a deadline of completing the program description.

The most critical people to be involved in this process are direct-service staff who know the most about the day-to-day operations of the program and may be empowered in sharing their views on the program (Rossi et al., 2004, p. 136). Consumer empowerment may be even more critical, as clients or members of the target population are also those most often left out and frequently overlooked in the process of describing a program. Staying with the notion of an empowerment evaluation will help emphasize the critical role of actual and potential consumers and staff of the program who need their voices heard. A strengths perspective can also be useful if the evaluator cuts the program some slack, allows for the strengths in possible program theories and interventions which may work, and recognizes creative approaches to achieve program goals.

Writing the Program Description

Writing program descriptions is again perhaps the most valuable part of program evaluation. Before a formal evaluation study can proceed there should be some consensus statement or at least agreement about what the program is. The program description can be based on previous program documents, interviews with staff, administrators, and consumers, and observational notes about the program in operation. Writing the description can be a key process in an empowerment evaluation in which all parties state their views about the program and become engaged in the evaluation.

The focus and content of data collection from those involved with the program should be the standardized content areas that need to be addressed in a comprehensive program description. Each program will probably have more or less description in any one content area, but an attempt should be made to cover every topic:

1. An overview of the program, the program rationale and purpose, the program setting, sponsorship, history, and the broad goals of the program
2. The broader program context and "state of the art" in the program's field, nationally and locally
3. The program setting and location
4. The program theory, program logic, and interventive methods
5. The goals and objectives of the program
6. The consumers, clients, or patients served
7. Characteristics of staff
8. Program cost and funding
9. Program planning and implementation issues

1. Overview of the Program, Program Rationale and Purpose, Setting, Sponsorship, History, and Broad Goals of the Program

The program description can begin with an overview of the program. What social problem was the program designed to meet? What is the general purpose of the program? The overview can include the program rationale, the setting and program history, and the broad goals of the program.

A good starting point can be the mission statement of the program. Although mission statements are usually very broad, for example, "to serve all the patients with HIV/AIDS in our community," they do provide the program's general focus or intent. Although mission statements are very general, they can lead to the overall rationale and purpose of the program and the general need the program was designed to meet. The rationale and purpose of the program can in turn lead to the overall outcomes and goals of the program.

The mission of the agency and the program may be to assist HIV/AIDS patients in the community. The program rationale and purpose may be to use volunteers to deliver meals to patients in the community and prevent social isolation of patients by seeing that they relate to their friends and family. The outcomes and goals may be to provide meals, increase relationships with friends, community participation, and the use of social services, and lessen feelings of isolation and depression that may be related to their diagnoses. Examining initial and general statements about mission, program rationale and purpose, and general outcomes and goals often provides a context for evaluation. For example, how does the program develop from the delivery of meals to preventing the social isolation of HIV/AIDS patients living in the community?

The overview can also present the history or origins of the program. The history may include the extent of the possible legislative or policy mandate for the program. This general overview statement can also include the need for the program and the problem the program was designed to solve; the program philosophy; an overview of the intervention and practice methods used; the theories, principles, and assumptions on which the program is based; the recruitment methods used; the setting of the program; funding and sponsorship of the program; and the consumers to be served. These general descriptions are then a prelude to more specific presentations of the broader program context and state of the art in the program's field, including the program setting and location; program theories and logic; interventive methods used; the goals and objectives of the program; the consumers, clients, or patients served; characteristics of staff; program cost and funding; and program implementation issues.

2. Broader Program Context and State of the Art in the Program's Field, Nationally and Locally

Specific programs can always be located within a broader program context. The broader program context can be the policy context, the program area or field of service, and the state of the art in that program field. The policy context of the program provides a link to the social, health, or educational needs that the program is designed to meet. This includes examining the literature and program documents that answer questions such as the following: How many people have this particular need? What are the current policies in place to meet this need? How many programs are there to meet this need nationally and locally? How are current legislation and policies designed to meet this need? How are national, state, and local governments responding to those needs?

The program's area of service or field of service is another part of the broader context. Where does this program fit in terms of the sponsoring agency, the local community, the state, the nation? Do all localities need to resolve these needs through programs? What is the current thinking about and the state of the art for programs in this area of service? Which strategies have proven successful in the past in such programs?

Which interventions have worked and how does this particular program add to the interventions tried in the past? What are the overall success rates? What types of program implementation issues usually surface in this program field?

One great way to provide the broader context is to review the policy literature related to the program, program descriptions in the literature, and previous evaluations of such programs. For example, in evaluating employee assistance programs (EAPs) in university settings, the program should be located within the policy context of the need for such programs and the program field of EAP program models. One such model is a "broad-brush" approach that provides a variety of wellness and counseling programs to the university population. In these programs, nutrition and health, personal counseling and advocacy services to assist people with personal problems, and assistance for employees in the care of elderly relatives and in finding day care service are emphasized. The literature on broad-brush programs generally in EAPs and especially programs in university EAP programs would be reviewed.

Another model of EAP is drug and alcohol–specific programs that target substance abuse. The literature on EAP programs focusing more on substance abuse should be reviewed if this will be the major model of service employed. Both the literature describing these EAP programs and the evaluation literature reporting on the implementation issues in these programs and success rates should be examined. Overall, the rationale for selecting a broad-brush or a substance abuse model should be documented and the emphasis on one or the other approach presented as an important policy issue for universities nationally and locally.

Researching the literature and presenting the program in a broader context are important because they help link this program effort to the knowledge base of other programs. For example, in evaluating a program using computer matching of senior citizens who need housing with people renting available apartments and houses an evaluator needs to examine the literature. In developing this program, the general thinking of the program planners was that through this computer matching of the elderly and housing vacancies maybe 50% of the matches would be successful and result in housing for the seniors. In conducting the literature review on these matching programs, however, the researchers found that usually only about 10% of the matches resulted in successful housing placement. With this information and data, this idealized notion of the effect of the program was replaced with a more realistic assessment of the program's impact.

3. Program Setting and Location

The organization and setting where the program is located can have profound effects on the program. For example, a patient representative or patient advocate employed in a large hospital will be greatly affected by the setting. Does the administration just pay lip service to the concept of patient advocacy or do they see the advocacy role as a way to level the playing field between health-care professionals and consumers? Will the patient representative or advocate be allowed to really advocate for patients' rights when the hospital's medical staff have violated those rights or will the patient representatives be constrained to resolving billing complaints or making sure that a patients' personal effects such as petty cash and eyeglasses are safe and secure? When the patient needs a patient representative to resolve a patient complaint, the patient could be a major contributor to the hospital or a low-income patient with limited health insurance. Will both parties be given the same service and the same commitment to patients' rights? The orientation of the hospital's hierarchical and power structure will have a great effect on what a patient advocate can do.

Naturally, the political climate of the organization will affect the program. Is this an organization with a charismatic leader or a bureaucratic leader? Does the program or agency executive want to make this program a major selling point on their resume and career? For example, one college president wanted to make a new employee assistance program a significant employee benefit that would fit the president's overall plan of "humanizing the institution."

What is the physical setting of the program? It is located in a place where consumers have easy access? If the program is a case management program in mental health, the clients need accessibility to the program and the case managers need accessibility to the community where the persons with mental illness live. What is the organizational structure? Do employees have job security? Are they paid the going wage for their respective professions? These are some of the questions to consider under the heading "organizational setting."

Another example of the effect of the setting on a program is a patient-care advocacy program within a managed-care insurance company that resolves consumer complaints. The patient advocacy program was crucial because of recent changes in managed care, such as contracting with more providers, increasing patient choice, and the company's response to current and proposed government-legislated consumer protection. The patient advocacy program was established to protect patients by resolving complaints, tracking grievances, and suggesting needed system changes. The overall purpose was to humanize the managed-care system, increase members' satisfaction with the health-care providers, prevent further investigations of bad medical practices, and resolve disputes.

Depending on how the organization views the program, the patient advocate could be seen in a neutral role or as a patient advocate. The issue is how aggressive the organization sees the advocate in terms of changing the patient's primary care physician, reducing the wait for a doctor, or obtaining a specialist. If not enough resources were available, staff could view the program as a "phantom program," a good public-relations move by the insurance company, but providing little in terms of service (Wilbrect, 1997). For example, in one advocacy program, most members were unaware of the patient advocate program. Also, the ratio of the large number of complaints to the small number of patient advocates was so high that the complaints could never be adequately investigated.

It is useful to organize issues in the program setting in a systems perspective. What role does the program play in the organization? In a systems perspective, the organization relates to its external environment. The program may bring in resources to the organization, which could be the only reason the organization has this program. The program could be strictly public relations because it "looks good" for this organization to have such a program. On the other hand, it could also be a positive way for an organization to meet the additional needs of the community it serves.

For example, staff at one large cancer hospital thought it needed some programming for the families of cancer patients, so hospital staff developed a group program for support of caregivers. Although a good program was developed, it clearly did not meet the needs of the very large number of patients served, but it was a way for the hospital to say it was relating to the community. An organization may feel the need to develop a program in a particular area just because it does not want to be criticized for not meeting the needs of a particular community. An agency may feel it needs to develop an HIV/AIDS program simply because it needs to show it is relating to the people in its environment, where there are large percentages of patients with HIV/AIDS.

4. Program Theory, Program Logic, and Interventive Methods

Considerations about program theories, the program logic, and the interventive methods used are crucial in program evaluation and, in fact, all program-planning processes. Theory, logic, and intervention methods need to be addressed in program descriptions. There are three types of program theory:

articulated program theory, implied program theory, and implausible program theory.

Articulated Program Theory

Theory that is an essential part of the program has been called "articulated program theory."

> *Articulated program theory* is an explicitly stated version of program theory that is spelled out in some detail as part of the program's documentation and identity or as a result of efforts by the evaluator and stakeholders to formulate the theory (Rossi et al., 2004, p. 168)

In articulated program theory, theory is an essential part of the program design and is documented as such. A good example of articulated program theory is presented in the program description of the Citiwide Harm Reduction outreach model (see below). This program serving previously homeless people involved in drug use and living in single room occupancy (SRO) hotels is based on low-threshold harm reduction outreach. The program begins by offering clean needles and supplies such as toiletries to intravenous (IV) drug users in SRO hotels. The theory is that by meeting the participants "where they are at" with their drug use and by offering clear services in a simple way, a trusting relationship can be established that will provide easier access to medical and social services. Once a trusting relationship is established, then health services are offered in the participant's own room or in the hospital for problems such as AIDS, hepatitis C, diabetes, substance abuse problems, and mental health issues. In addition, participants are referred to social services from the New York City HIV/AIDS services for the delivery of meals to other social-service and employment agency referrals. Thus the articulated program theory is that by providing practical, on-the-spot help, the participants will establish trusting relationships that they may not have found in their previous contacts with other, more bureaucratic social- and health-service agencies.

A similar theory was used in a voucher program to serve low-income families with developmentally disabled children in the South Bronx (McKaig, Caro, & Smith, 1989). By providing very practical help in the form of vouchers used to purchase needed food, clothing, furniture, and baby care supplies to families with developmentally disabled children, the family support program hoped to establish positive connections with the families. Direct and concrete help could clearly benefit these families. Once these relationships were established, the agency would be in an excellent position to provide advocacy for home care and educational and social services for the family in their extra duties related to caring for a developmentally disabled child. In both these programs, the provision of immediate help was intended to set this agency apart from other agencies serving the developmentally disabled that had more bureaucratic procedures for providing immediate and concrete help to families.

A Program Description Based on Program Theory: The CitiWide Harm Reduction Outreach Model

BENJAMIN SHEPARD, PH.D.

ASSISTANT PROFESSOR, NEW YORK CITY TECHNICAL COLLEGE OF THE CITY UNIVERSITY OF NEW YORK

PROGRAM DESCRIPTION[*]

The CitiWide Harm Reduction outreach model integrates low-threshold harm reduction outreach with home-delivered social and medical services. Its strength is a low-threshold manner for engaging with those living in single-room occupancy (SRO) hotels. The aim of the model is to meet participants "where they are at" with their drug use, providing easy access to services for those engaged in outreach who are placed in New York City's SRO hotels by the New York City HIV/AIDS Services Administration. The outreach program begins by offering clean needles and supplies such toiletries to those in SRO hotels. Once trust is established, participants are provided access to health-care services in their rooms or at Montefiore Medical Center and/or social services at CitiWide's drop-in center.

CitiWide Harm Reduction began as an underground needle exchange organized by former ACT UP (AIDS Coalition to Unleash Power) member Brian Weil, a New York artist in 1994. CitiWide began operations in 1995 with the support of La Resurrection United Methodist Church, providing services in a setting that few service providers had reached out to: SRO hotels throughout the South Bronx and Upper Manhattan (Lyons, 2001). Under Weil's leadership, CitiWide was founded to bring services directly to sites where the need for needle exchange was most profound; these SRO hotels served as emergency shelters for homeless people living with HIV/AIDS (PLWAs). Since the mid-1990s CitiWide has built on the basic non-judgmental low-threshold approach to the delivery of health-care services at the core of needle exchange practice.

---

[*] The author would like to thank Daliah Heller, the executive director of CitiWide Harm Reduction, for her innovation, the ideas and approaches behind this intervention model, and suggestions for this article.

CitiWide Harm Reduction was part of the second generation of needle exchange programs in New York City. Along with Housing Works, CitiWide assumed that the demographics of the AIDS pandemic would continue to shift as low-income women and people of color remained an underserved HIV/AIDS high-risk group. The agency was also New York City's first syringe exchange program to go to SRO hotels where homeless people living with HIV/AIDS are placed for emergency shelter.

The highly chaotic, poverty-ridden context of the SRO hotel environment contributes to risk behaviors. In addition to serving as a focal point for extensive sex work transactions, components of the black market economy, such as drug-dealing and loan-sharking that target residents at the site, take place at SROs. Thus women, men who have sex with men (MSM), and transgendered individuals in the SROs are impacted by these risks, including violence. In this dangerous and transient environment, fear, isolation, and lack of information create barriers to residents for obtaining social, mental, and physical health services, including access to HIV treatments (Heller & Shepard, 2001).

By bringing HIV prevention and care services to people at their homes and in a respectful, nonjudgmental fashion, staff can initiate trusting relationships with those who reside at the hotels. Staff members establish a comfort level for participants who may be wary or distrusting of or uncomfortable with service providers because the participants had negative experiences or interactions with providers in the past. Given the social isolation, stigma, and shame experienced by individuals residing in the SRO hotels targeted by outreach and the frequently chaotic and unsafe environment of the SRO hotel setting, it is essential that the team set out to build trust with this community of PLWAs to support and promote use of the services offered (CitiWide Harm Reduction, 2002).

PLWAs living in SRO hotels suffer from medical complications such as hepatitis C and diabetes, as well as substance and mental health problems. In the ensuing years, CitiWide has successfully built on its needle exchange and home delivery model to engage and care for this hard-to-reach population through Harm Reduction Services. The great innovation was expanding the home delivery model to a broader level of essential health-care services. Currently, a nurse practitioner, a doctor from Montefiore Medical Center, and a team of outreach workers are part of CitiWide's outreach team delivering services, which include food delivery to service referrals, all on site in SRO hotel rooms. As part of its joint program, Montefiore staff members deliver medical and mental health services, from blood tests to gynecological exams to medication prescriptions and counseling. They also set up appointments and travel arrangements for appointments to and from Montefiore's Comprehensive Health Care Center and CitiWide's drop-in center, where participants receive an additional

A Program Description Based on Program Theory (Continued)

array of case management, mental health services, and group and holistic counseling. Rides to and from the hospital can be arranged with CitiWide's full-time van driver.

Just reaching homeless people at risk can be a difficult first step. Building a trusting relationship is even more difficult, yet it is an essential step for creating a context that promotes behavior change (DeCarlo, Susser, & Peterson, 1996). The low-threshold harm reduction outreach model attempts to establish just such a context for change.

PROGRAM THEORY

The CitiWide Harm Reduction model was based on a significant amount of program theory. Much of harm reduction was developed in relation to Prochaska and DiClemente's transtheoretical model (2005). This framework delineates five stages of change: *(1)* precontemplative, in which individuals are not yet considering change; *(2)* contemplative, in which change is considered but ambivalence is high; *(3)* determination, in which the balance of ambivalence is tipped in favor of change; *(4)* action, in which change is initiated; and *(5)* maintenance, in which change results are maintained. The vast majority of substance users move back and forth between stages in anything but a linear fashion. These individuals are often unlikely to access health or medical services. Thus the health-care system is out of reach for many of those who need these services the most (Westermeyer, 2002).

CitiWide's program theory functions as an extension and a departure from this model and its limitations (see Marlotte et al., 2000). CitiWide does not ask people to change as much as it offers options and choices. It recognizes that drug use carries multiple meanings. Instead of assuming that abstinence is a starting point for treatment, CitiWide seeks to engage substance users across a broad continuum while working to provide a progressive perspective and alternative to traditional systems. A core assumption of this approach is that it is inhumane to take away one coping mechanism without replacing it with another (Tartarsky, 2002). Thus CitiWide's outreach team emphasizes bringing people tools—access to health care, dignity, respectful consultation, the opportunity for counseling and reflection, and partnership—while engaging participants in a supportive relationship. Most importantly, the model posits that the expressed desires of participants drive the program (ROMEO, n.d.).

CitiWide outreach workers use a harm reduction approach in which they try to learn from the reality of life for participants. In this model, outreach workers seek to understand drug, set, and setting; in other words, the meaning of the drug itself, the context, mindset of its use, and the specific setting of this use—where drug use is taking place and whether it is safe or unsafe. The program goal is to work with those on the periphery of the transtheoretical model, keeping all of these factors in mind. This approach, through which workers seek to learn, assess, and provide requested services, seems to be more effective in engaging hard-to-reach people than mounting a "knee-jerk" disease-model effort. When working with people who live in trauma or have experienced trauma, seeking to take away defenses, such as drug use, before there are services or enough room or psychological strength to deal with feelings can be considered cruel and contraindicated. The harm reduction outreach model strives to be more understanding, humane, and safe (Springer, n.d.; Zinberg, 1984).

TRANSLATING PROGRAM THEORY INTO PRACTICE INTERVENTIONS

Harm reduction–driven outreach interventions are based on the premise that these people must be met on their own terms, in their own communities and spaces if meaningful connections are to occur. Outreach is a harm reduction intervention that attempts to get people moving in the direction of change, even if change in high-risk behavior is not accepted. Outreach workers do not wait in an agency for the participant to come to the agency; instead they enter the external setting and offer aid. As stated earlier, CitiWide was New York City's first harm reduction needle exchange program to go to SRO hotels where the city places homeless people living with HIV/AIDS for temporary shelter.

CitiWide's emphasis was then and remains the provision of practical assistance without selling a bill of goods, through an approach of "how can we help you?" instead of "here's how I can help you." This shift in emphasis is important. While the answer to the question may produce more questions that have nothing to do with reducing drug use or stated goals of traditional substance use programs, it reflects CitiWide's emphasis on engagement with clients rather than on reducing drug use. Additionally, while there are those who are initially interested in referrals for shelter, medical care, food, and child care, many are not interested in these services. Outreach workers must accept that for many individuals living in the hotels, addictive behavior is of secondary importance, or not a concern. The primary concern is survival, and substance use is often part of that. In providing services, CitiWide's outreach team places emphasis on participant confidentiality, assuring that "my business isn't everybody's business." This point is essential for those living in cramped conditions in SRO hotels.

The aim of CitiWide's intervention is to provide individuals with little else than dignity and choice about treatments and service options. In the long run, those who feel respected for their priorities and values are far more likely to trust

A Program Description Based on Program Theory (Continued)

treatment providers and be open to various types of interventions. If workers show an interest in participants' interests, such as their drug use equipment, participants see there is no agenda. If participants see the worker actually providing services for these interests, such as clean needles or stem tips, then a rapport is established. Services then work all that much better. And participants may be open to engaging in other services, such as health care (CitiWide Harm Reduction, 2002; Westermeyer, 2002).

Outreach workers provide supplies that meet the basic and broad needs of those with HIV/AIDS living in the SROs. By providing regular evening and daytime door-to-door outreach at SROs, the outreach team reaches and engages those in need. The supplies provided to participants serve as tools for self-care and an improved sense of worth. For rapport to be established, outreach workers must go into areas where drug use is heavy, offering practical knowledge and services while building relationships (CitiWide Harm Reduction, 2002; Westermeyer, 2002). At its core, CitiWide seeks to cultivate the active involvement of users in their own health care and, if necessary, treatment action plans (Whittaker & MacLeod, 1998, p. 365).

CitiWide Harm Reduction's outreach model is made up of three specific components: *(1)* collaboration between CitiWide Harm Reduction and Montefiore Medical Center, *(2)* harm reduction outreach with a medical team, and *(3)* the joint CitiWide and Montefiore ROMEO program, designed to bring home-based primary care services to HIV-infected people living in the SRO hotels. Essential ingredients of the outreach model are CitiWide Harm Reduction and Montefiore working to establish trust with each other and with participants, lowering the entry-level threshold so that those living in SRO hotels can actually make use of these services, and allowing participants to maintain control of their decision to use services and the terms of usage (Heller et al., 2004).

Program engagement is a primary focus. Some participants who signed up to be part of the program were engaged in it, whereas others were not. A major hypothesis of the program is that participants who have more encounters with CitiWide Harm Reduction staff will subsequently initiate and maintain a greater degree of continuity in HIV medical care than participants with fewer encounters (Montefiore Medical Center, 2001, p. 27).

REFERENCES

CitiWide Harm Reduction (2002). Accessed December 11, 2002, from: http://www.citiwidehr.org.

DeCarlo, P., Susser, E., Peterson, J. (1996). What are homeless people's HIV prevention needs? http://people.virginia.edu/~gct2r/library/CAPS_Homeless.pdf.

Heller, D., & Shepard, B. (2001). The CitiWide Harm Reduction HOME model of services. Position paper.

Heller, D., McCoy, K., Cunningham, C. (2004). An invisible barrier to integrating HIV primary care with harm reduction services: Philosophical clashes between the harm reduction and medical models. Public Health Reports 119(1): 32–39.

Lyon, J. (2001, November). Back to the old neighborhood: The founder of a needle exchange dies from a dose, June/July 1996. Needle exchange renegade Brian Weil helped transform public health in New York. *CitiLimits*.

Marlotte, C.K., Jarvis, B., Fishbein, M., Kamb, M., Iatesta, M., Hoxworth, T., et al. (2000). Stage of change versus an integrated psychosocial theory as a basis for developing effective behaviour change interventions. The Project RESPECT Study Group. *AIDS Care* 12(3):357–364.

Montefiore Medical Center (2001). SPNS Outreach evaluation proposal. Project title: Outreach and Intervention Program to Reach HIV Infected Persons Living in Bronx New York Single Room Occupancy Hotels. Project Director: Chinazo Cunningham, MD. Co-Project Director: Daliah Heller, MPH.

Prochaska, J.O.& DiClemente, C.C. The Transtheoretical Approach. In: Norcross, J.C., Goldfried M.R., Editors. *Handbook of Psychotherapy Integration*. 2nd Ed. New York University Press; 2005, p. 147–171.

ROMEO. (n.d.). Vision statement. CitiWide Harm Reduction and Montefiore Hospital.

Springer, E. (n.d.). The psychological and cultural factors in drug use, "drug, set, and setting" (the basis for controlled intoxicant use). Dr. Norman Zinberg's work. Workshop handout.

Tartarsky, A. (2002). Harm reduction psychotherapy. In *Harm Reduction Psychotherapy: A New Treatment for Drugs and Alcohol Problems*. Northvale, NJ: Jason Aronson.

Westermeyer, R. (2002). Harm reduction and outreach interventions. Accessed December 10, 2002, from: http://www.cts.com/crash/habtsmrt/outreach.html.

Whittacker, A., & MacLeod, J. (1998). Care in the community. In Robert, R. (ed.) *Management of Drug Users in the Community: A Practical Handbook*. New York: Arnold/Hodder Headline Group and Oxford University Press.

Zinberg, N. (1984). *Drug, Set, and Setting: the Basis for Controlled Intoxicant Use*. New Haven, CT: Yale University Press.

Implicit Program Theory

Theory may or may not be part of the original program plan; however, program theory is always involved even if it is not stated. If a theory is not explicitly part of the program plan, it is implied in a program logic and through the interventive methods that are implemented. More typically, program theory is not explicitly stated in the program design. However, since a program is directed toward achieving some desirable consequence there are inherent beliefs that some type of intervention will achieve that result or outcome. Weiss (1998, p. 55) explains that theory does not need to be some broad, complex concept. The theory can be simply the beliefs that underlie actions. Thus a second type of program theory is *implicit program theory*: the assumptions and expectations inherent in a program's services and practices that have not been fully articulated and recorded (Rossi et al., 2004, p. 168). The program processes and interventions used reflect an implicit theory of why and how a particular result will be achieved.

An example of implicit program theory is the set of procedures that hospitals use to make patients aware of their rights as patients, discussed in the case below. While there is no explicit theory driving the model of implementation, the procedures used imply that patients will be more aware of their rights as they enter the hospital. In most hospitals, the Patient's Bill of Rights is given and explained to patients before they enter the hospital. It is assumed that their interaction with admitting personnel will make the patients aware of their rights as patients. Also, large posters are displayed prominently throughout the hospital for patients to read. While these procedures may change slightly from hospital to hospital, the implied theory is that the interaction with hospital staff, receipt of a copy of the bill of rights, and the display of the bill of rights throughout the hospital will increase the patient's awareness of and advocacy about their rights as patients.

Access to the Patient's Bill of Rights in a New York State Hospital
GAIL GARRICK, M.A.
GRADUATE OF THE MASTER'S PROGRAM IN HEALTH ADVOCACY,
SARAH LAWRENCE COLLEGE

According to hospital policy and procedure, the Patient's Bill of Rights and other federal- and state-prescribed material is mandated to be distributed to all patients admitted to the facility. The distribution of information is to be carried out by the emergency department or the admitting department of the hospital. All outpatients are also to be provided with the same patient's rights information when they register with the facility. This information was prepared by the federal government, along with the state and the Joint Commission [Public Health Law (PHL) 2803 (1)(g) Patient's Rights, 10NYCRR, 405.7, 405.7(a)(1), 405.7(c).]

In addition, the hospital provides information concerning the Patient's Bill of Rights on all bedside televisions in English and Spanish. Large-format posters containing patient's rights are displayed in public areas throughout the facility. These posters are printed in several languages. Training of the staff about patient's rights occurs during their orientation to hospital procedures and is reinforced on an annual basis.

The current Patient's Bill of Rights was prepared by the State of New York and is supposed to be enforced under state auspices by the State Department of Health. If the facility cannot provide a satisfactory conclusion to a patient's complaint, the next level of recourse for the patient is the State Department of Health. The rights protected by the patient's bill of rights, among other things, are as follows:

- Right to non-discrimination of any kind, including hearing, visual, and other disabilities;
- Right to know the names and position of any staff member present on your case;
- Right to know about your illness and treatment;
- Right to refuse treatment;
- Right to a written discharge plan;
- Right to review your medical record and to obtain a copy of same, for which a fee may be charged by the medical records department; and
- Right to a smoke-free room.

The hospital Patient's Bill of Rights is an offshoot of a federal Patient's Bill of Rights that addresses rights related to health insurance, recourse for patients who have been harmed by their health plan, protections from financial sanctions in emergency room care, access to necessary health-care specialists, and a fair and timely external appeals process to address health-plan grievances. Initiated in 1996, the bill, which has had incarnations as the Norwood-Dingell Act and the McCain, Edwards, Kennedy Act, has never been passed by both houses of the federal legislature and never has signed into law by a U.S. president. While our congressmen and women were busy debating or presenting their views on the health-care industry, states began preparing and implementing their own sets of patient's rights. Texas was the first state to establish a Patients' Rights Law in 1997. Other states followed shortly afterwards with their versions of patient's rights.

The Patient's Bill of Rights is presented to patients so that they can familiarize themselves with their personal rights after being admitted to a hospital and thus address any problems with their care in the facility. At the hospital, the admission packets have been professionally prepared for distribution. They are

Access to the Patient's Bill of Rights in a New York State
Hospital (Continued)

delivered to the Patient's Representative office from the printer and then distributed to the unit support associates for final distribution to the input units.

Each packet consists of the following items:

- *Your Rights as a Hospital Patient in New York State,* in English and Spanish (also available in Chinese, Japanese, Russian, and Yiddish);
- *A Patient's Guide to the Hospital,* which contains valuable information about the hospital and its services;
- *Medication Safety and You,* a patient guide to care with medications;
- Health care proxy form;
- Letter containing a listing of home health-care agencies;
- Patient notification record (PNR), which, when signed, indicates that the patient has received the admission packet. This executed form then becomes a permanent part of the patient's medical record: and
- An attractive folder in which all of the items are contained.

All of the information in the packet is presented in simple language so that it can be easily understood by most patients. If an interpreter is required for any reason by the patient (language barrier, visual impairment), the facility has an obligation to provide that service for them. There is a language interpreter's service available, conducted by telephone, which offers translations in obscure languages and dialects in addition to well-known languages. The hospital has the responsibility to ensure that each and every patient understands his or her rights. Family or friends, and hospital staff (probably the Patient Representative department) are permitted to provide assistance to patients who have a problem with understanding their rights.

Implementing the distribution procedure was not an easy task. The hospital's main function is to care for people who have medical problems. Many of those problems must be dealt with on an immediate basis. Paperwork or other nonessential administrative functions must take a back seat to the patient's physical condition. In times of physical immediacy, it is understandable that the distribution of written materials might not occur due to the impending situation, thus the facility may have to rethink the timing of the distribution of the packets. An alternative to distribution at admissions is to have packets distributed after patients are settled in their beds.

Clearly, a significant factor in the distribution of this material is the time pressure on the medical staff in the emergency room, admitting department, and unit staff. One knows that taking care of administrative business, albeit important, is not on the front burner for these staff members; life-threatening issues, as well as constant care, are their main concerns.

Implausible Program Theory

Both articulated program theory and implicit program theory suggest that there is a *program logic* or sequence of events that will achieve the program outcomes. However, programs have both logical and illogical aspects. The illogical side, or an implausible side can develop in programs as they are planned and initiated.

> [S]ocial programs [develop] from a mixture of what [professionals] learned in professional school, what they experienced on the job, what stories of other people's experience suggest, and perhaps some social science and evaluation learnings. Programs are not laid out in rational terms with clear-cut statements of why certain program activities have been selected and which actions are expected to lead to certain results. (Weiss, 1998, p. 55)

However, since programs often have illogical aspects, a third type of program theory is *implausible program theory*: when the program theory, whether articulated or implicit, is illogical and makes only a little sense or some sense given the conditions the program is supposed to change.

An example of implausible program theory is provided by an attempt by the City of Boston to prevent absenteeism in the Greater Egleston Community High School by buying students wristwatches with built-in alarms. The wristwatches were provided when it was found that less than 10% of the students had alarm clocks at home. While this may seem to be creative programming and it received a lot of media attention, the intervention has implausible elements and no logical base. First, there is no literature that provides a background that the wristwatches would work. Second, the logic would need to be accompanied by many far-fetched assumptions. The students would have to have their watch near then when they woke up, they would need to set the alarms, they would need to hear the alarms, and they would have to get out of bed when the alarms went off. Luckily, the watch intervention was also supplemented by other interventions throughout the district, such as incentives for attendance and hiring more truancy officers.

Programs that are quickly planned without reviewing the literature on interventions and without an extensive planning process are especially susceptible to implausible program theory. For example, in considering school truancy, a planning process that addresses the need for the program and spells out an intervention designed to address truancy would be a more logical approach than the "quick-fix" wristwatch approach. Such a plan for tackling school truancy is presented below.

A Multidisciplinary Intervention for Reducing School Truancy

MAURY BRANDE

DOCTORAL CANDIDATE, PH.D. PROGRAM IN SOCIAL WELFARE, GRADUATE CENTER
OF THE CITY UNIVERSITY OF NEW YORK

A needs assessment that employed a literature review on the importance of reducing school delinquency was conducted as a prelude to designing a delinquency prevention program. An overview of the major themes from the literature will be summarized here.

Truancy has been identified as a "first sign of trouble; the first indicator that a young person is giving up and losing his or her way" (U.S. Department of Education, 1996, p. 1). Research indicates that students who drop out of high school tend to have a history of absenteeism that can be traced back as early as first grade (Epstein & Sheldon, 2002). It is suggested that "serious social problems, such as illiteracy, unemployment, poverty, political powerlessness, alienation, social deviance and crime, intergenerational dependency, and racial discrimination, stem from truancy" (Cnann & Seltzer, 1989, p. 172). Further, students who drop out of school are significantly disadvantaged and not as likely to become productive members of society because of underemployment, an increased likelihood to need welfare assistance, or increased involvement in criminal behaviors (U.S. Department of Education, 1996).

Like marijuana, truancy has been called a "gateway" crime or the "kindergarten" of crime, as it tends to lead to future and serious juvenile crime (Davies, 2000; Gavin, 1997). Truancy inflicts a substantial expense on the community, local businesses, and taxpayers for training, welfare, and law enforcement of truant youth and youth who drop out (Epstein & Sheldon, 2002; Garry, 1996). Individuals with a history of chronic truancy and dropping out of school are more likely to have lower earnings, higher unemployment, and higher utilization of welfare and prison systems (White, Fyfe, Campbell, & Goldkamp, 2001). Clearly, truancy is not only an individual-student problem but also a problem that the family, school, and the whole community must pay attention to and take action to diminish (Davies, 2000).

THE MULTIDISCIPLINARY ECOLOGICAL INTERVENTION

In many large cities, school delinquency can be especially problematic with absenteeism rates climbing close to 50%. The multiple factors contributing to student truancy and its broad-reaching consequences require a multidisciplinary intervention to address this social problem.

School districts must employ assistance from offices such as the police department, district attorney and court system, social service agencies, and community-based organizations to work with the students and their families. An ecological theoretical framework that supports the idea that truancy affects not only the student but also his or her family and the community at large should be reinforced while developing a program to identify students engaging in truant behaviors. This framework needs to account for the complexity of truant behavior in the community and provide an effective intervention.

The first priority of such a program is to identify students who are truant—students who are absent from school without permission and are therefore not attending to their academic responsibilities. A simple premise is that in order for young people to achieve in their academic setting, they first need to be present. The next step is to ensure that the parent(s) or guardian(s) of the student is informed of the situation; this can be a challenge itself, especially in large cities. Once identified, the student and parent(s) need to work with attendance teachers and social workers to determine and assess the barriers to school attendance and develop a strategy for not only improving school attendance but also working at eliminating or diminishing the root cause. This is important to maintain attendance, well-being, and ultimately increase the student's chance at completing his or her full course of required education (i.e., completing high school). A concrete and specific action plan should be developed denoting the follow-up work necessary by each party. Due to the numerous possible contributing factors of school truancy, success is contingent upon the strength of the collaborating agencies' commitment to the program and to working together.

Finally, the students engaged in school truancy are often without connections to positive outside activities. Therefore, the social worker must also work with the student to establish involvement in extracurricular or community-based programs, such as sports recreation, arts, or music, centered on his or her interests and skills. Outreach workers are an ideal resource for this part of the intervention as they can work with students in the community to enhance their ability to attain their goals. Outreach workers may also conduct home visits and provide informal counseling services on an individual, family, or group basis as needed.

PROGRAM GOALS

The immediate goal of the program is to inform every student's parent or guardian of the truancy incident, to connect the parent with the student's school to facilitate appropriate interventions at the school and family level. The goal of the social-work intervention as well as the intermediate goal is to make an assessment and to involve these youth in appropriate after-school activities and counseling with the purpose of preventing further negative behaviors and

A Multidisciplinary Intervention for Reducing School
Truancy (Continued)

improving school attendance. Therefore, the theory is that if we help these young people remain interested and involved in their school and community they will have a stronger chance of graduating from high school. Monitoring the student's attendance following identification is essential to verifying his or her progress and ensuring that the planned intervention remains appropriate. Finally, tracking of specific program interventions provided will add to the knowledge base of this social problem and determine where additional resources are needed and which ones are most effective.

REFERENCES

Cnaan, R.A., & Seltzer, V.C. (1989). Etiology of truancy: An ecosystems perspective. *Social Work in Education* 11(3):171–183.

Davies, S.J. (2000, October 18). Truancy program targets problems before they start. Retrieved February 8, 2002, from: http://wwwkci.org/chanute.htm.

Epstein, J.L., & Sheldon, S.B. (2002). Present and accounted for: Improving student attendance through family and community involvement. *Journal of Educational Research* 95(5):308–320.

Garry, E. (1996). Truancy: First step to a lifetime of problems. *Juvenile Justice Bulletin,* January. Washington, DC: Office of Juvenile Justice and Delinquency Prevention, U.S. Department of Justice.

Gavin, T. (1997). Truancy: Not just kids' stuff anymore. *FBI Law Enforcement Bulletin,* March, 8–14.

U.S. Department of Education Safe and Drug-Free Schools Office (with input from the U.S. Department of Justice and in consultation with local communities and the National School Safety Center). (1996). *Manual to combat truancy.* Washington, DC: U.S. Department of Education.

White, M.D., Fyfe, J.J., Campbell, S.P., & Goldkamp, J.S. (2001). The school–police partnership: Identifying at-risk youth through a truant recovery program. *Evaluation Review* 25(5):507–532.

Programs based on implausible program theory are often those in which a charismatic leader or executive has an idea that he or she "knows" will work. If the program is implemented and is not working, no one may tell the agency or organization director that the program does not work. In that sense, it often becomes like the fable of the emperor's new clothes.

This situation draws attention to the need for a logic and sequence of program functions and activities that are more plausible and could lead to the desired result.

For example, in job-training programs for single parents with young children, a logical sequence of events would be the provision of child care for the children and transportation to child care and the job training before an effective job-training program could take place. This analysis is also referred to as *process theory* and related to process evaluations (Rossi et al., 2004, p. 156). Process evaluations can help establish if the theory on which the program is based is working. Should the theory be modified or enhanced, based on the reality of what is going on in the program and if or how human service workers are engaging participants?

Another example of an implausible program theory is from a local community's effort to reduce heart disease. The community had a number of initiatives to do this. One was to increase attendance at local greenmarkets, thus increasing the intake of healthy food and reducing the incidence of cardiovascular disease in the community. The community increased the advertisements and announcements about the local greenmarkets and tried to assess changes in the number and type of consumers using the greenmarket. This could be done with program evaluation. However, stating publicly that increased use of the greenmarket would reduce heart disease is not really recognizing the complex processes by which heart disease could be reduced in the community or the number of people who would need to participate in such a program to reduce heart disease in a whole community. The logical sequence of events, from the advertisement of the greenmarket, to people actually showing up at the greenmarket, to the right people going who could benefit from better diets, to the longer-term consumption of fruits and vegetables, to lessening heart disease is a complex chain. It may be implausible to assume that the role of the greenmarkets would be that pronounced.

Logic Modeling

Articulation of a program logic is an important aspect of describing the program. This process of describing the program logic can be assisted greatly by sketching out a full logic model (Chapel, 2004, p. 637). The Centers for Disease Control and Prevention (CDC) has found that logic models are the most effective way to develop program descriptions. Logic models produce graphical depictions of the relationship between a program's activities and its intended effects. The logic is the degree to which the program activities can possibly affect program outcomes.

Two variables in the CDC model seem especially useful: the distinction between program inputs and program activities. *Program inputs* are the resources that the program uses to generate program activities. Inputs include program funding, staffing involved, the service resources available, the physical resources and the setting, the training of staff, relationships and resources committed by other agencies, and the authority and auspice for delivering the service. *Program activities* are the actual work or professional interventions used by the program and its staff. Activities include program outreach, screening of participants, assessment of the consumers' environment, making referrals, diagnosis and triage, case management, the interventive methods used, and treatment techniques, for example, family work, crisis intervention, psychosocial treatment, behavior treatment, cognitive methods, psychoeducational training, and narrative approaches.

A logic model for a mental health program for clients with HIV/AIDS is described by Wheeler (see below). In developing the model, the evaluator and staff were involved in collaborative and participatory processes that greatly enhanced the evaluation plan. It seems likely that with such intensive staff input, the evaluation had the characteristics of an empowerment evaluation.

Wheeler's description below shows how valuable developing a logic model can be. The evaluator and staff were involved in collaborative and participatory processes that greatly enhanced both the program development and program evaluation. In the model, five major headings are specified: *(1)* program inputs, *(2)* program activities, *(3)* short-term outcomes, *(4)* intermediate outcomes, and *(5)* long-term outcomes. Program inputs include the program's resources in terms of its physical facilities, organizational model and staff, resources that clients receive from other agencies, and staff provided. Program activities include intervention provided to clients, including testing and assessment, ongoing individual and group treatment and therapies, training of staff in cultural competency and with a unique touch, meetings with a program evaluator to discuss and review program goals, and ongoing consumer surveys, which are feedback into program planning. Short-term outcomes are completion of comprehensive planning for patients, increasing client engagement in the program, increasing compliance with medication regimens, and increasing the number of mental health referrals to the program. Intermediate outcomes include increasing client knowledge about their mental health issues related to HIV and increasing staff responsiveness to the mental health needs of clients and staff sensitivity to the culturally diverse client populations. The long-term outcomes include increasing the coping skills of clients, ensuring client input in the types of services received, ensuring comprehensive treatment for each client, and increasing the number of services clients receive outside the agency. The overall model and agency planning that Wheeler presents is greatly enhanced by having a full logic model of inputs, activities, and outcomes. A logic model provides a framework for both program planning and program evaluation (see Fig. 4.3).

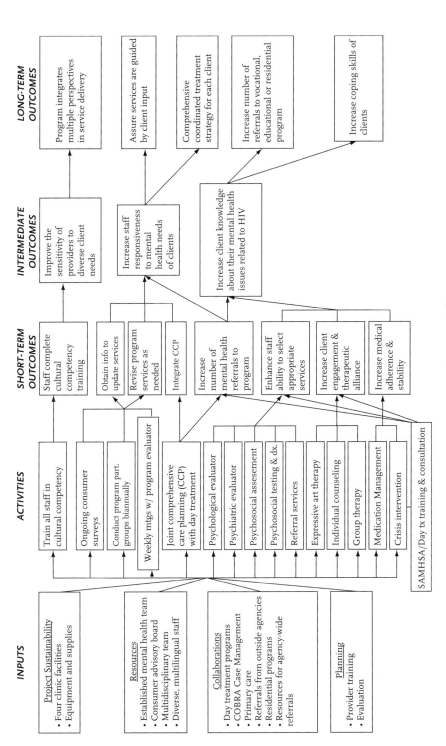

FIGURE 4.3. Agency–logic model.

Empowerment Evaluation in Logic Modeling: Participatory and
Collaborative Processes in Developing a Logic Model

DARRELL P. WHEELER, PH.D., M.P.H.

ASSOCIATE DEAN FOR RESEARCH, ASSOCIATE PROFESSOR

HUNTER COLLEGE SCHOOL OF SOCIAL WORK

As most program staff know, getting funded is only the beginning of the "real" work on a new project. Developing new programs from the ground up requires significant planning, oversight, quality controls, and "elbow grease." Planning a new mental health program for HIV-positive men and women was no exception. As we grappled with the complex issues of recruiting and hiring staff and securing site space, it became clear that we needed a mechanism to convey to new and "old" team members the intent and process of the mental health program. Developing a comprehensive picture of the intended goals, objectives, and activities of the new mental health services program was the major first step in our program plan. Logical modeling was required by the organization funding the program. However, the logic model became a vehicle for conducting an empowerment evaluation, emphasizing participatory and collaborative processes between the evaluator and project staff. Also, through logic modeling, the evaluator and staff were able to develop a truly comprehensive program description.

DEVELOPING THE MODEL—THE PROCESS

Creation of a visual representation of the program helped everyone see the relationships between planned activities, intended outcomes, and everything in between. For the project director, the schematic representation also needed to include resources to be obtained and/or justified within the program budget. The program evaluation consultant worked in a collaborative and participatory process with staff to ensure that as many anticipated program activities as possible were included in the planning document. If a program activity was omitted, it might also be excluded from the evaluation plan. This would greatly affect the evaluator's ability to monitor the fidelity of the proposed intervention delivery and ultimately outcomes attributable these interventions.

In the logic model, five categorical areas were addressed: program inputs, activities, short-term outcomes, intermediate outcomes, and long-term outcomes. The process was initiated by listing out discrete elements for each of the five categorical areas (e.g., under long-term outcomes we identified increased coping of clients). Each staff member was asked to participate in this initial process. At the time of this activity, there were five staff members (1.5 administrative and 3.5 clinical) and the evaluation consultant working on the project. The lists were collected and combined into one comprehensive listing of activities by category. From this comprehensive list the initial version of the logic model was created. In the initial version, inputs and outputs were the easiest to define by all participants. These two categories circumscribed the others and gave a start-and-finish framework to the modeling process. The discrete elements listed under activities were relatively clear-cut and easy to place within the emerging model. Short-term and intermediate outcomes were more difficult to situate in the logic model, and their ultimate placement required review in terms of logical ordering of events. Finally, a first draft of the logic model was completed and presented to the mental health team.

The initial reaction of the team members was that of being overwhelmed by all the boxes and arrows in the diagram. After the initial shock at the sight of the big picture, the staff were able to see the relationship with their earlier individual listing of inputs, activities, and outcomes. In discussing the relationship between the individual efforts and this amalgam of their efforts, the staff were able to critique and refine the first version. The revisions consisted primarily of relocating discrete items between categories and, to a lesser extent, including new items. No items were eliminated. The iterative process to refine and finalize the model went three rounds before the staff reached consensus on a version.

USING THE MODEL—ITS CONTENTS

Inputs for the logic model were seen as consisting of four elements: planning inputs, collaborative inputs, fiscal and personnel resources, and durable aspects of the parent agency (i.e., things to sustain the project). The team identified themselves as a critical resource and recognized their potential to shape and be shaped by the program. Collaborations, both internal and external, were identified as a necessary resource. These collaborations would help avoid unnecessary duplication of activities and would be a source for recruiting clients. Resources were broadly defined as fiscal resources and personnel that make the program run. These included the potential clients, staff, and an advisory body. Finally, the project was situated within a large and well-established organization. The organization's structure would provide a resource that helps in providing administrative and other services.

Activities identified in the logic model covered the full gambit of interventions done within the mental health program. These included assessments, evaluations, counseling sessions, and staff meetings and trainings. The activities portion of the model appeared to energize the staff's discussion and probably reflected their investment in their own work on the project.

Short-term outcomes were defined by the group as those things that were immediate outcomes of an activity or set of activities. So, for example, in earlier

Empowerment Evaluation in Logic Modeling (Continued)

versions of the model, "improving the sensitivity of providers to diverse client needs" was listed as a short-term outcome. However, in further discussions the team realized that completing the training was a prerequisite to achieving benefits from the training. Thus, "completing the training" became a short-term outcome and "improving sensitivity" became an intermediate outcome. This shift also made sense in terms of an evaluation plan, as the improved sensitivity on the part of providers could not be guaranteed, but was rather a desired outcome for those who completed the training. Listing and defining short-term outcomes helped the evaluator to develop process measures.

Intermediate and long-term outcomes were seen as the beneficial products of the work being done and the resources being put into the program. Particularly with the intermediate outcomes, staff members were able to identify the need for personal and professional development as a way of achieving client-centered outcomes.

THEORY, NOT MAGIC

In reviewing the logic model, another, unexpected outcome was achieved. Namely, the staff were able to see that there was a program theory, a program logic, and interventive methods for the program design and implementation. The theoretical basis was intricately linked to the agency's mission to empowerment and social justice. The logic model provided staff with a visual format that aided them in seeing their position in the clients' and organization's development and well-being. The time and energy put into developing and refining the logic model was questioned many times by staff; however, by the end of the process even the most skeptical staff member was assured that the effort was worth the outcome.

Interventive Methods

Since programs are efforts to achieve desirable consequences, something is being done to people. They are being trained for jobs, educated about a certain health condition, given some type of medical treatment, given therapy or counseling, or participating in a group. In the logic model, these activities are referred to as program activities—the actual work, the interventions given by a professional or paraprofessional. These methods can include individual counseling, group counseling, case management, advocacy, training, teaching, and methods of organizing people, among others. Interventive methods and program activities also include actions such as giving people access to money, benefits, food, or other tangible commodities.

A literature on interventive methods exists that examines the theories and assumptions on which the methods are based and how these methods may be used with different populations. There also is a literature on evaluative studies of particular interventions that may show program processes and success rates on the intervention with different groups. For example, if a program is treating clients suffering from agoraphobia, there is a clear literature available on the differential success rates of behavioral interventions such as desensitization in treating phobias.

Interventions or methods of how the program goals will be achieved need to be specified in a program description. The trend toward evidence-based practice (EBP), or practice based on methods that have been validated through research, usually research involving experimental designs and randomized control trials (RCTs), has meant that in some fields, only certain methods with clearly proven results have been adopted, because they are thought to deliver the optimal outcomes for consumers. For example, in the mental health field, cognitive-behavioral therapy (CBT), in which consumers are taught to change negative and distorted thinking, is purported to be the most effective treatment for a range of mental health disorders (Krieg, 2009). Through CBT consumers are encouraged to practice CBT techniques in a series of exercises about their cognition and thinking processes. CBT has been recognized as an evidenced-based practice because it has been well researched in over 100 RCTs. The range of studies indicate that CBT has been effective for the treatment of generalized anxiety disorders, panic disorders, adult and child depression, social phobias, and post-traumatic stress disorder (Krieg, 2009, p. 7).

In one recent process evaluation study of CBT, mental health professionals expressed their enthusiasm about the treatment and its results (Krieg, 2009, pp. 20–21):

> It works with a variety of diagnoses and it works here.
>
> This is a short, brief therapy and it fits like a glove.
>
> It's a strong treatment with a lot of structure. All the members of the treatment team play a role.
>
> I think it is a strong program that has a lot of structured groups and activities.
>
> The patient's thinking is less distorted and their behavior is less impulsive in terms of reacting.

As the above quotes suggest, the staff's commitment to interventive methods is important. Do they believe in the methods being used? Are there differing views and conflicts within the program about the treatment protocol? For example, in an alcohol treatment program, some professionals feel that attendance at Alcoholics Anonymous (AA) is a critical addition to the individual therapy and group therapy that the program offers. Other professionals may feel that what the program offers is enough, and that attendance at AA is not essential to quality treatment. Or, in a treatment program for adolescents, some professionals may think that the whole family needs to be involved in treatment, whereas the other practitioners think success can be attained by treating the adolescent individually. There can be legitimate debates over methods. For example, in a group program for increasing the cultural sensitivity of staff, would a didactic approach based on the literature of ethnicity or an experiential approach based on case examples be more effective?

The amount of the intervention received is another important consideration. Both the intensity (how many hours per day or week) and duration (over how long a period of time—1 month, 6 months?) of the intervention are important quantitative measures. There is a theoretical amount of intervention that is deemed appropriate and an actual amount that people attending the program are actually receiving. A good descriptive term that has been used in this setting is *dosage*, or the threshold level of participation in training, case management, or counseling that is needed to produce the intended effects.

In addition to dosage, the program probably needs to be provided at the right time of the day. For example, will parents be working at the time it is offered or will they have child care responsibilities for young children? The intervention should also be provided at the right time in the life cycle. A program that seeks to prevent the placement of children into foster care should offer substantial services before the family has reached a point of crisis when the placement of children into the foster care system can no longer be averted.

5. Goals and Objectives of the Program

In presenting the program logic, the connection between the program interventions and goals and outcomes has already been considered. In addition to presentation of a program logic, a logic model offers an analytic layout or diagram that describes program inputs, activities, and interventions. A full logic model spells out program inputs, activities, and interventions and adds specific intermediate program objectives and broader program goals and outcomes.

From the mission statements presented in the program overview broad goals of the program can develop. A program's mission statement is an important way of describing the overall program purpose. After all, a program must have a purpose.

While broad goals support the program's mission, the most important phase of program development is uncovering and documenting program goals and outcomes and more specific program objectives. Goals, outcomes, and objectives all indicate the direction that the program focus will take. Outcomes and goals are conceptual; they are the benefits to be received from the program. Program objectives are more specific; they indicate the progress and direction in meeting the program goals. Objectives tell the progress in achieving the goal. Program objectives should be measurable. Objectives also have a time frame set out during which they should be achieved and documented. For example, in a program designed to treat alcoholism in women, the overall goal may be to have the women abstain from alcohol and improve the quality of their lives over the length of the program, while one program objective may be to increase outreach to the population of women who abuse alcohol in one community during the current year.

The process of measuring goals and objectives, which will be presented in Chapter 6, begins with describing the goals and objectives in the program description. The program benefits, outcomes, goals, and objectives should be described as clearly as possible. Then, in the next step of evaluation, program outcome, goals, and objectives are spelled out more specifically. As a research design, methodology, or plan is developed for the program evaluation, that plan will set out how the outcomes, goals, and objectives will be measured.

6. Consumers, Patients, and Clients Served

Program planning and needs assessment include the specification of a target population of eventual consumers of the service who will benefit from the program. A crucial part of program planning is knowing the target population and directing services to that population (Rossi et al., 2004, p. 118). Definitions of a target population can change over time as the notions of who could benefit from the program change. For example, in the 1980s the homeless were identified as those living on the streets. Later, advocates for the homeless expanded the definition of people who could be helped by including persons without stable housing or those living in single rooms that are paid for daily or weekly (Rossi et al., 2004, p. 118).

Sometimes theorists in the program evaluation field can use impersonal terms to refer to human beings who participate in the program. For example,

Weiss sees consumers as "program inputs." Rossi et al. (2004) talk of program participants as "targets." A better definition might be to see consumers as "resources" of the program, recognizing the strengths that they bring to the program rather than seeing potential participants as "clients who are needy."

Principles of sampling can be applied to the participants of a program. As a program gets initiated, there are potential people from the larger target population who might benefit from the program. From this target population there is a sample of people who actually are enrolled in the program from program outreach attempts or contact with other organizations. Those who show up could represent an accidental or convenience sample of those attracted to the program. As criteria of eligibility are established, they may be a purposive sample from the target population.

Since the group in the program can be quite different than the target population, it is important to know their characteristics—that is, how much the "sample," or program participants, differs from the target population of potential participants. The characteristics of those using the program can be affected by the outreach strategies that the program uses. For example, if referrals to the program depend greatly on the other agencies and organizations, the program could be very dependent on those organizations. In a sense, the program may be "transferring accountability" when some other organization is needed to recruit a population and make the program successful (Chapel, 2004, p. 646).

Outreach, recruitment, and access cannot be overestimated as crucial and necessary parts of programs. Outreach and recruitment are the methods used to attract consumers to the program. Without consumers, there is no program. Methods of outreach to potential consumers are often labor intensive and programs rarely do too much outreach. More typically, too little outreach is done.

For example, a health advocacy program was set up to help older adults and their caregivers get reliable Medicare and general health information (Brosnan, 2009). Health advocates were positioned in two local libraries to provide seniors with health and Medicare information, counseling, and support. Opening events were planned in the two local libraries and a news conference was held with the county executive, state assembly representatives, library officials, and the sponsoring organizations. A number of local newspapers covered the opening and reported on where seniors could go to get help, but soon the coordinator of the program found that more outreach needed to be done as the program opened for business, because of the low turnout.

It became abundantly clear that a critical component for the program's success was left unattended—outreach. It is not always true that "if you build it, they will come." The program coordinator along with the volunteer health advocates embarked on a campaign to get the word out. The program coordinator reached out to 10 senior centers in the area and scheduled appointments to address the seniors at each center. The presentation included a general announcement about the program and a description of the services provided. The coordinator also "worked the room" and went around to each individual table of seniors distributing bookmarks advertising the program and sat down to chat with the seniors about the program, their health care needs in general, and, of course, the prescient news of the day—the ongoing presidential primary.

The health care volunteers made significant personal investments to getting the word out about the program. They distributed bookmarks and flyers in their local senior centers, shopping centers, shopping malls, the local "Curves," supermarkets, laundromats, etc. The health care advocates were part of a program from a sponsoring agency where they made presentations to senior centers about Medicare, and they incorporated a description of the program in their presentations. (Brosnan, 2009, pp. 6–7)

All this outreach generated between 20 and 30 seniors per month who were given services in the two local libraries. As an additional component of outreach, later on in the program year a public relations (PR) firm got involved in getting the word out.

A significant increase in the number of patrons served in November and December 2008 was attributed to the public relations campaign conducted in October and November 2008. The publicity campaign was launched at this particular time frame to precede the annual November 15 to December 31 Medicare Part D open enrollment. The PR firm along with the program coordinator crafted press releases with a cost saving message geared to how people could save money if they chose the right drug plan to draw people to the library program. (The increase from the PR campaign made the number of seniors go from 20 to 30 to around 60 seniors in each of the 2 months.) (Brosnan, 2009, p. 9)

"Creaming" is another process that often happens in recruiting consumers for programs. Sometimes programs select consumers or clients who are a little better off than the traditional client who would be part of the target population. For example, a program serving families who are in danger of their children being placed in foster care may select or recruit only cases where there is neglect rather than physical abuse, since physical-abuse cases may have more likelihood of being placed in foster care. Or, a program designed to prevent nursing home placements of the elderly may select or recruit only families that score high on the activities of daily living scales and may not really be in danger of a nursing home placement. In a university employee assistance program that provided personal counseling to all employees of the university, upper middle class groups such as faculty and administrators may be more easily disposed to psychological counseling. The program may be less available to building maintenance and secretarial staff, for whom more outreach might be needed to explain the value of the program.

In addition to outreach and access, program attrition, or determining who drops out of the program, is an important part of describing who uses the program. Often, however, no data are available for those who have dropped out. Staff members can be interviewed to get their hunches and ideas about the types of clients that the program is serving and which types of clients are dropping out. The best source of data on the characteristics of those in the program can come from an agency's or organization's client information system (CIS) or management information system (MIS). These systems comprise computerized records that describe the characteristics of clients. A CIS provides simple data on the client's age, gender, socioeconomic status, ethnic background, income and income sources, diagnosis and severity of problems, and services used. Most likely the organization itself or its funding source requires that this type of data be compiled for accountability purposes. An MIS would be more extensive and include types of data such as attitudes toward the program, motivations for participation, aspirations and expectations from the program, degree of support from family, treatments and services and their cost, and outcome or the achievement of program goals (Weiss, 1998, pp. 134–135; Rossi et al., p. 177).

The data from the CIS or MIS is a crucial part of describing the program and often can be found in the program's quarterly reports to a funding agency or annual reports to the organization's board. This type of data may be more readily available. If further data analysis on client characteristics is required, this may take the agency more time. Client data are critical in program-monitoring studies and accountability studies as it indicates who showed up. The characteristics of those who become part of the program in total are an important part of the program environment.

7. Characteristics of Staff

The type of staffing in the program is a key area of program description. The number of staff involved, the number of staff per clients or caseload size, previous experience of staff, professional backgrounds of staff, racial and ethnic characteristics, and turnover of staff are all important factors in a program. Often the program is based on the assumption that a certain type of professional—a psychologist, a social worker, a patient advocate, a nurse—will be the best person to provide this service. There may be a team approach and a group of professionals that is required to provide optimal service. Past staff experiences in relation to the problem being addressed can be helpful, as can in-service agency training for the program.

The overall tradition of agency service may be important. For example, in evaluating a small information and referral direct-service unit in a United Way planning agency where most the staff are program planners and fund raisers, the majority of agency personnel may not appreciate the work of direct-service work, and this may affect the program environment. Likewise, an organization may have a history of providing personal counseling from a psychodynamic perspective, while the new program requires practitioners with expertise in behavioral and cognitive approaches to practice. One way in which a program might resolve this potential conflict is to "retool" and train the agency direct-service staff in these new methods. Another way is to bring in new direct-service staff with expertise in behavioral and cognitive methods. How staff is recruited is another important area of program description.

Staff members' beliefs about the service being rendered are also important. Interventions are never fool-proof; they need practitioners who can deliver them. The personalities of staff and their approach to service and belief systems also need to be considered. Program evaluation often presents the service independent of the personalities and approaches of those delivering the service, but this is certainly not the case in the real world.

8. Program Cost and Funding

The way in which a program is funded and its cost are critical variables. Yet surprisingly, cost and funding are often not considered or are considered indirectly in evaluation studies. Basic questions about cost need to be answered. What is the level or amount of program funding? Is the funding limited in relation to the goals the program hopes to achieve? Is the program funded through a number of small funding sources from foundations and local government? Have substantial amounts of federal, state, or local government funds been allocated to the program? Is the program funded for a short or a long period of time? Could program stability be threatened by the length of time funds are available? The amount of funds, the funding source, and the longevity of the funding are important parts of the program description. The amount, source, and longevity of funds are also clues as to the values placed on the program and the role the program plays in the local community and in society in general, which will be referred to later as the "utility" of the program.

Suchman's comment that "few programs can be justified at any cost" (1967, p. 146) is still relevant today. By believing in the programs and services, which is a good thing, professionals may act as though the program is essential at any cost for all times and all consumers. However, it is also the professional's, administrator's, evaluator's and program planner's job to see that costs are documented and justified.

In planning the program, "projective or anticipated costs" need to be considered. As the program becomes operational, actual and changing costs should be documented. Sometimes it is difficult to find out the cost of a program, especially if it is part of the overall operating budget of a large organization. Direct costs of the program such as professional and secretarial salaries as well as indirect costs such as money paid for office space within the larger organization need to be considered. As the program is planned, approximations of direct and indirect costs can be projected. Eventually, cost factors can be used to answer the evaluation question of what the most desirable allocations of money are for the program to perform in an efficient and effective manner.

Examining costs is always a good idea. All the stakeholders in an evaluation should be concerned with documenting costs, given the mandate for evaluation and accountability.

Costs and Benefits

The whole field of relating program costs to benefits in program evaluation is called "efficiency analysis."

> The basic idea is to add up all the costs . . . and compare them to benefits. This is conceptually easy to imagine, but, in practice, it is difficult to do. (Weiss, 1998, p. 244)

Many evaluators do not have the technical skills needed to measure costs and relate them to the benefits of a program.

Weiss (1998, pp. 244–245) has outlined four types of economic analysis on relating costs to benefits:

1. Cost minimization analysis
2. Cost-effectiveness analysis
3. Cost–benefit analysis
4. Cost utility analysis

Each type of efficiency analysis provides a different perspective on studying costs and benefits.

A first look at costs could begin with *cost minimization analysis*, in which a range of programs or program methods is compared and the least expensive program strategy to achieve a certain outcome is selected. Different program options are costed out and the least expensive method is chosen. Rather than thinking about the least cost, however, it may be useful to think of cost–cost analysis, that is, the different costs associated with providing the program in a different manner in relation to an outcome. Since measuring outcomes in health and the human services is sometimes difficult, cost–cost analysis can help spell out different program options in relation to one another because dollar amounts can be put on different program interventions. Of course, the danger here is to ignore measuring benefits and just choosing the cheapest form of the program.

The cost of programs should be recognized as a particularly sensitive issue. For example, the costs of health care, the costs of education, and the costs of entitlement program have been hotly debated. When the debate is only about costs, all the stakeholders in an evaluation should tread lightly. Usually, the interest in cost might reflect strong values in reducing costs and scaling back programs. Since outcomes and benefits are harder to pin down than costs, and cost is much more easily quantified, the simple solution may be cutbacks or the elimination of the program. The commitment to measuring costs should be made with a caveat or an awareness that sometimes the simple value of reducing costs may be the goal without even considering program outcomes or benefits.

In the second type of analysis, *cost-effectiveness analysis*, several program strategies are compared in terms of costs and how much each strategy achieves a certain program outcome. In cost-effectiveness analysis, *effectiveness* is defined as a conceptual outcome that is measured much as it would be in traditional evaluation studies. So, for example, in an employee assistance program, the costs of individual counseling compared with the cost of providing group programs designed to help employees in caring for an elderly parent could be calculated. Then outcomes such as better care for the elderly relative and reduced stress for the employee engaged in elder care would be measured to determine the most cost-effective way to achieve these desired outcomes.

How can these outcomes be measured and how can the outcomes measured be linked to the different program strategies? Ways to measure the outcomes, for example, which stress scales to use, or how to measure better care for the elderly, must be developed or selected from the literature. Also, impact assessment and quasi-experimental designs need to be used to determine that in two similar groups of employees either personal counseling or offering support groups on elder care is the most cost-effective way to help with elder care. Of course, group programs to all employees caring for elderly relatives usually cost less than individual counseling, and in many interventions, groups are used because they have less costs than individual counseling.

In *cost–benefit analysis*, costs are measured in dollar amounts and benefits are translated into dollar amounts. Then a cost–benefit ratio is computed. So, for example, in an employee assistance program to help employees with their personal and family life, benefits would be calculated as the dollars saved from an employee's taking less time off from work, reduced costs from employees performing better at work, and reduced costs from reduced personal stress. The costs saved through these benefits would then be compared to the costs of the program or intervention. Theoretically, the costs saved from the benefits should outweigh the costs of the program. Cost–benefit analysis is used more often in business, where the benefits are increased profits or revenues and can be more easily measured. In health and the human services, measuring outcomes is tough enough; assigning dollar amounts to the outcomes that were achieved is doubly difficult. Nevertheless, the exercise of translating positive outcomes into dollars saved can help conceptualize and compare program interventions with program outcomes. Program planners, policy-makers, and funding organizations may be especially persuaded by the findings from a cost–benefit analysis.

A final type of efficiency analysis is *cost utility analysis*, which closely examines the values of outcomes for a person or society as a whole. Personal and societal values come into play. So, for example, the value of health outcomes such as extending a person's life if the quality of life is preserved may be clear-cut, given certain cost ranges for health programs. However, if an employee assistance program is reducing the stress of employees through helping an employee with caring for their mother or father, the organization's commitment to paying for such a service may be much less than extending a person's life. Or, while providing needle exchange programs to IV drug users to prevent the spread of AIDS might seem like a very important and useful thing to do, politicians and society in general might balk at providing needles that people use to continue drug use, even if lives will be saved.

Weiss (1998, p. 245) has introduced the notion that *perspective* is important in efficiency analysis. The perspective can be from the viewpoint of various stakeholders in the program. Every stakeholder in the program and in the program evaluation has a perspective that relates to cost in relation to achieved benefits. The administrators in the program, direct-service staff, and consumers all have their own perspective and stake in efficiency analysis. For example, the cost to an administrator may be viewed as high, while to a consumer who values the program the cost may be a lot less in view of the benefit of the program to them. The perspective can vary, from one individual's point of view, to the organization's view, to the view of local or state government, to that of the federal government or of society at large.

The values and perspective of one person may affect how cost is viewed and efficiency analysis is conducted. For example, one university president's perspective was extremely positive toward the cost of a new employee assistance program that she initiated as a benefit for employees. She perceived the program as a benefit for employees that would provide such services as personal counseling, access to services such as daycare or elder care, and help with supervisory issues at work. The original cost of the program involved hiring an administrator and some direct-service staff. The program office was an indirect cost, as the space was within the university complex. From the perspective of that president, the cost was well worth the benefits received. Over a period of about 10 years, the program budget and amount of employees served stayed constant and the program was viewed as a success. When a new college president was installed, his perspective was that the cost was not worth the number of employees served. He simply took the budget divided by the number of employees served and computed the cost per employee, which he said was not worth the benefits that the employees were receiving. The values and perspective of this new president changed everything.

9. Program Planning and Implementation Issues

Programs always change and evolve from the time when they are planned to when they are initiated and implemented. There is usually a large difference between what the program was planned to be and what it became. In the initial stages of implementation, a location and physical setting for the program must be found, staff need to be recruited, outreach and referral methods need to be developed, and funding must be received. Coordination is needed among members of the program, between the program and the larger organization where it may be located, and between the program and the larger community. As the program is implemented, it can be determined if the theories upon which the programs is based seem correct. Assessments need to be made about how the program is operating. Are consumers using the program? Are outreach and referral procedures working? Are they from the target population of consumers who were to be recruited? Were the right staff members hired? Were they given proper training? Are the program theories working? Is there consensus on where the program should be headed?

Descriptions of the evolution of the program and how it developed and solved issues in implementation are critical to understanding the program and its implementation. The early successes and failures and how the program surmounted obstacles will give a true program context.

Implementations issues can be seen in a church-based outreach program to immigrant populations (McKaskie, 2004). The program used employed staff and volunteers to provide help with immigration to immigrant groups, along with assistance with language issues, access to government benefits such as food stamps, and referrals to health services. The program also had a food pantry, which interfered greatly with implementing the other parts of the program.

The demand for food was such that as many as 100 people could be seen waiting for food at one time. Staff and volunteers had to relinquish other duties to tend to the food pantry. As resources became limited, the program developed eligibility criteria for the food service. To receive food, a person had to be an immigrant who had used the program for other services or be a member of the church. For those who did not meet these criteria, staff and volunteers were asked to "make a judgment" about who needed food and who did not. Program staff and volunteers had real difficulty in making these judgments and made statements such as the following:

> People who really need food come to the pantry. If we have the food, we need to give it away and we should not be making judgments on who needs it.
>
> I just see them as clients who come in here for the service. For me, it's hard to see someone and just say, "You need it and you don't."

Another problem was the anger and resentment of some staff and volunteers in implementing the program when they encountered clients with demanding and aggressive attitudes:

The big thing was before Thanksgiving and Christmas. "Where's my turkey?" People had higher expectations than we were able to fill . . . but I couldn't produce the turkeys! It was almost the same reaction as the immigrant clients. They think I can change the law for them.

There were some who wanted food when they wanted it, and we have to give help to more people. Sometimes, they wanted more of something. Some of them received a particular thing one time, for example, chicken, and they would want that again and again . . . . They aren't the only ones who need food. There are many.

People didn't like the way staff treated them . . . . They wanted more food and we didn't have it. Or they wanted meat and we didn't have it. Yes, I agree with those complaints because I saw the way they were treated. But, sometimes they were nasty too.

Clearly, implementation of the food pantry program was affected by the attitudes of staff about program policies concerning which community members should be eligible for food. In turn, program implementation issues in the food pantry affected staff's ability to meet the other needs of the immigrant community in relation to help with legal issues, access to benefits, employment issues, and language issues. Documenting implementation issues is a major focus in program-monitoring studies, which will be described in the next chapter.

Example of a Comprehensive Program Description

This chapter would not be complete without an example of a comprehensive program description. In completing this "Description of the Jefferson Houses NORC Supportive Services Program for the Elderly" (below), Guiffre employed the methods used in evaluability assessment studies described earlier in this chapter. National, state, and local publications and documents about naturally occurring retirement communities (NORCs) and the programs designed to serve those communities were one source of data. Program descriptions from the local Jefferson Houses Program were another source. In addition, original data were collected from interviews with program administrators, direct-service staff, and senior residents who participated in the program. This programs description was designed to capture all of the elements of program description that have been discussed in this chapter. As with all program descriptions, some areas of the program were described more completely. However, the data in some areas, particularly cost of the local program, number and characteristics of consumers served, and characteristics of staff, were less well developed. Nevertheless, this excellent program description was welcomed by all involved in the program and was an excellent precursor to a monitoring study of how NORC residents used the program and how they rated the quality of the services.

The Jefferson Houses NORC Supportive Services Program
DEBORAH GUIFFRE, M.A.
GRADUATE OF THE MASTER'S PROGRAM IN HEALTH ADVOCACY,
SARAH LAWRENCE COLLEGE

The following program description examines a supportive service program directed at seniors who reside in a community defined by its unique demographic profile, a naturally occurring retirement community (NORC). As the first part of a program evaluation, the evaluation task was to provide a detailed description of one NORC supportive service program in lower Manhattan. The eventual program evaluation would be a monitoring study measuring how residents of this NORC use and rate the quality of NORC supportive services available to them. The results of this study would eventually serve to provide the basis for understanding several of the strengths and weaknesses of the supportive service program relative to its goals, and suggest actions to maintain and improve services.

OVERVIEW, PROGRAM RATIONALE, AND PURPOSE AND BROADER PROGRAM
CONTEXT: NATURALLY OCCURRING RETIREMENT COMMUNITIES

It is well established that the aging of the U.S. population has impacted and will continue to affect many aspects of American society. Two areas that have emerged as particularly affected by this trend are health care and housing. These inextricably linked factors of well-being provide the basis for the existence of naturally occurring retirement communities (NORC) supportive service programs.

Following World War II, government agencies, unions, and business developed apartment building and housing complexes for low- and moderate-income individuals. Many tracts of private homes were also established in this era. These communities were populated by large numbers of young adults. In some locations, residents remained in these homes, thus "aging in place" occurred. This phenomenon has resulted in large concentrations of older adults in some communities. Communities with a majority of residents 60 years and older were coined NORCs by American sociologists in 1985.

The desire of individuals to continue to live in their own homes is not unique to the population of seniors currently living in a NORC. In surveys conducted by the American Association of Retired Persons, 85% of seniors expressed the desire to remain in their own homes. The April 2003 U.S. Department of Commerce Current Population Survey showed that 42% of U.S. homes are occupied by individuals age 55 years and over. In 2003, 26.6 million men and 33.0 million women in the U.S. population were aged 55 years and over. By 2010, the U.S. population 55 and over is expected to increase by more than 5 million. By 2030, it is estimated that there will be more than 70 million people in the country who are 65 or older. These statistics create issues that are not hard to see.

New York City is a notable reflection of these national trends. Many New Yorkers have aged in place, and at present, New York City has approximately 350,000 seniors over the age of 60 living in approximately 30 recognized NORCs. An overwhelming majority of seniors in New York City, 89%, greater than the national norm—live in their own homes. Nearly half of all residential developments created with assistance from the government could now be considered a NORC. This concentration of seniors in NORCs has provided an unprecedented opportunity to plan and develop innovative models for meeting the social and health-care needs of these elders.

Among the growing number of seniors remaining in their homes, most will experience some level of decline in physical or mental health, largely due to chronic disease, or will encounter other factors that will compromise their ability to continue to live independently. According to the 2000 census, more than 39% of seniors aged 65 and older had a disabling condition. New York City seniors realized a 55% increase in disability since 1990. This trend and the associated need for support provides the basis for the establishment of NORC supportive services programs.

PROGRAM THEORY AND LOGIC

NORC supportive service programs promote independence and healthy aging by engaging seniors before a crisis occurs and aim to respond to seniors' challenges as they change over time. Eligibility for services and programs is based on age and residence in the NORC, rather than on functional deficits or economic status. NORC supportive service programs strive to be proactive and take a holistic, preventive approach to the health and well-being of seniors.

Around the country, NORC supportive service program are slowly emerging as a viable program model to meet the needs of seniors. At all levels—national, state, and local—demonstration projects are being funded to advance this model. Many of these projects draw from the early experiences gained in New York City NORCs.

The Jefferson Houses NORC Supportive Services
Program (Continued)

Most of the services available to individuals through a NORC supportive service program can be obtained independently and outside of an organized program. However, the underlying premise of a NORC supportive service program is that comprehensive, integrated, on-site services provide an opportunity for improved quality and efficiency of service delivery.

PROGRAM GOALS AND OBJECTIVES

NORC supportive services programs share some basic goals and objectives. The extent to which particular goals or objectives are given greater priority within a housing community is dependent upon the structure and composition of a particular program and the unique needs of the population. Some common basic goals and objectives include the following:

• Improve residents' access to high-quality services and programs by bringing them on site in housing units
• Maximize individual choice and control and promote resident autonomy
• Strengthen housing quality, i.e., safety, security, and maintenance
• Promote and/or increase residents' activity and sense of community
• Increase residents' activity and community involvement
• Prevent or delay institutionalization

PROGRAM IMPLEMENTATION: DEVELOPING NORC SUPPORTIVE SERVICES PROGRAMS

Upon recognition that a community bears the demographic profile of a NORC, and the associated recognition of unmet needs of seniors residing within them, several NORC communities work to bring a range of services to their residents. The processes by which the needs of seniors are established and the types of services made available to residents vary considerably by NORC. This variation is reflective not only of the unique needs of a population, but also of who leads the effort to assess and advocate for the needs of the community, the means by which needs are established, and the funding available.

A leadership role associated with the establishment of residential needs and the development of a supportive service program may be assumed by any number of players, including a board of directors, a tenants association, a philanthropic group, or a public housing authority. Such a determination is highly dependent upon the structure and nature of the housing community. Similarly, variation can be observed in the means by which NORCs determine the specific program needs of their residents. In some cases, experienced evaluation consultants are engaged to conduct formal needs assessment surveys and analysis of population needs, to engage partners and secure funding and, to promote program access. In other cases, this process can be described as more "grassroots" or "homegrown" and is often marked by an informal analysis of needs and a less comprehensive and/or integrated supportive services program. Under most circumstances, senior residents play a key role in shaping programs through their participation in the planning process, governance, and, in some cases, service provision.

NORC supportive services programs in New York City represent the spectrum of possibilities related to who has led efforts to establish them, the processes by which resident needs were determined, and the services that were implemented. In fact, New York City is often cited as a pioneer in the development of NORC supportive services programs and serves as national model. A frequently cited example is PennSouth, a NORC in Manhattan's Chelsea neighborhood. Under the leadership of the board of directors of a moderate-income housing cooperative, a comprehensive NORC supportive services program became operational in 1986. The program components resulted from a formal survey of the needs of residents, partnership with established social and health service agencies, and grant funding from a large foundation.

PROGRAM INTERVENTION—NORC SUPPORTIVE SERVICES PROGRAM COMPONENTS

While each NORC designs its own program for its population, there is general consensus on the types of service program elements that serve to maintain independent living among NORC residents. These services are typically provided on site or in close proximity to the NORC.

- *Social services*: Evaluation of individual and family needs, individual and group counseling, and referral for utilization of other professional disciplines or services to outside agencies. Services can include assistance with securing a wide range of social services entitlements such as Medicaid, transportation, Meals-on-Wheels, or other services such as housekeeping or chore services.
- *Care coordination and management*: Help individuals and families assess, advocate for, and coordinate their social, medical, and/or other needs.
- *Health services (including mental health)*: Provide on-site services of nurses and other medical professionals; referrals to off-site services of medical personnel; development and/or implementation of preventative health programs and services. Services can include short-term home care, senior daycare programs.
- *Recreation, educational, and cultural activities*: On-site activities that enhance the quality of life; off-site trips.
- *Legal and financial services*: Referrals to off-site services, on-site information distribution, and/or lectures on key financial and legal topics.

The Jefferson Houses NORC Supportive Services
Program (Continued)

NORC supportive services programs strive to reflect a collaborative effort between housing, health, and social service organizations to organize and locate the mix of services within a housing community. Services are generally coordinated by one service agency. NORC supportive services programs typically provide care for healthy seniors as well as frail elderly individuals within the NORC. Once a program is in place, social and health services are generally provided free of charge to all residents age 60 years and older. Funds to pay for these services are frequently funneled through and managed by one agency. Some social or recreational services offered may have a small fee. In some instances, services are brought on site by NORC supportive services program coordinators, but are not paid for by the NORC program-coordinating agency. An example of such services is some medical services that are billed as per typical third-party procedures.

NORC housing is not licensed or regulated by a government agency. Each individual or organization associated with providing supportive services regulates their respective services, as they would do under any other circumstance.

NORC SUPPORT SERVICE PROGRAM FUNDING

NORC program funding sources vary widely and are strongly influenced by the NORC's location, its sponsors, and its supporters. To date, most NORC public funding is at the state, city, or town level. Philanthropic groups also play a role in providing funds to establish and maintain NORC supportive services programs. Federal government involvement in NORC programs has begun, arguably, at a relatively modest level. In 2001, the largest non-profit NORC consulting group was awarded a $1 million dollar grant by the federal government's U.S. Department of Housing and Urban Development to develop programs in three states (Michigan, Illinois, Maryland). In 2002, the federal government began the National NORC Demonstration Project, which chose five cities—Baltimore, Cleveland, Pittsburgh, Philadelphia, and St. Louis—to investigate how to help the elderly who remain in their own homes. In 2003, the U.S. Department of Health and Human Services, Administration on Aging awarded $5.6 million to support community services for seniors in NORCs in 12 cities.

Pending legislation (S. 2222/A. 8912) in the New York State legislature would expand services to the elderly in NORCs by changing the definition of NORC from "a majority" to 45% of seniors 60 years and older comprising the housing community, or where 250 residents are elderly.

In New York City, NORCs receive funding from the state legislature, the City of New York (through the Department for the Aging and the New York City Housing Authority), housing units, and philanthropic groups. In the 2004–2005 budget for the New York City Department of Aging, $3.8 million was earmarked for direct-service support to NORCs. In some cases, public funds are matched by housing units or grant-making organizations. In addition, some NORC supportive services are provided through in-kind services. One philanthropic organization considered to be on the forefront of developing and sustaining NORC supportive programs in New York City is the United Hospital Fund (UHF). Through their Aging in Place Initiative, UHF, in partnership with the United Way of New York City, is credited with effectively creating partnerships among housing corporations, medical providers, and social service agencies throughout the city.

PROGRAM SETTING AND LOCATION: NORC SUPPORTIVE SERVICES PROGRAM AT
JEFFERSON HOUSES

Jefferson Houses is a 2000-unit, city-supervised and city-subsidized housing complex located on the Lower Eastside of Manhattan. Jefferson Houses residents total approximately 3500, with approximately 50% of residents aged 60 or older, many of whom occupied apartments there since its inception in 1978 and who have "aged in place." This demographic feature characterizes Jefferson Houses as a NORC. Residents there have been integral to the development of several community-based resources, including a supermarket and other commercial businesses, a local elementary school, a park and gardens, and a library. This point is mentioned because it amply defines this group of seniors–decidedly self-reliant and with a history of grassroots activism.

The Jefferson Houses community room is the hub of the NORC Supportive Services Program within this housing community. The following will describe this program, its history, goals, structure, and components.

A HISTORY OF SENIOR-ORIENTED SERVICES AT JEFFERSON HOUSES

Long before a formal NORC support services program was developed, residents saw to it that its seniors (and other residents in need) were tended to. For many years, small fees were paid by seniors to an industrious retired police detective to provide escort and chore services. Similarly, because the physical plant of the complex housed several community rooms, including one designated for seniors, gatherings of neighbors in a common space was the norm. Some residents cling to this model and reject a formal programmatic approach to service delivery of the NORC.

The Jefferson Houses NORC Supportive Services
Program (Continued)

Jefferson Houses was home to a New York City council member as the trend toward NORC supportive services programs was developing. As an active participant in the Jefferson Houses Tenants Association, she was aware of the residents' demographics, the housing complex's physical space, and the fact that some social services, such as Meals-on-Wheels, were being used by senior residents. She was also aware of city council legislative activity to expand NORC funding. As such, she was instrumental in establishing a relationship between a local senior-oriented service agency, the Senior Alliance, and Jefferson Houses.

THE SENIOR ALLIANCE

The Senior Alliance and Jefferson Houses forged a relationship that would become the backbone of the NORC supportive services program. The Senior Alliance is a 10-year-old social service organization with a mission of "serving the active and frail elderly of Manhattan in a manner that fosters independence, dignity and respect." Their goal is to assist and empower senior citizens so that they may live safely in their homes, and remain in their homes and in their community for as long as they are willing and able.

THE PHYSICAL SETTING—THE COMMUNITY ROOM AT JEFFERSON HOUSES

In 2000, using the community room at Jefferson Houses as its hub, the following services were introduced and managed by the Senior Alliance with funds provided by the City of New York Department for the Aging (DFTA). Each program element was mandated by the DFTA and was centered around a lunch program, as senior malnutrition was identified as an important issue among New York City seniors:

- *Lunch*: 5 days per week for a $1.00 donation by the resident
- *Social work services* for both homebound and ambulatory residents as requested, 2–3 days per week
- *Recreation and education*: four types of classes per week (with a budget of up to $40 per class)
- *Blood pressure checks* weekly
- Nutrition classes: six per year

Program funding also covered a Center Director who is now on site Monday–Friday, 9:30 AM–3:30 PM, and is responsible for managing program components on behalf of the Senior Alliance. In addition to these services, the Senior Alliance also coordinates (but does not fund) Meals-on-Wheels, shopping and escort services staffed by Senior Alliance volunteers, and other recreation and education programs that are at no cost or provided as in-kind services. Time has been incorporated into the weekly schedule each Monday for the discussion of any number of current events or topical issues.

While not paid for through funds earmarked for the NORC, the following services are also available to seniors there. Senior Alliance social workers and the Center Director are often involved in helping facilitate these services on behalf of Jefferson Houses residents.

- *Visiting Nurses*: A visiting nurse program was established in 2000. A registered nurse (has been the same individual since the program inception) maintains a caseload of 25–30 individuals, most of whom are seniors. The nurse provides a range of services including postoperative care, medication management, wound care, pain management, and care coordination with physical therapists, occupational therapists, and nursing aides, either in an individual's apartment or in a designated treatment center in one of the Jefferson House's buildings. The nurse also provides referrals to additional services such and mental health and nutrition services.
- *Physician Home Care program*: Jefferson Houses residents are part of the Physician Home Care program. Upon request by the visiting nurse, or as part of discharge planning from local hospitals, a physician will provide home-based services.
- *Podiatry services* are provided by a neighborhood podiatrist in a designated treatment area near the senior center, once per week or by appointment.
- *On-site health promotion programs*: A neighborhood gynecologist provides periodic health promotion programs to seniors at the center and at her nearby office.
- *Off-site trips* are paid for on a fee-for-service basis, and subsidized by a grant made by a local bank.

PROGRAM PLANNING AND IMPLEMENTATION

For all intents and purposes, minimal organized planning was conducted to assess the current or anticipated health and social services of senior residents at the time the program was initiated. As such, the core program elements, centered on the lunch program in the senior center, were somewhat "boiler plate" based on DFTA mandates. Other hosted programs evolved on the basis of what was available in the community, or was introduced on an as-needed basis by residents. While the Senior Alliance maintains a general mission to help

The Jefferson Houses NORC Supportive Services
Program (Continued)

maintain senior dignity and autonomy, and hosted programs are generally believed to contribute to these factors, it is concluded that explicit, intentional planning in relation to specific needs was not undertaken at the onset of NORC programming.

While some components are mandated by their funding sources as noted above, many of the program elements available to seniors are flexible and under the direction of the Senior Alliance Senior Advisory Council. The purpose of the Advisory Council is to represent the general membership, advise staff, and make recommendations that reflect the interests of the program participants. Consisting of five elected resident members (aged 60 and older), the Council meets monthly. The Council has three subcommittees: Program Committee, Menu Planning Committee, and Grievance Committee. General membership meetings are also held monthly to solicit input from the larger senior community. Examples of the types of issues this group has addressed include the choice and frequency of recreation and education classes, and the decision to change lunch from a catered service to on-site preparation. The Council has also been instrumental in planning a number of fund-raising activities that enabled the senior center to raise money for additional recreational and educational activities.

This comprehensive program description, based on the literature on NORC senior programs, and on data collected from program administrators, direct-service staff, and the seniors themselves, was the basis for the monitoring study that followed. In this study, seniors rated the different types of services provided and how well they thought these services met their needs. With a solid program description, the evaluation could proceed within a framework that provided a strong foundation for program evaluation.

Summary

1. Describing the program is a critical part of program evaluation. Accurate and comprehensive program descriptions help prevent the black-box phenomenon in which evaluators and evaluation designs focus more on goals and outcomes and less on describing the interventions.
2. Evaluability assessment studies are used to determine if a program has developed to the point where it can be evaluated. The techniques of data collection in evaluability assessment studies,

including examination of all program documents, observation of the program in operation, meeting with groups of administrators, staff, and consumers and interviewing some of them individually, and examining the literature in the program area, are all useful strategies for writing a comprehensive program description.

3. Program descriptions are important because often there is no program description or a very limited one. Also, programs change over time and need to be updated. There can also be different perceptions of the program among administrators, staff, and consumers.

4. Program description is central to the research purposes of exploration, description, replication, and knowledge building.

5. As a rule, program descriptions address a number of areas:

   a. General program overview, the rationale and purpose of the program, and general goals of the program;
   b. The broader program context nationally and locally, including the literature describing and assessing similar programs;
   c. The program setting;
   d. The program theory, logic, and interventive methods used;
   e. The program goals and objectives;
   f. Characteristics of consumers, clients, and patients served;
   g. Characteristics of staff;
   h. Program funding, cost, and budget; and
   i. Program planning and implementation issues

6. There are three types of program theory: theory that is articulated in the program design, theory that is not stated but is implicit in the interventive methods and goals, and implausible theory, which lacks a program logic.

7. A logic model can be a very important method for specifying inputs, activities, and short- and long-term goals. All relevant stakeholders can be involved in developing a logic model.

8. A description of the methods of intervention used is important because the choice of methods clearly affects the program's ability to achieve its goals.

9. The program's funding, cost, and budget are crucial variables to study and greatly affect outcome. Programs always operate in a cost–benefit framework. Cost minimization, cost-effectiveness,

cost–benefit, and cost utility analysis are all ways to study costs of a program in relation to outcome.

REFERENCES

Brosnan, M. (2009). Health advocacy resource center initiative. Sarah Lawrence College, Program Evaluation and Assessment Course.

Chapel, T. (2004). Constructing and using logic models in program evaluation. In Roberts, A.R., & Yeager, K.R. (eds.) *Evidence-Based Practice Manual: Research and Outcome Measures in Health and Human Services.* New York: Oxford University Press, pp. 636–646.

Krieg, S. (2009). Process evaluation: Mental health program specializing in cognitive behavioral therapy. Sarah Lawrence College, Program Evaluation and Assessment Course.

McKaig K., Caro, F.G., & Smith, M.J. (1989) *Comprehensive Support for Families: Final Report of the Family Partnership Program, A Demonstration to Assist Families with Developmentally Disabled Children.* New York: Community Service Society of New York.

McKaskie, K. (2004). An exploratory investigation of a food pantry program: The benefits and dilemmas at a street-level agency. Hunter College School of Social Work.

Rossi, P.H., Lipsey, M.W., & Freeman H.E. (2004). *Evaluation: A Systematic Approach.* Thousand Oaks, CA: Sage Publications.

Rubin, A., & Babbie, E. (2005). *Research Methods for Social Work (fifth edition).* Belmont, CA: Wadsworth/Thomson Learning.

Suchman, E. (1967). *Evaluation Research.* New York: Russell Sage Foundation.

Weiss, C.H. (1998). *Evaluation: Methods for Studying Programs and Policies.* Englewood Cliffs, NJ: Prentice-Hall.

Wholey, J.S. (1994). Assessing the feasibility and likely usefulness of evaluation. In Wholey, J.S., Hatry, H.P., & Newcomer, J.E. (eds.) *Handbook of Practical Program Evaluation.* San Francisco: Jossey-Bass, pp. 15–39.

Wilbrect, A. (1997). A corporate survey of the Office of the Health Ombudsman Program, December 18, 1997. Sarah Lawrence College, Program Evaluation and Assessment Course.

5

Needs Assessment Studies

Programming planning and the designing of programs are crucial elements of the work in social and health organizations. A very important part of the field of program evaluation is needs assessment studies, which are integral to social and health planning and programming activities. Professionals in social and health organizations can benefit greatly from needs assessment activities, which can include reviewing the literature on social and health needs, analyzing census data on people who might use the program, and reviewing the work of other social and health organization practitioners who have diagnosed needs, the extent of that need, and possible programs designed to meet certain needs. Attention to needs that have been defined and to methods for meeting needs can lead to thoughtful program planning and will help build an excellent foundation for a program. Sometimes in a planning process an organization's staff is not sure whether to develop a program or not, and needs assessment studies can help them make a sound decision.

There are three things to remember about needs assessment:

1. Needs assessment is a part of professional practice.
2. Needs assessment is important both in the initial stages of planning a new program and for ongoing or established programs because needs can change.
3. Having a program assumes that a need for that program exists, so all programs and all evaluation studies have needs assessment aspects to them.

All professionals in the health and human services have at least some program planning and development responsibilities. Meeting program planning and program development responsibilities should help ensure that the *best* program and interventions are offered to consumers. Needs assessment is an essential tool for program administrators and practitioners alike in carrying out this responsibility. For example, in the field of community organization and planning in social work, the concepts and skills involved in needs assessment have been identified as central to professional work (Mizrahi, 2002).

While needs assessment studies are essential in the initial planning and program development stages, assessment studies can also be useful for assessing programs already in operation as part of the ongoing program development for established programs. For programs in operation, needs assessment studies can document whether the need for the program still exists and how much the needs may have changed. For example, in the early days of treating AIDS when the mortality rate was high, short-term hospice arrangements were greatly needed. Later, as fewer people died from the disease, long-term housing and community supports were needed.

Needs assessment concepts are used in all types of program evaluation studies; they are not used simply for program planning and development. In monitoring or outcome studies, needs assessment is relevant. All evaluation studies, including those that assess the program in operation and those that assess program goals and outcomes, have needs assessment components. All programs assume that an established need exists that the program is trying to address. All program evaluation has implications in terms of whether or not the need truly existed and whether consumers recognized those needs and came to receive services that met those needs. This is true when assessing program operations in program-monitoring studies and in outcome evaluations where the outcome determines whether consumer needs were met or not. So for the student of program evaluation, needs assessment is an important type of evaluation used in all program evaluations.

The discussion of needs assessment will be presented here in the following order: *(1)* the essential elements of needs assessment; *(2)* the process of needs assessment studies; and *(3)* the types of data collected for needs assessment.

Essential Elements of Needs Assessment
Studies—Defining the Need

The following are the essential elements of needs assessment:

1. Define the problem or the need. This means defining the health, social, or educational problem and possible needs that may exist, then the ways the program or programs could meet those needs.

2. Diagnose or assess the problem.
3. State the prevalence or rate of occurrence of a need in a particular population (Rossi et al., 2004, p. 123).
4. Define the target population that has the need or problem and that might benefit from the intervention.
5. Define the needs of the population and the describe the nature of those service needs.

Clearer definitions and descriptions of need are critical because they will lead to more productive statements about what the services should be and, ultimately, to comprehensive and clearer descriptions of the program as outlined and discussed in the previous chapter. The systematic procedures of research help document the need in a reasonable and orderly way.

As any good program evaluator knows, in social, health, and educational programs the word *need* is a soft concept. Needs assessment studies are sometimes initiated in the world of speculation and the hypothetical, which is the challenge of needs assessment. The assignment is to make the speculative and hypothetical real by collecting data about problems and needs. Strong values are involved in determining what people need and what they do not need. *Need* includes both the community's attitudes about the needs and programs to meet those needs that would be "acceptable" in terms of policy.

Need itself can be a deep and complex concept. Documenting need has been identified by Mizrahi (2002) as a sociopolitical process that includes values, power, resources, and ideology. Need is most specific when it implies a connection to resources. At some point, a program is planned to meet and resolve the need represented by the social problem being considered. Needs assessment is most valuable to planners when it includes the concept of needs-resources, in which need is examined in relation to possible program services that meet that need; focusing on need alone can be an empty and totally philosophical enterprise.

While the concept of need can be somewhat philosophical, needs get translated into program design. In addition to the question of what the needs are is the question of which services will meet those needs. Is the service suggested reasonable and logical? Is there a valid conceptualization of the problem and the solutions to the problem? A very practical side of addressing needs is program outreach, outreach strategies, and directing services to the target population. Suchman (1967) has noted that needs are problems that affect a whole group of people and needs are translated into immediate and ultimate program objectives. Thus needs assessment studies contain the seeds for program development and for future monitoring and outcome studies in program evaluation.

The complexity of recognizing need is illustrated in the example of parents raising developmentally disabled children. It is clear that these parents have many needs because of the daily tasks of caregiving and parenting. The medical and educational needs of disabled children are clearly recognized in the United States through publicly funded Medicaid health services and special education services aimed at mainstreaming children into classrooms. However, the parents' extra effort with the daily care of disabled children is not recognized as a need in this country as much as it is in Great Britain (Smith, Caro, & McKaig, 1988, p. 118). Whereas the United States has recognized the value of home care for aging populations to improve the quality of life of the elderly and prevent nursing home placement, home care for developmentally disabled children and their families to help ease the burdens of caregiving is less clearly established as a need. Some may view the provision of home care to families with developmentally disabled children a waste of public funds or a service that should be provided only through private funding by families that can afford a "housekeeper."

The recognition of need can also progress slowly to the program level, so that home care providers specializing in the needs of developmentally disabled children and trained to work with such children and their families may not be available. Overall, the concept of need gets formulated within needs and the resources available to meet those needs, and eventually programs are designed to meet those needs. However, the needs first must be identified, recognized, and studied. This is where needs assessment studies come in. Even after the need is diagnosed and recognized, the political process will have to acknowledge the need and the depth of the need so that resources and services can be allocated to addressing it.

Sometimes the recognition of need comes slowly. For example, there has been a great increase in families in which both parents work. When no parents were home to provide after-school care, communities gradually saw an increase in unsupervised children going to public libraries after school, which often created overcrowded conditions and disruptions in libraries. Communities eventually recognized the need for an increase in after-school care in the schools to help alleviate this problem.

The answers provided by needs assessment studies are often tentative ones. Needs vary and program interventions may have yet to be defined. Surveys often ask people about needs and what types of programs they would attend to meet those needs. These data may be somewhat hypothetical, since the need exists in a person's mind and the program has yet to be planned or initiated. Resources are also based on estimates and prognostications about how many staff are needed, what type of staff is needed, and how much staff would need to be trained, since the program does not yet exist.

Need is also highly dependent on who is defining the need. In this context, the concept of stakeholders is again relevant. As described in Chapter 3, the primary stakeholders are the population in the community, the consumers, clients, or patients who might be the target population in need, the agency and program administrators who might design and implement the program, and the practitioners and staff who may have seen people with the need and may be trained to provide service in the new program. Clearly, consumer input to needs assessment can greatly increase the empowerment of consumers. Likewise, professional input can greatly increase the implementation of an empowerment evaluation.

Other stakeholders are the governmental agencies interested in looking at the social need, and local agencies and private foundations. A third group of stakeholders could be the public in general, who must agree that this is a social problem; national and local agencies in this area of service; and experts and scholars who know about the issues addressed in the need.

Program stakeholders will define the need. They may vary in their definition of need. They should also be involved in the planning process of articulating the program design, the program logic, and the program model. Historical development is important; for example, only community agencies and small foundations were initially involved with family preservation programs to prevent the placement of children in foster care. Now the need for family preservation programs is accepted nationally in laws written to support families with children, at the state level through state family and child services departments, and at the local level through child welfare agencies and the child welfare administrations and child protection agencies. In the field of the aged, services for the elderly in naturally occurring retirement communities (NORCs) were first advocated by local groups planning services for this population. Later, larger foundations and state governments planned and funded NORC programs.

It seems that needs assessment studies are more suspect than they used to be, and program monitoring and process evaluations are being called for more than needs assessment studies. The idea behind monitoring studies is to offer smaller versions of the program and monitor people's use of the program. The aim is to get a better sense of whether the needs exist to the extent that consumers would show up for services to meet those needs. In this process, needs assessment moves from being a soft concept of need and a hypothetical program into the real world of programs that exist. In other words, need can often be established by developing a small pilot program that determines if the program can connect to the population that needs the service.

A Strengths Perspective and Consumer Empowerment

Needs assessment studies that do not address strengths should be judged as unacceptable. The very term *need* can present problems from a strengths perspective. While it can be determined that needs exist, this does not mean that no strengths are present in the communities and individuals chosen as the target population. Strengths assessment should be an important part of needs assessment. The concept of need should not preclude the strengths inherent in populations and communities; people have often survived without the services that may now be seen as essential based on the needs assessment study. People have needs, but they also have strengths, which should be documented in needs assessment studies. All needs assessment studies should have a section that addresses consumer, client, and patient strengths as well as community strengths.

The Process of Needs Assessment Studies

In needs assessment there are really two processes involved. The research process comprises the steps of how a needs assessment study is conducted. In the program planning process a needs assessment study must fit in the overall planning.

In conducting a needs assessment study, a research process similar to the steps in program evaluation is followed. However, the first two steps are different. In the first step, instead of describing the program, the possible needs that the program could address and some of the program options are described. Then, unlike in traditional program evaluation, where the goals are described, the needs and possible resources are more fully refined and described. The remaining steps in a needs assessment study are similar to those in traditional program evaluation. A methodology and a research design are planned. Data are collected and analyzed, and a report of the needs and possible ways to meet those needs are described.

Needs assessment works best when viewed as part of a participatory planning process that involves stakeholders in the process of needs assessment. Empowerment evaluations and consumer empowerment are both part of these participatory processes. At the broadest level, federal government and legislative bodies, state and local governments, and foundations are involved in needs assessment. At the program level, the administrators and staff of the program and potential consumers are empowered through the process of determining the need and possible services for those needs.

Through needs assessment studies the following major research questions are answered: Is there a need for this program? What types of services might meet those needs?

Methodologies and Types of Data in Needs Assessment Studies

There are eight different methodologies, strategies, and types of data that could possibly be involved in a needs assessment study:

1. Survey of the community and/or potential consumers
2. Survey of related programs in other organizations
3. Survey of consumer utilization data and/or agency records in the current organizational setting
4. Survey of key informants or experts in need and program area (e.g., community leaders, national experts, staff)
5. Review of census or population data on potential consumers, including health, education, and social indicators (e.g., trends in poverty, income, unemployment, health insurance, homelessness)
6. Review of the literature in the need and program area
7. Lists of resources in community to meet needs
8. Review of professional training programs for professionals who will staff the program

Take the example of planning and developing an employee assistance program in a university. For a needs assessment study, the major research questions concern the kinds of needs the university's employees have, and the kinds of services that could be provided to meet those needs. At this point, need is highly hypothetical and speculative. The program planners have at least determined, however, that they want to provide assistance to help employees with work, personal, and family problems.

Typically, employee assistance programs have used a number of interventions that are helpful. The program could provide services directly related to personal counseling around family and work issues or be directed toward the treatment of alcohol and substance abuse problems or integrate both approaches. A university-based employee assistance program could develop group discussion programs on issues such as divorce, single parenting, child care, and caring for elderly relatives. Likewise, groups could offer information and activities related to health and wellness, such as weight reduction, stress in the workplace, and nutrition and exercise. Or the program could offer group discussions of work-related issues such as how to supervise a difficult employee or how to deal with employees with suspected substance abuse problems. There are a number of ways to collect data to move into a needs assessment study that could provide data to document employee need. Actually, before the needs assessment study even began, one stakeholder, the president of the university, had determined that there was a need and that this program could help employees with the everyday problems of life and work rather than substance abuse issues alone.

In the needs assessment study, first the planners could survey potential consumers of the program to assess which types of services they could use and to see if the judgments of the university president were correct in terms of employee needs. For example, employees could be asked to assess their own needs in relation to supervising a worker, communicating with workers, needing help with an elderly relative, balancing work and family demands, issues in substance abuse, and mental health issues such as anxiety and depression. Employees could rate the different types of group programs that might be offered through the program. A university-wide survey could determine the types of services the employees might utilize and if there were different problems for different parts of the university population. For example, the needs of building maintenance staff may differ greatly from the needs of professors at the university. A survey could also be conducted at another similar university to determine which types of services they provide, which groups and individual counseling and assistance are offered, and what the hours of operation are.

In addition to surveys of different populations, census reports could also be used in this needs assessment study. Whereas most needs assessments would focus on the population in a geographic area of a city or neighborhood, a needs assessment for a university employee assistance program could focus on the numbers of different types of staff in the university community—how many employees are in each department, how many professors are at the university, how many clerical staff and maintenance staff. Staff in different positions probably have different needs. Also, the characteristics of staff such as age, gender, marital status, and length of employment might give clues about the types of services needed.

In assessing the needs of a university population, reviews of literature on employee assistance programs and university-based employee assistance programs can provide descriptions of how the programs work, what types of personal issues staff members bring to the employee assistance program, and what types of outreach the programs use. A review of program evaluations of employee assistance programs and their success levels with addressing different problems that staff bring would be especially useful. For example, how successful are these programs with drug and alcohol problems, family problems, elder care, and day care issues? How successful are they in preventing absenteeism or reducing the cost of medical benefits, if that is the major purpose of the program?

In terms of using pilot programs to determine if needs existed, the employee assistance program conducted some group programs to assess the needs of employees. Group discussion on parenting and psychological needs were used less than concrete programs that addressed the concerns of employees' everyday life. Groups offered for older employees to explain Medicare health options and eligibility in relation to retirement were well attended, as were groups to help employees who were considering purchasing condominiums or coops as their primary form of housing. Yoga groups also got large turnouts in the area of wellness programs. Attendance at these pilot programs was another way to assess need and the employee response to services.

Another strategy for needs assessment could be use of a key informant or expert opinion survey in which experts in the employee assistance field are asked about the main issues in setting up an employee assistance program and in planning the types and scheduling of service that should be offered. Pertinent administrators in the university could also be surveyed as key informants on the types of employment and personal issues that university employees seem to have and when employees might attend a relevant program.

In the first case study presented here, a needs assessment study was conducted for a cancer information center at a hospital. This was a traditional needs assessment study in which two methodologies were used. First, a review of literature was conducted on the need for cancer information and the resources used to meet those needs. Second, a survey of potential consumers was conducted to determine which types of information people could use and how the information could be accessed.

Needs Assessment Study for a Cancer Information Center
ELEANOR SCARCELLA, M.A.
GRADUATE OF THE MASTER'S PROGRAM IN HEALTH ADVOCACY,
SARAH LAWRENCE COLLEGE

A cancer hospital wanted to plan and develop a cancer information center. The basic idea was to give accessible information to patients and their families, prospective patients, and the community at large to empower consumers in the areas of cancer care and prevention. The rationale and conceptualization of need for this program were based on a number of background issues in the literature.

Needs Assessment Study for a Cancer Information Center (Continued)

BACKGROUND ISSUES

Patient self-determination and health-care professionals' obligation to ensure that treatment is delivered with fully informed consent by the patient are, by law, standards of care and practice. In the setting of managed care, health organizations can have control over the choice of care and choice of caregiver, so the patient or prospective caregiver *must* get consumer information as a type of "consumer defense." Professional and public-advocacy groups have developed consumer and patient health-information resources to meet this need. Not very long ago, medical librarians resisted serving consumer needs and worked exclusively with medical staff. Now consumer health-care kiosks are present in public libraries and in hospital libraries. The federal government has acknowledged this trend by allowing World Wide Web access to MEDLINE, the preeminent collection of medical information managed by the National Library of Medicine.

The managed-care environment also challenges health-care providers to care for patients with cost-consciousness in mind. Expenditures in developing patient education programs have proven to be cost-effective, as studies have shown that patient outcomes are better for patients who are informed and involved.

Statistics show that one American turns age 50 every 8 seconds, and an older population means an increasing overall incidence of cancer. The initial diagnosis of cancer can open a world of hopelessness and isolation for an individual. However, by empowering individuals with knowledge about cancer, patients can improve their ability to respond more rapidly to symptoms and the demands of treatment. Patients and their families can anticipate and become involved in a plan for their treatment and not rely solely on emergency care services. Access to cancer information may also help the public seek preventive measures to protect their health and create greater awareness of potential carcinogenic hazards.

THE PROGRAM: THE CANCER INFORMATION CENTER

Media attention to "hot topics" in cancer detection, prevention, and treatment can be confusing and contradictory at times. Professional help offered through doctors and a cancer information center can assist in deciphering the hype. The research can be translated into practical terms for the consumer, and variables customized to a patient's individual case.

At the hospital discussed in this case, the initial idea for such help was to plan a cancer information center on site in a specialized department of the hospital. Through a combination of outpatient and inpatient cancer programs the hospital had 250 patient contacts per week, in addition to lists of former patients treated at the cancer facility. Space would be provided on the hospital floor accessible to both the inpatient and outpatient facilities.

In the program planning for the center a number of possible program strategies and methods were described. Information and assistance would be given to cancer patients and their families along with guidance from library and volunteer staff working at the center. A person just diagnosed with cancer might be given information about the type of cancer, the various treatments, the options in medical care, and the literature on the emotional support, coping strategies, and psychological and self-help services needed to fight the disease. Support groups of patients with varying types of cancer and caregiver support groups run on a regular basis were to be located at the center so that information and support could be centralized in one place.

The information provided at the center was to include periodicals, textbooks, popular literature on cancer, audiovisual tapes, CDs, and access to the Internet for information and support. Materials from major cancer groups such as the American Cancer Society and the National Cancer Institute, consumer materials from pharmaceutical companies, and information on outreach programs in the local community and Web sites specializing in different types of cancer and support would also be provided, along with information about the perceived reliability of these informational resources. Program funding would need to be sought for these important functions and for staff, such as a director of the institute, library staff, and computer resources.

REVIEW OF THE LITERATURE

A review of the literature on consumer health-information service was part of this needs assessment study. The review described the approaches taken by many public libraries, many of which have developed bibliographies on specialized health-care issues. Hospital libraries are also serving patients and their families. A number of cancer-specific information centers are present in hospitals, such as one developed at Inova Health Systems in Fairfax, Virginia, where in-person assistance is provided by program staff. Data from these centers were used to compare the services provided, the ratio of paid staff and volunteers, the level of assistance provided, whether the center specialized in one type of cancer or many

Needs Assessment Study for a Cancer Information Center (Continued)

types, and the types of support groups and self-help groups sponsored at the center.

One survey of a health library's service found that 79% of consumers reported increased knowledge of treatments or procedures and 54% reported lower fear and anxiety levels. When these information centers develop outreach to those who need information but are unlikely to access the information themselves, the centers may be especially effective. Not surprisingly, income and education are significant factors in the ways in which health information is consumed. The "health-poor" are much more likely than the "health-wealthy" not to seek information when they have a health problem and often have problems getting health information.

PATIENT SURVEY

As a primary part of the needs assessment study, a survey was conducted to assess patient and family needs in relation to cancer. In the needs assessment approach, the responses of potential users of the center were sought to provide guidelines to possible program objectives being developed and to specify directions for the allocation of funds. Some obvious goals were to increase knowledge of the disease for the newly diagnosed patient so that the disease process and treatment options could be clearly understood, and to increase patients' knowledge about the resources available in the hospital and the community, such as financial assistance and eligibility for home care upon release from the hospital and throughout recovery. Goals could also include an increased sense of empowerment for the patient and family members, improved attitudes toward the disease, improved knowledge about symptoms and the demands of treatment, better anticipation about the course of the disease and treatment, and fewer instances of using emergency care services. Ultimately the goal was to improve health outcomes for the patient.

The change in level of a person's knowledge base can be studied in a pre–post study design in which the patients' information base is assessed before and after exposure to the cancer information center. A needs assessment study in which patients are asked about information they need and about their current knowledge can help in developing a baseline of a person's present knowledge of cancer and access to informational and medical resources. This type of needs assessment study has the seeds for further process evaluations and outcome-oriented evaluation studies.

The plan of the hospital's needs assessment study was to survey the population of patients and families visiting the hospital for outpatient cancer services. Patients and families were asked about their current level of information about the disease and treatment, how they received the information, and what additional materials, support, and assistance they might need.

OTHER NEEDS ASSESSMENT STRATEGIES

In future surveys patients could also be asked about their level of informed consent, to assess whether they are knowledgeable about their current course of treatment and other options that may be available. In addition to the structured quantitative data gathered from a survey of patients, at a later point, focus groups of outpatients receiving cancer treatment, family members, and other caretakers could be conducted to collect qualitative data to determine patient needs and the best means of accessing information. Another way to develop accurate needs assessment is to develop pilot programs intended to reach the affected patient populations and engage them in seeking out relevant health information.

In the current survey, a convenience sample of outpatients seeking cancer diagnosis and treatment was chosen as a first strategy. The objective was to identify the knowledge level of the patients and to determine whether they would use a cancer information center. The questionnaire developed asked first about demographics, such as gender of the patient, their age, education, and usual language spoken and language used for reading. Comfort level with traditional and electronic information gathering was another area selected. Patients were asked how often they used libraries for pleasure and for personal and professional information, and whether they used a computer for word processing and Internet searches. They were also asked how accessible books, CDs, magazines, and television were. They were asked if they wanted more information about the biology of the disease and how it affects the body, the diagnostic procedures, and treatments such as drugs, surgical procedures, and radiation. Patients were also asked if they wanted information on clinical trials, research, public policy issues, home health care instructions and eligibility, and support groups for patients, family, and caregivers. A unique aspect of the survey was determining which information sources had been helpful in getting useful information up to this point, for example, talking to doctors, talking to nurses, talking to others with cancer, videotapes, books, or the Internet. Finally, patients were asked if they would volunteer at an information center and if they would use the center.

Needs Assessment Study for a Cancer Information Center (Continued)

FINDINGS OF THE NEEDS ASSESSMENT STUDY

The majority of the patients were adults over age 55 years; 60% had education beyond high school and 35% were college graduates. They used the library for reading for pleasure more than for personal or professional research. Some patients did not use the computer for Internet searches. The major types of cancer that patients had been diagnosed with were breast cancer (30%) and prostate cancer (30%). Patients wanted "much more" information about the biology of the disease (39%), drug treatment (37%), radiation (26%), diagnosis (25%), and surgical treatments (15%).

One major finding was the great need for information and access to clinical trials. Eighty-seven percent wanted more information on clinical trials and cancer research. In terms of their current information, 64% found "talking to doctors" very helpful; for 54% "talking to nurses" was very helpful; 60% found pamphlets very helpful, and "talking with other cancer patients" was very helpful 57% of the time. Almost half of the respondents had read books of personal cases dealing with cancer and everyone who had read personal cases found this helpful.

In terms of uses of the cancer information center, 58% wanted to get informational material; 28% wanted assistance with research; 26% would drop by and browse in the center; 16% wanted to get involved with cancer issues; and 15% would use it for going to a support group.

Perhaps one of the most useful sections of the questionnaire was when patients were asked an open-ended question about which types of information and services they would like. Therapeutic use of diet and herbs and alternatives to surgery was one area where information was sought. Another request was for guest speakers and contacts at pharmaceutical companies. Some expressed exasperation with the information available: "This is my second go-round with lung cancer. I continue to be amazed by the limited specific information that is available."

CONCLUSIONS AND IMPLICATIONS

Just one part of this needs assessment study, the survey of cancer patients, revealed important information for program planning. Patients tended to be an educated group for whom English was their spoken and read language. Some patients would need help with Internet searches and patients were more likely to use magazines and newspaper articles directly. Patients were especially interested in current research and clinical trials, which may be a labor-intensive type of knowledge delivery, matching type of cancer and stage to the clinical trial information. This information should supplement information provided by physicians and other health-care professionals that patients have found helpful. Personal contacts seemed especially effective, so a personal approach to information and the empathy of a trained staff person would be especially valued. Also, providing personal accounts of people's experiences with cancer and getting people to read personal accounts might be a useful approach.

Further data collected from the focus groups and surveys of family members and caregivers of cancer patients could provide even more information about the needs of patients and their supports and the types of information needed to empower them as health consumers. A comprehensive needs assessment approach can assist greatly in program planning, so that pilot programs can be planned and monitored as the program shifts from the planning to the implementation stage of development.

The second example of needs assessment is a needs assessment study of the state Children's Health Insurance Program (CHIP) in Indiana, which provides medical care to lower-income families without medical insurance. The state of Indiana launched a program-planning and program development process involving experts in the health-care field. Public hearings on the new programs were conducted. In the literature, public hearings and community forums have been identified as democratic, grassroots approaches, as all stakeholders are invited to attend (Royse, Thyer, Padgett, & Logan, 2001, p. 62). There are nonetheless concerns about how well each stakeholder group is represented in such hearings and how well the group represents the attitudes and experiences of the larger community.

A qualitative analysis of the data was conducted on the basis of public hearings in which expert testimony, the concerns of service providers, and potential consumers of CHIP reported on the value and need for public health insurance and issues in the design and accessibility of the program. Themes generated from the qualitative data greatly aided the program development process. Comprehensive coverage, the need for specialty services, outreach strategies, reduction of stigma and bureaucracy, and lack of health-care providers were all identified as formidable issues in planning and developing the new health-care program.

A Needs Assessment Study of Indiana's Children's
Health Insurance Program

SHERISSE WEBB, M.A.

GRADUATE OF THE MASTER'S PROGRAM IN HEALTH ADVOCACY,

SARAH LAWRENCE COLLEGE

In 1997, The Social Security Act was amended in Washington, DC, with the addition of the state Children's Health Insurance Program (CHIP), or Title XXI. The purpose of this legislation was to assist states in expanding children's health insurance coverage to children whose families' incomes exceed the requirements for Medicaid but are insufficient to pay for private insurance coverage. Beginning on October 1, 1997, and continuing for the next 5 years, the federal government made $24 billion in grants available to the states to expand Medicaid and/or create a new CHIP to provide coverage for children below the age of 19 with family incomes up to 200% of the federal poverty level.

States needed to submit and obtain approval for a child health plan that detailed how eligibility would be determined and how the plan would be coordinated with other existing health-care programs (including Medicaid), how services would be delivered, and how access and quality would be assured. The legislation also called for the provision of federal funds to promote the development of outreach strategies to identify and enroll all uninsured children in either Medicaid or CHIP.

INDIANA'S STATE PLAN FOR THE CHILDREN'S HEALTH INSURANCE PROGRAM

In October, 1997, Indiana's Governor Frank O'Bannon announced that a panel consisting of 21 health-care professionals, insurance executives, legislators, educators, and parents had been created to evaluate the State Children's Health Insurance Program and recommend the manner in which the state of Indiana ought to participate. The panel members were granted responsibility for reviewing the current Medicaid program, recommending how CHIP might be coordinated with other state and federal block-grant programs, and suggesting how the program should be designed and implemented in Indiana so as to achieve the ultimate goal of providing health insurance coverage to the uninsured children of working-poor families.

The advisory panel identified five proximate goals to guide development of the program. Panel members agreed that CHIP should *(1)* be a family-centered, integrated program offering preventive and acute-care services to measurably improve the health status of the children of Indiana; *(2)* encourage participation by being accommodating to the needs of both families and providers; *(3)* be coordinated with and contribute to existing and future health-care initiatives; *(4)* be sensitive to the diverse interests and cultures of health-care consumers; and *(5)* promote healthy behavior and responsible utilization and distribution of health-care resources.

INDIANA'S OUTREACH CAMPAIGN

The initial state plan developed by the advisory panel included an outreach campaign composed of program objectives intended to make the application process simple and convenient for families, ensure that the application and income verification processes were executed so as to avoid visits to the welfare office, encourage local development of outreach strategies to reflect and serve the interests of the communities, and improve outreach and enrollment in a manner that did not overburden the existing infrastructure.

One of the measures included in the outreach proposal was a de-linking of Medicaid from Temporary Assistance for Needy Families (TANF) and Food Stamps in the computer system used by the Department of Family and Children, the agency responsible for administration of all three programs. The panel members anticipated that the separation of Medicaid from other social-assistance programs would remove the stigma traditionally associated with Medicaid.

The panel members also recommended that Indiana *(1)* establish a toll-free hotline from which potential enrollees could obtain information and applications; *(2)* develop a simplified two-page application form for both Medicaid and CHIP; *(3)* initiate a media campaign to inform the public about the availability of the Medicaid program; and *(4)* create a new training curriculum for caseworkers and other individuals involved in the administration of the program. These outreach activities were supplemented by the efforts of the local Department of Family and Children directors to establish enrollment centers and outstation eligibility workers throughout their communities with the assistance of local hospitals, schools, health centers, and social service agencies.

TESTIMONY AT PUBLIC HEARINGS—DATA FOR THE NEEDS ASSESSMENT STUDY

Prior to the development of its recommendations for the design and implementation of the Children's Health Insurance Program, the Governor's Advisory Panel held 11 public meetings throughout the state of Indiana to familiarize themselves with the issues and concerns of state residents regarding health insurance

A Needs Assessment Study of Indiana's Children's
Health Insurance Program (Continued)

coverage for children and to involve the public in the program development process. Specifically, the Advisory Panel sought responses to the following questions:

1. What changes in health care need to be made to help children stay healthy and get sick care immediately?
2. What can we do to encourage parents to get regular health care for their children?
3. How should CHIP differ from the Medicare system?
4. How should CHIP differ from the Medicaid system?
5. What can we do to encourage parents to sign up and use the new program?

The forums were held at various sites and at different times so that public awareness and participation would be maximized. As well, brochures and informative literature about the significance of CHIP and the importance of the public input process were distributed to several health-care organizations, including community health clinics, county health departments, Women and Infant Children (WIC) programs, and health-care provider networks. Many members of the Advisory Panel and advocacy groups also notified interested parties and organizations. Finally, press releases were distributed to various radio, television, and newspaper outlets and resulted in pre-publicity interviews, articles, and media coverage of the meetings themselves.

The extensive publicity succeeded in enticing more than 450 persons to the meetings and convinced several others to submit written documents. Approximately 100 parents, advocates, providers, and others who attended the meetings shared their thoughts and perspectives with the Advisory Panel members.

The following qualitative data analysis of the transcripts of the proceedings was conducted to gain an understanding of the needs of Indiana's uninsured and Medicaid-eligible children and to suggest how the Children's Health Insurance Program might be used to meet those needs. Assessment of the qualitative data found that, although many different issues were raised by the participants, several common themes emerged that seemed to transcend the traditional boundaries between and among parents, advocates, and providers. Participants' quotes presented here link the themes to the participants' experiences with and perceptions of public health insurance programs.

The health status of individuals is often a reflection of their particular personal, environmental, and socioeconomic circumstances. Many individuals who attended the Advisory Panel's public hearings noted that to serve the various medical needs of all uninsured children in Indiana, the program would have to include a comprehensive benefits plan that recognizes and addresses all of the factors affecting the health status of children. Those responding to the new program mentioned medical, social, educational, housing, and transportation issues as such factors.

> Poor housing conditions affect children's health. CHIP should dovetail with well-being programs of decent housing and welfare reform. (Retired city planner)
>
> Address medical and social needs like reading and education. They are all interwoven. (Caseworker)
>
> Medicab needs to be more creative in rural areas with regard to transportation. Medicaid should pay for the cost of transportation, or maybe cover the extra liability insurance of the caseworker who drives them. (Caseworker)
>
> Transportation is the biggest selling point in our Healthy Families Program. It should continue in CHIP. (Caseworker)

Participants at the public hearings maintained that CHIP had to be able to address the particular health-care concerns and needs of adolescents.

> Adolescents get forgotten. We couldn't serve them because of parental consent. So we opened a clinic in the alternative school. We had 538 visits through December, and now are over 1000. (Open Door Health Center)

Many commenting at the hearings were concerned that specialty services such as dental and vision care would not be offered in the CHIP package. Federal guidelines did not require that beneficiaries in Medicaid or CHIP have access to specialty care. Participants pointed out that preventive dental and vision services are equally as important as preventive care offered by general practitioners and that low- and moderate-income families may not be able to afford dental and vision services if such services were not offered by CHIP.

> Teeth are not optional body parts. Dental care must be included as it is vital to overall children's health. Prevention services such as sealants, etc., are effective in reducing damage. (Professor, Indiana University)

A Needs Assessment Study of Indiana's Children's
Health Insurance Program (Continued)

> I came here with a passion for dental health – to get knowledge
> and help to the needy public. As I sat and listened to everyone speaking,
> I saw a passion for every angle of health. *All needs should be addressed.*
> (Dental worker; emphasis mine)
>
> Vision care is often overlooked. Make sure it is available and
> accessible. (Optometry professor, Indiana University)
>
> I am here to ask that you include optometrist visits as part of this
> Comprehensive Health Plan for Children. (Teacher)

OUTREACH PROGRAMS

Those who testified noted that many low-income working families would not realize that their children qualified for the new program or would not believe that their children needed health coverage if they were not currently sick. Several persons who participated in the hearings proposed ways of informing parents about CHIP and encouraging them to enroll their children by linking to the schools, putting ads on TV, and including incentives for parents to enroll their children in the program.

> CHIP should be in the schools. Enroll the kids where they are. Get the
> kids who are already on free school lunches. (Neighborhood association
> president)
>
> Schools are accessible and convenient. Parents wouldn't have to
> miss work. Kids would miss less school, and they are in a familiar
> setting and stable environment. (School nurse)
>
> Put ads on TV. Even the best programs fail if they don't reach the
> kids. (County health department worker)
>
> Include incentives for parents for enrolling their kids. Reinforce
> preventive care as a family process. Don't get so focused on the kids
> that you forget about the families. (Worker from Minority Health
> Coalition)

THE STIGMA OF MEDICAID AND WELFARE DEPENDENCY

Many, many participants noted that families might be reluctant to enroll their children in Indiana's health care programs because of the stigma associated with public assistance and Medicaid and the poor treatment they receive from caseworkers.

I have a part-time job and go to school full-time. I am on welfare, but will be off in a year. When you are on welfare, they make you feel like doo-doo—how they treat you and talk about you. CHIP should be about treating people right. If it's not, it is a failure. It's about people, not just the children. (Welfare/Medicaid recipient)

The temptation to stigmatize and/or punish people who receive assistance is pervasive. Let's take the attitude of "them versus us" completely out of the effort to keep children healthy. (Parent of child who would be eligible for CHIP)

It is imperative that this program be separated from the Medicaid program. CHIP needs to have a good image. People shouldn't be ashamed to use CHIP. (School nurse)

I know several people, including pregnant women, who refused to sign up for Medicaid because of poor treatment and/or the attitudes of caseworkers. (County health care services worker)

I am concerned about the lack of knowledgeable people working in the current Medicaid system. Caseworkers don't know the rules about immigrants—53 percent of their cases are overturned. Who are we placing in these positions? (Worker from Hispanic center)

The enrollment process for Medicaid often involved long forms and excessive documentation. It was hoped that CHIP could avoid these problems and that Medicaid itself could be reformed.

No need to expand Medicaid. The application, approval, and claim process at Medicaid is disastrous . . . . The caseworkers, overall, are rude and uncaring, and treat clients like they are stupid. The bureaucracy is unwieldy, confusing, and concerned mainly with the convenience of the worker and the state, not the care of the client. (Member of AIDS task force)

Parents need help with the forms, but that doesn't mean they are stupid. (Boys/Girls Club county worker)

Could we please put a stop to the red tape and bureaucracy? Too much paperwork, too much wasted money to get the health services that are really needed. (Parent)

Too often people have to leave work only to be told, "Oh, you brought the wrong forms." (Member of Indiana Caregiver Network)

The key is simplicity. No more hoops for people to jump through. (Family shelter worker)

A Needs Assessment Study of Indiana's Children's
Health Insurance Program (Continued)

> There should be more humane, courteous, fair, and
> nonjudgmental screening. (Case manager)
>
> I've mapped the paths clients have to take to get services. CHIP
> must streamline the process. More single points of entry. Combine it
> with other forms. (Member of Indiana Caregiver Network)

THE LIMITED NUMBER OF HEALTH-CARE PROVIDERS

Participants also commented on the limited number of Medicaid providers. The unwillingness of physicians to treat low-income patients was identified as a significant and persistent barrier to care. Many of the medical professionals who shared their thoughts at the meetings argued that insufficient reimbursement rates would discourage providers from participating in the program and may be responsible for the limited umber of Medicaid providers.

> I am concerned with the limited amount of Medicaid providers. Our
> families are having to drive to other communities to receive services.
> (School corporation employee)
>
> There are obstacles in Indiana's Medicaid program.
> Reimbursement can take 4 to 6 months on some claims, and there are
> no dental providers because of the low reimbursement rates.
> (Caseworker)
>
> I strongly feel CHIP should recognize the needs of providers—
> reasonable fee for services. Historically, Indiana dentists stopped
> providing services when Governor Bayh reduced reimbursement rates
> to below provider costs. Current providers, on the whole, are not
> providing quality care. (Dental hygienist)

SUMMARY OF FINDINGS

This analysis of the qualitative data from the transcripts of testimony from hearings on the CHIP program indicates that most people agreed that uninsured children require the following: *(1)* comprehensive benefits, including specialty health service such as dental and vision care and transportation services, especially in rural areas; *(2)* outreach and enrollment strategies that remove existing barriers to participation and encourage parents to seek primary health-care services for their children; and *(3)* convenient access to affordable health care. The data suggest that everyone desired a program that is family oriented, accommodates the needs of working families, incorporates existing local and regional health-care services, is compassionate and respectful of consumers, and promotes health lifestyles by emphasizing preventive health care. This type of needs assessment data was invaluable in the program planning and development of Indiana's Children's Health Insurance Program.

This last example clearly shows how the concerns identified in the planning and development of the program will be issues in the later stages of implementing the program and in future monitoring and evaluation studies. For example, as the CHIP program begins, research questions arising out of the needs assessment will also be relevant. How comprehensive was the coverage? Which specialty health services were included? Was the program effective in reaching consumers in rural areas? How was outreach implemented? Were the application process and bureaucratic procedures simplified? Were eligibility workers sympathetic to the health needs of lower-income participants? In this way, a good needs assessment process can set the stage for a quality program as the program proceeds from the program planning to the implementation stage.

Summary

1. Needs assessment studies are an important part of the field of evaluation.
2. The needs assessment process is part of professional practice for administrators and practitioners.
3. Needs assessment is useful in the initial stages of program planning as well as in the later stages of program development for both new and established programs.
4. All evaluation studies have needs assessment aspects to them. Programs should always be fulfilling some meaningful needs in people's lives.
5. While *need* can be a vague and abstract concept, needs assessment studies help make the needs concrete and operational.
6. One of the goals of needs assessment is to see that all stakeholders, the community, potential consumers, government agencies, program administrators, and staff are involved in the process of assessing and defining need.

7. In assessing need, the strengths of communities and consumers should also be assessed. Less powerful groups, usually consumers and the community, should be empowered through the needs assessment process.

8. In needs assessment, the first two steps of the research process are different from those of program evaluation. The first step is describing the possible needs, and the second is describing needs in relation to resources and possible interventions to meet those needs.

9. A comprehensive list of methodologies for needs assessment studies includes a survey of the community and/or potential consumers, a survey of related programs, consumer utilization data and data from agency records from current programs, a survey of key experts or informants, reviews of census and population data, reviews of literature in the need or program area, lists of community resources, and reviews of staff training and qualifications of staff for providing the needed services.

10. Needs assessment studies contain the seeds for further evaluation studies that examine program implementation and program outcomes.

REFERENCES

Mizrahi, T. (2002). Community organizing principles and practice guidelines. In Roberts, A.R., & Greene, G.J. (eds.) *Social Worker's Desk Reference*. New York: Oxford University Press, pp. 517–524.

Rossi, P.H., Lipsey, M.W., & Freeman H.E. (2004). *Evaluation: A Systematic Approach*. Thousand Oaks, CA: Sage Publications.

Royse, D., Thyer, B.A., Padgett, D.K., & Logan, T.K. (2001). *Program Evaluation: An Introduction* Belmont, CA: Wadsworth/Thomson Learning.

Smith, M.J., Caro, F.G., & McKaig K. (1988). The role of home care service in family care of developmentally disabled children: An exploratory study. *Home Health Care Services Quarterly* 9(1):117–134.

Suchman, E. (1967). *Evaluation Research*. New York: Russell Sage Foundation.

6

Determining Program Goals

Nothing happens until we plan, and good plans have goals and objectives. Setting goals and objectives correctly go a long way helping in the achievement of goal and objectives.
—G. Ambler, "Setting SMART objectives" (2006)

A program was defined as a strategy or intervention planned and conducted for a group of people to achieve some desirable consequence or outcome. For desirable consequences or outcomes to occur, the program's goals and objectives need to be central to the definition of a program.

Goals are essential for programs in the same way that goals are important for our personal and professional lives. For instance, in our first years of marriage, my wife encouraged me to sit down with her to determine and rank our goals for the next 10 or so years. In this way, the nature and priority of each of our goals could be seen. The goals were not dramatic and included buying a house, having children, and finishing our education. However, this process did help clarify our overall goals and the priority of each person's goals. Now after 37 years of marriage, these goals have been redefined and recalculated, as goals change over time. Program goals also are not static; they change over time.

Goals should be clearly thought out and described to the extent that they could also be measured, through either quantitative or qualitative measurement. Program outcomes are the gains and successes that can be documented as a result of the program. In a full evaluation, program strategies and interventions are also measured, along with goals, to assess the relation between the program, the program interventions, and the program goals.

While the importance of goals is stressed in the chapter, it is important to remember that goals and objectives always develop in a program environment. Program evaluation is not a field made up totally of efficiency experts using a strictly quantitative methodology in which every goal must be concretized and broken down and measured in statistical terms. The program context, philosophies, and environments and a program ethos are also important parts of a program even if they cannot be sketched out on a chart of program goals and measured concretely or clearly. These more amorphous, descriptive parts of the program may be more easily studied through qualitative methods. For example, consumers might be asked to thoroughly describe what they thought about the program and how they experienced the program, rather than simply rating how easy it was to make an appointment or how much they felt respect from the staff. The many descriptive aspects of a program that create the overall program environment, philosophy, and "feel" of the program were discussed in Chapter 4. Put simply, a program is not merely a collection of goals and objectives.

All evaluation studies involve program goals. In needs assessment studies, as a program concept is developing and needs are being documented, the eventual purpose of a program and some program objectives will be established, even if at first the needs are not completely known. Program monitoring and process evaluations are directed at studying program inputs and program processes, but inputs and processes are always in relation to program goals and objectives. Outcome-oriented evaluations focus much more on specifying and measuring goals and objectives so that the evaluation can determine whether or not those goals and objectives were achieved. In impact assessment studies, experimental designs are used to focus on very specific goals such as changes in knowledge, behavior, attitudes, skills, and status. Impact assessment studies set out to establish a causal link between the program and the achievement of program outcomes and goals.

Part of describing the program (Chapter 4) includes the program concept, the mission statement, the general purpose and rationale of the program, and the program goals and objectives. Logic modeling was presented as a method for charting goals and delineating short-tem, intermediate, and long-term outcomes. After describing the program, the program goals need to be defined and eventually measured; then the program is evaluated by collecting data on those goals. As they are measured, program outcomes, goals, and objectives are *operationalized*, that is, defined specifically to the extent that they can be measured. Program goals and objectives should be measured well in accordance with the principles of measurement, especially the *reliability* and *validity* of measurement, which will be discussed toward the end of this chapter.

The quantitative measurement of goals depends on the reliability and validity of measurement. Reliability and validity are also involved in qualitative measurement, but concerns about the reliability and validity of qualitative data come *after* the data are collected, in the process of analyzing the data. For this reason, reliability and validity in qualitative research will be discussed in Chapter 9, on data analysis.

Creating and Developing Programs and Program Goals

Program goals are both identified and developed during the initial stages of planning an evaluation. The evaluator most definitely takes a *proactive* stance in helping to identify more of the goals of the program. The goals are usually not clear, and the evaluator, with the help of other stakeholders, needs to develop, list, and spell out the goals. In the spirit of paradigms such as participatory evaluation, consumer empowerment, empowerment evaluation, and demo-cratic evaluation, *all* of the stakeholders should be involved in identifying established goals and recently conceptualized goals of the program. This is the same type of collaborative process discussed in developing the comprehen-sive program description (Chapter 4). Rossi, Lipsey, and Freeman (2004, p.209) indicate that "stakeholder perception of outcome" is very important. For example, what do staff, administrators, and consumers think are the goals of the program? Are they assuming that the program is achieving its goals? Do they agree in their assessment of what the goals are? Assessing stakeholder perception of outcome can help accomplish the task of developing and creating a comprehensive list of goals or outcomes. A very important task then is collaborating with relevant stakeholders to identify program goals and trans-form very broad goals and outcomes into more specific outcomes and program objectives (Rossi et al., 2004, p. 89)

This proactive goal development process can be aided by examining the context of goal orientations and perspectives. These include the following: *(1)* the mission statement of the program; *(2)* the dependent variables in the program; *(3)* practice goals; *(4)* program goals and program objectives; *(5)* process objectives; *(6)* short- and long-term goals and objectives; *(7)* tender-hearted and tough-minded goals; *(8)* unanticipated goals; and *(9)* changes in knowledge, behaviors, attitudes, skills, and status (the KBASS model).

1. Mission Statement of the Program

Programs and organizations usually have mission statements that express the overall purpose and intent of the program. While these statements can be broad, vague, and all-encompassing, they often can provide a good start for the development of program goals and interventions. In addition to providing the overall intent, and perhaps the program philosophy, these statements can lead to the overall rationale and purpose of the program, which then leads to more specific program outcomes, goals, and objectives. For example, the mission statement of an employment program might be "to have people who were previously unemployed and underemployed lead productive lives." While "lead productive lives" is vague, this phrase can be used to develop a comprehensive list of outcomes and goals meant to measure what "leading a productive life" can mean. So, increased job skills, better interaction with co-workers, and maintaining steady employment can all be seen as program goals related to the mission of "leading a productive life." At the same time, the goal "to have previously unemployed and underemployed people lead productive lives" is specific enough to begin to identify a target population that can be investigated in a study of unemployed and underemployed individuals receiving job training.

In one program for homeless women with chronic mental illness, the mission statement was "to create a therapeutic community among homeless women with serious mental illness to help them develop to the best of their abilities so they can lead productive lives." While this statement is vague, it provides a sense of the overall purpose, focus, and philosophy of the program and really contains a broad statement of the goals. For example, "therapeutic community" suggests there are some clinical goals for the women and the phrase "lead productive lives" suggests that an increase in social functioning and obtaining of employment will be part of the program goals. The phrase "develop to the best of their abilities" is vague and means that a list of possible abilities needs to be established to further develop the program and practice goals and objectives.

As the program description proceeds from the mission statement to a description of the services provided, goals can be developed even further. For example, the program for homeless women provided housing, therapeutic groups, social work and case management services, life skills groups, housing readiness programs, and creative arts such as dance therapy and a visual arts program. Thus there are general goals in relation to long-term housing, improvements in quality of life, use of housing services, coping with mental illness, and personal growth. There can be specific program objectives for each of the eight service areas.

The mission statement can be made more specific by relating it to a target population of consumers and to the needs the program should address and the services given so that it can be a jumping-off point for the development of program goals and outcomes. However, sometimes the mission statement can be just "pious platitudes" written about the program, such as "to help people become productive members of society," and essentially say nothing if left at this primitive level. While mission statements can be a jumping off point for the development of the program, until the target population and their needs are defined, the services given more clearly described, and the explicit goals stated, the mission statement itself can only be considered a descriptive part of the program context, not a specification of program goals and objectives.

2. Dependent Variables in the Program

In research terms, *dependent variables* are variables considered to be the "effects," the goals, the outcomes, the objectives. *Independent variables* are variables that are thought to be "causes." Independent variables are the program inputs, such as the resources and the consumers who are served. So, in an employment program, obtaining employment would be an "effect," or dependent variable, and the program's efforts to train people would be an independent variable that might "cause" the effect of becoming employed. The words *cause* and *effect* are between quotation marks because if program outcomes or effects are being studied, it does not necessarily mean that the outcomes achieved were caused by the program. Pre–post studies and experimental and quasi-experimental designs, discussed in Chapter 7, are designed to rule out the other non-program variables that may have caused an outcome.

Program goals or outcomes fit the classification of dependent variables— the effects. At this point, the program goals should already be present in the formal description of the program. As the program evaluation develops, all possible program goals or outcomes should be sketched out and developed in a thorough and proactive program-development stance and in the initial stages of planning an evaluation study.

As an example, in a program providing counseling services, program goals could be to increase a person's level of self-esteem or efficacy, reduce a person's social isolation, increase marital satisfaction, increase communication between partners, or improve parents' relationships with their children and reduce the number of arguments. In a substance abuse program, the dependent variable or outcome might be the cessation of taking drugs or alcohol or for clients to stay sober and get off drugs for a period of at least 2 years. A short-term goal might be for consumers to be sober for a 2-month period. In a seniors program the program outcomes or goals could be to increase the overall quality of life of elderly people, increase their socialization and participation in social activities, improve consumers' feelings about themselves, decrease their social isolation, or obtain greater access to social services such as home care and case management services. In a sex education program a dependent variable could be imparting a better sense of what sex means in a person's life, increasing knowledge about HIV/AIDS or sexually transmitted diseases (STDs), increasing consumers' safer sex behaviors, or increasing their condom use.

What then are the independent variables? The program services, program inputs, or the intervention is one major class of independent variable. The program theory, program philosophy, practice methods, different types of services given, number of service contacts, overall intensity and duration of the service, outreach strategies and recruitment methods, and types of staff giving service and their skill or orientations are all independent variables. So, for example, in a program to treat substance abuse, one set of program inputs could be individual sessions with counselors, attendance at Alcoholics Anonymous, and support groups conducted by professionals to prevent relapse. In Chapter 8, research designs will be presented that can be used to contrast different forms of program inputs to determine which form of intervention or input is achieving the optimal result.

Another major type of independent variable is the type of consumers or clients given service. The demographics of the consumers being served, their types of problems, the severity of their problems (as assessed through diagnostic tools such as the *Diagnostic and Statistical Manual of Mental Disorders* [DSM] or the severity of addictions index), their strengths and what they have done well in life, their sense of power over their lives, and their family backgrounds are all independent variables. Since consumers come to the program and receive services, they are "put in" to the program and are classified as "program inputs" (Weiss, 1998, p. 134). At one time, Weiss called the consumers "thru-puts" as they advance through the program.

Program outcomes and program inputs and consumer–client variables can all be sketched out as a beginning plan for an outcome-oriented evaluation. So, for example, in an outreach program to increase the number of Latina women getting mammograms, follow-up care, and routine medical exams in a community, the independent variables are the program inputs. The program inputs are the outreach efforts such as newspaper and TV ads and articles, contacts with staff about the mammograms, and the mammograms, follow-up, and routine medical exams. The women themselves who initially contact the program and those who go for mammograms and medical care are also program inputs. The major goals, or *dependent variables*, are the earlier detection of breast cancer, better cancer treatment, increased longevity rate, and better health care in general.

Based on the above, the researcher could develop an evaluation model that would track the independent variables, or program inputs, and the dependent variables, or the major outcomes, goals, and objectives, of the program. A useful exercise is to write "dependent variables" at the top of a page and start making a list of program goals and keep refining the list. Then on the left side of the page write "independent variables" and make a list of program variables, service variables, and consumer variables.

3. Practice Goals

An excellent way to develop a comprehensive goal list is to consider the interventions or practices of professionals providing service in individual cases and examine and list the variety of practice goals they have for individual consumers. This process can be initiated by reviewing cases and talking to program staff and administrators about their work and what they are trying to achieve. Then the researcher can ask if this individual case goal applies widely to all the consumers in this program.

For example, in examining case goals of a marital counseling program, reducing the number of marital conflicts, increasing communication, and increasing socialization with other couples might be case goals. However, reducing marital conflict and increasing communication are more clearly program goals and can be evaluated as goals in all cases, while increasing social interaction with other couples might only be a goal in a number of cases and should be studied for those cases, but it may not be an overall program goal. When case goals fit those of most of the cases, they may be synonymous with program goals.

In evaluating the goals of a counseling program for adolescents, a review of some cases and talking to the counselors may indicate that some of the adolescents have issues with controlling anger, but not enough that it could be considered a major program goal. However, other case goals such as improving self-image, improving clients' functioning at school, reducing discipline problems at school, and better social adjustment could be thought of as program goals that affect all cases in the program and can be assessed for all cases in the program.

Case goals can also be studied in an evaluation; however, data must be collected on the number of cases that had this goal. If there are very few goals that apply to all cases, the researcher probably needs to use a Goal Attainment Scale (GAS) for evaluation (see Royse, Thyer, Padgett, & Logan, 2001, pp. 181–190). In this method, individual case goals are tracked and rated in terms of accomplishment. Then the goals are generalized under broad topic areas and each broad area is rated. The Goal Attainment Scale was developed by Kiresuk in the 1960s as a system of evaluation based on individual goals. Since then some enhancements have been made in the system (Kiresuk & Lund, 1994). On each goal, a case is rated from +2 for best-anticipated results with current treatment to −2 for most unfavorable results thought likely. Goals are then summated and scored through the scoring system. Goal attainment scaling is especially relevant in clinical evaluations where individualization of cases is especially valued. However, many critiques of this research strategy have been offered, not the least of which is that it is based on highly subjective ratings by therapists. One major critique of the GAS system is that in rating different individualized case goals and summating them, the researcher may be adding apples and oranges.

4. Program Goals and Program Objectives

All programs have purposes and these purposes are expressed in program goals. A program goal is an outcome toward which effort is directed, the ends or outcomes the program hopes to achieve. A program goal is a more specific statement of the program's mission and philosophy. Goals are usually more substantive, conceptual, longer term, and deeper than program objectives. Broader program goals can be usually be defined into more specific goals and program objectives.

Program objectives are more concrete and specific than goals. Objectives include the events and activities leading to the goals and are a useful way to track the program's direction and progress in meeting the goals. Objectives indicate the direction and progress made in achieving the goals. Objectives usually have a time frame and an end point when they will be achieved. Program objectives are more specific and measurable and they often suggest how the program goal can be achieved. Setting objectives is crucial in both program planning and evaluation. Developing objectives helps set program priorities and establish the focus of interventions and program activities.

One of the great values of logic models is that they use the concepts of specific objectives and short-term outcomes. So, for example, in a mental health program for HIV-positive men and women, Wheeler (Chapter 4) described specific objectives, such as increasing the number of mental health referrals to the program, increasing client engagement and therapeutic alliances, and increasing medication adherence and stability, and broader goals, such as increasing the overall number of clients who are employed, increasing clients' knowledge about mental health issues related to HIV, and increasing clients' coping skills.

Goals and objectives usually have action words, such as *increase* outreach to minority women needing health care, *reduce* the number of children in foster care, have clients *continue* in drug treatment, and *provide* 200 counseling sessions to people with chronic mental illness. As other examples of goals and objectives, the program goal of a public-health nursing program might to keep the children in a community healthy. The objectives might be to get children to doctor's appointments and see that they receive inoculations to prevent disease. In a program where the goal is to increase the socialization of the elderly, one objective under that goal might be to increase an elderly person's interaction with friends.

5. Process Objectives

Process objectives are objectives clearly related to the means of achieving the program goal. The means of achieving the goal is, of course, the intervention, the types of activities implemented by the program for consumers. Process objectives can be distinguished from outcome objectives that measure an amount of change in some behavior or attitude changed by the program (see the KBASS model later in this chapter). Process objectives help explain the rationale of how the program is to work. So in the program for IV drug users, process objectives included the distribution of 100 safe-sex kits at a community outreach event, distribution of clean needles and personal-care items to IV drug users in three SRO housing complexes, and to provide 2-hour HIV education and risk reduction groups to 100 people who had tested positive for HIV/AIDS. Program goals might be to see that consumers receive quality health care, increase their knowledge of the disease and their health-care options, prevent possible social isolation, and increase consumers' use of social services.

In a seniors program having the goal of increasing socialization of the elderly and improving the quality of their lives, a process objective might be to have the seniors increase their social interaction in a support group they are participating in or to increase involvement of the seniors in more activities at the senior center.

In a program designed to increase attendance of physically disabled students in mainstream classes, a process objective might be to discuss with teachers about the disabled child in order to ensure participation of the teachers in the program. In a program with the goal of reducing stress in parents of developmentally disabled children, a process objective might be to help the parent pay for a washing machine so that parents do not have the extra stress of going out of the house to a laundromat with their three children.

In the low-threshold harm reduction model for servicing IV drug users living in SRO hotels (described in Chapter 4), one process objective was to engage the consumers in the program and form trusting relationships by offering concrete services such as needle exchanges and personal-care items. Rather than focusing on the program goal of getting people off drugs and get them medical services, the process objective was to have consumers form a positive view of the agency and then to provide case management, counseling, mental health services, and transportation to the program.

An example of the difference between goals and objectives is described in an outreach and service program to IV drug users in New York City, VIP's Project STRIVE. The first goal of the program was to reach out to African-American and Latino substance abusers who had been incarcerated on drug-related charges and enroll them in HIV pretreatment support services and in long-term care programs. Under the goal of achieving program outreach, the first objective, a *process objective*, was to conduct outreach and contact 500 substance abusers recently released from prison in New York City and to enroll at least 100 or 20% of 500 in the VIP STRIVES project. These process objectives pointed the way toward people's involvement in the program.

The second set of program goals was for clients who were enrolled in the program, to reduce their risk of HIV transmission and infection and improve the quality of their lives. One process objective under the goal of reducing risk of transmission is that clients attend groups teaching the reduction of risk behaviors. Monitoring of attendance of the program groups, and examining substantive program outcomes such as the use of safe sex practices could be measured. Reduced risk of HIV transmission includes the behavioral goals of consistent condom use, reduced number of sexual partners, reduced drug use, and increased use of clean needles and syringes. Likewise, the program goal of improved quality of life includes the objectives of clients obtaining stable housing, maintaining low-risk behavior, enrolling in GED classes, obtaining a GED degree, keeping parole officer appointments, and reuniting with family members.

Goals and Objectives From the VIP STRIVES Project
DANIELLE STRAUSS, M.P.H., DOCTORAL CANDIDATE
PH.D. PROGRAM IN SOCIAL WELFARE, GRADUATE CENTER
OF THE CITY UNIVERSITY OF NEW YORK

In response to the disproportionate impact of HIV on African-American, Latino, and other racial and ethnic minority IV drug users, many of whom have histories of incarceration, the Substance Abuse and Mental Health Services Administration (SAMHSA) started the HIV outreach grants initiative in 1999, with funding from the Minority AIDS Task Force (formally known as the Congressional Black Caucus) (SAMHSA, 2002). The purpose of this funding was to reduce drug-using behavior and encourage treatment by successfully employing outreach techniques to reach these high-risk populations (SAMHSA, 2004). VIP Community Services (VIP), a multi-service community-based organization (CBO) located in the Bronx, New York, was among the first group of CBOs to receive this funding, which lasted through September 2002. In the fall of 2003, VIP was awarded a second HIV outreach grant from SAMHSA, which funded the VIP STRIVES (Substance abuse Treatment Referral through InnoVative Education and Support) Project for 5 years.

The VIP STRIVES Project is based on the program theory that low-threshold, harm reduction services that focus on HIV prevention act as entry points for substance users into treatment for substance abuse, mental health issues, and/or HIV. Entry into such treatment helps substance users reduce their vulnerability and strengthen their ability to make sustained life changes. Thus, the project engages substance users in a continuum of low- to medium-threshold services prior to entering higher-threshold services such as substance abuse treatment, in order to assist them in developing a readiness for treatment prior to being referred. The premise behind this theory is based on Prochaska and DiClimente's (2005) transtheoretical model of behavior change (more commonly known as the stages of change). The transtheoretical model of behavior change suggests that people move through a series of stages (precontemplation, contemplation, ready for action, action, and maintenance) in the process of changing their behavior. In the setting of the VIP STRIVES Project, those who are ready for treatment have a greater likelihood of succeeding in treatment, as compared to those who enter treatment before they are ready.

The program consists of three major intervention types (services): outreach, individualized and client-centered counseling, and education and supportive counseling administered in a group setting. The overall goal of the project was to provide outreach to these high-risk substance users, including ex-offenders (individuals recently released from prison or jail) and engage them in these medium-threshold services (individualized and group counseling and support) in order to prepare them for and refer them to the higher-threshold services (substance abuse treatment, mental health treatment, and/or HIV medical treatment) when they were deemed ready.

The following details the specific goals and objectives for each component of this program. The goals and objectives (short-term, realistic and attainable targets) were developed on the basis of literature and past experience working with this target population.

Goals and Objectives From the VIP STRIVES Project (Continued)

GOALS AND OBJECTIVES FOR OUTREACH TO RECENTLY
RELEASED PRISON POPULATIONS

Program Goal 1: To provide outreach and enroll African-American and
Latino substance abusers who were incarcerated on drug-related charges
in HIV pretreatment support services and referrals into long-term care
programs.

Objective 1: To outreach and contact 500 substance abusers recently released
from prison or jail in New York City per year and inform them about the
services available through the VIP STRIVES Project.

Objective 2: To enroll at least 100 or 20% of these 500 substance abusers with
histories of incarceration in the VIP STRIVES project per year.

GOALS AND OBJECTIVES FOR OUTREACH TO COMMUNITY
POPULATIONS IN THE BRONX, NY

Program Goal 2: To provide outreach and enroll high-risk African-American and
Latino substance abusers from the Bronx, NY in HIV pretreatment support
services and referrals into long-term care programs.

Objective 1: Of the 2000 African-American and Latino substance abusers from
the Bronx who were reached by VIP's Outreach Team, to enroll 150 of them in
the VIP STRIVES Project per year.

GOALS AND OBJECTIVES FOR PROGRAM SERVICES

Program Goal 1: To reduce the risk of HIV transmission or acquisition to clients
enrolled in the VIP STRIVES Project.

Objective 1: To have 60% or 150 of the 250 clients enrolled in the program
successfully complete the program by attending at least 80% of the assigned
groups.

Objective 2: To have 60% or 150 of the 250 clients enrolled in the program
self-report reduced risk of HIV transmission 180 days after enrollment in
the program. Clients of the program will demonstrate at least one of the
following:

1. Consistent condom use
2. Reduced number of sexual partners
3. Reduced drug use
4. Increased use of clean needles and syringes

Program Goal 2: To improve the quality of life of the 150 clients who successfully complete the program. Clients of the program will achieve at least one of the following:

1. Obtain stable housing
2. Maintain low-risk behavior related to HIV transmission
3. Enroll in GED classes
4. Complete a GED degree
5. Keep consistent appointments with parole officers
6. Reunite with their family members

Program Goal 3: To prepare the 150 clients who successfully complete the program for long-term treatment and refer them into such treatment when they are ready. Clients of the program will enroll in at least one of the following long-term treatment programs upon completion of the program:

1. Substance abuse treatment
2. Mental health treatment
3. HIV primary care (if HIV positive)

REFERENCES

Prochaska, J.O. & DiClemente, C.C. (2005). The Transtheoretical Approach. In: Norcross, J.C., Goldfried M.R., (eds.) *Handbook of Psychotherapy Integration.* @nd Ed. New York University Press, p. 147-171.

SAMHSA. (2002, April 19). Substance Abuse and Mental Health Services Administration, HIV/AIDS: Overview. Retrieved April 20, 2004, from: http://search.samhsa.gov/...query=HIV+AIDS.

SAMHSA. (2004). SAMHSA FY 2004 budget: Government Performance Results Act Plan and Report (GPRA), 2.29 TCE: Community-based substance abuse treatment and HIV/AIDS outreach program. Retrieved May 2, 2004, from: http://www.samhsa.gov/budget/content/2004/gpra/gpra2004-33.htm.

6. Short- and Long-Term Goals and Objectives

Rossi, Lipsey, and Freeman (2004, p. 209) discuss *proximal effects* on program participants, which are immediate, short-term goals for change, such as in psychological attitudes, knowledge, awareness, skills, and behaviors, which have hopefully been changed by program activities. Short-term, proximate goals can be linked more easily to specific program activities to achieve them as they are similar to process objectives; however, they do not necessarily have program activities included in the statement. The phrase "to develop groups to increase clients' socialization" is a process objective. "To increase socialization" is a short-term goal, as there in no mention of the process to achieve this goal.

Long-term effects are referred to as *distal effects*, which are broader and more policy-oriented goals, such as increasing the quality of life of seniors, increasing their social integration in many areas of life, or avoiding nursing home placement (Rossi et al., 2004, p. 209). Distal effects in programs can include goals such as reducing delinquency, reducing substance abuse, reducing family violence, and increasing IQ scores.

Proximate and ultimate outcomes are similar to short-term and long-term goals. So there can be proximal, proximate, immediate, short-range, formative goals and more ultimate, distal, long-range, substantive, summative goals Proximate–ultimate goals can be thought to be on a continuum. It is often helpful to write out and develop goals on this continuum from proximate goals to ultimate goals.

For example, in a day treatment program for persons with chronic mental illness such as schizophrenia, the more ultimate, long-range goals might be to prevent hospitalization in a group of patients, decrease psychological symptoms, promote occupational and vocational functioning, improve quality of life and personal adjustment, improve social functioning, reduce social isolation, gain and continue employment, obtain long-term and quality housing, and increase independent living. Intermediate goals might be to increase compliance with medication, increase the social supports available to the person, attain more satisfaction with treatment, improve the self-image of those with serious mental illness, improve physical appearance and relationships with people, increase the amount of time spent in the community, and reduce any fears associated with using public transportation. Short-range proximate goals could be to provide a supportive atmosphere to consumers, maintain attendance at the day treatment program, make a therapeutic connection to clients (a process objective), or ensure that consumers have a positive attitude toward the program.

Proximate goals are not inconsequential. For example, proximate goals such as connecting with consumers and providing a supportive atmosphere are important. If consumers are initially turned off by the program and how it is offered, very few may attend and no ultimate goals will be achieved. Only in connecting and coming to the program will it be possible for consumers to maintain better health, improve their quality of life, or obtain better employment.

Rossi, Lipsey, and Freeman (2004, p. 205) feel that there should be a clear distinction between program effects or goals and program services. So for them providing meals to 100 homebound seniors is not an outcome, but an aspect of service delivery. However, providing meals to 100 homebound seniors can be an important short-term goal. Factors such as whether they attended the program, whether they found it useful, and whether they felt it was a positive atmosphere are all important proximate goals and are especially important in doing monitoring and process evaluations, as these more formative approaches improve the overall quality of the program. So, although providing five inter-ventive contacts or creating a therapeutic community is not a goal, it can be a short-term process objective leading eventually to successful program outcomes.

An old joke among evaluation researchers is ask the staff what the goal of the program is, and they will say the goal is to provide service, while technically that is not a goal at all. However, providing service to 50 consumers can be an important short-term goal or process objective. Considering all the programs that do not become operational and provide no service, and, of course, never achieved the program's other short-term and long-term goals, these short-term goals and process objectives are important as early indicators on the health of the program.

The Centers for Disease Control and Prevention (Evaluation Guide, 2009) has developed a model of SMART objectives. In developing program objectives, they advise that objectives should always have the following characteristics:

Specific—objectives need to be clear and well defined in terms of what the program will achieve. When objectives are specific, both practitioners and administrators will know the expectations of the program in terms of the target population, the interventions, and the objectives of those interventions.

Measurable—the objectives should be specific to the point where they can be measured in some way. Measuring objectives means having a set of methodological procedures and quantitative and/or qualitative procedures, and deciding on a set of questions you will ask or how you will observe whether or not the program is achieving its objectives. Measurement also means applying principles or procedures that conform to the standards of reliability and validity.

Appropriate—the objective needs to fit the purpose of the program, the larger program goals, and the purposes of the interventions. As discussed in program description in Chapter 4, there should be a logical connection and a logic between what is delivered and what the program hopes to achieve. Achievability implies consideration of implementation of the intervention. Are appropriate professionals delivering the program? Are they operating at a certain level of skill? Is there access to services for the target population?

Realistic—the amount of change sought is logical given the *dosage* of the level and type of intervention. Are enough resources committed to the program? Are there enough service contacts to realistically consider the possibility of change?

Time-based or Time-phased—there is a concrete time frame within which the program objectives can be achieved. The time limits for achieving objectives cannot be open-ended. Also, some objectives need to be achieved before other objectives and program goals are achieved. For example, seniors must attend socialization groups at the senior center, where they will be taught and advised about the importance of increasing their social contacts, before the objectives of increasing their socialization outside the home is achieved.

Although there is overlap between the above SMART characteristics, all programs need specific objectives that are Specific, Measurable, Achievable, Realistic, and Time-based. SMART objectives tend to be very quantitatively focused statements, such as the following: There will be a 25% increase in the social interaction of the elderly over the first 6 months of the program. There will be a 35% increase in the use of social programs by elderly clients over the first 8 months of the program. There will be a 30% increase in the number of elderly attending the low-impact exercise group over the next 3 months. The only downside to SMART objectives is if qualitative measures of goal achievement, such as the consumers' feelings about the program and their statements on how the program was helpful and not helpful, are left out of the evaluation so that only quantitative goals are studied.

7. Tender-Hearted and Tough-Minded Goals

Many years ago, Kogan and Shyne (1966) used the terms "tender-hearted" and "tough-minded" to refer to approaches to evaluation. This typology might be applied to the development of program goals. Tender-hearted goals can be more formative goals and service objectives, while tough-minded refers to the achievement of ultimate, substantive goals that program funders find more acceptable. So, for example, in a Head Start program a tough-minded goal would be an increase in children's IQ scores or other standardized scores on cognitive functioning. A more tender-hearted goal would be parents' satisfaction with the particular Head Start Program that their child attended or the child's connection to his or her teacher.

The general idea here is to not have all tender-hearted goals or all tough-minded goals. Some balance should be achieved between formative, tender-hearted goals, such as a consumer's connectedness and loyalty to a program, and tough-minded goals, such as gaining housing, being employed, preventing hospitalization, and avoiding family dissolution.

A good example of contrasting a tender-hearted with a tough-minded approach to assessing goals is an evaluation of a university-based employee assistance program that helps employees with their personal, interpersonal, marital, and family problems. A tender-hearted approach to evaluation would be to have 100 employees who use the program be satisfied with program services. A tough-minded approach would be to measure the employees' success in their personal and professional lives to see if their personal and family situations had improved, if the quality of their work had improved, or if work attendance had improved as a result of these personal services. Or their quality of life could be measured through reliable and valid research instruments to determine quantitatively if their quality of life had improved as a result of the employee assistance service.

Tender-hearted versus tough-minded evaluations follow the formative versus summative orientations to evaluation discussed in Chapter 2. Tender-hearted goals are more likely to appear in formative evaluations, and tough-minded goals are more related to summative evaluations.

The following statements might be personal and contextual views of researchers, staff, and organizations that are more likely to study tender-hearted goals:

1. It is difficult to connect with patients or clients and then hope that they enroll in a program.
2. Health and human service practitioners have a difficult job implementing programs.
3. Offering help to someone is often a complex endeavor.
4. If patients or clients feel connected to a program, the program is on its way toward achieving the program goals.

The following statements might be the personal views of researchers who are more likely to study tough-minded goals:

1. Programs funded through either private or public funds need to justify funding by showing outcomes that are achieved.
2. Evaluators need to take a hard look at programs.
3. Programs that do not show substantial achievements should not be funded.
4. The only true model of a program evaluation is the experimental model that assesses different forms of the program against substantive goals.

8. Unanticipated Consequences

Unanticipated consequences are outcomes that were not considered or not thought of as goals during the program planning and implementation stages of a program. They may also have been overlooked when the evaluator was planning to evaluate the program. In planning an evaluation, the research and the major stakeholders try to develop, expand, determine and brainstorm all the possible program goals. The better the process is, the more the evaluation is thoroughly planned and organized, and the fewer the number of unanticipated consequences which will be found during the evaluation. However, all goals cannot be anticipated and studied, so strategies are needed for finding unanticipated consequences of a program.

One way to look for unanticipated consequences is to employ qualitative research methods. For example, in collecting data from consumers, a series of open-ended questions can reveal unanticipated goals. Examples of such questions are the following: What did you find helpful in the program? What did you get out of the program? What else did you find useful about the program? The researcher could have consumers and staff interviewed about what they think is being achieved by the program. Direct observation of the program would also uncover consequences that neither consumers nor staff thought to be goals of the program. Unanticipated consequences can be made into goals can be studied if researchers and stakeholders have an inquiring mind and attitude and are not "locked in" to only the formal goals of the program. While structured or quantitative data on unanticipated consequences will not be available in the first round of evaluation, these goals, which were unanticipated consequences in the first evaluation, can be formalized and studied more comprehensibly in subsequent evaluations as program goals and outcomes.

An example of unanticipated goals can be found in the development of a single-parent family program in New York City. The purpose of this single-parent family program was to provide technical assistance and help develop a local group of single parents through support groups in which they could discuss their status as single parents and how to raise their children on minimal resources or advocate for themselves in family court in securing child support payments. The groups were designed to resolve issues of child care and child support payments and provide employment and career guidance. In addition, however, the program developed good contacts with the media, which meant that the program tried to improve the image of single parents by providing many newspaper articles and TV programs that projected a positive image about the single-parent family and lifestyle. The program had articles on single-parent issues published in all the major newspapers. Creating a positive image for single parents in the community was not an initial goal of this program in its first year of operation.

Programs can also experience unanticipated consequences that are negative. For example, in a psychoeducation group for relatives of persons with chronic mental illness, increasing relatives' knowledge about mental illness may make them more frightened or at least less optimistic about their ability to help the person with mental illness.

Weiss (1998, p. 51) notes that all program evaluations start with the *official goals* of the program, however, as the evaluation is planned and more goals are uncovered, an exciting development in program planning occurs: translating unanticipated consequences into anticipated goals of the program. If all possible goals and outcomes are sketched out and developed in a planning process involving all the stakeholders, there is less of a possibility that unanticipated consequences will be found once the evaluation is conducted.

9. Changes in Knowledge, Behavior, Attitudes, Skills, and Status (KBASS Model)

The KBASS model can assist in the development and measurement of a whole series of program goals and objectives. The KBASS model is on the ultimate side of the proximate–ultimate goal typology. Programs need to make substantive changes, not merely achieve proximate goals or process objectives. At some point in their development, programs need to make major positive changes in a person's life. Changes in knowledge, behavior, attitude, skill, and status are more clearly program outcomes and goals rather than process objectives. These program outcomes and goals specify a change—in **K**nowledge, **A**ttitudes, **B**ehavior, **S**kill or **S**tatus (KBASS). Formative evaluation would be more in the genre of saying that the program is "moving in the direction" toward making these changes. Impact assessments and pre–post studies that measure change and seek to make causal connects between the program and major changes are more often within the KBASS model as changes in knowledge, attitudes, behavior, skill, or functional status are measured.

Changes in knowledge are especially important in educational programs, training programs, support groups, psychoeducational groups, and other group work programs in which the group needs to learn specific areas of knowledge. Evaluations of many of these programs have some elements of knowledge gain as goals of the program. For example, in a group for caregivers of people with Alzheimer's disease, one of the program goals is to increase caregivers' knowledge about community resources so that they can use more community services, such as day treatment facilities for the relative with

Alzheimer's disease. Caregivers could also benefit from increased knowledge about Medicare issues, access to transportation, and other services. Another knowledge-related goal would be to increase caregiver knowledge about the disease of Alzheimer's and its progression.

In many programs an increase in knowledge is a major program outcome. For example:

- An increase in knowledge could be a major goal for a senior citizens' group at a local senior center if the program is designed to increase knowledge of entitlements, such as eligibility issues and where to apply for home care, Medicaid, Medicare, transportation, and other health and social services.
- In-service training programs for new social workers or other types of professionals frequently target increased knowledge about the job and the procedures used on that job as goals. In-service training for social workers might be focused on increasing knowledge about professional concepts such as different psychopathologies and defense mechanisms, or increasing knowledge about theories of child development, family theory, and individual and family counseling theories and perspectives.
- In-service training for hospital staff in how to present issues of advance directives might be conducted to make sure that patients learn the issues related to heath-care proxies and the importance of choosing whether or not extraordinary measures should be taken when serious health-care decisions are being made.
- In an adolescent after-school program in which teenagers are being taught about sexually transmitted diseases, increased knowledge of these diseases could clearly be measured, and a pre–post study could document whether or not such knowledge was increased.
- In a group program for recovering alcoholics, increased knowledge about the effects of drugs and alcohol could be a program goal that can be documented.
- In a community mental health setting, psychoeducational groups could be conducted for relatives of persons with mental illness. One program goal could be to increase a family's knowledge about mental illness.
- In a support group of cancer patients a program goal could be to increase a person's or family's knowledge of the disease and what they should do behaviorally to help treat symptoms. An increase in knowledge about cancer-care resources and the various treatments available for their disease could also be a major program goal.

- Psychoeducational groups on HIV/AIDS for IV drug users could increase knowledge about the disease and how it is transmitted.
- In substance abuse programs increased knowledge about the effects of drugs and alcohol would be important goals.
- In a program designed to provide outreach to medically underinsured populations of people the program goal would be to increase knowledge of the child health plus or family health plus programs for low-income people without medical insurance.

Behavioral changes may be the most concrete goals to measure but the hardest goals and objectives to achieve. Programs for clients may impart knowledge about the community resources that exist, but getting people to actually obtain more services and *use* community resources may be more difficult to achieve. For example:

- Some programs for the elderly might try to decrease social isolation and increase the social interaction of seniors. Movement toward this goal might begin with more participation in program activities and extend to more community involvement, which reduces social isolation.
- Abstaining from the use of drugs and alcohol is the ultimate goal of drug abuse and alcohol treatment programs and may be the hardest program goal to achieve.
- The increased use of condoms and reduction of risky sexual behaviors can be major goals in safe sex programs for populations that are at risk for HIV/AIDS.
- In a senior housing program, a decrease in hoarding behavior and increased cleanliness of the apartment may be behavior changes for seniors who exhibit such behavior and have cluttered apartments. These behaviors endanger their personal safety and make them at risk of losing their apartments because of the lack of cleanliness and the possibility of fire.

Changing the attitudes of people is a major, substantive goal in many programs. Attitudes encompass deep values and beliefs, or how a person feels about particular issues. Sometimes attitudes can be of a very personal nature, such as feelings of self-esteem or self-worth. Personal efficacy or belief in one's own power within a system such as the health-care system has been a current research interest in attitudes that might move a person to act or to change their behavior.

As an example, in measuring attitudes about health care, the multidimensional health locus of control scales (MHLC) measure how much a person feels in control of their health (efficacy) compared to what health professionals do for the person (powerful others), and what factors are outside one's control (chance) (Fischer and Corcoran, 2007, p. 498). The internality of health locus of control score is a subset of the scale and measures the degree to which a person's health is determined by their own behavior. A person's personal health-efficacy score would be calculated by adding together a person's scores on their level of agreement and disagreement with items such as the following:

1. If I become sick, I have the power to make myself well again.
2. I am directly responsible for my health.
3. Whatever goes wrong with my health is my own fault.
4. My physical well-being depends on how well I take care of myself.
5. When I feel ill, I know it is because I have not been taking care of myself properly.
6. I can pretty much stay healthy by taking good care of myself.

The idea is to assess a person's efficacy with how much they think what they do matters in relation to health care professionals in the system or is due to the power of luck or chance in relation to health. Attitudes scales such as these especially lend themselves to the measurement of pre–post changes. For example, a health-care program might want to see whether or not people's efficacy or power over their health care changed because of the program.

Attitudes encompass a wide domain. For example:

- In a mediation and conflict resolution program for students in a high school, how does the overall program change the students' attitudes toward peers and authority figures in the school system?
- A community campaign to improve community attitudes toward developmentally disabled children could study changes in community attitudes as the program is implemented.
- A hospice program could study the change in people's attitudes toward end-of-life issues and death.
- A foster care program could study social worker and foster parent attitudes toward biological parents of children in foster care.

Many, many programs seek to teach and *improve the skills* of those who attend. A concrete example is a vocational and job-training program in which participants are taught specific skills and learn new job tasks. Changes in job skills following from increased knowledge about job tasks are integral to these programs. Employment programs usually also teach job-search skills, such as how to prepare a resume, how to conduct a job search, and how to perform at a job interview.

Professional skills are developed in many educational programs, and through in-service programs staff are often trained in new techniques and skills. Group and individual counseling skills, skill in family interaction techniques, skills in psychosocial social work, among others, may be important. Skills in advocacy on behalf of clients or patients, skills in referring clients or patients for services, skills in outreach to certain populations of clients, skill in leading case conferences, and increased skills in family treatment are all possible improvements in skills in professional development programs.

Skills are often complex and are based on professional knowledge, attitudes, and the values of a profession. For example:

- In a new medical school program, medical students were taught improved skills in relating to the patients and the patients' families.
- Training of home care workers and home health care workers would help them be skilled in the tasks they need to accomplish for families or clients, such as monitoring the taking of medications, and performance of personal-care tasks such as bathing and grooming.

Status changes are perhaps the most substantive, long-range goals to be achieved. Status changes fit the goals of a wide variety of programs. For example, in an employment program a change in status would be going from being unemployed to employed, a critical status change. Or it could mean going from part-time to full-time employment. An increase in income would also be a status change in employment programs, as would graduation from a high school equivalency program.

In a weight-loss program a status change would be a decrease in weight, from being overweight to being at the proper weight. In a program for the homeless, going from being homeless to being housed would be an important change in status. In child welfare programs, foster children can have a status change from living in foster care to returning to live with their biological parents, or from living in foster care to being adopted.

In a Head Start program a change in status could be an increase in IQ score or a change from a below-average IQ score to an above-average score. In many programs, improvements in the quality of life would be an important substantive status change. In health programs, a status change could be an improvement in health or going from being unhealthy to healthy. In juvenile delinquency programs a reduction in the number of arrests would be a status change.

In the field of mental health programs, a reduced number of psychiatric hospitalizations would be a major program goal reflecting a change in status. Also, if the goal of a mental health program is to reduce symptoms in persons with serious illness, this would be a status change. If the goal is to provide treatment so that people can move from being depressed to not being depressed, depression scales can be used to see if the program met that goal, by measuring features before and after treatment to see if depression was reduced.

Many comprehensive goals are studied once the program goals and objectives that include areas of knowledge, behavior, attitudes, skills, and status are defined. Usually the results of program evaluation are that some goals are achieved and others are not. For example, in Strauss' example of goals in the VIP STRIVE HIV program presented earlier in this chapter, attitudes were examined as well as behavior. One goal was to increase clients' awareness of the importance of disclosure of HIV status to sexual partners, an attitude. Behavioral goals included clients actually disclosing their HIV status to sexual partners, or increasing condom use to prevent the spread of AIDS and STDs. Program evaluation helps all the stakeholders to define the goals and determine which goals are being achieved and which are not being achieved.

Likewise, in a program on adolescent sexual behavior for female adolescents in a local community center, a number of goals were developed. Attitude changes included fostering comfort with, respect for, and appreciation of human sexuality. Knowledge changes included enhancing knowledge about puberty and reproduction as well as HIV and STDs. Skills included developing decision-making and conflict management skills in relation to sexual behaviors. It is also possible to study the program process of achieving goals. For example, initially knowledge about puberty and reproduction may be increased, which could then influence more positive attitudes about human sexuality. Such attitudes could in turn ultimately result in improved decision-making skills in relation to sexual behaviors. So, in addition to looking at differential goal achievement, one could also examine the causal connections between different types of goals.

In addition to examining which goals were achieved and the possible sequencing of goal achievement, there are questions of *how much* change has been achieved, *how long* it may take for certain goals to be achieved, and how long the goals will be *maintained* after the program is completed. Usually goals are achieved closer to the delivery of the program intervention, although Weiss (1998, p. 124) has noted the possibility of "sleeper effects" in which changes are not seen initially but are seen months after the program.

On the basis of previous programs and the literature of program evaluation in certain fields, there may be norms of how much change is expected given the dosage or level of intervention in the program. For example, substance abuse programs that use a certain type of intervention will have recovery rates associated with them in the literature.

Initially, beginning evaluations can have ratings to determine if consumers think that changes have occurred. Later evaluations can have pre- and post-tests to study real changes in knowledge, behaviors, attitudes, skills, and status.

In implementing an advocacy model for health and human services professionals, the KBASS model could be an appropriate example of the intensive program needed for professionals to pursue advocacy roles. Professionals may need knowledge about the field of advocacy, what it is, and how to be an advocate. In terms of behavior, they need to practice advocacy in their work with consumers. Attitudes can make a big difference in practicing advocacy to ensure that consumers get needed health and social service benefits. Skills in advocacy need to be learned and refined. And, ultimately, the advocacy work should make a difference in status changes for consumers, based on the worker's knowledge, behavior, attitudes, and skill. Status changes can be from no service to getting service, no day care to having day care, no home care to getting home care, from no health care to having health care, from no advance directive to having an advance directive, from no mammogram to getting a mammogram.

In the two case studies that follow, the KBASS model was used. In the first example the KBASS model was used to present a comprehensive model for program goals and objectives in the field of mental health. The second case study describes changes that seemed to occur in a qualitative pilot evaluation study in a master's program in social work in health and aging.

Development of a KBASS Comprehensive Model for Program Goals and Objectives in Mental Health Programs
MICHAEL J. SMITH, D.S.W., PROFESSOR
HUNTER COLLEGE SCHOOL OF SOCIAL WORK

In any program area, program goals can be conceptualized into the five themes in the KBASS model. The following is an outline of goals for programs operating in the field of mental health. Under each of the five themes of knowledge, behavior, attitudes, skills, and status, program goals will be identified. To evaluate mental health programs the selected program goals would then need to be operationalized and measured in the program evaluation design.

*Development of a KBASS Comprehensive Model for Program
Goals and Objectives in Mental Health Programs (Continued)*

KNOWLEDGE

Increase in knowledge about mental illness and symptoms

Increase in knowledge about diagnoses, such as paranoia, schizophrenia, etc.

Increase in knowledge about the symptoms of various diagnoses

Increase in knowledge about drug therapies used in mental health field

Increase in knowledge about community resources

Increase in knowledge about employment or job tasks

Increase in knowledge about how to find a job, create a resume, interview for jobs, etc.

BEHAVIOR

Increase in social functioning

Increase in interaction with family and friends

Increase in leisure-time activities

Increase in program participation

Increase in trips to local stores, etc.

Reduction in symptoms

Reduced delusional symptoms

Reduced depression

Reduced number of suicidal attempts

Increase in medication compliance

Reduction in use of alcohol and/or drugs

Reduced drug or alcohol use in a 3-month period of time

Increased attendance at day treatment program

Increase in use of personal counseling

ATTITUDE

Attitudes about mental illness

Attitudes toward professionals and staff

Satisfaction with mental health programs

Satisfaction with treatment services

Satisfaction with mental health housing

Satisfaction with employment services

Satisfaction with case management services

Satisfaction with long-term housing placement services

Attitudes toward medication and medication compliance

SKILLS

Increase in vocational and occupational functioning and skills

Increased skill in employment interviews

Increased skill in housekeeping and personal-care tasks

STATUS

Reduced number of hospitalizations

Reduced number of emergency room visits

Reduced number of arrests

Reduced homelessness, more time housed

Increase in amount of earned income, steady income

Increased quality of life

Constructing a comprehensive list of program goals and objectives can be a great method for considering the larger program context of goals in a program field. Then the comprehensive list of program goals can be examined in relation to the goals in the particular program being evaluated. In this instance, in the field of mental health, consideration of all the possible program goals in mental health can provide a good context for program goals in one particular program. Having a comprehensive KBASS context of program goals is another method for the development of more substantial goals to be studied in the evaluation.

Example of Use of the KBASS Model: Changes in Knowledge, Behavior, Attitudes, Skills, and Status in a Master's in Social Work (MSW) Program in Health and Aging

ROBERTA GRAZIANO, D.S.W., PROFESSOR, AND BARBARA RINEHART, PH.D.

HUNTER COLLEGE SCHOOL OF SOCIAL WORK

The Aging and Health Work-Study Master's in Social Work Program at the Hunter College School of Social Work was a grant-funded pilot project designed to address the shortage of MSW social workers who have expertise in meeting the social and health needs of older adults. The students recruited for this program were full-time employees of agencies serving older adults in New York City who would be educated as professional social workers.

An initial, formative qualitative assessment of the program was conducted to examine the initial goals of the program and possible program objectives. Follow-up telephone interviews with graduates of the program asked both open-ended and close-ended questions so that both qualitative and quantitative data could be collected. Examination and analysis of the initial trends indicated that

Example of Use of the KBASS Model (Continued)

the formative changes clearly followed the KBASS model. The most substantive and concrete changes found were changes in job status.

CHANGES IN STATUS

Of course, the status change of graduating from the program with a master's degree in social work was a major part of the program goals. These students had worked in gerontological settings before and while they were in the MSW program. After graduation, they were asked if they had changes in status, job status, job title, or job responsibilities. In all, 65% experienced a change in job status or a significant increase in job responsibilities. Thirty percent got promoted to new positions in their agencies or found new positions at a higher level in other gerontological programs. The average salary increase for the cohort was $12,155 a year. The most common pattern was graduates with case management or case aide positions being promoted to professional social work positions. A second pattern was the promotion from assistant program director to program director.

Sixty-five percent of the graduates had increasing job responsibilities. They usually had increases in administrative and managerial, or supervisory functions. There were also increases in professional social work functions such as conducting biopsychosocial assessments, professional counseling, or clinical supervision of other social workers. Ninety percent of the graduates thought their training resulted in better services to clients, friends, and caregivers.

CHANGES IN KNOWLEDGE

The qualitative data pointed to a number of areas where the graduates gained professional knowledge. Graduates of the program thought they increased their knowledge about aging and the psychosocial needs of the aged, medical issues of the aged, and issues for caregivers of the elderly. In an answer to an open-ended question about the value of the program, 66% cited knowledge of the special content in aging and health and 41% reported on the support and guidance they received from the program as key program benefits. Within the context of an MSW program, they also mentioned more general professional knowledge such as cultural diversity, human behavior, and knowledge of group work. The areas of knowledge gain were represented by a few selected direct quotes from the graduates:

> I now view the aging process as a normal process rather than accepting the myths of aging.
>
> I am much more knowledgeable about the needs of the elderly and that they are not a homogeneous group.

Much more knowledgeable about the medical issues in aged populations

I now keep caregiver issues in mind in direct client work and in supervising workers.

Learned the importance of cultural diversity.

Better understanding of cultural diversity.

Better understanding of client behavior.

Increased knowledge of groups and group behavior.

CHANGE IN ATTITUDES

The graduates also talked about having a "different" attitude, a more professional attitude about their work. Previously, they may have personalized practice issues. They now had a greater awareness of the elderly and how to advocate for clients and empower the elderly and their families. Professional attitudes were intertwined with professional behavior and skills as corroborated by the following selected quotes:

My attitude has changed, more positive, more self-aware. No longer focused on "doing for" my clients. I pick up more now on details in assessments with clients. Now I empower them to do.

I see my clients differently. I do more to go out of my way to help clients. I do differential assessments, intervene with the clients and their family. I take more initiative using Adult Protective Services and get families more involved now.

I now see things in a much broader gerontological perspective and I don't personalize issues.

I have new perspectives on clients and their issues. I don't personalize.

I am more attuned to the physical problems of the aged and their medications.

More aware of health care needs and issues.

CHANGES IN BEHAVIOR

In addition to attitudes, graduates reported changes in professional behavior and skills. This included more advocacy and outreach with clients, caregivers, and their families, and more involvement with health issues. There was also a switch from solely case management tasks such as referrals to professional counseling of the elderly and their families, as illustrated by the following selected quotes:

Example of Use of the KBASS Model (Continued)

> More involved with psychosocial care with MDs and psychiatrists. More involved in the medical needs of my clients and linkages with doctors. I now do more formal, structured one-on-one work with clients.
>
> More contact with families and more outreach.
>
> More comfort doing counseling, not just concrete services.
>
> Improved ability to provide more resources to caregivers. More family-oriented work.

The graduates also were doing more professional tasks such as making professional presentations, and had more involvement with group work, supervision, and program planning and development. The increase in professional job tasks was evidenced in the following selected quotes:

> I make presentations on living wills, health care proxies, credit card problems of the elderly, etc.
>
> I run workshops, do groups, do outreach to clients.
>
> I now run support groups.
>
> New approaches to supervision. Now I have a commitment to workers and stress the need for teamwork and getting the workers involved. I pick up on things quicker in supervision. I am more fully aware of family dynamics and client support systems.
>
> I am providing more training for staff and have enhanced awareness of client needs.
>
> I realized that family support for elders can be very important. I developed a family project for elderly substance abusers and their families with groups and family therapy.
>
> I developed a caregiver support group for Alzheimer's patients.

CHANGES IN PROFESSIONAL SKILLS

In the area of professional skills, the graduates talked about increases in clinical skills in interviewing and assessment, more empathy toward clients, better skills in advocacy and referral for community services, and skill in working as a member of a professional team. Increase in skill was noted in the following selected quotes:

> Better assessment and clinical skills.
>
> Can partialize and do better assessments.

> Listen more to clients, empathize, and [have] a better understanding of my clients. Improved listening skills, which enable me to know more when to refer for specific health-related services/programs and where to send people.
>
> Working creatively with the community and learning to use other types of community resources.
>
> I do more client advocacy, how to cut through red tape.
>
> My advocacy skills have improved.
>
> I learned empowerment skills and information and referral skills.
>
> Can work collaboratively with health professionals on a team to promote continuity of care.
>
> I am better, more comfortable collaborating with doctors and other health-care professionals.
>
> Can work with families now more comfortably then before. Before this I was referring cases to other workers.

In addition to direct practice skills, the graduates mentioned better skill in administration, management skills, and grant-writing skills:

> Administrative skills such as the ability to take on more responsibility, how to prioritize, and time management.
>
> I do everything differently now. I manage staff more efficiently and effectively. I also manage clients more effectively and can meet their needs.
>
> I now have grant-writing skills.

SUMMARY

This formative evaluation helped conceptualize goals and objectives in terms of changes in knowledge, behavior, attitudes, skills, and status—the KBASS model. Sixty-five percent of the graduates had changes in job status and moved to more responsible positions after they graduated from the program. The initial qualitative data seemed to indicate that the graduates increased their knowledge in the field of aging, which affected the way they practiced, and they made the switch from beginning human service workers to professional social workers.

In this formative evaluation, the graduates, the consumers of this educational service, were asked "if they thought" the program goals and objectives were achieved. Further evaluation of the program would come through more quantitative assessments that document the relative success of the program. In more outcome-oriented evaluations, the goals can be operationalized more to determine which goals were more successfully achieved. Eventually, pre–post tests on

Example of Use of the KBASS Model (Continued)

knowledge, behavior, attitudes, skills, and status can be developed to examine change quantitatively. Then, in impact assessments, different forms of the health and aging MSW program can be compared to determine the optimal effect of the different forms of the program.

Measurement of Program Goals and Objectives

Use of Standardized Scales

The measurement of program goals and objectives can be greatly advanced by the use of standardized scales that have been already developed to measure a whole range of knowledge, behavior, attitude, skill, and status changes (see Fischer and Corcoran, 2007). Consulting these measures can assist in implementing the KBASS model. For example, in evaluating a program of support groups for caregivers of the elderly with senile dementia that are designed to decrease stress, the caregiver burden scale, made up of 29 items to measure feelings of burden experienced by caregivers of elderly persons, can be used (Fisher and Corcoran, 2007, p. 136).

The burden scale includes items where people rate how often they feel a certain way, from "nearly always" (scored 4) to "quite frequently" (3) to "sometimes" (2) to "rarely" (1) to "never (0)." Example items include the following:

- It's painful to watch my relative age.
- My relative does not allow me much privacy.
- I am afraid what the future holds for my relative.
- I wish my relative and I had a better relationship.
- I feel my relative is dependent.
- I am embarrassed by my relative's behavior.

A person's score on the burden scale is computed by adding all their ratings. With 29 items scored from 4 to 0, the highest possible burden score would be 116 (29 × 4) if a person said they felt every attitude "nearly always (4)," and the lowest would be 0 if a person said they "never (0)" felt that way to all the items. In testing out the scale on caregivers, the average score for daughters caring for the elderly with senile dementia was 28.3 and the average score for spouses who were caregivers was 32.5 (Fisher and Corcoran, 2007, p. 136). In a pre-post evaluation, The average burden score before and after a support group program could be compared to determine if the program reduced the caregiver's feelings and attitudes that caregiving is stressful.

Likewise, a program outcome could be more behavioral and focus on the reduction of caregiver role strain, using the index on caregiver role strain (Fisher and Corcoran, 2007, p. 134). The caregiver role strain index is a 13-item instrument designed to measure strain among caregivers of physically ill or functionally impaired older adults. The index includes items such as whether or not a caregiver's sleep is disturbed, whether or not they have felt a physical strain, or the whether or not the caregiver thinks caregiving is confining by restricting their free time or limiting their social life. So in addition to seeing if burden is reduced, it could be determined if the program reduced role strain or not.

Even if a measure does not directly measure a program goal, these standardized measures should be consulted to determine if there are goals that can be measured in this way or if these measures can be modified to fit the goals of the program. Standardized measures can provide a context for the possible measures that can be developed if the measure in the literature does not quite fit with the goals of the program. If standardized measures are used without any modification, the measures are especially useful because they may have proven reliability and validity. Either way, consulting the literature on measurement and examining how others have measured concepts related to program goals is an important exercise in developing and measuring program goals.

Reliability of Program Measures

Since program evaluation employs research methods, the measurement of goals and objectives is important. The measurement of goals and objectives takes place within the principles of standardized measurement from social science research. The concepts of reliability and validity help us assess measurement error and the stability of measures. To measure aspects of the program well, the measures need to be judged against standards of reliability and validity. This includes measuring program inputs such as the number of service contacts, consumer variables such as the demographic characteristics of those who attended the program, and, most importantly, the program goals and objectives.

Variables such as client characteristics or the number of service contacts are often easier to measure. However, many program goals and objectives are based on broad concepts measured by a number of variables. For example, decreased anxiety, increased family functioning, increased social functioning, and better health are complex and require use of measurement instruments made up of a number of variables needed to measure these concepts well. Social isolation in an aging program would be measured by a number of questions or variables such as the number of times the elderly person goes out of the house, attends social activities, and visits with friends and relatives. The breaking down of program concepts and variables into questions or methods for measuring those questions is called *operationalization* or creating *operational definitions*. Measurement of concepts in words by specifying what needs to be included is called a *conceptual definition*.

Reliability has more to do with operationalization. Reliability means clarity or consistency of the measurement process by having an organized data collection process and asking clear questions when data are collected. The best way to collect consistent data is to ask clear questions and create instruments based on the principles of questionnaire construction, which will be presented in Chapter 8. For example, in asking a question such as "Were our services easily accessible to you?" a consumer might not know what you mean by "accessibility." Did you mean, "Was the service close to your home?" or "Was the service provided at a convenient time of the day?" Also, which "services" were you talking about—the counseling service, the employment service? If consumers are confused about the questions asked you will not get reliable data. They might say services are accessible one week because the program is close to their home, but might say services are not accessible the next week because they were thinking about the hours of service that were not convenient. If individual questions were asked about how close the program was to their homes and whether the hours of service were convenient, confusion would be reduced and reliability would be increased. These clear, specific questions would more likely to achieve a cornerstone of reliability: test–retest reliability, or a measure that is consistent and produces the same results.

Test–retest reliability means that the data are reliable if independent administrations of the same questions or data collection instrument produce the same results. For example, in a program designed to reduce isolation in seniors, a scale measuring social isolation was used. For such a scale to achieve test–retest reliability, it would be administered to a sample of seniors not in the program this week and a month from now. If the same level of isolation is found now and a month from now, the measure would seem to have stability in measuring social isolation and have high test–retest reliability. Test–retest reliability is measured by a correlation coefficient, the correlation between the score now and that a month from now. The correlation coefficient can range from +1.00, a perfect positive correlation through 0 or no correlation, to −1.00 a perfect negative correlation. While the standards for judging reliability are not hard and fast, to be reliable a correlation of +.65 +.70 +.80 or above would need to be achieved. In other words, +.80 would mean the equivalent of 80% agreement between consumers' ratings of the program from one month to the next.

Often measures are used where the test–retest reliability is known. For example, if the program goal is to increase self-esteem, a measure of self-esteem that has test–retest reliability of .80 means the measure has been assessed on general populations of people where their self-esteem levels were consistent over two or more time periods. Then, if we know the measure is reliable, the program has more assurances that changes in self-esteem from the beginning to the end of the program are not produced from the inconsistency of measurement but perhaps from the program itself.

In addition to conducting test–retest, another way to establish reliability is through the *parallel forms* technique. In this technique, two different scales or questions measuring the same variables or concepts are administered at the same time. For example, in a program designed to decrease caregiver stress, two different scales on caregiver stress scales would be used in the same questionnaire at the beginning and end of the questionnaire. By correlating the two scale scores and obtaining a correlation coefficient of around .80 or above, parallel forms reliability has been achieved. Again, often instruments and measures have been tested and proven for parallel forms of reliability. Another example is if consumers were asked questions about the quality of the program at the beginning and end of the questionnaire. Parallel forms reliability would be achieved if their ratings were similar at the beginning and end of the questionnaire. If a program was designed to increase a patient's efficacy, two efficacy scales might be used. Or, if a program was designed to reduce depression in clients, two depression scales might be used to corroborate whether or not depression was decreased.

In certain types of situations, reliability can be established through *inter-rater* or *inter-observer reliability*. For example, in a program to decrease abusive discipline of parents, researchers may observe parents' interactions with their young children in a group. Two research observers could watch the same group and rate particular interactions between parents and their children to determine the percent of agreement on whether a particular interaction was positive or negative in terms of abusive discipline. The observers would be trained and establish rules about what is a positive or negative interaction, and try to achieve at least 80% agreement between their ratings.

Likewise, if a program was assessing the types of mental illness present in a group of consumers, DSM criteria could be used and a number of practitioners would assess the same cases to see how often they agree on a particular mental health diagnosis. Also, if case records are kept on consumers in a program, two expert clinicians could be used to assess how often they agree that a particular case is successful or not successful. A *kappa coefficient* is a measure used for inter-rater or inter-observer reliability. The kappa can range from 0 for no agreement between the observers to 1.00 for perfect agreement. Improved reliability in data helps greatly in improving the quality of data and reducing measurement error.

Researchers use scales or questions with proven reliability in measuring concepts. These measures have established reliability because of additional reliability procedures that have been used in research studies measuring similar concepts and in studies that psychometricians use to improve measurement with different populations varying by income, class, ethnicity, and gender. Data on the reliability of particular scales can be found in research studies and in compendiums reporting the results of reliability studies. This includes item analyses and split-half methods of reliability.

In *item analyses*, all the items thought to measure a particular concept are put into an instrument. If a scale on "caregiver stress" is being developed, a number of items can be used. For example, items such as "I don't have enough time for myself," "I am embarrassed by my relative's behavior," and "My relative asks for more help than they need" could be used in the stress scale measured for the categories "strongly agree," "agree," "disagree," "strongly disagree." If all the items used are measuring stress, a person with high stress on one item should also be relatively high on stress for another item. If the person is low in stress on one item then they should score relatively low on another item. So there should be high *inter-item correlations* of .60, .70, .80. Also, there should be high *item-to-total correlations*, meaning each item should be correlated with a person's total stress score.

Another measure to assess the reliability of a scale is the *split-half method*. For example, if there are 20 items measuring caregiver stress, the scale can be spilt into two scales of 10 items each and there should be a high correlation between the stress scale scores on each of these two subscales. All computerized statistical programs have routines for assessing reliability. For split-half reliability, the computer randomly splits the items into two scales and computes the reliability coefficient or the correlation between the two total scores. For example, the Beck Depression Inventory, a 21-item test to measure intensity of depression, was found to have a split-half reliability coefficient of .86 (Fisher and Corcoran, 2000 p. 202).

The gold standard in assessing the reliability of a scale in measuring a concept is the statistic *Chronbach's alpha*. The alpha coefficient is based on a summary correlation similar to all the combinations of split-half reliability coefficients. If the Chronbach's alpha is .80 or above, the scale is considered to have internal reliability. Statistical programs also provide a measure of the alpha you would get if a particular item were removed, called "alpha if item deleted." For example, a researcher can start out with a scale of 23 items measuring caregiver stress that give an alpha of .70, but by removing 3 items that are not good measures of caregiver strain, the computer would tell us that the alpha is .81, and achieves reliability or scalability. The caregiver strain index (CSI) achieved a Chronbach's alpha of .88, indicating that the 22 items used to measure caregiver stress had internal reliability (Fischer and Corcoran, 2007, p. 134). Likewise, in one study, a scale measuring job satisfaction achieved a Chronbach's alpha of .88, and an emotional exhaustion scale indicating a feeling of exhaustion had an alpha of .82, while a depersonalization scale indicating a feeling of not being able to relate to clients had an alpha of only .62, not a reliable scale (Acker, 1999).

Validity of Program Measures

Validity in measurement is more conceptual and related to the word definition of the concept. Most people remember validity as measuring the concept you wish to measure. How well is the concept being measured? Validity has more to do with words, concepts, and theories and is based on the descriptive conceptual definition in words. There is no doubt that the number of service contacts means something in terms of the program. However, in measuring concepts such as caregiver stress, self-esteem, efficacy, or depression, which are made up of a number of factors, the concern of validity is whether all the items included represent the particular concept.

The first type of validity is *face validity*—are the questions asked or the items the researcher chose in order to measure the concept related to that concept "on the face" of it? For example, in measuring the concept of "caregiver stress," "feeling that you do not have enough time for yourself" can be judged as a valid measure of stress. Clearly, items that ask about the general "health of the caregiver," which may be related to their stress, do not measure stress directly, as people can be in good or bad health regardless of their stress levels. On the face of it, level of health does not measure level of stress. Each item used to measure caregiver stress can be assessed to determine if the item seems to fit the concept of caregiver stress, and items or questions that do not seem to fit the concept are deleted.

Beyond face validity is *content validity*. In using content validity, researchers determine if they have all the items that are "thought" to measure the concept. Do all items that are usually related to the concept in either general thinking or in the literature appear in the measurement instrument? For example, feeling angry more often, having a strained relation to the relative, and feeling you are the only one who can care for the relative may be things recognized generally by experts or in the literature on caregiver stress.

The third type of validity, *construct validity*, involves looking at the theory behind the concept and determining whether the theory is adequately represented in the measure. For example, in creating a measure of caregiver stress, theories of stress can be consulted to help construct the definition. Are theories of psychological stress or those of physical stress being used in the definitions of caregiver stress? If the measure is based on theories of psychological stress, more of the feelings of stress would be included in the instrument. Items reflecting psychological stress would be feeling overburdened and feeling alone in the caregiving role. Depending on the psychological theory selected, feeling depressed may be part of stress or it may be a different concept that is not directly in the theory of psychological stress. If theories of physical stress are included, the instrument would reflect physical aspects of stress such as changes in blood pressure and problems with health, such as back problems and headaches. If the theory selected includes both psychological stress and physical stress, then both types of items would appear in the instrument.

The most concrete and empirical measure of validity, and the most difficult to achieve, is *empirical or criterion validity*, in which the measure used is correlated with some external criteria known to be associated with the concept. For example, if caregiver stress is measured, there should be a high correlation between caregiver stress and the number of hours of the hours of the day that the relative cares for the elderly relative. Likewise, caregiver stress should be related to levels of depression, restrictions on social life, and social isolation. Also, there should be a correlation between caregiver stress and the level of assistance with personal-care tasks needed by the elderly relative or their overall level of disability. This is similar to parallel forms reliability, only instead of correlating two measures of the same concept, the measure and some external criteria are being correlated. Again, the measure is a correlation coefficient where a high correlation would be .70, .80, or above.

There are two types of empirical validity. *Concurrent validity* tests the correlation between a person's score on one measure and some external criterion when they are measured at the same time or in the same questionnaire or instrument. *Predictive validity* occurs when the scale score is correlated with external criteria when the external criteria are measured at a later time. In other words, in a program for caregivers, if their initial stress level is correlated with their level of depression after 6 months of intensive caregiving, then the measure has some predictive validity in that caregiver stress predicts depression.

Example of a Reliable Measure Lacking Validity

Patient satisfaction surveys are now used routinely in hospitals and health-care organizations. The use of patient, consumer, or client satisfaction surveys extends from health care to mental health agencies, community agencies, social agencies, child welfare agencies, employee assistance programs, and other organizations that what work directly with consumers. In Chapter 3, consumer satisfactions surveys were described as important to achieving goals of consumer and client empowerment. But what do measures of satisfaction really measure? At issue is the use of these patient satisfaction surveys in health-care organizations as a measure of the "quality" of health care (Chang et al., 2006).

Usually satisfaction measures have been shown to be reliable. If a patient likes one aspect of care, they usually like other aspects of care. For example, if they felt they were treated well by physicians, they are usually satisfied with other aspects of physician care such as communication with the physician, the physician's attitude, the treatments the physicians prescribed, and the physician's kind, caring manner. Patient satisfaction can be measured with reliability. This means that items measuring satisfaction with the physician's communication are strongly correlated with an overall positive attitude toward the physician. An overall physician satisfaction scale could easily produce high correlations among satisfaction items that produces an alpha coefficient well above the .80 level, indicating reliability.

What can be at issue is validity of whether the concept of satisfaction is related to the concept of quality medical care. One of the ways to prove validity is to test for empirical validity or concurrent validity. If concurrent validity is achieved, a high correlation would be needed between the overall satisfaction rate of patients and the quality of their medical care. One study, at least, suggests that this is not the case.

In a survey of 236 elderly patients in selected health maintenance organizations (HMOs) in the Northeast and Southwest, patients were asked about their satisfaction with how frequently the doctor listened to them, if they showed respect, and explained things in a way they understood, among other things. Then the researchers looked at the medical records of the patients. They studied 22 medical conditions and whether the HMO physician met treatment guidelines for the elderly patient. For example, were the patients asked about recent falls or about their balance, or were they screened for diabetes.

What the researchers found is that the patient's overall satisfaction had a very small correlation with the quality of care found in the medical records. Thus the level of patients' satisfaction may not have concurrent validity when the quality of medical care is looked at as the external criterion. Both the patients' satisfaction with care and the quality of health care are important outcome criteria or program goals for health care; they just may be two separate outcome criteria in measuring the care that patients are receiving.

Summary

1. Programs have purposes, outcomes, goals, and objectives that need to be measured in program evaluation. Stakeholders in the evaluation collaborate with the evaluator in identifying program goals. While goals are important, the program context such as program philosophies and the program environment should not be overlooked. Evaluating a program is not just a mechanical exercise.

2. Program outcomes, goals, and objectives can be developed by using a context of mission statements, dependent variables, practice goals, program goals versus program objectives, process objectives, short- and long-range goals, tender-hearted versus tough-minded goals, unanticipated goals, and changes in knowledge, behaviors, attitudes, skills, and statuses (the KBASS model).

3. Reliability, or consistency of measurement of goals, and validity, or how well the goals measures reflect substantive and substantial changes in program participants, need to be considered. The use of standardized scales with proven reliability and validity can help. Even if the standardized scales do not actually fit the program goals, examining them can be useful in developing new measures based on program goals.

REFERENCES

Acker, G.M. (1999). The impact of clients' mental illness on social workers' job satisfaction and burnout. *Health and Social Work* 24(2):112–118.

Anonymous (n.d.). SMART objectives. Retrieved July 26, 2006, from: http://www. changing minds.org/disciplines/hr/performance-management/smart_objectives. Htm

Evaluation Guide:Writing Smart Objectives Retrieved June 18, 2009 http:// www.cdc.gov/dhdsp/state_program/evaluation_guides/pdfs/smart_objectives.pdf

Chang, J.T., Hays, R.D., Shekelle, P.G., MacLean, C.H., Solomon, D.H., Reuben D.E., et al. (2006). Patients' global ratings of their health care not associated with the technical quality of their care. *Annals of Internal Medicine,* 144(9):665–672.

Fischer, J., & Corcoran, K. (2000). *Measures for Clinical Practice: A Sourcebook (1st ed.) Volume II. Adults.* New York: Simon and Schuster Adult Publishing Group.

Fischer, J., & Corcoran, K. (2007). *Measures for Clinical Practice and Research: A Sourcebook (4th ed.) Volume II. Adults.* New York: Oxford University Press.

Kiresuk, T.J., & Lund, S.H. (1994). Implementing goal attainment scaling. In Kiresuk, T.J., Smith, A., & Cardillo, J.E. (eds.) *Goal Attainment Scaling: Applications, Theory and Measurement.* Hillsdale, NJ: Lawrence Erlbaum.

Kogan, L.S., & Shyne, A.W. (1966). Tender-hearted and tough-minded approaches in evaluation research. *Welfare in Review*, 55(2):12–17.

Rossi, P.H., Lipsey, M.W., & Freeman H.E. (2004). *Evaluation: A Systematic Approach.* Thousand Oaks, CA: Sage Publications.

Royse, D., Thyer, B.A., Padgett, D.K., & Logan, T.K. (2001). *Program Evaluation: An Introduction.* Belmont, CA: Wadsworth/Thomson Learning.

Weiss, C.H. (1998). *Evaluation: Methods for Studying Programs and Policies.* Englewood Cliffs, NJ: Prentice-Hall.

7

Formative Evaluations

Program Monitoring and Process Evaluations

The most common and frequent types of formative evaluations and perhaps all evaluations are program monitoring and process evaluations. Both program monitoring and process evaluation focus more on program processes rather then outcomes. Program monitoring and process studies have less emphasis on goals and more emphasis on questions such as who is using the program, what services are provided, and the process of how the program attracts and serves consumers.

Program Monitoring

In Chapter 2, *program monitoring* was defined as an assessment of the program and program operations that helps to determine whether the program was implemented as planned, which members of the target population are using the program, if program outreach seems successful, and what the initial successes and failures of the program are. Program monitoring does not measure goals and outcomes comprehensively and looks at proximate outcomes and goals such as connecting with a target population and giving people quality service.

Program monitoring helps to achieve basic *accountability*. Weiss (1998, p. 50) notes that monitoring is often used by funding agencies that provide the financial support for the program, and it helps fulfill the oversight function for government agencies or foundations that have a responsibility for seeing that programs are operating efficiently and ethically. Basically, as Weiss states, program monitoring is used "to be sure that local projects are doing what they are supposed to do." On the most basic level, if no one is being served, if participants do not engage with the program, or if the program has tremendous operational problems, the program has no chance of achieving its goals. A formative, monitoring study will uncover this basic information about a program.

In program monitoring more structured quantitative data tend to be used. These include data from the program in the form of program records, program budgets, and agency management or consumer information system (MIS or CIS) data about program participants and the services they are receiving, and surveys such as consumers' initial satisfaction with services. In essence, program performance is being monitored. Rossi, Lipsey, and Freeman (2004) note that monitoring looks at the integrity of program operations and service delivery. More importantly, they maintain that "it is not advisable" to do more summative evaluations without first conducting program monitoring and process evaluations that focus on the program intervention. So process and monitoring studies are needed before evaluation proceeds to outcome-oriented and impact assessment studies.

Evaluators using program monitoring ask simple, straightforward research questions. Basic information about the program is considered, such as the following:

1. How many participants are in the program?
2. How did they find out about the program?
3. What are their sociodemographic characteristics?
4. Are the participants part of the intended or target population?
5. Does program outreach seem effective?
6. How do consumers perceive the program?
7. What is the intervention?
8. Does the intervention seem to be working?
9. How are program funds being used?
10. Are consumers satisfied with the service and their encounters with program staff?

By answering these simple questions, program monitoring uncovers basic facts about the program. The hope is that these results can then be feedback to program planners and staff to improve the operations of the program. Weiss (1998, p. 50) indicates that the results of program monitoring studies should not be examined rigidly and should be viewed flexibly. For example, the program staff may have found that it takes longer than expected to connect with consumers, thus implementation of the program is delayed, so a much smaller number of consumers might be entering the program until the bottlenecks in outreach and referral procedures are corrected.

In a program to help 50 low-income parents raising developmentally disabled children receive SSI and Medicaid-funded home care, a program-monitoring study could be used to see if the outreach to the 50 families was successful. Then the 50 families could be tracked with case records to see how many receive SSI and how many were referred for home care services, and how many actually received home care to help the parents with child care and home tasks. The home care itself could be monitored to see which tasks the home care person did for the parent and if the parent thought quality care was being provided. Later in the evaluation the study could be extended to an outcome- or goals-oriented evaluation to study the effects of home care services on reducing parental stress from household tasks and supervision of the disabled child. In this example, program monitoring can lead eventually to more summative outcome studies.

Sometimes program monitoring can be done within a goal-oriented evaluation. For example, in a goal-oriented evaluation of a program to help families care for the frail elderly in the community where the goal was to maintain the elderly in the community and prevent nursing home placement, a few telephone interviews were conducted with family members to determine if there were any problems implementing the service and which parts of the program had strengths and which parts were weak. Program monitoring was done within the context of a much larger outcome assessment study (Frankfather, Smith, & Caro, 1981).

Program Monitoring of an Employee Assistance Program

Program monitoring involves simple attempts to document what the program is doing. For example, program directors from a university-based employee assistance program providing referral services and counseling to university employees developed a simple information system based on client case records. To monitor the program simple, straightforward questions about the program could be answered:

1. How many employees are using the service?
2. What types of problems do the employees bring to the program?
3. Which types of employees, i.e., faculty, administrative staff, program associates or assistants, secretarial staff, building operations and maintenance staff, use the program?

4. What are the demographic characteristics of the employees using the program in terms of ethnicity, gender, age, and years employed at the university?

5. Do employees use the program for information and referral about day care, home care for an elderly relative, or nursing home placement for a relative?

6. Do employees use the program for personal counseling about depression or anxiety? Do they use the program for marital counseling?

7. Do employees come in with substance abuse problems for themselves or a family member?

8. Do employees use the program for assistance with a child's academic or behavioral problems?

9. Did employees seek professional help for the problem before they came to the employee assistance program?

These monitoring questions can be answered by analyzing simple numbers and percentages—that is, how many were there and how many different types of employees were served over a 6-month or a year's period of time? Data from this monitoring are used in reports to the university sponsoring and funding the employee assistance program. The data on how many employees were in each job title and how many were faculty or administration, etc., were compared with data on the target population of the whole university. Through this analysis, under- or overserved groups were discovered.

In addition to satisfying the need for accountability, employee assistance program staff used the results to give them an overview of how the program was operating, not just in relation to the caseloads of individual staff but also in relation to the whole program. How many were served? Who were they? Staff valued looking at the effects of all their hard work. For example, they were pleased to learn that a high percentage of faculty used the program, as this amount of faculty use exceeded standards of most employee assistance programs in the literature. Results and findings from the program monitoring became feedback to make changes in the program. When it was found that the number and percentage of program operations and building maintenance staff served was low, outreach to this group of employees was expanded.

Monitoring studies can examine what was originally intended in the program and if the policies and practices that the program was supposed to implement were actually achieved. For example, the employee assistance program did not accept supervisory referrals; the employee was given autonomy about whether or not to use the employee assistance program. Thus examining data on how employees found out about the program to determine if there were employees who were referred by supervisors would indicate if program policies were being implemented correctly. Assessing why they came would also help answer this question. Also, substance abuse cases were planned to represent less than half of the cases since the plan was to establish a "broad-brush" program that would offer personal counseling for those with other personal and inter-personal problems. In all, substance abuse cases represented less than 20% of all cases and personal counseling comprised the largest percentage of cases, so monitoring helped establish that the program had been implemented as planned.

In addition to simple analysis of examining one piece of data at a time, cross-tabulation of one variable by another answered critical questions. For example, did particular groups of employees use the program for particular problems? Did faculty use the program differently than secretaries or administrators? Was the custodial staff more likely to use the program for services such as referrals to day care or help with elder care? Was secretarial staff more likely to use the program for issues of job stress?

After a few years of issuing reports from the information system, the program monitoring was expanded to include an employee satisfaction survey for those who had used the service, which is an increasingly popular form of program monitoring. There were a number of questions that could be answered in the employee satisfaction study:

1. How did they hear about the employee assistance program?
2. Was the problem that brought them to the program affecting their experiences at work (e.g., less satisfaction from job, less motivation, reduced ability to concentrate, not doing work as well as usual, more absences or lateness)?
3. Did a staff member from the program respond quickly? Were the employees offered service? How often did they meet with the staff person?
4. How helpful was the program? What was the most helpful part of the service?
5. Did the problem that brought employees to the employee assistance program become better, worse, or stay the same?
6. Did employees feel they experienced improvements in work life, personal life, or feelings about themselves?
7. Would employees come with another problem to the program? Would they recommend the program to a friend? Is it useful for the university to have such a program?

Another use of program monitoring is provided below by McConnaughy, a licensed social worker, who monitored her private practice caseload. Examination of who was being served, the referral sources and presenting problems, and whether or not clinical goals seemed to be achieved provided a useful framework for her to look at trends across all cases and assess her private practice in total. The formative results had many implications for her continuing practice as a social worker and any changes she thought she should make to her interventions.

A Monitoring Study of Private Practice Social Work

SUSAN MCCONNAUGHY, LCSW DOCTORAL CANDIDATE

PH.D. PROGRAM IN SOCIAL WELFARE, GRADUATE CENTER OF THE CITY UNIVERSITY OF NEW YORK

Over the past 5 years, *monitoring* and *accountability* have become watchwords of the managed-care environment of private practice social work. The need to assess practice and use research strategies to determine effective methods of practice has taken center stage in many settings. A prime example is the push for evidence-based psychotherapy (EBT) in the mental health field. While the number of social workers in private practice use evidence-based models of psychotherapy is unknown, the need for accountability continues to loom large and requires a response.

In view of the increasing pressure for private clinicians to respond to expectations of accountability, social work clinicians would do well to promote their own views on how psychotherapy might demonstrate its usefulness based on criteria intrinsic to their own practice processes and outcomes.

In the context of accountability, I decided to conduct a program monitoring study to look at my own private practice cases for questions that could be easily answered. Four general research questions guided this practice monitoring study: What practice issues would be clarified by descriptive data? What types of cases were being seen overall? Which cases seemed more successful? What were the characteristics of successful and of unsuccessful cases?

In the old research terminology, this monitoring study uses "available data" or "secondary data" to answer basic questions about the current private practice. The study can come under the current parlance of "data-mining," whereby practitioners answer their own practice questions through an analysis of basic monitoring data that exist in any practice or program (Epstein, 2010).

TABLE 7.1 Client's Stated Reason for Termination

Reason for Termination	Frequency	%
Treatment completed	17	56.7
Financial problem	6	20.0
Not satisfied with results	2	6.7
Scheduling difficulty	4	13.3
Moved	1	3.3
Total	30	100

INTRODUCTION TO THE DATA

The practitioner-researcher looked at all closed cases from January 2003 to September 2004 in order to determine the factors associated with clients completing treatment and those associated with clients terminating treatment before completion (see Table 7.1).

A little more than half of the clients (56.7%) gave indications that they were satisfied that they had completed treatment for their presenting problem(s). One-fifth of the clients (20%) reported terminating because a financial problem that prevented them from continuing in treatment. Two clients (6.7%) terminated because they were not satisfied with the results, and another four clients (13.3%) said they had to quit because of scheduling difficulties. One client terminated before the project was complete because she moved.

Because it is hard for some clients to tell a therapist directly that they are not satisfied with their treatment, it is possible that clients who terminated prematurely, citing financial problems or scheduling difficulties, might in fact have terminated because of dissatisfaction with the counseling or its effectiveness. On the other hand, financial problems may have been underreported because they may have exerted a strong pressure that clients may not have wanted to admit.

Taking into account the possibility of problems with the data, the results still proved useful for practice. The treatment glass was either half-full, with 56% completing treatment, or half-empty, with 44% not completing treatment. At this point the monitoring study became more interesting and compelling to pursue, with the possibility that it might uncover factors related to satisfactory and unsatisfactory terminations.

Other descriptive, measurable factors from the case records were also examined. These factors were referral source, presenting problem, number of sessions attended, number of months attended (with the idea that the last two together might gauge the intensity of the work involved), and satisfaction of the therapist in the outcome.

The client population was drawn for the most part from people who knew the clinician's work very well (see Table 7.2). One-third (33.3%) of the clients in

A Monitoring Study of Private Practice Social
Work (Continued)

TABLE 7.2. Referral Source

Referral Source	Frequency	%
Client had seen therapist previously	10	33.3
Colleague	9	30.0
Former or current client	5	16.7
Medical setting	3	10.0
Other	3	10.0
Total	30	100

this study had been former clients who had come back to deal with another problem. Nearly a third more (30.0%) were referred by colleagues whom the clinician knew professionally and socially for at least 15 years. Another important source of referrals (16.7%) was former or current clients referring people they knew.

During the past year and a half, the therapist has sought to build the practice by networking with other medical providers, but these sources of referral represent only 3% of the client base. It will be interesting to see whether certain sources of referral are more associated or less associated with certain outcomes of treatment.

By far the greatest number of clients (46.7%) presented depression as their reason for coming to therapy (see Table 7.3). It will be interesting to see how depressed clients fare in terms of outcome. If they complete treatment, the therapist will be encouraged by her work. In fact, it will be most interesting to compare how many clients within each category of presenting problem complete treatment. If, for example, clients with work or addiction problems do not do well, additional outside services might be needed. If depression and relationship

TABLE 7.3. Presenting Problem of Client

Presenting Problem	Frequency	%
Depression	14	46.7
Relationship problems	7	23.3
Loss	3	10.0
Addiction	3	10.0
Anxiety	2	6.7
Work/career	1	3.3
Total	30	100

problems are most successful, perhaps it is because the therapist has more expertise in theses areas. This monitoring exercise clearly has practice relevance.

Once a week was the intensity of the therapeutic sessions and the duration of treatment was from 4 months to 3 years. The median case was 46 sessions attended or just under 1 year of treatment. A sizeable number of clients (6, or 20.0%) terminated shortly after 30 sessions (31–35 sessions). It should be noted that Oxford Health Plans puts a limit of 30 sessions a year on the number of psychotherapeutic contacts. Altogether, nearly half of the clients (46.7%) terminated after 35 sessions. Since most clients attend once-weekly sessions, this represents approximately 9 months of therapy.

After the basic data were computed, cross-tabulations were made to analyze the connections between the outcome of termination and other variables that might impact the reason for termination. This variable separated the cases into two categories: those who completed their treatment goals and those who terminated before completing their goals.

Two cross-tabulations were analyzed and had practical significance even if the sample size was very small, and one cross-tabulation had statistical significance where $p < .05$. These are displayed in Tables 7.4 and 7.5.

There was clearly a descriptive association between clients completing their treatment goals and their source of referral (Table 7.4). Successful outcome patterns were found for clients referred by former or current clients or those who were former clients themselves and returned for service. It was found that 80% (4) of those who were referred by former or current clients completed their goals, and 80% (8) of those who had themselves been former clients completed their goals. Clients referred by colleagues were the least successful cases. Only 22.2% (or 2) of clients who were referred by colleagues completed treatment; in other words, nearly 80% (77.8% or 7) of them did not complete their goals.

TABLE 7.4. Outcome of Treatment by Source of Referral

	Source of Referral					
	Former or Current Client		Colleague		Client Was a Former Patient	
Outcome of Treatment	N	%	N	%	N	%
Completed goals	4	80	2	22.2	8	80
Did not complete goals	1	20	7	77.8	2	20
Total	5	100	9	100	10	100

Although there were not enough cases to use a Chi-square test, the Chi-square probability was .09.

A Monitoring Study of Private Practice Social
Work (Continued)

Clients who were referred by other clients or who themselves were once the therapist's clients were far more likely to achieve their goals in treatment than clients referred by colleagues. The therapist notes that in order to serve the latter group of clients better, she would do well to understand why this disparity exists and seek to remedy it.

It may be that those who reach their goals in therapy are drawn from a self-selected group who know the therapist and how she works, so the fit is likely to be very good from the beginning. If there are not immediate good results, these clients probably trust that if they stick with it, they will have success because they have seen the success that they or others have had.

It is more likely that a client who comes without this advantage will quit immediately if there seems not to be a good fit with the therapist at the beginning. In a climate of increased suspicion about the effectiveness of therapy, compounded by greater consumer empowerment, if not sophistication, the client is more likely to shop for a new therapist rather than try to make it work with a particular therapist. This may not always be a good thing for the client.

Clients referred by colleagues obviously need and deserve more attention during the induction phase of treatment, so that the therapist can ascertain what it is they are looking for so as to develop and fine-tune goals for treatment.

For example, since January 2004, the therapist received eight referrals from two psychiatrists. These clients seemed to be people who preferred or needed a medical approach rather than talk therapy, but their psychiatrist suggested they "needed to talk" more with a therapist. They were used to meeting with their psychiatrist for 15 minutes every 1 to 3 months, and depended on medication related to their diagnosis. With this background, this group of clients may have expected to take the same rather passive or receptive stance, and would therefore bridle if results were not produced by the clinician after a few 45-minute sessions. The expectations of these clients require closer scrutiny at the beginning to address their hopes and set very realistic short-term goals with them. In this way, they will have a relatively successful outcome in therapy, with the possibility of engaging again at a later point for other work.

In these cases, the therapist could do a better job of ascertaining who initiated the referral—the psychiatrist or the client—and for what reason in the context of the medication agenda. She would do better if she kept an ongoing dialogue on this agenda with the psychiatrist and with the client, because these treatments have the potential to be collaborative, even if the psychiatrist thinks of the clinician's role as merely supportive.

Another finding from Table 7.4 is that the therapist is doing quite a lot of repeat business with former clients. This is usually quite productive for the client and rewarding for the therapist because of her previous investment in these people. It might be a good idea to reframe goal-setting with these and all clients to anticipate this series of working periods over time, rather than to set the goal of conducting a "definitive analysis," as the therapist's training had coached her to do.

There was a statistically significant connection between outcome of treatment and number of sessions clients attended (Table 7.5). Two categories were created by dividing the data on number of sessions attended at the median: 46 and fewer sessions attended and more than 46 sessions attended. It was found that 81% (81.3%, or 13) of the clients who completed their goals attended more than 46 sessions, whereas only 28% (28.6%, or 4) of the clients who attended 46 and fewer sessions completed their goals. Fully 71% (71.4%, or 10) of the clients who attended less than 46 sessions did not complete their goals in treatment.

The findings in Table 7.5 refer to and build on the implications of Table 7.4. Since half of the clients attended less than 46 sessions, the therapist needs to base goal-setting on this expectation. More care is needed in the goal-setting stage of therapy to address the expectations of the client and the therapist regarding how much can be accomplished in a particular time frame. Together client and therapist can set realistic short-term goals, perhaps within a context of optional longer-term goals.

At this point, it has become clear to the therapist that she must change her own expectation: that embarking on a long-term treatment is possible in most instances. The era of long-term treatment as a major modality, however, is now gone and, while the past was a tremendously satisfying time in working with clients, it is now time to shift gears. Not changing with the times can affect the ability to "meet clients where they are" and it can affect the therapist's satisfaction with the work. This monitoring study can be used by the therapist to plan short-term services and take a step in the right direction.

TABLE 7.5. Outcome of Treatment by Number of Sessions Attended

| | Number of Sessions Attended | | | |
| | ≤ 46 Sessions | | >46 Sessions | |
Outcome of Treatment	N	%	N	%
Completed goals	4	28.6	13	81.35
Did not complete goals	10	71.4	3	18.8
Total	14	100	16	100

Fisher's exact probability =.004.

*A Monitoring Study of Private Practice Social
Work (Continued)*

TABLE 7.6. Outcome of Treatment by Presenting Problem

	Presenting Problem										
Outcome of Treatment	Depression		Anxiety		Relationship		Loss		Work		Other	
	N	%	N	%	N	%	N	%	N	%	N	%
Completed goals	7	50	1	50	4	57.1	3	100	1	100	1	33
Did not complete goals	7	50	1	50	3	42.9	0	0	0	0	2	66
Total	14	100	2	100	7	100	3	100	1	100	3	100

Outcome was not significantly related to the presenting problem (see Table 7.6). Fifty percent (7) of the clients whose presenting problem was depression completed their goals, and 50% (7) did not. A similar pattern was found for relationship problems, where 57%, or 4 cases, were successful and 43%, or 3 cases, were not.

Severe depression is notoriously intractable, and in this era of short-term therapy it was gratifying to see that as many people reached their goals as did not. Up to now, the therapist has set two goals for clients with depression: *(a)* understanding the causes, and *(b)* feeling significant relief. Going forward, it would be wise to set shorter-term goals and help all clients feel some success on the long road to well-being. Shorter-term goals with depression might include understanding the diagnosis and current symptom picture; understanding the disorder of depression itself; understanding the impacts that depression is having on the client's functioning; helping the client cope with the symptoms; helping the client talk to important others about what is happening; and dealing with reactions to depression's long and tight hold. Previously, the therapist had been leaving these goals unstated and had been aiming only for the "big relief." But when clients don't feel relief soon enough, they doubt the benefit of the work altogether and may discontinue treatment. That can contribute to feelings of hopelessness. In the future, clients who are not able for one reason or another to stick with the work long enough to get some relief will at least leave treatment knowing they got some small help and that they might get some small help in the future.

IMPLICATIONS FOR A MONITORING STUDY

Monitoring studies voluntarily undertaken may provide useful insights for private clinicians who want to improve their services to clients. Monitoring can be used to help gauge efficacy of private practice based on the shared goals of client and therapist, which is more likely to have validity in the eyes of consumer and practitioner than outcome studies based on external criteria such as simple decreases in symptoms.

This small study has been useful in redirecting practice efforts to help more clients complete realistic goals. Cases referred by outside professionals merit special consideration in relation to treatment planning. The implications of these findings suggest adopting a shorter-term therapy model with tightly framed goals. This, in fact, is a managed-care model that could have been imposed on the therapist by a supervisor or insurer. In investigating the therapist's own practice, this direction now seems inevitable.

REFERENCES

Epstein, I. (2010). *Clinical Data-mining: Integrating Practice and Research*. New York, NY: Oxford University Press.

Process Evaluation

Process evaluation was defined in Chapter 2 as an evaluation study that describes the program model and program activities, determines how the program is being implemented, and assesses initial program goals. In these evaluations researchers look at how the program is implemented and whether the program was "faithful" to the program design, known as *program fidelity*. Process evaluations address how the program is managed and organized, and address issues of participant enrollment, activities offered, actions taken, staff practices, and client outcomes. Process evaluations study what the program actually does, not just outcomes but process. (Weiss, 1998, p. 9). These studies can uncover simple flaws such as not enough staff being hired or the program model being implemented in a different way than it was planned.

The questions answered in process evaluations are very similar to those answered in monitoring studies. The difference is that program monitoring tends to use more structured data, whereas process evaluations are usually characterized by a number of more informal types of data collection reflecting program process and activities. Process evaluations employ qualitative data more often. As Weiss (1998, p. 130) states, "program processes may sound too flexible and spongy to withstand (quantitative) measurement and evaluators often choose to study them through qualitative methods." These qualitative methods include observing the program in operation and conducting qualitative personal interviews with staff, consumers, and administrators, asking broad, open-ended questions to get qualitative data on how the program is being implemented. Weiss (1998, p. 49) further notes, "The evaluator has to discover the reality of the program rather than its illusion."

Process evaluations are very useful in preventing the black-box phenomenon in which evaluators do not pay enough attention to how the program is delivered. Process evaluations can be studies in themselves or can be part of more comprehensive summative evaluations using impact assessment designs (Rossi et al., 2004, p. 57). Either way, process evaluations uncover and shine a light in the "black box" and describe how the program works. If a more summative evaluation shows that the program works, conducting a process evaluation will give clues as to why it worked. Likewise, if the program did not work, the process evaluation may uncover why it did not work (Rossi et al., 2004, p. 57)

Overlap Between Program Monitoring and Process Evaluation— Program Process Monitoring

In the example of the monitoring study of the employee assistance program discussed earlier in this chapter, the integration of a satisfaction survey contributed significantly to overall monitoring of the program. Most of the survey used structured, closed-ended questions and examined quantitative data; this part was clearly program monitoring. Some of the questions in the satisfaction survey were open-ended, for example, "In your own words, tell us what was helpful or not helpful about your contacts with the employee assistance program staff?". Thus qualitative data were also collected and analyzed. This more clearly represents process evaluation, explaining the process whereby the employee benefited or did not benefit from the program. As staff developed qualitative case examples from their records, even more data on the process in a particular case were included in the overall monitoring.

Although most evaluation texts treat program monitoring and process evaluation as separate types of evaluation, Rossi, Freeman, and Lipsey (2004, p. 171) use one integrative term, "program process evaluation and monitoring," in recognition of the similar processes involved in program monitoring and process evaluation and the overlap between the two types of formative evaluations.

Examples of Process Evaluation Studies

Two process evaluation studies are provided as examples of the usefulness of the findings on program process and implementation from these formative, process evaluation studies. In the first example, Irish presents a process evaluation of the

Seniors Out Speaking on Medicare (SOS Medicare) Prescription Drug Benefit Presentations Program, which was developed in the very early days of Medicare Part D. The study highlights the aspects of training that the volunteers found useful in making presentations on the confusing changes in Medicare prescription coverage to community groups. The study showed how training the volunteers, preparing them, and giving them skills helped the program achieve some of its initial goals. The reports of the most experienced volunteers who made the presentations and a focus on "successful cases" or positive approaches to helping seniors with Part D was found in the analysis and reported back to program administrators so that future interventions and presentations could be refined.

In the second example, Whittemore presents a process evaluation of the "Everybody Needs a Proxy" campaign of the Westchester End of Life Coalition in Westchester, NY. This formative evaluation highlights the successful aspects of program implementation, such as the strong training given to the volunteer presenters, the enthusiasm of the volunteers, the program model of a saturation approach, the usefulness of closed presentations with lectures instead of setting up a table at a street fair or festival, and the value of using the Terri Schiavo case as an example. Best practices included having the head of the organization committed to the importance of a proxy and having the presenter go through her own proxy and explaining how it was filled out. Future summative evaluations could include outcomes variables such as how many of the people contacted actually filled out their health-care proxies and which approaches were more successful in terms of this outcome

Seniors Out Speaking on Medicare (SOS Medicare) Prescription Drug Benefit Presentations

SHAWNA IRISH, M.A.

GRADUATE OF THE MASTER'S PROGRAM IN HEALTH ADVOCACY,

SARAH LAWRENCE COLLEGE

Seniors Out Speaking on Medicare (SOS Medicare) is a program of the Medicare Rights Center, an independent non-profit consumer advocacy organization. The Medicare Rights Center is located in New York City and does the majority of its outreach within New York City, in addition to providing a statewide Medicare hotline. The SOS Medicare Program focuses solely on Westchester County, the county nearest to New York City to the north. With funding from Westchester County and the connection to the Medicare Rights Center, the program is both connected to Westchester County and has access to the resources provided by the Medicare Rights Center, affording the program respectability in the county, and accountability through the backing of the Medicare Rights Center.

Seniors Out Speaking on Medicare (SOS Medicare) Prescription Drug Benefit Presentations (Continued)

The Medicare Rights Center began the SOS Medicare Program in June of 2001 as a pilot project "to test the idea that ongoing, proactive personal assistance and communication can make a significant difference in the health care people receive" (SOS program description, p. 1). The mission of the SOS Medicare Program is to educate people about their Medicare benefits, rights, and options and to encourage them to think about their own health care (SOS program description). The program has since grown from an initial 10 sites to 37 current monthly locations.

The SOS Medicare Program has recruited retired professionals who volunteer to present "Medicare Minutes" in area senior centers and senior nutrition centers. A Medicare Minute is a brief presentation on a current issue in Medicare, ranging from deciding whether to enroll in a private plan or spelling out the services covered by Medicare. The SOS Medicare volunteers consistently frequent a core group of centers—30 in southern Westchester and 7 in northern Westchester. Through these monthly presentations the volunteers have built rapport with the center leaders and members. The volunteers themselves represent an articulate and intellectually active group of people.

In 2003, legislation was passed that called for prescription drug coverage for recipients of Medicare. The benefit was scheduled to begin January 1, 2006, requiring seniors and people with disabilities to research and enroll in one of 68 prescription drug plans offered by upwards of 20 private insurance companies. In addition, a low-income subsidy program has been administrated through Social Security to absorb some of the costs of the drug benefit for qualifying seniors and people with disabilities. The benefit model that the government itself released caused confusion among seniors and people with disabilities. Even the best-educated consumers found the task daunting.

The Kaiser Family Foundation (2005) reported that only 16% of surveyed Medicare recipients sought out community organizations and groups to help them make a decision about enrolling in a plan, and 14% had spoken with someone from a community organization about the benefit. For individuals without family or knowledgeable providers, community organizations were one of the few resources outside of Medicare itself. What is disheartening is that the Kaiser Family Foundation (2005) also found that 33% of Medicare recipients had not spoken to anyone about the prescription drug benefit. In general, there seemed to be a great need for information dispersal on all levels.

The SOS Medicare Program received new funding from various sources to expand the program to include outreach to seniors regarding the Medicare prescription drug benefit, which began in January of 2006. For SOS Medicare, prescription drug benefit outreach included presentations about the prescription drug benefit to seniors and people with disabilities across Westchester County, to inform recipients of the changes and refer them to additional counseling about the benefit when needed. The goal of this expansion included change in knowledge, attitude, skills, and behavior of seniors and people with disabilities. The presentations were an effort to educate and inform people how to make the best decision for their own care. The objectives of the prescription drug benefit outreach included beginning a dialogue on the benefit, soliciting audience participation, forming peer-to-peer connections, and using knowledgeable volunteers to clarify the coverage. Many of the SOS Medicare volunteers rose to the challenge, as they had to "tool-up" quickly to meet the coming demands of Medicare Part D. They expanded their responsibilities as volunteers and began presenting information about the prescription drug benefit in old and new venues, in a new format.

A PROCESS EVALUATION

To assess how program implementation was proceeding and to suggest the beginning effectiveness of the prescription drug benefit outreach, a process evaluation focusing on the preparedness of the volunteers, the methods the volunteers used to make their presentations, and the initial reactions of seniors to the presentations was conducted. This process evaluation was seen as a formative step in the overall evaluation of the program. Through interviews with the volunteers who have presented information about the prescription drug benefit at various venues in Westchester County, program administrators could measure impressions of the training and preparations the volunteers received, how they implemented the intervention, and the impact the volunteers thought they had on seniors and people with disabilities.

As noted previously, the volunteers for the SOS Medicare Program are a well-educated group of retired professionals. For the past 4 years many of these volunteers have been visiting senior centers on a monthly basis, building relationships and a core base of sites for information dispersal. The new prescription drug benefit has allowed these volunteers to further educate the public and perhaps go into areas where they had not gone before. Being themselves Westchester residents, they have been a part of some of the communities in which they speak, and because of their ages, they may be able to relate to the audience more than younger volunteers would. In both respects, the volunteers bring peer-to-peer connections that may be useful in reaching Westchester residents.

Seniors Out Speaking on Medicare (SOS Medicare) Prescription Drug Benefit Presentations (Continued)

The volunteers are at the core of the SOS Medicare Program. They learn about, teach, and interact on all aspects of Medicare. Since the volunteers are most involved in these presentations, they have a good initial sense of audience reaction and the benefit of the presentations to the audience. An important resource for staff of the SOS Medicare Program and the Medicare Rights Center is to know their resourcefulness to volunteers committed to educating a vulnerable group about a complicated topic. Through this process evaluation, the volunteers can provide feedback and enlighten the program staff about the needs of seniors and people with disabilities.

This process evaluation assesses the volunteers' initial program experiences regarding how they proceeded and the possible beginning effectiveness of the program to present clear and concise information in a manner that enables seniors and people with disabilities to be proactive in their health-care options. For the purpose of this evaluation, the volunteers chosen had participated frequently in presentations of the prescription drug benefit across various venues in Westchester County. While 29 of the original volunteers had participated in at least one presentation, only 9 had presented more than two times. These are the "seasoned" volunteers that were interviewed for this evaluation. Through these in-person interviews where descriptive, qualitative data could be collected, the volunteers were able to relate the effectiveness of their own preparations and the impeding benefit to the audiences.

RESEARCH DESIGN AND TYPE OF SAMPLE

In the hopes of obtaining a sample of "best volunteer practices," the nine volunteers who had presented more than twice were all interviewed. This non-probability purposive sample reflects the experiences of the most experienced volunteers, but it does not represent the population of all SOS Medicare volunteers. Personal interviews with open-ended questions to collect qualitative data and some rating scale items were conducted to evaluate the presentations about the prescription drug benefit. The data from these interviews represent rich, descriptive data on the impressions left on the volunteers and provide excellent data for feedback that enables adjustments to be made in the program.

The interviews were designed to address the Part D presentations solely, not the "Medicare Minute" work that the volunteers continued to participate in. The interview questionnaire delved into the volunteer perspective on the benefits of the Part D presentations. Included in this inquiry were questions pertaining to the training of and support to the volunteers, and how this affected the benefit to the audience. The prescription drug benefit has been described as confusing and complicated, and the SOS Medicare volunteers have been positioned so that they bear the burden of educating a somewhat vulnerable group. Through this task, the volunteers developed their own theories and perspectives about the issue as a whole, much of which they shared through these interviews.

The questions asked during the interviews sought a variety of information. First we wanted to find out the volunteers' opinion on what the purposes of the presentations were and their responsibilities. Second, how did they think the training worked and what other forms of preparation were successful in helping them to meet the purposes of the presentation? The final aspect of the interview was the volunteers' perceptions of the their interaction with the audience and possible benefits that occurred from the presentations. Did the presentations seem to be beneficial? How did they help and why did the volunteers feel that way? What problems did they experience in making the presentations?

ANALYSIS OF PRESENTATION STATISTICS

In structured data that more closely represents data from a program monitoring study, it was found that, at the time of the interviews , the nine SOS Medicare volunteers had done 60 presentations in Westchester County on the prescription drug benefit. To date, the SOS Medicare Program has provided 95 presentations to Westchester County residents; this includes 8 town hall meetings, in which the presenter was a staff person at the Medicare Rights Center.

The volunteers reported the number of presentations they made. The number of presentations given ranged from 3 to 12. The three volunteers who each did 12 presentations were clearly the most experienced volunteers. The remaining 6 volunteers did between 3 and 5 presentations. The mean or average number of presentations was 5. The median number of presentations was 4 and and the modal number of presentations were 4, as the highest number or 4 volunteers made 4 presentations each. The number of presentations that a volunteer participated in had no correlation with how beneficial they perceived the presentation to be for the audience.

The volunteers presented to various audiences sizes. Based on the average audience size that each volunteer reported, the mode audience size was 60 and the median audience size was 50.

PREPAREDNESS

Preparation was a recurrent theme in the interviews with the volunteers. The interviews focused on preparedness in regard to training, knowledge of

*Seniors Out Speaking on Medicare (SOS Medicare) Prescription Drug
Benefit Presentations (Continued)*

information, readiness of the sites, presentation format, and the personal abilities and experiences of the volunteers. The volunteers themselves seemed to
have high confidence in their own preparation.

The volunteers received training that was 3 hours a day for 4 days. The training
was conducted by the Medicare Rights Center and it involved Medicare basics, the
prescription drug benefit, and tips for presenting. All of the volunteers seemed to
view the training as beneficial in that the training helped them breakdown the
material and emphasize key points. The volunteers also tended to supplement the
material with their own research, as noted in the following selected quotes:

> It was clear and concise as far as the material we knew about. There
> were changes along the way but that was to be expected. The slide
> presentation helped to impress the material in my mind.
>
> I had to supplement it with my own reading.
>
> It emphasized and brought out the important points we need to
> get across. It simplified the information we needed to understand—it
> broke it into parts.

It made sense to have the volunteers do a presentation quickly after the training.

> But I think that to remain effective the training has to occur close to the
> presentation. I don't find it helpful to get the training and then 4
> months later do the presentation.

Since Medicare Part D was new, it was suggested that more training was
needed on the new drug benefit. Upon the expansion of the program to
include presentations about the prescription drug benefit, volunteers had to
tread into new territory.

> I think the training could have had less emphasis on Medicare
> mechanics and more on Part D. More training would be better.

In addition to the training, the volunteers were given scripts to relay the
information in an organized manner, as drafted by staff of the Medicare
Rights Center. The scripts were developed to keep the volunteers on message
and to form a structure by which to present the information. When asked if the
scripts were helpful to the presentations, 88.9% of the volunteers expressed that
they were. In addition to the scripts, the volunteers were given handouts to
distribute on the topic. The volunteers were split on the handouts, as 55.6%

thought that they were beneficial. Those who did not like the handouts felt that people do not pay attention to the presentation when there are handouts passed around and that people just throw them away anyway. Those that liked the handouts, however, expressed great enthusiasm for them.

> I always give handouts. Most people are visual and appreciate something to look back on. They are essential.
>
> I am a handout person! I believe they're a great tool for education. Having a handout enlarges the presentation.

For the overall format of the training programs, however, the volunteers voiced little dissatisfaction.

> I feel that the parts that I've done were fine. When we were training there was so much information and then when we started to make the presentations—I guess the main purpose is to get the idea across, not in so much detail. So I thought it was really watered down. This again depends on the audience. I might give them more details and vice versa.

The information that was given to and available to the volunteers played a major role in their concept of preparation. Much information was provided to the volunteers through training, but as noted previously, many volunteers sought information from additional sources. Overall, the volunteers were content with what was provided to them, and felt that they were able to use it in their presentations.

> Given the problem we have with information changing all the time, the Medicare Rights Center does a wonderful job training volunteers.
>
> I believe from the groups we presented to I was able to answer their questions.
>
> The information is available to me.
>
> There's an awful lot of information and I try to review it all.

Since the inception of the SOS Medicare Program, the volunteers have been developing relationships with people and leaders at the sites they go to on a monthly basis. This has helped to build a core group of sites where SOS volunteers have rapport and credibility. All of the nine volunteers interviewed had been in the program for many years. They were all retired professionals and had much experience with public speaking. This was represented in their answers regarding their preparations and apprehensions. They all felt confident in their ability to disseminate accurate information in a clear manner.

Seniors Out Speaking on Medicare (SOS Medicare) Prescription Drug Benefit Presentations (Continued)

> I know the people, I have the chemistry down pat. When you have been doing this as long as I have, it's easy.
>
> If I wasn't very prepared I couldn't get my message across so I better be well prepared and know my subject matter.
>
> Now, I've been going there over 4 years. I know these people, we're sharing information on what's important to all of us.
>
> If you like people it's reciprocated, you can't be phony.

Some volunteers affirmatively answered that they believed that age did indeed increase their ability to connect with the audience.

> I think some seniors get turned off by younger people.
>
> I think it does have some influence. I think when they know I'm in the same boat they feel better, misery loves company.
>
> When you bring in a personal situation. It's more credible —more understandable.

Some of the volunteers cited being a member of the community as a positive influence.

> I think because I am a senior citizen also, I live in the community, they know that I took the training. They really respect that they feel it's wonderful that our community has this type of service.

Not only were some of the seniors in the audience affected by the age of the presenters, but perhaps the volunteers were also affected by the age of the audience.

> I didn't have the apprehension I would have with a younger group.

Many, however did not feel that it was really directly related. Knowledge and confidence ruled out the factor of age. As the following quote suggests, knowledgeable old and decrepit volunteers were valued more than unknowledgeable, old and decrepit volunteers.

> I don't know whether they judge me by my age—they judge me by my mannerisms more than anything. You can be old and decrepit; they look upon you as old and decrepit. But if you're old and decrepit and you know what you're talking about, they'll respect you.

EFFECTS OF PRESENTATIONS ON THE AUDIENCE

The volunteers were asked to rank their perception of the benefit of the presentations to the audience (1 = Not Beneficial, 2 = Somewhat Beneficial, 3 = Very Beneficial, 4 = Extremely Beneficial). Through audience participation and the questions that were asked the volunteers gave their impression on how the audience was affected by the presentation. The mean and median responses were that the presentations were very beneficial (or 3 out of a possible 4 rating). Overall, the volunteers believed that the audiences were leaving less anxious and better off than before the presentation, as can be seen by the qualitative data which corroborated their ratings.

> They have a lot of research to do. I've had people kiss my hand, hug me, whatever, who are just so thankful. That allows them to lessen their anxiety. We're doing a good job basically and people appreciate it.
> I think I clear things up in their mind for them.
> At this point they still don't understand but they're getting there.
> It always ends on a high note; they always know that they're responsible. I think they're grateful for what we have to offer. When we leave they feel they've participated in some small way.

On the other hand, some volunteers weren't so optimistic. There were some concerns voiced that people still don't have much understanding, which was not necessarily a reflection of the presentation. The reasoning may have been the need for further individual consultation or that no amount of information was helpful to people who were unable to do anything.

> I don't think they quite get it.
> I think these people are going to need counseling and that's because of all the uncertainty around this.
> As clearly as we present Part D some people cannot sit down to figure it out and some people don't want to.

The volunteers had the understanding that the audience would not be able to make decisions on prescriptions drugs after one presentation, but that it was a step in obtaining knowledge about what was happening to their drug coverage.

VOLUNTEER DISCRETION

The expansion of the SOS Medicare Program to include presentations about the Medicare prescription drug benefit allowed the volunteers to take on greater roles. The volunteers who were interviewed saw these presentations as a chance to "inform seniors and others about the new Medicare drug law." The primary

Seniors Out Speaking on Medicare (SOS Medicare) Prescription Drug Benefit Presentations (Continued)

objective for the new outreach was the education of Medicare recipients. In addition, the volunteers saw their own responsibilities begin to expand.

> I see myself as one to deliver the facts as accurately as possible and to try to interpret the information for them and to dispel any misunderstandings.
>
> To know more than the printed material. To be able to distinguish between times when I have the expertise and times I have to pass it on to someone with more expertise than I do—to make the presentations interesting and accessible.

The volunteers seemed confident in the role that they played in these presentations. In addition to the training that they received, most of them supplemented their knowledge with their own research into the latest media coverage. Through this confidence in their knowledge and abilities, the volunteers took discretion with the material in which they presented.

> I do review the scripts, I do try to incorporate information that's not in the script but part of the script—more details depending on the audience. I try to anticipate the audience questions.
>
> We adapt ourselves to the audience. We adapt ourselves to the scripts.

Perhaps it was the confidence displayed to the audience that lessened anxiety and helped the audience to understand the material somewhat better. Although age may not have played a factor in audience reception of the volunteers, it seemed that the volunteers' competence was the major player. In this respect, the volunteers felt an obligation to be knowledgeable about resources for seniors and people with disabilities.

Whether the audience was able to handle their own health-care decisions after the presentations did not seem to be the largest indicator of benefit to the volunteers. Rather, making sure that seniors and people with disabilities were well informed with accurate information and had access to reliable resources was the top priority. This perspective fits in with the mission of the Medicare Rights Center, whose advocacy lies in presenting accurate information to consumers about their health-care options. Since this was in the early days of Medicare Part D, the volunteers thought people would need further intervention to select a drug coverage option.

FINDINGS AND IMPLICATIONS FOR THE SOS PROGRAM

The addition of a new prescription drug benefit for Medicare recipients posed a challenge to the SOS Medicare Program to educate a large number of seniors and people with disabilities. As the program expanded to include outreach for the prescription drug benefit, the roles of the volunteers in the program also grew. The volunteers had a grueling task ahead of them, but rose to the challenge. To date, SOS Medicare volunteers have reached nearly 4800 individuals through their presentations alone. With the knowledge and expertise they developed from their professional lives and their experiences with the program previously, they were able to reach out to Medicare recipients with knowledge and empathy.

The support of the Medicare Rights Center provided useful resources to the volunteers. Not only did Medicare Rights Center staff train them, but they were armed with the Medicare Rights Center as a resource to answer their questions or to refer people to when they did not have the answer. The Medicare Rights Center provided the volunteers with scripts and handouts for the presentations, which for the most part the volunteers deemed useful. The training simplified the information that needed to be conveyed, provided scripts to keep volunteers "on message," and provided a structure for the presentations. In addition, while the volunteers found the expertise of the Medicare Rights Center to be beneficial, they were able to use discretion in their roles as educators and counselors. The fact that the volunteers were assigned on an ongoing basis to particular senior centers or sites where they made the presentations increased their rapport and credibility. With their confidence and personality, and being of similar age to that of the seniors, they were able to connect with the audience on a level that provided trust, and the volunteers thought the presentations were well received.

While the process of the presentations was useful and informative, the outcome in relation to Medicare Part D could not be assured. The benefit of the presentations to the audience was not necessarily a reflection of their ability to make their own decisions afterwards, but to get on their way to understanding what was ahead of them. The new prescription drug benefit has presented itself to a group of seniors confused by the new program. After an hour-long presentation, an individual might not have the magic answer, but they would be equipped with the appropriate questions to find their answer.

These findings were feedback into the program to suggest improvements that could help the seniors select a drug program. The findings

Seniors Out Speaking on Medicare (SOS Medicare) Prescription Drug Benefit Presentations (Continued)

suggest that in addition to the group presentations, there is a great need for one-on-one counseling about their individual prescription needs. The SOS Medicare Program has planned in its prescription drug benefit outreach to provide in-person counseling to residents of Westchester County. Many of the same volunteers who have been presenting the information at the various sites around the county will be providing counseling for the individuals they reached through these presentations. They will be in a few sites around the county, speaking with Medicare recipients on a one-on-one basis. This will be especially helpful in reaching the population of individuals who do not have family and friends to guide them in making an informed decision.

This process evaluation of the presentations on the prescription drug benefit shows a great need for the education itself, and for follow-up such as counseling. Through these interviews, all objectives appear to have been met. These include beginning a dialogue on the benefit, soliciting audience participation, forming peer-to-peer connection, and using knowledgeable volunteers. With a group of committed and talented volunteers, successful outreach can be provided to seniors and people with disabilities. With funding from county resources, a knowledge base shared by the Medicare Rights Center, and the skills of retired professionals, a program can be expanded for large-scale Medicare programs, such as the prescription drug benefit.

The formative, process evaluation should now proceed to more summative, outcome-oriented evaluations. This should include pre–post studies to see how much the seniors' knowledge of Medicare increased and which types of knowledge increased and which did not. With the launching of individual counseling, follow-up interviews were being conducted to determine what decisions seniors made in relation to Medicare Part D and the effect of those decisions on the cost and accessibility of their prescription drugs.

REFERENCES

Kaiser Family Foundation/Harvard School of Public Health. (2005). The Medicare drug benefit: Beneficiary perspectives just before implementation. Retrieved December 14, 2005, from: http://www.kff.org/kaiserpolls/upload/The-Medicare-Drug-Benefit-Beneficiary-Perspectives-Just-Before-Implementation-Chartpack.pdf
Seniors Out Speaking on Medicare (SOS Medicare) program description.

Process Evaluation of the Everybody Needs A Proxy Campaign,
Bronxville, Eastchester, and Tuckahoe, NY

NIKE WHITTEMORE, M.A.

GRADUATE OF THE MASTER'S PROGRAM IN HEALTH ADVOCACY,

SARAH LAWRENCE COLLEGE

In recent years, Terri Schiavo has become a household name, sending shivers down most people's spines because of the pain and suffering that the prolonged end of her life entailed. In essence, Terri Schiavo did not have a health care proxy.

For over 10 years Terri Schiavo, a severely brain-damaged young Florida woman, had been kept alive by feeding tubes. Because prior to her incapacity Terri had not documented her end-of-life care wishes or appointed a person (called a "health-care proxy") to make health-care decisions for her, a bitter struggle ensued between her husband, who believed Terri would not have wanted to continue living on life support and advocated for the removal of her feeding tube, and her parents, who believed that Terri would want to continue on life support and believed that one day she would recover, advocating for the maintenance of her feeding tube. As the nation watched with horror, Terri's feeding tube was removed, reinserted, and removed again because of an unprecedented series of court rulings and political interventions. A few days after the final removal of her tube, Terri died.

Perhaps the most important lesson gleaned from the Terri Schiavo ordeal is that adults need to plan for their future medical treatments, including life-prolonging procedures, while they still have the ability to do so. Different states have varying laws about advance directives. New York has the Health Care Proxy Law that was enacted as Article 29-C of the New York Public Health Law in 1990. By appointing a health-care proxy, "an individual (principal) can designate a health care agent who will have authority to make any and all health care decisions on the principal's behalf. Unless the principal specifically limits authority in the health care proxy itself, the agent's authority to make health care decisions will be unlimited. The principal can also provide detailed instructions, orally or in writing, to the health care agent expressing his or her wishes" (Ecker, 1991). Under current New York law, unless a patient has formally designated a proxy or provided "clear and convincing evidence" of their end-of-life care wishes in some other format (i.e., living will), the patient's family members (i.e., parents, spouse, siblings) *do not* have the authority to refuse life-prolonging treatments for their incapacitated loved one (*New York Times*, 2005). This is unique to New York and Missouri only, which is why patient advocates are so motivated to get individuals to appoint and sign a health-care proxy while

Process Evaluation of the Everybody Needs A Proxy Campaign,
Bronxville, Eastchester, and Tuckahoe, NY (Continued)

clearly stating their wishes about artificial nutrition and hydration at the end of life. Considering that 80% of New Yorkers have not signed health care proxies or living wills, patient advocates are faced with a tall order (*New York Times*, 2005).

Although the federal Patient Self-Determination Act of 1990 requires hospitals that accept Medicare and Medicaid to provide information to adult patients about their right to prepare advance directives such as the health-care proxy, "the material usually gets ignored among the pile of papers patients receive at admission in a moment of crisis" (Davis, 2005) Mary Ann Jezewski, Associate Dean of Research at the University of Buffalo School of Nursing, says her studies indicate that "patients and nurses tell us that this [hospitals] is not the appropriate place to do this," and suggests that "wider acceptance of advance directives will come as people are introduced to the idea at less stressful settings, such as churches, synagogues and senior citizen centers" (Davis, 2005).

It is interesting to note that another study, conducted by the University of Wisconsin Medical School, revealed that "the main difference between those who do and do not complete advance directives is an understanding of the documents and their purpose" (Marchand, Cloutier, Gjerde, & Caq, 2001). The researchers concluded that physician efforts to educate patients about advance directives, especially routinely in the office, or preferably in community settings, were important (Marchand et al., 2001). With that said, however, another study conducted by the University of Pittsburgh suggests that doctors are ill-prepared (by lack of training) to initiate end-of-life care discussions with their patients. Researchers studied fourth-year students at Georgetown University School of Medicine and Mayo Medical School and found that most of the students felt unprepared to discuss end-of-life issues with their patients. "All (99%) recognized the importance of advance directives and anticipated discussing end-of-life issues with patients in their practices (84%). However, only 41% thought their education regarding end-of-life issues had been adequate, only 27% had ever discussed end-of-life issues with a patient themselves, and only 35% thought they had had adequate exposure and education regarding advance directives" (Buss, Marx, & Sulmasy, 1998).

These research findings give a broader context and establish the program need for outreach efforts such as the Everybody Needs a Proxy campaign, which educates people about the New York health-care proxy outside the medical setting. The campaign's theory has a certain program logic: If people are handed a proxy outside the medical setting, walked through it by a knowledgeable volunteer, educated about its importance, and have their questions answered, they will have more time to process the information, thoughtfully choose the person they would like to designate as their proxy, have a conversation with that person about their end-of-life care wishes, and then sign the actual proxy form.

PROGRAM DESCRIPTION

The Everybody Needs a Proxy campaign is a program of the Westchester End-of-Life Coalition in Westchester, NY, that "promotes the signing of health care proxies in Westchester by persons 18 years and older." The goals of the program are to help people think about their health care, values, and wishes, and whom they would want as their health care proxy (agent), and to assist them in completing a health-care proxy form. The first stage of the Everybody Needs a Proxy campaign targeted those living, working, meeting, and studying in ZIP Code areas 10707, 10708, and 10709 (Bronxville, Eastchester, and Tuckahoe) (Everybody Needs a Proxy campaign brochure, 2005).

The initial phase of the campaign kicked off in April 2005 and ended in June 2005, using a "saturation approach" (a hard-core sell for a limited amount of time). This initial phase was funded by a $5000 grant from the Community Fund of Bronxville, Eastchester, Tuckahoe, Inc., which paid for a part-time coordinator, and, coupled with a $3000 donation from Lawrence Hospital for the printing of 10,000 health-care proxies. The Everybody Needs a Proxy campaign anticipated being an on-going, community-based effort and has relied heavily on the recruitment of volunteers from local academic institutions and health organizations who are then trained by a health-care attorney and bioethics consultant (who is also a board member of the Coalition) about the New York health-care proxy. The training, offered three times per year, is free of charge and consists of two 3-hour sessions held 1 week apart at either Sarah Lawrence College in Bronxville or Gilda's Club Westchester in White Plains. Upon completion of the training, volunteers are requested (through e-mails from the campaign's coordinator) to give 10- to 15-minute presentations at select civic, health, or social meetings and/or staff information tables at local venues, such as schools, banks, libraries, and street fairs.

THE PROCESS EVALUATION

The objective of this evaluation was to investigate the processes of the Everybody Needs a Proxy campaign through the eyes of trained campaign volunteers and to discover patterns that illuminated and could help improve the program's overall effectiveness. A process evaluation was conducted, focusing on the campaign's processes and the program methods that seemed to be working and the issues

Process Evaluation of the Everybody Needs A Proxy Campaign, Bronxville, Eastchester, and Tuckahoe, NY (Continued)

that arose from program implementation, as well as participant judgments about outcomes. This was a qualitative, ex-post facto, formative process study because it emphasized broad-based questions to elicit the trained volunteers' perceptions of the campaign *after* participating in it. The evaluation also had elements of a pre–post study, since a few questions tried to document change, such as pre- and post-knowledge of the proxy, in campaign volunteers and consumers, or those whom campaign volunteers educated about the proxy.

Data were collected from program literature, conversations with program administrators, pre-existing quantitative data compiled by the program coordinator, and in-depth interviews with campaign volunteers through a questionnaire with closed- and open-ended questions. (The questionnaire is presented in the next few pages.) Of the 21 questions on the interview questionnaire, 14 were purely open-ended, qualitative (66.5%) questions and seven were closed-ended, quantitative questions with the option of qualitative elaboration (33.5%). This latter type is known as the "inverse funnel" approach, where the questioning proceeds from specific, closed-ended questions to broad, open-ended questions. Questions in different categories expanded the data collection: experience/behavior questions solicited descriptions of the respondents' experiences and actions in the program; opinion/belief questions revealed their values and their thoughts about the program; feeling questions elicited their emotional responses to their experiences and thoughts; and knowledge questions brought out the facts they knew about the program.

The entire questionnaire was given systematically during an in-person or telephone interview, and was focused on gathering detailed descriptions about the campaign volunteers' individual perceptions of the inner workings of the program and its overall effectiveness. To enhance reliability, I, the evaluator, wrote respondents' answers to each question *during* the interview (rather than relying on memory), and paid special attention to quoting verbatim what was relayed. Each interview lasted approximately 20 minutes. The questionnaire is presented next.

QUESTIONNAIRE FOR EVERYBODY-NEEDS-A-PROXY-CAMPAIGN VOLUNTEERS

Please note that this is a confidential survey and that there are no right answers.

1. In your opinion, what is the purpose of the Everybody Needs a Proxy campaign?

2. In your opinion, how effective has the program been in meeting its purpose/goals?

3. What population is the program designed to target? In your opinion, has it been effective in reaching that audience? Is there anyone the program leaves out or doesn't reach?

4. Please describe the type of interventions/services the program provides. What types have you performed and what have been your experiences?

5. In your experience, what intervention method seemed to work BEST in achieving the goals of the program?

   a. Which venues?

   b. Which approach styles toward individuals and/or groups?

   c. Do you find it most useful to go through the proxy question by question?

   d. What other strategies have you found to be most effective?

6. When you first meet consumers, how knowledgeable are they about the New York health-care proxy? (Please circle one)

1	2	3	4
(No knowledge)	(Very little knowledge)	(Some knowledge)	(A great deal of knowledge)

Please elaborate:

7. Do consumers connect to the program?

8. In your experience, which consumers were the most receptive to the program's services? What were their comments?

9. In your experience, which consumers were the least receptive to the program's services? What were their comments?

10. How knowledgeable would you say consumers are after your presentation? In other words, do they seem to "get it"? (Please circle one)

1	2	3	4
(No knowledge)	(Very little knowledge)	(Some knowledge)	(A great deal of knowledge)

Please elaborate:

11. What do you see as some of the strengths of this program?

12. What do you see as some of the weaknesses of this program? What do you perceive as the barriers to service? How could this program be improved?

Process Evaluation of the Everybody Needs A Proxy Campaign, Bronxville, Eastchester, and Tuckahoe, NY (Continued)

Now I'd like to ask a few questions about the training provided to you in the program.

13. How much knowledge did you have prior to the program's training on New York health-care proxies? (Please circle one)

1   2   3   4

(No knowledge) (Very little knowledge) (Some knowledge) (A great deal of knowledge)

Please elaborate:

14. How would you rate the trainer's knowledge of the New York health-care proxy and delivery of that knowledge? (Please circle one)

1   2   3

(Inadequate)   (Good)   (Excellent)

Please elaborate:

15. How much knowledge did you have after the program's training on New York health-care proxies? (Please circle one)

1   2   3   4

(No knowledge) (Very little knowledge) (Some knowledge) (A great deal of knowledge)

Please elaborate:

16. Do you think that the Everybody Needs a Proxy campaign is helpful? Do you think it's the most effective way to educate the target population about the New York health-care proxy outside the medical setting? Why or why not? What, in your opinion, would be a more effective route?

Now I'd like to ask a few questions about your satisfaction as a volunteer of the program.

17. How satisfied are you with volunteering for this program? (Please circle one)

1   2   3

(Dissatisfied)   (Somewhat satisfied)   (Very satisfied)

Please elaborate:

18. What suggestions do you have to make the volunteer experience more rewarding?

19. Do you like the process by which you are asked to volunteer? Why or why not?

20. What are your thoughts about the "summary sheets" you're asked to fill out during or after a program event?

21. Do you yourself have a health-care proxy? ___ Yes ___ No

    a. Under what circumstances did you decide to sign or not sign a health-care proxy?

THE SAMPLE

This study used a non-probability, purposive sample. Each volunteer in the population pool (those who had completed the training and were labeled "active") was identified on a list provided by the campaign's coordinator and e-mailed a participation request. Self-selection was a factor in eliciting the sample because those who responded and were willing to be interviewed became members of the sample population. There are no assurances that this sample of eight participants from a population pool of 24 reflects the population. However, the sample did include some different types of volunteers, as the respondents included medical professionals, students of health advocacy (both past and present), and campaign administrators (who are also trained campaign volunteers)—all characteristics of those in the overall population pool.

As a program evaluator, it is important to acknowledge my own biases that may affect the assessment process. First, I am a master's-level student who is focusing my studies on end-of-life care, including the promotion of advance directives. Second, I am a trained volunteer in the Everybody Needs a Proxy campaign and have experienced first-hand the strengths and weaknesses of the program. Third, I am the daughter of elderly parents, one of whom wants to talk about advance directives and the other who would rather not. And fourth, I admit to having a hard time filling out my own health-care proxy, appreciating that it takes considerable thought and is a process, not a flippant decision.

PLAN FOR DATA ANALYSIS

For consistency of measurement, this study used more than one data collection approach, which enabled the use of triangulation to enhance the reliability and validity of the findings. Triangulation, discussed fully in Chapter 8, is the comparison of two data sources or two types of data to see if they show the same finding. *Data triangulation* was used by soliciting a variety of data sources (i.e., interviewing people with different

Process Evaluation of the Everybody Needs A Proxy Campaign, Bronxville, Eastchester, and Tuckahoe, NY (Continued)

points of view) and *methodological triangulation* was used by incorporating a variety of data-gathering methods (i.e., questionnaires, interviews, program documents). Both qualitative data (i.e., themes) and quantitative data (i.e., frequency distributions, percents, correlation coefficients, and paired *t*-tests to compare judgments about pre–post changes) were gathered and compared using triangulation to verify if the responses from the qualitative data was backed up by the quantitative data. (Some of the quantitative data will be presented as an exhibit in Chapter 8 on triangulation in data analysis.)

Presenting the same questions systematically during each interview, regardless of who the person was and whether the interview was conducted in person or on the phone, also enhanced reliability and validity. The use of multiple case examples, some of which revealed best-practice approaches, reinforced emerging patterns, as did the incorporation of negative cases (cases that didn't fit the pattern), which demonstrated exceptions that prove the rule.

Content analysis of qualitative data involves identifying coherent and important examples, themes, and patterns. Therefore, I looked for descriptions that fit together and revealed the same underlying issue or concept. I also chose to focus on a strengths-based perspective, so my evaluation will emphasize the strengths and best practices of the campaign, touching on the perceived weaknesses only periodically for the sake of improvement.

PROGRAM STRENGTHS: ENVIRONMENT AND APPROACH

Program volunteers perceived the Everybody Needs a Proxy campaign as having numerous strengths. When asked what these strengths were, responses varied, including solid training, volunteer enthusiasm, raising awareness, the timing of the Terri Schiavo case, the geographic location, the use of a saturation approach, and legitimization.

The training provided to the volunteers and the person delivering the training were valued by some volunteers, as expressed in the following selected quotes.

The trainer is a huge strength to the program. She's so knowledgeable and experienced.

> A strength would be the good solid training which turned out to be two-fold: it raised consciousness about proxies in both the volunteers and the people they reached out to.
> Fabulous training is the campaign's strength.

The enthusiasm of the volunteers and their concerns about the issues of advance directives were also mentioned.

> The enthusiasm of the volunteers is a strength because most of us are very concerned and are dedicated to getting the word out.

This enthusiasm translated into raising awareness about the proxy.

> Going out to the public to make them aware of its [the proxy's] importance is a strength.
> Awareness and well organized are strengths.

The timing of the Terri Schiavo case and the geographic location of the program were also valuable to the overall effort.

> I think the strengths of the campaign are being out there, the timing of the Terri Schiavo case, and the geographic location (it's Westchester, not the Bible Belt).

The use of a saturation approach was also valued.

> A saturation approach was a strength because it concentrated on a specific time for a specific population and used every avenue to reach them.

The campaign proved a legitimate way to discuss advance directives and the more general topics of death and dying, which are germane to the mission of the Westchester Coalition.

> I can comfortably get up and give a 5-minute presentation in any health-related forum about the proxy because I have the campaign to refer to. The campaign legitimizes why I'm bring up the topic. That's a strength.
> The campaign gives us an entry into talking to people about how they want to die—a difficult subject to bring up socially if you don't have a lead-in.

The campaign used two approaches: open discussions at tables set up at street fairs, banks and libraries, and closed presentations to community groups. In response to which campaign approach the volunteers perceived as being the

Process Evaluation of the Everybody Needs A Proxy Campaign, Bronxville, Eastchester, and Tuckahoe, NY (Continued)

most successful and satisfying, study participants (almost unanimously) favored closed presentations.

> The best thing is to talk to groups when people are actually there to listen.
> I think the most successful were ones that included a lecture since people had a reason to be there.
> Presentations are the most effective because people are actually sitting down to listen to the information and can ask thoughtful questions.

Volunteers also revealed common approach styles that seemed to work well, such as mentioning the Terri Schiavo case and giving consumers different case scenarios.

> Referring to the Terri Schiavo case was very helpful. People may not have known what a proxy was, but when I said Terri Schiavo, they instantly knew what I meant and said they didn't want to end up like her.
> Bring up the Terri Schiavo case. Most people know about that.
> I've found it to be effective to show a group of people an 8- to 10-minute video of a specific scenario (I gear the scenario according to the audience) and then give a short talk about the proxy, leaving time for questions.
> I like to give them different scenarios.

One respondent gave a detailed account of her positive presentation experience, attributing the success to the enthusiastic introduction by the meeting's organizer and the "very attentive" audience. This could be an example of a best practice.

> The best experience I had was doing a 10-minute presentation for the Lion's Club at a restaurant in Bronxville. We had a private room and sat eating dinner together at a large conference style table. Before I got up to speak, the organizer, who was a dynamic speaker, got up and said "You know, I think this is so important. I have taken this to other clubs I belong to and they think it's great, too." That was a great entry. I spoke for 10 minutes tops about the benefits of having a proxy, exercising your autonomy and making it easier on your family. I then answered

five or six questions and told them that I would be there during dinner if they wanted more information. People were very attentive and took lots of forms.

Another respondent revealed a best-practice example as well. This volunteer described her experience of starting off her presentation at her temple by asking two adults from the audience to come up and sign her own proxy as witnesses. This volunteer reported that this was an extremely effective approach, because it encouraged audience participation as well as demonstrated how easily the proxy could be filled out and validated without the need for a lawyer or notary. She further personalized the presentation with real-life anecdotes.

I found it extremely helpful to open a presentation by asking if anyone in the audience was over 21 and then inviting two volunteers to come up to the front of the room and witness my own proxy. Then I said, "I just extended my autonomy— it's that easy." Also, offering personal anecdotes to the audience is helpful because you, as a health-care professional, can say, "I had a patient who either did or didn't have a proxy and this is what I saw with my own eyes."

PROGRAM WEAKNESSES: ENVIRONMENT AND APPROACH

At the other end of the spectrum, there was a clear consensus and emerging theme about the least favorite environment and approach in terms of effectiveness and reward, chiefly staffing information tables (especially those at street fairs and outside banks). Campaign volunteers used descriptions such as, "I felt like just another vendor"; "People aren't interested in stopping to talk"; "It's a touchy subject and people don't want to think about it, especially at a fair"; "People thought we were trying to sell them insurance and were reluctant to stop"; "People walking by seemed to have a purpose, a place they wanted to get to and seemed pretty busy"; and "It was hard to just stand outside a bank and park a table."

The street fair in Bronxville was not as good. I felt like just another vendor. People walked by and ignored you if they weren't interested. It wasn't as effective or as rewarding an experience.

I did a street fair and another outdoor info table that wasn't a street fair, but was something similar. The fairs are good, but people aren't interested in stopping to talk. It's a touchy subject and people don't want to think about it, especially at a fair.

I did a sidewalk festival in Bronxville—that required a very aggressive stance. People thought we were trying to sell them

Process Evaluation of the Everybody Needs A Proxy Campaign,
Bronxville, Eastchester, and Tuckahoe, NY (Continued)

insurance and were reluctant to stop. Only the people who had an ill relative or lost a loved one recently were interested in hearing what we had to say in that setting.

I did a sidewalk thing twice in Bronxville. It was okay, but people walking by seemed to have a purpose, a place they wanted to get to and seemed pretty busy. They'd simply take the information with them.

It was hard to just stand outside a bank and park a table.

TARGET POPULATIONS

There was a common perception among campaign volunteers that although the program was intended to target all adults over age 18, the younger generation was being left out.

The campaign's designed to target, generally, the adult population, not just seniors ... but we didn't reach the young adult population.

It's not getting out to enough people or to the right people, like younger people with families. Terri Schiavo was young and look at what her family went through because she didn't have a proxy!

The campaign should target everyone 18 years and older, but those under age 40 are not interested.

People are reluctant to talk about end-of-life issues until they are eligible for AARP. This limits the voluntary population.

Unless the "younger than 50" population has had a personal experience with this issue, they are not motivated to hear about it.

This finding was underscored by an overwhelming agreement that the most receptive consumers were those who were older, with volunteers using terms such as "mature in age," "older," "seniors," and "people over 40."

The more mature in age were the most receptive. One quarter of them said they already had a proxy. Others said, "Oh, I have to do this" or, "Oh, I know how important this is."

Older people naturally connect to the program.

Seniors are the most receptive. They say something like, "Oh, I'm really glad you're doing this. I know it's something I should have already done. Thanks for reminding me."

People over age 40. They say, "It's a very good idea. It's important."

Only one respondent perceived the older population as being left out of the campaign, which demonstrated an exception that proves the rule.

> Because of restrictions of money and time, we haven't been able to reach enough elderly in nursing homes and senior centers, as well as veterans. I think those are the people we're leaving out.

MOST EFFECTIVE WAYS TO EDUCATE THE PUBLIC ABOUT A HEALTH-CARE PROXY

There was a mixed review among volunteers as to whether the campaign was the most effective way to educate the target population about the New York health-care proxy. Some agreed that it was:

> It's the best way I've come across to reach a broad population.
>
> It's an effective tool among many.
>
> For this geographic area, yes, I think it is an effective way to reach the target population. Many of us who are volunteers live and work in this area and know a lot of people. We can identify with them and they trust us. That's an important factor and one we'll have to consider as we go into other communities.
>
> Yes, I think it's helpful.

Other volunteers had some suggestions for making the campaign even more effective, such as giving presentations at corporate health fairs and handing out proxies to corporate human resources (HR) departments, standardizing presentations to include an introductory video of different scenarios, expanding into other parts of Westchester; and setting up a multi-ethnic conference to discuss how different groups perceive the health-care proxy.

- Presentations at corporate health fairs:

> I think it's a helpful campaign, but it could be executed differently. I buy into the concept, but they need to do more. Why not go to places like IBM and PepsiCo and do presentations at their health fair day or give proxies to their HR departments? The campaign needs to find venues where there is a captivated audience.

- Standardizing presentations to include an introductory video:

> Yes, I think it's helpful, but it would be most effective to make it standard at the beginning of our presentations to show a short video of a specific scenario (geared toward the audience). I think this approach would

Process Evaluation of the Everybody Needs A Proxy Campaign, Bronxville, Eastchester, and Tuckahoe, NY (Continued)

generate more questions because people would have a better idea of what to ask.

- Expanding into other parts of Westchester:

  There was an unanticipated snowball effect—organizations outside the targeted ZIP Code have requested the campaign's participation.

  This is an ongoing campaign and we're going to focus on covering all of Westchester, going to groups where we're asked to speak (such as the Teacher's Union), rather than stay within the three ZIP Codes.

- Setting up a multi-ethnic conference to discuss different groups' perceptions of the health-care proxy:

  There's been some talk about setting up a multi-ethnic, multi-religious conference in Westchester that's focused around how different groups think about end-of-life care and the health-care proxy.

Finally, there were other volunteers who believed that the Everybody Needs a Proxy campaign was *not* the most effective way to educate the public about proxies, and offered alternative interventions such as, including proxy training in all health and education classes, reimbursing physicians for sitting down with families to discuss the proxy (while people are still healthy and coherent), encouraging insurance companies to send a letter to their subscribers explaining the proxy, and including a proxy in local and state politicians' annual mailings.

- Including proxy training in all health and education classes:

  No, I don't think the campaign's the *most* effective way to educate people about proxies. Learning about proxies should be in all education and health classes.

- Reimbursing physicians for sitting down with families to discuss the proxy (while people are still healthy and coherent):

  No, I don't think the program is the best way to reach the public. Doctors themselves should talk to their patients about the proxy when they are healthy and coherent. When people are sick and in pain, they don't want to think about a proxy. It would be beneficial for doctors to do this since the doctor would know where he/she stands.

Doctors should be reimbursed for sitting down with families and explaining it.

- Encouraging insurance companies to send a letter to their subscribers explaining the proxy:

  I also think that insurance companies should get involved and that it would be mutually beneficial for them to do so. They could send a letter to all their subscribers, suggesting that they fill out a proxy.

- Including a proxy in local and state politicians' annual mailings:

  I think that asking local and/or state politicians to include the health care proxy in their annual mailings would be helpful.

SUMMARY AND IMPLICATIONS OF FINDINGS

Because this study used a non-probability, purposive sample, there are no assurances that the sample reflected the population. With that said, however, a number of findings from the process evaluation legitimized the program strategies and had implications for improving the program through the reported results and findings.

1. There appears to be a clear need for alternate approaches to the hospital setting in educating people about the health-care proxy. This finding was underscored by the Everybody Needs a Proxy campaign volunteers' experiences with consumer confusion about the meaning of and need for a health-care proxy.
2. The Everybody Needs a Proxy campaign appears to be an effective alternative to educating the public about health-care proxies outside the medical setting, especially in offering closed presentations that either stand alone or piggy-back onto other organization's (e.g., civic, health, social) meetings. Therefore, in going forward, it might be advisable for the campaign to focus more on this specific outreach effort (rather than on general information tables), while incorporating the newly revealed best-practice approaches such as inviting audience members to witness the speaker's proxy, mentioning the Terri Schiavo case and offering other real-life anecdotes, and showing a brief video about different end-of-life care scenarios (tailored to specific audiences).

*Process Evaluation of the Everybody Needs A Proxy Campaign,
Bronxville, Eastchester, and Tuckahoe, NY (Continued)*

3. There are clearly many strengths of the Everybody Needs a Proxy campaign, as perceived and reported by program volunteers. These strengths include solid training, volunteer enthusiasm, raising awareness, the timing of the Terri Schiavo case, the geographic location, the use of a saturation approach, and legitimization.

4. The Everybody Needs a Proxy campaign appears to be reaching the older population and is, for the most part, well received among this population. The campaign, however, is not reaching or appealing to the younger population. Considering that the campaign's goal is to target *everybody* over age 18, the campaign may want to devise more creative ways to connect to the younger generation, such as making health-care proxy presentations to teachers (e.g., Teacher's Union) and to parents' organizations (e.g., PTA) so that children and young adults learn about the proxy through school and at home, and including young adults in the campaign's training so there are younger speakers who can better identify with and reach younger audiences. The campaign could also add public service announcements (PSAs) or buy advertising on local radio (e.g., rock music) stations that would educate young listeners in a young adult's voice (using age-specific lingo) or in the voice of a beloved celebrity about the need for a health-care proxy. As suggested by a campaign volunteer in the study, the campaign could become more involved in corporate culture, for example, by handing out proxies to human resource departments to pass on to their employees, many of whom are young adults, and making presentations at corporate health day fairs.

5. The unanticipated snowball effect of the initial stage of the Everybody Needs a Proxy campaign—that other communities within Westchester would like the campaign to expand into their area—highlights the need for and effectiveness of the campaign in educating the public about health-care proxies. Perhaps, then, the campaign could focus on broadening its target area by recruiting and training volunteers who live and work in other towns. By keeping the volunteers local, trust and an identification level can be established that, as seen in the initial phase of the campaign, is crucial for generating interest in the program's mission and opening doors to otherwise closed forums.

REFERENCES

Buss, M.K., Marx, E.S., & Sulmasy, D.P. (1998). The preparedness of students to discuss end-of-life issues with patients. *Academic Medicine*, 73(4):418–421.

Davis, H.L. (2005, March 24). Avoiding doubt at the end of life: Schiavo case underscores need to plan for a proxy to resolve treatment issues when the patient can't. *Buffalo News*, A1.

Dignity for the dying. *The New York Times*, May 29, 2005.

Ecker, R.L. (1991, April). Health care proxy law. *The CPA Journal*. Retrieved November 14, 2005, from: www.nysscpa.org/cpajournal/old/10691663.htm

Everybody Needs a Proxy campaign brochure. (2005). Westchester End-of-Life Coalition, Bronxville, NY.

Marchand, L., Cloutier V.M., Gjerde, C., & Caq, C. (2001). Factors influencing rural Wisconsin elders in completing advance directives. *WMJ*, 100(9):26–31.

Summary

1. Program monitoring and process evaluations are two types of formative evaluation studies in which there is less emphasis on goals and more emphasis on documenting program operations.

2. Program monitoring usually uses more structured data, such as the number and types of program participants, and the number and types of services given.

3. Process evaluations are more likely to use qualitative data based on direct observation of the program, focus groups of program participants, or personal interviews with staff.

4. "Program process monitoring" (Rossi et al., 2004, p. 171) is a term used for formative evaluations in which both program-monitoring and process evaluation methods and techniques are used in relatively equal amounts.

5. *Program fidelity* is a term used to show how much congruence there is between the program as planned and the program as it operates.

REFERENCES

Frankfather, D., Smith, M.J. & Caro, F.G. (1981). *Family Care of the Elderly*. Lexington, MA: D.C. Heath and Co.

Rossi, P.H., Lipsey, M.W., & Freeman H.E. (2004). *Evaluation: A Systematic Approach*. Thousand Oaks, CA: Sage Publications.

Weiss, C.H. (1998). *Evaluation: Methods for Studying Programs and Policies*. Englewood Cliffs, NJ: Prentice-Hall.

8

Designing the Evaluation Study

The research design is the overall plan for the evaluation study. Just as planning is the most important step in quality program planning and practice, planning is the most important step in quality program evaluations. Evaluation studies must be planned well.

Having a plan or an overall study design is crucial. Typically, health or human-service professionals new to the field of program evaluation think they can interview all the program participants, interview all the staff and administrators, analyze all the case records, and then maybe even conduct some focus groups of program participants or staff as well as analyze the minutes of some program-planning sessions or board of directors meetings. All of this could be done if there were unlimited funding or resources for research. However, the researcher is usually lucky if 5% or 10% of the program budget has been allocated for evaluation. In the fields of social work and health, there is usually not enough funding to provide the services in the manner planned. Thus a design needs to be realistic and planful; every part of the design, data collection, and analysis must be planned. In developing the plan, the systematic research methods are specified that set program evaluation apart from program development or health or social work practice.

The research design is the logic of how an evaluator will answer questions about the program. Evaluators specify whether they will conduct a survey interviewing clients after they received program services, whether they will interview or test clients both

ʻefore and after the program, or whether they will conduct an experimental study to compare two different forms of the program. In short, this plan, or study design, describes how evaluators will answer the research questions of whether the program is being implemented well and/or whether the program is achieving its goals. The study design has four parts:

1. Selecting a research design or a type of study that fits the purposes of the evaluation.
2. Deciding on the most efficient and effective data collection strategies
3. Constructing the data collection instrument or instruments
4. Selecting a sample of people to interview or the parts of the program to observe

Selecting a Design or Type of Study

The basic designs used in program evaluation are formative designs, survey designs, pre–post designs, and impact assessments in the form of quasi-experimental and experimental designs.

Formative Designs

Formative designs are used in process evaluations, program-monitoring studies, or combined program process–monitoring studies. As described in Chapter 7, process evaluations and program-monitoring studies provide useful information about program implementation to determine if the program is operational and if there are any bottlenecks in the program and if the program is being implemented as planned. Formative studies such as these assess whether the program has strayed from the original design or achieved program fidelity. *Program fidelity* is a judgment about how much has the program is congruent with its original design and conception.

Formative-exploratory and explanatory designs can be a good way to implement a strengths perspective or asset-based program evaluation that looks at the positive elements in the program first and then seeks improvement when program processes are not productive and need to be improved. As such, these formative designs focus less on outcomes and goals and more on program processes and implementation. However, since goal achievement is the point of all programs, program processes and implementation are always examined in relation to goals and outcomes. No program evaluation is goal-free.

Formative evaluations are characterized by answering simple research questions such as the following: What progress is the program making? How is it functioning in its day-to-day operations? Formative evaluations also have simple and more informal types of data collection that could include the use of case records or data from a client information system on the characteristics of program participants, the motives that brought them to the service, and the services they received. A focus group could also be used to collect qualitative data on the initial experiences of the first participants in the program, as well as a survey or personal interviews with staff or administrators in the program, a consumer satisfaction survey about program services, or direct observation of the program in operation.

Good examples of formative studies are the program-monitoring and process evaluations illustrated in Chapter 7. McConnaughy looked at the case records of her clients to reveal trends in her clinical work, such as where the clients were referred from, their primary reason for service, the length of time in service, and the possible achievement of clinical goals. By examining these data, she achieved a better sense of how her interventions were implemented and of her approach to the clients she counseled. Irish interviewed volunteers who had been trained to make community presentations about Medicare prescription drug coverage, to determine how the presentations were being implemented, what the volunteers saw as the most effective ways to do their work, and how they felt their presentations were received by the seniors. Whittemore interviewed volunteers responsible for increasing community awareness of the need for health-care proxies. They reported on initial program implementation, the level of success of the presentations, their reactions to the training they received, and what they did to make the most effective presentations. Later, more summative impact assessment evaluations could be conducted to examine the effect of their presentations on the consumers of the service. Did the consumers solve their Medicare part D dilemmas or did consumers complete their health care proxies and understand more about end-of-life decisions. However, these beginning evaluations of what is actually happening in the program should not be undervalued.

Process evaluations are more exploratory, formative evaluation designs that describe and evaluate program process; usually qualitative data are collected on how the program is implemented. Formative designs can also be explanatory as in a monitoring study examining quantitative data and the statistical relationships between quantitative variables. For example, data from an employee assistance program's client information system could be examined to determine the relationship between a person's position in the university (e.g., faculty, secretarial, administrative, building maintenance staff) and the type of problem that brought them for service (e.g., personal counseling, marital counseling, substance abuse disorders, family caregiving issues, health issues, seeking services such as day care or nursing home service). These monitoring studies can be explanatory and answer important questions about the program. For example, they could tell program staff in a university employee assistance program that faculty members were using the program more for personal counseling than for referral to service such as day care or health services.

Survey Designs

A more summative survey of most of the consumers in the program is another type of design that is more formal and geared to the evaluation of some goals or outcomes in relation to consumers. A survey design may be the most typical type of program evaluation. In a survey, data collection usually takes place *ex post facto*, or "after the fact." In the case of program evaluation this means collecting data after consumers have received services to determine what they got out of the services.

A major consumer satisfaction questionnaire handed out to all 100 of a program's participants would be a good example of a survey design. A typical survey would not employ pre–post measurement and is an "after-only," or an *ex post facto*, design. It also is a "one-group-only" design, since program participants are not being compared to a group of similar people who did not attend the program. The simple survey design can be outlined at follows:

$$X \text{ (the program)} \quad O_1$$

People attend the program, X, then they are observed or measured once, O_1. They are given a questionnaire to fill out or they are interviewed after they attended the program.

A survey design and surveys in general have many strong points. Surveys generate sound, systematic data in an efficient manner on a range of consumer experiences from initially finding out about the program to what happened in the program and what the perceived effects of the program were. Surveys usually have some generalizability to many of the program participants, depending on the response rate.

Generalizability means that surveys can have *external validity*, which is the degree to which findings generalize to the larger population of program participants and programs in other settings. If a consumer satisfaction survey is conducted of all 100 program participants in a program and all 100 complete questionnaires about the program, the findings generalize to all program participants. Even without a 100% response rate, a survey usually gives a larger sense of how the program is doing for a broad number of consumers. The survey would be a next logical step after a formative study with personal interviews with only 10 consumers. External validity also refers to the generalizability of the evaluation to other programs in other settings. In evaluating a Head Start educational program for young children for instance, if a survey is conducted in a wide variety of different programs the study might generalize to those different programs and not just be an evaluation of one Head Start program.

Survey data can also be essential for program planning. Surveys are adaptable to different groups of consumers, staff, and program administrators in the program. They can ask about every aspect of a program experience: How did the consumers find out about the program? What happened in the initial contacts? Were people treated with professionalism and respect? What services did people receive? What outcomes do they think they achieved? Would they come again to this program for service?

The analysis of survey data can be straightforward, examining frequencies (e.g., do they think the program gave them more knowledge or made them feel better?) and relationships between variables (e.g., which groups of participants in terms of demographics, gender, age, and ethnicity rated the program more highly?). A survey can be easy to implement in the beginning stages of evaluation when less is known about the program. The feedback provided by surveys can supplement professionals' knowledge about the program. Surveys can provide a wide range of information from how the program is working to which goals are being achieved.

Surveys can be limited by a number of factors. A small sample from a larger number of program participants may not be generalizable to everyone's experience in the program. In a survey, program participants or staff would be asked "if they thought" change had occurred, change would not be measured directly as in a more summative pre–post study. Also, The survey does not approach assumptions of cause-and-effect relationships between the program intervention and program outcomes, since there is no control or contrast group as in experimental and quasi-experimental studies.

Surveys are usually weak in *internal validity*, or the degree to which it can be proven that it was the program alone that caused the improvement in people or an outcome to occur. For example, since the survey conducted is about the person's program experience, factors outside the program, such as improvements in a person's family, may have contributed to a positive result. An impact assessment or experimental study is considered better at internal validity because parts of the design control for these other factors that may have caused the outcome. Likewise, experimental studies are usually weak on external validity because they use small samples in one or two program settings that might not generalize to all program participants or to program participants in other settings where the program provides service.

Pre–Post Designs

Real change can be measured through a pre–post design, also called a "one-group-only pre–post design." This is the one design that people most equate with program evaluation and is the first design they think is needed in doing an evaluation or establishing a program's usefulness. The reason is that there is a simple logic about this design that appeals to people. Using just the knowledge component of the knowledge, behaviors, attitudes, skills, and status (KBASS) model, program participants come in with little knowledge. They attend the program and then they increase their knowledge. So the model looks like this:

$$O_1 \text{ X (the program)} \quad O_2$$

O_1 refers to observation 1, the pre-test or testing of participants' knowledge at time 1, before entering the program. Then they experience X, the program. O_2 refers to observation 2 at posttest, when knowledge is again tested after participating in the program. It is hoped that a person's knowledge is greater after taking part in the program and has increased by the end of the program. Thus:

$$O_2 - O_1 = \text{Net change}$$

Similarly, one could study changes in behavior, attitude, skills, and status in the same way. These variables can be measured before and after the program to determine the net change in behaviors, attitudes, skills, and status (KBASS) that result from participation in the program.

For example, if a psychiatric hospital had a psychoeducational group for relatives of persons with mental illness, knowledge about mental illness could be assessed before and after the program to see if the relative's knowledge of the person's mental illness had increased. Likewise, attitudes toward their relative could be assessed before and after the group meetings to see if their attitudes toward the relative had improved. The study could also assess if their stress level in caring for the relative improved as a result of the groups. This gives three major outcome areas that could be measured.

The pre–post study adds another dimension and depth to the survey, as change can be studied. The pre–post study represents a more summative design in that the program has developed to the point where clear indicators and measures of program outcomes and goals are agreed upon and are chosen as the main indicators of program success.

In the posttest, questions can be asked that are similar to those in the survey design about the participants' experiences in the program, such as their satisfaction and ratings about different parts of the program and their own assessment of what the program meant to them. In the pretest of a pre–post study, basic information, such as how people found about the program and reasons for attending and basic demographic information, is collected.

As an example, let's consider a program that provides counseling and informational services to adoptive parents after the adoption of a child. The service would be planned to assist the adoptive parents and support their parenting, to help them learn more about parenting in an experiential and didactic way, and to underscore and teach major issues in adoption. Following is an outline of a pre–post study of post-adoption groups for adoptive parents. It lists the types of data that would be collected in the pretest and the posttest.

PRETEST-ONLY MEASURES.

1. How did parents find out about the program?
2. Why did they choose to attend the groups? What types of adoption issues did they want information about? How much support did they want from other adoptive parents?
3. Their own experiences with adoption. Type of adoption, and difficult issues for them. Positive experiences with the adoption.
4. Characteristics of the adopted child
5. Demographic information about the family

PRETEST AND POSTTEST MEASURES. Here items were measured before and after the study to determine the net change.

1. Knowledge about adoption issues.
2. Feelings of support for themselves as adopted parents
3. Parenting skills
4. Understanding of children's behaviors
5. Interactions with the child and within the family
6. Relationship with the child's teachers and school environment

POSTTEST-ONLY MEASURES.

1. Overall ratings and satisfaction with the program
2. Ratings of the trainer or group facilitator
3. Ratings of individual group sessions and topics
4. Parents' perceptions of which parenting skills they used from the training
5. Ratings of how much adoptive parents supported each other inside and outside of the groups

Note that on the pretest basic demographic and background information regarding how the parents learned about the program and their experiences with adoption are recorded. Then a set of change measures in KBASS is measured on the pretest and posttest to determine the amount of change. The posttest has rating scales about the program and program process that are similar to the questions asked in a satisfaction survey. This is the basic protocol for data collection in a pre–post study.

There are some immediate concerns about and issues with pre–post studies. First and foremost is the possibility of a "ceiling effect," where participants already have the proper knowledge, behavior, attitude, skills, or status *before* the program starts. If this happens, there may be little room for progress or change by the end of the program—thus the term *ceiling effect*. For example, in a group program on the detection of breast cancer, the pretest showed that the women who attended were already quite knowledgeable about the disease, how to detect it early, and how the disease is treated. While this was valuable information in terms of program planning, so the program could shift to issues the women did not know about, it was impossible for this pre–post evaluation to show change in a positive direction since the respondents already knew the correct answers. The rationale and format of the program needed to change. But in terms of positive change, there was little chance of that. Generally speaking, in program evaluation, "ignorance is bliss" if it's on the pretest, because there is more room for improvement.

Sometimes there can be *a measurement* or *testing effect*. In this effect, program participants might score higher on the posttest solely because they took the pretest with the same items or questions. Taking the pretest may have helped them clarify their knowledge or they might have sought out the answers to particular questions and found the correct answers. In the example of the post-adoption services groups, the possibility of a testing effect can be measured by using a control group of adoptive parents who are similar to the group being given services. The control group can be given the test over the same time period of the program. If the control group shows increased scores on knowledge or parenting scales but did not attend the program, there may be a testing effect where just taking the pretest helped improve their scores. However, if those attending the program had increased scores over time and the control group did not show such increases, there is a greater possibility we can sssume that it was the post-adoption groups that caused the effect. It takes resources to find and recruit a similar group of adoptive parents to act as a control group. While a control group may be hard to locate, sometimes parents on a waiting list for the services can be used. Notice, too, that pre–post studies in themselves take extra time and resources to implement. The data collection needed can detract from the time given to provide the services, as parents will need to complete pre- and posttest forms. Nevertheless, pre–post studies are excellent ways of measuring change, which is, after all, why programs exist in the first place.

Impact Assessment Studies: Experimental and Quasi-Experimental Studies

Impact assessments are the most summative types of studies that determine ultimate program effects or outcomes. In impact assessments there are more assurances that the "program effect" or outcome was the result of the program, and only the program. The assumption is that the program effects would not have occurred if the participants had not attended the program or had used an alternate type of program. Obviously, these are the types of studies that funding sources like to see to assure their constituencies that funds spent on the program are being used wisely.

The ultimate impact assessment studies employ experimental and quasi-experimental designs. Experimental designs come the closest to determining that it was the program and not other factors such as factors in a person's life that caused the outcome. This reflects the concept of internal validity, which is based on another concept, *equivalence of groups*: if the groups of program participants are similar in all respects, except that one group received service and the other group did not receive service or that the groups received different forms of service, it can likely be concluded that the program alone caused the program effect or outcome. Equivalent groups are more safely assumed if program participants are *randomly assigned* to the groups from similar populations of people.

In the example of post-adoption services for parents, if two different forms of service were to be tested, parents would be randomly assigned to one of two service groups and maybe a third control group who would have no service. Contrast groups are a more ethical alternative. Parents could be randomly assigned to two contrast groups or two different forms of service and the control group where no service is given might not be used. In the case of contrast groups, the first parent entering the program would be assigned to a didactic, lecture-discussions group. The second parent would be assigned to a more experiential group experience where the experiences of adoptive parents would help set the agenda. The third parent would be assigned to the didactic group, and the fourth to the experiential group, etc. Assuming that the parents were similar, for example, that all had adopted children who were from 2 to 4 years of age, and assuming they were recruited from similar neighborhoods, etc., the two groups may be *equivalent* in many, if not all, respects, except that group 1 had didactic learning and group 2 had experiential learning. Thus the only thing that might differ is the type of service they received.

Most experimental designs test for this equivalence in the groups by comparing the characteristics of one group with the other in terms of family background, demographics, and type of adoption experience. In theory, if the groups are equivalent and the program effects are being measured by comparing pretest and posttest scores, it can be determined which group had the larger net changes in awareness of adoption issues, child behaviors, use of outside resources, and interaction with teachers.

A diagram of the classic experiment is shown below:

Experimental Group	R	O1	X (the program)	O2
Control Group	R	O1	__ (no program)	O2
Contrast Group	R	O1	X1 (different form of program)	O2

In this diagram, R stands for random assignment to the different groups, O_1 represents the pretest, and O_2 represents the posttest. The second group, the control group, would receive no intervention. In the adoptive-parents program, adoptive parents waiting to enter the program might be used as a control group and studied over the same period of time that the other groups are studied and the results from this no-treatment group would be compared with those for the two intervention groups. At the end of that period of time, to be ethical, the parents receiving no service could enter the program and receive service so they don't miss out on the program. In the contrast group, the two different forms of service would be compared to see which intervention produced a better result. Again, the posttest result would be subtracted from the pretest result to study the net change.

The ethical issues of random assignment of potential program participants to a control group of no treatment is rather obvious. However, random assignment to different forms of intervention may also cause ethical problems.

Random assignment determines whether the consumer receives program A or program B; the decision is not made by a professional in terms of which form of service the consumer could merit from best. For example, if experiential program groups are deemed to be the best form of post-adoption service for parents struggling with raising adopted children, a professional might want adoptive parents with more parenting issues to attend those groups. If this happened, the characteristics of the experiential group might differ greatly from those of the contrast group, especially in terms of their parenting experiences, and the groups might not be non-equivalent, but the ethical commitment to serve consumers was maintained.

Quasi-experimental designs have the characteristics of experimental design and impact assessment studies with one important feature left out: there is no random assignment of program participants to different groups. *Randomization* means assignment by chance to different forms of intervention or to no intervention. Randomization helps ensure that there are equivalent groups. When random assignment is not used, the groups could be different.

One way that researchers try to make equivalent groups is through *matching*: for a group of participants in the program, the researcher tries to consciously find a control or contrast group that has similar characteristics. Individual participants might be matched by gender, age, ethnicity, income, level of service needed, or initial problems. Matching often results in undermatching. So, for instance, the ages and gender might be similar, but the incomes could differ among the various groups. If this happens, all is not lost. There are statistical procedures that can control for undermatching so if one group has a higher income, for instance, statistics can help control for the effects that a higher income can have on one group.

If matching is not done, the researcher could assign people to different groups, and let the chips fall where they may. Usually program professionals decide which type of program group a person should be assigned to, on the basis of some professional diagnosis or diagnostic criteria or hunch about which program would work better for which person. This could be thought of as a "naturalistic" experiment. However, in terms of experimental design, this represents a selection bias in terms of who was chosen for the program, and the comparison groups of two different forms of the program would probably be groups with different characteristics.

The professional practice of program staff—good professional practice—can often subvert randomization. Professional staff members are trained to make judgments that certain people are better candidates for the program or for a particular form of the program. Note that "subversion" of the experiment is clearly the word of the researcher committed to experimental design. On the basis of their expertise and experience, program staff feel that they can determine who the program can best benefit. Clearly, the resulting groups would be non-equivalent groups. For example, in a program for the homeless, those without any families may be judged to need the program more quickly, and they might be overrepresented in the experimental or program group.

Non-equivalent groups can be a problem in impact assessments that assess the overall outcome or effect. For example, in a program training medical students to communicate with and relate to patients' families, age could be a factor in interpersonal relationships and communication. Older medical students returning to school from other careers might be more able to relate to patients' families and communicate information about a serious medical condition than younger students. If there were more older students in the training program than in a control group and age contributed to better communication, the program could show positive outcomes that were more the result of the group being older than the training itself. Statistics can help here. By statistically controlling for age, it can be determined whether or not the program achieved results for both older and younger medical students. If this is true, it can be established that the program, rather then the age of the medical students, caused the positive outcomes of increased communication with patients' families.

Threats to Internal Validity—Opportunities for Growth in Impact Assessment Studies

Impact assessment studies employing experimental designs are stronger at resolving issues in internal validity. The concept of internal validity means that it was the program and the program alone that caused the effect. These threats to internal validity, which experimental studies help resolve, were described and developed in a classic work by Stanley and Campbell (1966). Especially in quasi- or non-experimental designs, the threats suggest the possibility that something other than the program or treatment caused the effect.

For some, experimental designs are considered the only form of evaluation worth their salt. Furthermore, if experimental designs have threats that can weaken their value, the value of data from more formative studies such as program monitoring and process evaluations can be diminished even more in the eyes of those who only believe in experimental design. Creative program development and the useful data produced from process and program-monitoring studies that is fed back into program development should not be devalued because of more summative experimental designs may be valued.

In presenting threats to internal validity, a novel approach is presented here. Why not consider these "threats" to internal validity as "opportunities for growth" in terms of awareness of how programs develop and are planned. Each opportunity for growth has a lot to say about the nature of programs, how they operate, how they develop, and what is involved in evaluating programs. The opportunities for growth described here are selection bias, program attrition or experimental mortality, outside events or history, maturation or the passage of time, testing, instrumentation, and Hawthorne and placebo effects.

Selection Bias

Programs are initiated, they grow, and develop. Health and social work professionals design methods for outreach and recruitment to try and *select* people who could benefit the most from the program. Program participants choose the programs from which they think they can benefit and are motivated to attend. Those who are selected or enrolled in the program can be very different from those who are not selected. Those who are motivated to attend the program can be very different from those who are not motivated. For example, in group work in social work, group workers are encouraged to do preplanning, which often involves interviewing people to determine their compatibility with and need for a certain group program. This is the traditional way in which programs develop, and should be described fully in an evaluation.

Experimental designs control for a selection bias through random assignment. As program participants are recruited and enrolled in a program, if they are randomly assigned to different forms of treatment, there is a greater likelihood that the groups receiving different treatments will be similar. If a control group is used and some people are randomly assigned to no treatment or program, that group should also have equivalent characteristics. As mentioned before, a control group could be recruited from a group of potential consumers waiting for service, rather then withholding treatment from the group.

Use of a contrast group of people receiving a second form of the program who are recruited in the same way as the experimental group would help control a selection bias even more, because that group was most likely recruited in the same way as the experimental group. Recruitment of a control group could differ because they are not being promised services right away. So a contrast group with random assignment should make for equivalent groups.

The good news is that a selection bias can be tested by comparing factors such as demographic characteristics in the experimental group, a contrast group, and a control group to see if the groups have similar demographic characteristics. Hopefully, the characteristics of an experimental group, a contrast group, and a control group will be similar, and the groups will be equivalent.

The "opportunity for growth" in a possible selection bias, is recognizing and describing how people are selected for programs and why professionals make decisions about who should get the service. These are important parts of a program and should be described to see how selection is affecting the program. Knowledge from formative evaluations about why people select programs and how professionals are making decisions are important program variables. Once groups are established, regardless of whether they are randomly assigned or not, they can be tested to see if the groups are equivalent. Describing how consumers are recruited and selected is an important part of describing the program, and helps prevent the black-box phenomenon and allows for future replications of the program.

Program Attrition or Experimental Mortality

A pervasive characteristic of most programs is that people drop out or do not complete the program for a variety of reasons. Group workers often say, "people vote with their feet." A high dropout rate can be an indicator that consumers are not connecting to the program as it is currently designed. Factors such as not having adequate child care or the time of the day when the program is offered could affect program participation. In experimental studies, "dropping out" can be referred to as "program attrition" or "experimental mortality" (which does not mean programs or experimental designs are killing people). In terms of experimental design, if people have dropped out of the program, the group that received the program or intervention could wind up being very different at the end of the program from the group that started out in the program. If an experimental group has a significant dropout rate but a control group does not, then the characteristics of those who completed the program would probably not be similar or equivalent to the characteristics of the control group. If two different forms of the program are compared and there is a high dropout rate in one group during the program, the groups might not be equivalent at the end of the program. If the dropout rate is similar in both program groups, there is a better chance that the groups may be equivalent by the end of the program. In all cases, the researcher compares the characteristics of the groups to see how equivalent or non-equivalent they are on the basis of characteristics such as gender, ethnicity, income, and types of help needed.

The opportunity for growth in terms of experimental mortality is to realize how important the attrition rate is in *all* programs. How many people are dropping out and why did they drop out? In the early stages of program development, attrition rates tell how well the program is connecting with the target population. All programs need to track the dropout or attrition rates. Sadly, this type of data is often missing because of difficulties following up with people who have left the program. Yet, it is crucial data, both in formative evaluations and in impact assessment studies. In formative evaluation, describing who dropped out and why they dropped out an tell you a lot about program processes.

Outside Events or "History"

Outside events, or factors outside the program, can contribute to program outcomes and change in program participants. In the experimental literature, outside events are referred to as "history." Suppose program participants in the experimental group had much more support from their families, but the control or a contrast group had no significant family support. Clearly, family support rather than the program could have created a positive effect in the experimental group, whereas the contrast or control group did not have a positive effect because they had no or lower levels of family support. Likewise, suppose some consumers in the experimental group found services outside of the program that really helped them. If the consumers were not referred to these services through the program, these outside events could have caused the outcome as much as the program did.

In a special high school program to reinforce the dangers of smoking to adolescents, some students in the program could be learning this information in the regular health classes of one teacher while students in another teacher's class might not be getting information on the dangers of smoking. So was it the presentations in the special program or the information given in their health classes that caused the effect? In establishing a program in which community residents were supposed to complete advance directives about health-care decisions at the end of life (see Chapter 7), what if one community had a newspaper that ran many articles on health-care decisions and the Terri Schiavo case that showed the problems of not having advance directives, while in another community the newspapers did not run articles about end-of-life health-care decisions. Clearly, this outside event could have created a positive outcome as much as the program the residents were enrolled in.

Program evaluation needs to be sensitized to events outside the program that can help or hinder the program in achieving its objectives. In theory, experimental design can control for outside events if the events are experienced in a similar amount and fashion in both the experimental and control group or a contrast group. Since it is difficult to know if an evaluator is controlling for these outside events, they should be studied as a part of the evaluation to see their effect in comparison to the program's effect. Thus collecting data on variables such as additional services received outside the program or the level of family support should be part of the evaluation. In that way, the researcher can determine if "history" or "outside events" were not equivalent in the experimental, contrast, or control group.

The opportunity for growth here is the need for program planners and evaluators to speculate on which types of outside factors could be related to achieving program goals. These outside events should be conceptualized and studied in all evaluations, both formative and summative, to determine the effects of outside factors on the program. Social work and health professionals can develop a list of outside events that could be affecting the program meeting its goals based on their experience from individual cases in their practice. Then these events could be studied in the evaluation be it a formative evaluation or a summative, impact assessment study.

Maturation

Maturation means that program participants may "mature" or change over periods of time and the changes may not be directly attributable to the program. For example, it is known that a certain group of adolescents who get in trouble with the law "age out," or mature out of delinquent behavior (Weiss, 1998, p. 184). In evaluating a program to reduce delinquent behavior, the program might appear to be effective as delinquency is reduced from the pretest to the posttest. However, maturation may be the cause, not the program. A control group or a contrast group would control for maturation; if all groups were the same ages. If maturation is occurring it should occur in both groups and the net change in the different groups should show what additional change was produced from the program. If the program is effective at all, the program groups should have a higher overall or net change than a control group or a comparison group, even if maturation is occurring in both groups.

In a group counseling program to help overcome the trauma that people experienced on 9/11, maturation could definitely be an issue. It is possible that as time elapses from the trauma of 9/11, the effects of trauma could be reduced simply by the passage of time. If the participants were randomly assigned to two different forms of group experience the researcher could assess net change in the reduction of trauma to see which intervention was more effective, even if maturation or time was healing the trauma. In addition, a control group of people on the waiting list for the program could help assess the net change in program versus no program. So, even if the passage of time was reducing the trauma in both the experimental and control groups, the net change for those who attended the program should be higher than for those who did not attend the program. If the reduced trauma found in the control group is at the same level as the experimental group, then the reduced trauma could have been caused by the passage of time as people recovered from the trauma of 9/11.

The growth experience around maturation is appreciation of the fact that people change even without programs to help them change. Thinking about change in program participants and how and why it is happening is the legacy of maturation for program planners, evaluators, and practitioners.

Testing and Instrumentation

As discussed in pre–post designs, sometimes just taking the pretest or being studied before the program can affect people's responses and scores on the posttest. People simply may score higher on a second testing in the posttest once they have taken the pretest. The pretesting may make program participants more aware of the goals that the program planners would like people to achieve and the participants might want to please program planners or practitioners by acting as though they have achieved the goals of the program. Participants may also figure out the "correct" responses at the end of the program or they may have sought out the correct answers to knowledge-type questions. If a testing effect is occurring, then the control or contrast group should show as much improvement as the experimental or program group. If the experimental or program group has a higher net change than that of the control or comparison group, then the program can be judged to be effective because the pretesting took place in all three groups.

There may also be interactions between the program and the pretest. The pretest may make people more amenable to change in the program by highlighting and helping people focus on the kinds of interventions and changes being sought. Participants taking the pretest may do better in the program. If an interaction between the pretest and the program is occurring, it should occur in both the experimental and a comparison program group. If net change in the experimental group is larger than net change in a comparison group, the program may be effective even if a testing effect is operating.

The growth opportunity for testing is the realization that test-taking and measurement can affect future tests and measures. Tests and measures that have not shown a testing effect when used in previous studies should be considered better than tests that have not been examined for a testing effect.

Just as a testing effect can be present in evaluating a program, a change in instruments or the way in which data are collected could occur from the pretest to the posttest; this is called "instrumentation." By asking the same question in the same way or administering a test in the same way and using the same instruments in the pretest and the posttest, the effects of instrumentation can be avoided. If the people in the experimental group, the control group, and a contrast group are tested in the same way, instrumentation may not be an issue. If one group, say, a control group, is tested in a different way because no program was attended, then instrumentation or a difference in measurement could have occurred.

Instrumentation highlights the importance of measuring outcomes and collecting data consistently in program evaluation. The better the process of instrumentation, (i.e., clearly specifying the data to be collected and specifying how the data are collected) is described in the research, the more assurance that effects of instrumentation are not occurring.

Hawthorne and Placebo Effects

There are two threats to internal validity that relate to the way in which the program or treatment and research is presented to program participants. Hawthorne effects and placebo effects are produced by the experiments themselves.

In a *Hawthorne effect*, just being interviewed or observed can cause a positive effect by paying attention to subjects or by the program participants trying to please the researcher or the professional involved with the program. Program participants may react differently because they are being studied. If a Hawthorne effect is present, it should be present in all three groups; they are all being studied, and net change can still be assessed to see if the experimental group did better.

The *placebo effect* is the psychological impact of program participants thinking that they are receiving the effective treatment—this in itself can cause an effect. In medical-research testing of a drug, people are given a "sugar pill," or a pill without the drug. This is called a "single-blind" study. If the researchers and program staff also do not know whether the person is receiving the drug or a placebo the study is a "double-blind" study.

In program evaluation, creating a "sugar-pill program" is not thought to be useful and has unethical implications of deception. A placebo effect could be controlled for by use of a comparison group if it was really thought by the program participants and the professionals in the program that the comparison group would achieve strong results. In that case, both groups could experience a placebo effect and the net change between the experimental group and the contrast group would tell which program model was more effective.

Both a Hawthorne effect and a placebo effect can be uncovered by experimental debriefing at the completion of the program. Program participants are asked how being tested may have affected them, if they knew about a contrast group, and whether they thought they were in the group in which the most improvement was suspected. They could be asked if they may have inflated their scores because they were being studied or to please program professionals or researchers.

The opportunity for growth in the Hawthorne and placebo effect is to consider how participation in the research is presented to and effects program participants in *all* evaluation studies, in formative studies and in more summative studies. Did participants want to show positive results that were not there? Were they excited about the program and its potential to help them? Over the past years, the strength of the placebo effect has been found to be especially strong. In fact, a placebo effect may be sought by professionals who want consumers to experience change from the program. While this presents problems in terms of internal validity, programs that truly engage participants and give them hope and enthusiasm about achieving outcomes are programs that may be more valuable and successful. In formative evaluations the question of how the program was presented to people is a key question. How *are* the program and the research being presented? Are people being engaged in this program or not? These questions can be answered through qualitative interviews with program participants, which can be a major part of formative studies. In experimental and impact assessment studies, these qualitative interviews conducted after the experimental study are simply termed "experimental debriefing."

Summary of Opportunities for Growth

Consideration of threats to internal validity has shown the value of experimental design in relieving some of these threats through the use of equivalent control and contrast groups. This comparative framework, for example, thinking about different forms of service and their effect, or different levels and amounts of service and their effect, is a useful way to plan and evaluate all programs. The concepts of experimental design can be useful in thinking about programs and professional practice more generally because all programs and practice processes are about assessing changes and trying to cause positive and desireable consequences – in other words – program gaols.

Likewise, by considering these threats as opportunities for growth, positive value is placed on consideration of these threats to internal validity, even in formative evaluation designs. A number of principles based on these opportunities for growth are salient for all types of program evaluation:

1. Pay attention to how people are selected for the program.
2. Study factors outside the program that could affect program success or failure.
3. Track program attrition, people who drop out of the program, their characteristics, and especially why they left the program.
4. Be aware that people can change because time has elapsed or people mature in or out of certain conditions
5. Pay attention to the effect of pretesting in pre–post and experimental designs, and be observant as to how data are collected in both the pretest and the posttest.
6. Pay attention to how the program is presented to people, and get qualitative data on their feelings about the program and the research and whether they felt the program was supposed to be successful in the minds of the researchers or program staff.

Selecting a Data Collection Strategy: Deciding How to Collect Data

An essential part of the research design or plan is deciding how to collect data. Planning for the collection of data should be initiated when an evaluation study is first considered. There are a limited number of choices for collecting data. The major types of data collection are the questionnaire, personal interview, telephone interviews, focus group, direct observation, and use of secondary data. The type of data collection is based on the type of data being sought—structured, quantitative data, or in-depth qualitative data. Self-administered mailed, handed-out, and Internet questionnaires are best for structured data; personal interviews, focus groups, and direct observation are best for collecting in-depth qualitative data. Telephone interviews and the in-person administration of a questionnaire lie somewhere in between. Usually in a particular study, one or at most two data collection possibilities make sense.

In the following section, each type of data collection procedures will be described along with their advantages and disadvantages.

Questionnaires

A *questionnaire* is an instrument with mostly closed-ended questions and Likert and other types of summated scales. A questionnaire is usually mailed or handed out, sent out on the Internet, or completed within a group. In doing a survey over the Internet a package such as Survey Monkey (www.surveymonkey.com) is helpful, as a questionnaire can be constructed using various formats. It is especially helpful when a list of e-mail addresses can be provided for the survey's recipients.

ADVANTAGES OF QUESTIONNAIRES

1. Questionnaires are inexpensive to administer and involve just copying the questionnaire and mailing or handing it out, or filling it out in a group context.
2. Questionnaires more typically use close-ended questions, "yes–no," "degree of," and rating scales. The data from questionnaires are structured and can be more easily analyzed quantitatively into percentages, averages, etc., in a straightforward manner through computer analysis.
3. Questionnaires can produce normative data for programs on consumer satisfaction and are the most common way for accountability agencies to think of evaluation.
4. Because questionnaires need to have great clarity in their wording, they should be easier to complete for the respondent than a personal interview.
5. There are no interactional effects between interviewer and interviewee if the questionnaire is mailed or handed out.

DISADVANTAGES OF QUESTIONNAIRES

1. The largest disadvantage of questionnaires is the low return rate. Return rates of 10%–30% are not unheard of, and even if a 45% to 65% return rate is achieved, this means that data on 35% to 55% of those surveyed are not available. Additional follow-up is often needed to achieve an acceptable return rate. The response rate can also be improved by recruiting a group of consumers or staff and having them complete the questionnaire in a group context. Or, at the end of a group program, consumers can be given the time to complete the questionnaire at the

end of the last group session and thus would not need to mail or bring the questionnaire back to the program. Any confusion about completing the questionnaire or what certain questions mean can be clarified in the group.

2. Questionnaires cannot be used for qualitative research when thick, rich descriptions of peoples' experiences in the program are needed. Responses to open-ended questions in a questionnaire will not yield comprehensive rich, descriptive data. There is no personal interaction and no one to probe or ask people to expand their answers. Sometimes good qualitative data from questions such as "What was the most useful thing the program did for you?" might yield answers from 30%–40% of those completing the questionnaire if consumers or staff were especially involved in participating in the program. But, the data obtained would not be in-depth qualitative data in the form of thick, rich descriptions which could only be produced if someone administers the questionnaire or if personal interviews or phone interviews are used.

3. Questions and directions must be very clear and simple in a questionnaire, since no interviewer is there to provide clarification or directions.

4. Questionnaires are usually more productive with literate, knowledgeable, motivated respondents with fewer vision, physical, emotional, or developmental disabilities. In some cases, where respondents have literacy, vision or disabilities issues, the questionnaire should be administered in-person rather than being mailed, handed-out, or sent on the internet.

Personal Interviews

A *personal interview* is an in-person contact in which the interviewer asks questions directly of the respondent.

ADVANTAGES OF A PERSONAL INTERVIEW

1. Personal interviews are excellent for collecting rich, descriptive data because open-ended questions can be asked and the interviewer can probe for a depth of response by asking the respondent to provide detailed information. Questions such as "Is there anything else?" or "Can you tell me more about that?" are useful.

2. Personal interviews are the most flexible form of data collection. Questions can be rephrased if they are unclear, and close-ended questions and structured data can also be collected. Open-ended,

checklist-type, and scale items can be asked at the same interview in which qualitative data are collected.

3. Personal interviews enable interviewers to record respondents' affect, mood, and body language, which might reveal a lot about their experiences with the program.

4. Personal interviews have a higher response rate than that for questionnaires because interviewers make arrangements to interview people rather than just handing–out or mailing a questionnaire.

DISADVANTAGES OF A PERSONAL INTERVIEW

1. This is an expensive form of data collection as the interviewer must be paid for setting up the interview. There may also be travel costs, and and an interviewer needs to be paid to conduct the interview.

2. If detailed qualitative responses are being collected and tape-recorded, the creation of a transcript of qualitative data is required for analyzing the data which can be a major cost. Analysis of trends from qualitative data is generally more costly and complex than quantitative analysis of structured data.

3. In the personal interview there can be interactional effects of the interviewer "putting words" into the respondent's mouth. This can be mitigated by training interviewers how to ask questions and how to ask neutral probes (e.g., "anything else?" *not* "yes, it sounds like the program really helped you").

Telephone Interviews

Telephone interviews have some of the advantages of both the questionnaire and the personal interview. The response rate is better than with a question-naire. The cost can be lower because there are no travel costs for the interviewer, and the personal interaction is similar to that in a personal interview. Telephone interviews can obtain both qualitative data from open-ended ques-tions and structured data through close-ended and structured questions such as rating scales. Respondents must have a telephone and be accessible for an interview at certain times. Also, telephone interviews might not be completed if the respondent is pulled away from the phone.

Focus Groups

Focus groups have enjoyed increasing popularity as a means of collecting data (see Krueger & Casey, 2008). A *focus group* is a group of 6 to 12 people who have had a similar experience. This could be a group of consumers who have been in the program, or staff members who have provided service in the program. Focus groups can be used at every stage in program evaluation. In assessing the need for the program, potential consumers can be asked about their needs and different program models to help them, as is done in market research when people are asked about new products in a focus group. More traditionally, these groups are conducted in the initial phases of the program to monitor program implementation. However, focus groups can also be used later on toward the end of the program to assess program processes and goals.

In the methodology of focus groups, group participants are asked a series of not more than 10 topics or open-ended questions. A researcher is the group leader who convenes the group and asks the questions and probes answers by asking for more detailed answers. The group leader needs to establish rapport and create a supportive environment for discussions. A second research-recorder is often present to record responses, and this person may also be trained to advance the discussion. Peoples' comments in focus groups are usually tape recorded. Later the taped recordings are transcribed and the transcripts are analyzed using the qualitative analysis techniques described in Chapter 9. The researcher looks for common trends and themes. In addition, the field notes of the recorder and the group leader should be written up. Focus groups are especially good for obtaining qualitative descriptive data, as the interaction allows for probing for detailed responses. In addition, usually at the end of the group, quantitative or structured data can be collected by handing out rating forms on the program process and how consumers or staff would rate the relative success of the program in relation to the program goals.

The interactional effects in focus groups can affect the process. The researcher-group leader needs to avoid affecting the types of data by asking probes in a neutral manner. "Snowballing" in a group refers to the group process of moving in one particular direction. For instance, when asked about the value of the program, consumers may provide a lot of detail about the positive elements in the program. When all of these positive parts of the program are discussed by participants the leader needs to make sure that other elements of the program are included, and needs to direct the discussion toward the limitations and negative points of the program. The group leader can also encourage the quieter persons in the group to participate and may even conduct individual interviews with the quiet group members after the focus group session.

As with personal interviews that collect a lot of qualitative data, the data from focus groups take an investment of time to analyze the qualitative data and look for trends in the data. Sometimes, however, focus groups are not part of an intensive research study. The group experience itself may be valued, and intensive qualitative analysis is not conducted on the data as it should be in social research and formal program evaluation. Often a focus group can be just a simple exercise to get consumers' impressions of the program. However, if the groups are carefully planned and the data are thoroughly analyzed, focus groups can be a significant way to assess beginning and more developed program efforts and can provide great data for program-planning based on the real experiences of consumers and staff.

Direct Observation

Direct observation of the program is the most naturalistic form of data collection and is a less structured form of data collection. While a questionnaire or a personal interview is a relatively contrived situation in which preconceived questions are asked, direct observation of the program might entail fewer preconceived notions about the program. Direct observation is especially good in process evaluations that thoroughly describe how the program operates and how consumers are responding to it.

As an example, a researcher could observe the processes in a group program designed to increase the socialization of the elderly in a senior center. The program design and rationale in the program description would indicate how the program is designed to increase socialization and what areas of socialization the program is meant to improve. As the researcher engages in direct observation of the program he or she would take copious notes on program processes and possible outcomes. Then the researcher would use qualitative analysis of the notes (outlined in Chapter 9) to compare the themes in the notes to the areas originally outlined in the program description and design to determine how the program is being implemented. Both program process and possible effects on the socialization of the seniors could then be determined.

Direct observation is sometimes more structured and quantitative. For example, in a group program for parents who have abused their children the researcher could observe parent–child interactions. The researcher could train a number of observers to develop rules for what constitutes an interaction between parent and child. Rules could also be set up for what constitutes a positive or a negative interaction. If two independent observers could eventually make reliable judgments about negative versus positive interactions, then it could be determined how many parent–child interactions there are, and whether the number of positive interactions is increasing and the number of negative or abusive interactions decreasing. In addition to these structured observations, the observers could take process notes on their observations of parent–child interactions and the interventions and whether the parents are engaging in the interventions. This more traditional observational study provides rich, descriptive data, especially when programs are in their formative stages of development in a process evaluation study.

Use of Secondary Data

Some evaluation studies can be conducted without collecting original data. Program data could be the data required for accountability by funding sources or it could be the data that direct-service professionals routinely collect as part of professional and agency-based accountability. Data could also be the academic records of students in a school-based program or court records of young offenders, or hospital records of patients who entered the hospital with a particular diagnosis.

Secondary data are also referred to as "available data." This type of data has great appeal because no funds are needed to collect,the data and the only cost may be for data analysis. This use of case-record databases has also been referred to as "data-mining," as the data that help in evaluating the program are "mined" from the records and available from program documents. Epstein (2010) describes how such data-mining can answer practical questions about the program and the practices and policies of the program.

There are a number of limitations to secondary data. The evaluative questions that can be answered are limited to the data in the case records or program documents. If case data are to be analyzed, rather than a questionnaire, the researcher needs to develop a data collection form to take the data from the record. These data can then be fed into the computer for data analysis.

Problems with the reliability of case records are another limitation of secondary data. The lack of reliability may come from a number of factors:

1. Case records and "paper work" may not be the most important priority of health and human-services professionals. Often some of the data are incomplete or missing or forms are not filled out. Often there are serious gaps in the data.
2. The data in case records are sometimes colored by the administrative and practice content in which the information is collected. For example, health and social work professionals may describe a consumer in a certain way or select presenting problems or a diagnosis that makes the consumer eligible for a certain program or service.

3. Secondary and case-record data are not usually screened for consistency and comprehensiveness, so there are no checks against unreliable and missing data with procedures such as inter-rater reliability, where two researchers read the same case record to determine if they agree that certain characteristics are present in a particular case.

Because of the difficulties in developing complete and comprehensive secondary data, use of secondary data is best seen as one minor method for analyzing data about a program. Case records could be used in comprehensive evaluation in which the major data collection is based on personal interviews with consumers and staff. For example, to evaluate a school counseling program, interviews with students who attended the program might be the primary data, which could be supplemented by students' records on their academics and behavior in school.

Given these caveats, analyzing the data available from program records should not be dismissed. Case-record data can be useful in beginning evaluations to determine what the program has been doing. More important, secondary data are also part and parcel of monitoring studies that answer simple research questions such as who uses the service and what do they seem to be getting out of the service. Finally, the lower cost associated with available data or case-record data is a huge argument in favor of using secondary data.

An example of the types of data that might be found in case records is presented in the following example of the case records from a university-based employee assistance program.

Example of the Use of Case Records in Monitoring a University
Employee Assistance Program

The case record form below is from a university-based employee assistance program (EAP). The case-record data include a number of important variables and fields that are crucial for accountability purposes to determine who the program is serving and why employees are coming in for service. This set of monitoring data is especially useful in the beginning stages of the program as it can be used to see if there is program fidelity and that the program is staying faithful to its plan. Eventually these monitoring data can be supplemented by questionnaires given to consumers in order to determine their experiences with the program.

The data (see Client Information Form below) include the following:

A. *Consumer data:* Who are the program consumers? Are they employees, their spouses, or family members? Who are they in terms of age, gender, marital status, and race? Are they administrators or higher education officers, faculty, or clerical or custodial staff? Are they supervisors? Are they employed full- or part-time? How long have they been employed at the university?

B. *Program data:* When did they first come into the program? Was the initial contact in person or by telephone? Who referred them for services, or were they self-referred? What was the reason for contact? What was the problem that brought them to the EAP (financial, housing, personal adjustment issues, job-related stress, family problems, alcohol abuse)? What services were to be provided by the EAP? Were referrals made to other programs or agencies?

Simple data analysis of the numbers and percentage of employees who used the EAP and why they came for service can be analyzed monthly, semi-annually, and annually to determine trends in consumers and their problems. For example, how many faculty members are being served? How long have consumers been employed at the university? Did they come because another employee or a supervisor requested them to come? What problems did they have that required service? What was the primary problem? The simple numbers and percentages can be compared to population data for the university community, the target population, to determine which groups are being served. Relationships between variables in the data set can then be examined. For example, do different employees (faculty, administrators, or secretarial or maintenance staff) come to the EAP for different kinds of problems? Is employees' age, gender, or ethnicity related to how employees use the program?

Serious issues in terms of equal access to services and the possibility of "stigmatized" services are at stake. For instance, is the program only being used for substance abuse services rather than personal counseling? Are only secretarial and maintenance staff using the program, and are they using the program for different reasons than those of faculty and administrative staff?

This is only part of the data originating from case records that a monitoring study can provide. Ultimately, an employee satisfaction form developed by the program can also become part of the whole program evaluation. The employee satisfaction questionnaire focuses more on program interventions once employees came to the program and outcomes that employees thought they achieved.

The actual client information form for an employee in the EAP is presented below. Notice that the form is precoded; categories are given numbers (example: type of contact, 1 = in person, 2 = telephone). This makes it easier for computer analysis and statistical analysis of these monitoring study data.

CLIENT INFORMATION FORM

1. Date of first contact: _____/_____/_____
   Month Day   Year

2. Type of contact: _____ (1) in person _____(2) telephone

3. Is the client (check one)

   ____ (1) an employee

   ____ (2) an employee's spouse

   ____ (3) an employee's child

   ____ (4) another relative

   ____ (5) other (list): _____

4. Age: ____

5. Gender: ____ (1) male ____ (2) female

6. Marital status:

   ____ (1) Married

   ____ (2) Single

   ____ (3) Divorced/separated

   ____ (4) Widowed

7. Race:

   ____ (1) White, non-Hispanic

   ____ (2) Black, non-Hispanic

   ____ (3) White, Hispanic

   ____ (4) Asian

   ____ (5) Other (list): _____

8. Employee's job classification:

   ____ (1) Administrative, higher education officer

   ____ (2) Faculty

   ____ (3) Secretarial/clerical

   ____ (4) Custodial/maintenance

   ____ (5) Other (list): _____

9. Employee is ____ (1) a supervisor ____ (2) non-supervisor

10. Employment status: ____ (1) full-time ____ (2) part-time

11. Number of years employed at the university: ____

CONTACT INFORMATION

12. Primary referral source (check one):

    ____ (1) Self

    ____ (2) Other employee

    ____ (3) Supervisor

    ____ (4) Union

    ____ (5) Family

    ____ (6) Other (list): _____

13. Reason for contact (check one):

    _____ (1) Information and/or referral

    _____ (2) Problem assessment and service

    _____ (3) Consultation to supervisor or management

    _____ (4) Other (list): _____

14. Service needs (check all that apply):

         _____ (1) Financial
         _____ (2) Legal/consumer
         _____ (3) Housing
         _____ (4) Social services
         _____ (5) Personal adjustment
         _____ (6) Mental illness
         _____ (7) Job-related stress
         _____ (8) Alcohol abuse
         _____ (9) Substance abuse
         _____(10) Interpersonal
         _____(11) Couples/family
         _____(12) Physical health
         _____(13) Physical/sexual Abuse
         _____(14) Alcohol abuse in family/significant other
         _____(15) Substance abuse in family/significant other
         _____(16) Other (list): _____

15. Number of *primary* problem from above list: _____

16. Services to be provided at the employee assistance program (check all that apply):

         _____ (1) Information
         _____ (2) Individual
         _____ (3) Couple/family
         _____ (4) Group
         _____ (5) Advocacy

17. Referrals made to other agencies (check all that apply):

         _____ (1) Financial
         _____ (2) Legal
         _____ (3) Social services
         _____ (4) Educational
         _____ (5) Housing
         _____ (6) Health care
         _____ (7) Mental health
         _____ (8) Family
         _____ (9) Inpatient
         _____ (10) Self-help
         _____ (11) Union
         _____ (12) Other: list_____

Constructing the Data Collection Instrument

After deciding how to collect data, the next step in the plan or research design is the actual construction of the data collection instrument. Be it a personal interview, a questionnaire, a focus group, guidelines for direct observation, or a form to obtain data from case records, an instrument needs to be constructed and questions need to be formulated. The data collection instrument comes out of the initial conceptualization of the program processes and/or goals defined in the program description and evaluation plan. If a consumer is interviewed, the questionnaire or personal interview most likely contains questions about the background and demographic characteristics of the consumer, their experience of the program, and the program outcomes.

Constructing a questionnaire or interview with clear questions and directions is really an art form. At one time or another, most people have experienced incomprehensible questionnaires that are confusing and frustrating to read, and they probably landed in the garbage. If the wording and directions are clear and the questionnaire is formatted nicely, however, it is easier to complete. The questionnaire or interview should not have the respondent reaching for Advil; a "no-Advil" questionnaire is the ideal. Along these lines, a questionnaire usually undergoes many drafts.

When the data collection instrument is in order, *the most important principle is the pretest*. This means trying it out with someone who is a potential respondent (for instance, a consumer who used the program). If that is not possible, it can be tried out with anyone—a colleague or a significant other—because *pretest, pretest, pretest* is the most important principle of questionnaire construction. After the pretest, the person filling out the questionnaire should be asked if there were any problems in completing it. What were confusing questions or directions? What parts of the program were not asked about? Then, based on a few pretests, changes can be made in the questionnaire to provide more clarity and less confusion.

The principles of questionnaire construction that come partly from some of the principles in the reliability and validity of measurement were discussed in Chapter 7. For example, ask simple, clear questions, and avoid complex terms and professional jargon. These principles will be presented here using a consumer satisfaction questionnaire developed for an employee assistance program.

Development of a Satisfaction Questionnaire for a University
Employee Assistance Program

A beginning evaluation plan for an employee assistance program in a major university was developed. One part of program monitoring and accountability was an information system based on case records that recorded which types of employees came to the program, what kinds of problems they sought to resolve, and how many service contacts they had with program staff. As a second part of the evaluation, a questionnaire was developed for employees who used the program to assess what problems they had, their satisfaction with the services, and possible self-perceived employee outcomes. Consumer satisfaction surveys such as this one have become a major part of accountability in health and human service programs. The quality of the questionnaire developed is a key element in the success of satisfaction surveys.

Principles of Questionnaire Construction

Example questions from an employee satisfaction questionnaire will be used here to illustrate a number of the principles of constructing a questionnaire or questions for personal interviews or focus groups, or forms constructed to retrieve data from case records. As the questions used in the questionnaire are presented, the principles illustrated will be described. This section will conclude with a list of the most important principles of questionnaire construction. (The Complete Employee Assistance Program Questionnaire is presented in the appendix.)

EXAMPLE QUESTIONS. Which of the following best describe the kind of situation or problem for which you sought help at the employee assistance program (EAP)? (Check as many as apply)

———— Trouble getting along with a spouse or someone with whom you share a close personal relationship

———— Trouble with a child in your family

———— Trouble getting along with a family member or friend

———— Stress from a change in living circumstances

———— Trouble carrying out responsibilities at home

———— Physical or health problems

———— Financial problems

———— Trouble carrying out responsibilities at work

———— Trouble getting along with someone at work (e.g., co-worker or supervisor)

———— General irritability at work

———— Trouble dealing with feelings or emotions

———— Drinking or drug problems

———— Other; please describe: _____

- Since a handed-out questionnaire was used, at least 80% of the questions need to be close-ended, checklist, rating-scale types of questions such as the above checklist. This is one example of a close-ended question.
- If respondents were asked an open-ended question about describing the kinds of situations that brought them to the EAP, without any personal interaction and probing, their responses would be slim (e.g., "hard to deal with my supervisor") and would be hard to develop into standardized reports.
- Wording of the question was simple and clear, without professional jargon, for example, "What kind of situation brought you to the EAP?", rather than "What was your presenting problem?" or "Was your child acting out?"
- Directions were clear, the employees were asked to "check as many as apply" rather then leaving it to the employee-respondent to figure out if they were supposed to check one problem or check as many as apply.
- Note that in a "check as many as apply" question, each problem category must be coded and analyzed as a separate yes/no question. If the category is checked it is coded as a "yes"; if it is not checked it is coded as a "no." So in the computer analysis question1 represents 13 questions, one for each of the 13 categories in the question. In this way, quantitative analysis such as "45% of the employees came to the EAP because they had trouble dealing with emotions or feelings" can be made. If it was treated as one question in the computer and in the analysis, every possible combination of problem category would have to be coded under one variable or question.
- By having the employee check as many items as apply, quantitative analysis on the computer could include adding up the total number of problems checked to determine how many problems each employee reported. Patterns in the problem areas that were checked or clusters could also be analyzed, for example, how many employees with problems carrying out responsibilities at work also had trouble carrying out responsibilities at home, and physical or health problems.
- This is the first question asked and illustrates the order and natural flow of questions. "Why did you come to the EAP?" is the first order of business, then a series of questions will be asked concerning what happened when they came to the EAP and the possible results or outcomes of the service.

EXAMPLE QUESTION. Did anyone suggest that you go to the employee assistance program? (Check one)

____ No
____ Yes, a co-worker
____ Yes, my supervisor
____ Yes, someone else, for example, family member, personal friend, etc.
Please list their relationship to you (not their actual name): _____

- Notice that professional jargon was avoided—"Did anyone suggest that you go to the EAP" instead of "Who *referred* you to the EAP?".

EXAMPLE QUESTION (CLOSED-ENDED QUESTION). How frequently did you meet with the EAP staff person? (Check one)

____ More than once a week
____ Once a week
____ About every other week
____ About once a month
____ Less frequently than once a month

- Frequency of contact or "how often" is another type of rating scale to use in which categories are constructed to reflect how frequently things happen. In this program, once a week was typical of how often the employee came to the program for counseling.

EXAMPLE QUESTION. What would you say the EAP staff person did for you?

- This is an open-ended question and should be used sparingly (not more than 20% of questions in a mailed, handed-out or internet questionnaire). A personal interview can have many open-ended questions and a focus group can have all open-ended questions. In a personal interview or focus group, the interviewer could probe (e.g., "What else did they do for you?"). In a mailed or handed-out questionnaire an open-ended question should not be a critical question, since you want everyone's response and a lot of people skip those questions. In yearly satisfaction data only about 30% of employees responded to this question. Nevertheless, the answers to this question that were received provided great data about what the service was in the employee's own words.
- Inserting some open-ended questions in a questionnaire might also improve the flow of questions, helping to vary the question format and reduce fatigue in completing the questionnaire.

EXAMPLE QUESTION. In general, what do you think of the service you received from the employee assistance program?

____ Very satisfied
____ Satisfied
____ Neither satisfied nor dissatisfied
____ Dissatisfied
____ Very dissatisfied

- Rating scales should be used more often than simple yes/no questions and should be balanced. In this example, from "very satisfied" to "very dissatisfied" with a midpoint of "neither satisfied or dissatisfied" shows balance.
- Here all levels of satisfaction and dissatisfaction are presented. This illustrates that closed-ended questions should be totally exhaustive, that is, they should include all possible levels of response, from very satisfied to very dissatisfied.

EXAMPLE QUESTION. How do you feel your situation or problem has changed since you first contacted the EAP?

____ Has become much better
____ Has become a little better
____ Not much change
____ Has become a little worse
____ Has become much worse

- *Comparative rating questions* are extremely useful in a survey. Here the consumer is asked to state if they think their situation or problem has changed, compared to when they started services. Comparative rating scales are especially important when there are no pretest–posttest data to measure change. In other words, the consumer is asked to rate how they think their situation has changed.

EXAMPLE OF QUESTIONNAIRE ENDING. In the space below, please make any additional comments about the service that was provided to you by the employee assistance program or make suggestions about new ways we might help you or others.

Thank you. We appreciate your help.

Now simply place the questionnaire in the stamped envelope and mail it back to us.

- A questionnaire, interview, or focus group needs to have an ending. Generally, respondents are given an opportunity to add comments about perspectives on the program that may have been missed. They are told what will be done with the results. They are thanked. They are told where to return the questionnaire.

Additional Rating-Scale Formats

The above example of the employee assistance questionnaire presented a few different rating-scale formats. One was the *comparative rating-scale format,* where someone who had used the service was asked, "How has your situation (problem) changed since coming to the program?" In one-time surveys, the comparative scales "much better," "better," "same," "worse," "much worse" are very useful. However, in the evaluation of a group program where the actual problem could be measured before and then after the program in a pretest–posttest design or in impact assessment studies using a quasi-experimental or experimental design, the actual impact or change from pretest to posttest would be studied. Then more substantial measures of concepts would be used in the scale formats. The most common of these is the Likert scale format.

For example, in a program designed to improve the self-esteem of adolescents, a self-esteem scale could be used. Such a scale might use a Likert scale format ranging from "Strongly Agree" to Strongly Disagree." For example:

	Strongly Agree	Agree	Disagree	Strongly Disagree
I feel good about myself	4	3	2	1
I am an important person	4	3	2	1

Notice that the presentation of rating scales such as a self-esteem scale is clear and precise using a *double-column format* in which the items appear on the left column and the categories of agreement are in the right columns. Having respondents circle a number that represents level of agreement makes it easier for them to fill out. It is easier than making a checkmark (X) on a line. These numbers will also be the codes or numbers that go into the computer for data analysis. A person's score could then be easily computed by adding their scores on the items. Here, if there were 10 items, a person's score could range from 40 (scores of 4 on all 10 items, or 4 × 10), the highest possible self-esteem if they "strongly agreed" with each item, to 10 (scores of 1 on all 10 items, 1 × 10), the lowest possible esteem if they "strongly disagreed" with all the items.

Sometimes a neutral category of "uncertain" is used and the Likert scale is a 5-point scale:

	Strongly Agree	Agree	Uncertain	Disagree	Strongly Disagree
I feel good about myself	5	4	3	2	1

If a health program was designed to exercise a person's sense of power over their own health care, a health-efficacy scale could be used. One part of this scale measures a person's sense of how powerful health-care professions are seen in determining a person's health. The scale uses a 6-point scale with "moderately" and "slightly agree" and "slightly disagree" so that more finely determined attitudes about health-care professionals are measured. One of the items reads:

	Strongly Agree	Moderately Agree	Slightly Agree	Slightly Disagree	Moderately Disagree	Strongly Disagree
Health-care professionals keep me healthy	6	5	4	3	2	1

Again, people are asked to circle the codes matching their attitude and the double-column format is used. Items are on the left, and ratings are in columns across the top.

In addition, to Likert scale formats, formats used to examine the degree of time a person feels or acts a certain way are common. For example, in a mental health program, a person's depression score can be obtained before and after the program to see if depression was reduced. One item from a depression scale or one question to elicit a person's self-rating of their depression could be the following on a 5-point scale.

	Most or All of the Time	A Good Part of the Time	Some of the Time	A Little of the Time	Rarely or None of the Time
I feel depressed	5	4	3	2	1

A 7-point format could also be used to get at fewer distinctions in self-perceived depression level.

	All of the Time	Most of the Time	A Good Part of the Time	Some of the Time	A Little of the Time	Rarely	None of the Time
I feel depressed	7	6	5	4	3	2	1

Another format type lists percent of the time or percent of cases a staff person provides service to. For example:

Appoximately what percentage of your cases have a diagnosis of schizophrenia?

0%	1–10%	11–20%	21–30%	31–40%	41–50%	51–60%	61–70%	71–80%	81–90%	91–99%	100%
0	1	2	3	4	5	6	7	8	9	10	11

Smaller percentage breakdowns could also be used if you know that these will be large differences and that not all respondents have 1–24% of clients have a diagnosis of schizophrenia.

0%	1–24%	25–49%	50–74%	75–99%	100%
1	2	3	4	5	6

A bipolar scale with only two or three categories or anchor points is another popular way to get a generalized opinion, behavior or attitude. For example:

How would you rate this program?

Outstanding									Poor
10	9	8	7	6	5	4	3	2	1

Or one could use three anchor points and five rating points:

How effective would you say this program was?

Extremely Effective		Somewhat Effective		Not Effective
5	4	3	2	1

One thing to avoid is rank-order items, where the respondent is asked to order or rank items from "best" to "worst" or from "most important" to "least important." For example, in a hospital patient satisfaction survey, a question could be as follows:

Rank-order the following parts of your hospital stay from the best experience to the worst experience. Five (5) is the best and one (1) is the worst. Fill in rank here from 1 to 5:

_____Admissions experience
_____Nursing staff
_____Doctors
_____Food services
_____Discharge experience

Rank-order items take time for people to fill out and often go unanswered, or people will rank three items but leave out the last two. Instead of rank ordering, patients should be asked to rate *each* aspect of their stay. For example:

How would you rate the nursing staff?

Excellent	Very Good	Good	Fair	Poor
5	4	3	2	1

This way a person gets to vote on each area separately to determine the strengths and weaknesses of their hospital experiences and no areas go unranked.

Key Principles of Construction of Questionnaires and Interviews

Based on the previous discussion and corresponding examples, 15 key principles of the construction of questionnaires and interviews are presented here. Five of those principles have to do with the process and order of questions, and 10 principles have to do with formulating or constructing individual questions.

A. Process and Order of Questions

1. A proper introduction is needed. The introduction should explain the general purpose of the study and address the principles on the ethical treatment of human subjects and institutional review board (IRB, see Chapter 2) concerns. It should also state how long it will take to complete the survey and that the responses are confidential.
2. There should be an organized and natural flow of questions in the questionnaire or interview. Group similar questions together reflecting the order or process of the service, beginning with how a consumer found out about the program, what happened, why they came to the program, and the possible effects of the program.
3. Usually questions related to the purpose of the study appear first, so the person interviewed sees this as a professional encounter. Demographic questions are left for the end of the questionnaire. The only exception might be for sensitive topics (e.g., a program evaluation of a drug or alcohol program), demographic questions might go first and be used as warm-up questions.
4. Closed-ended questions may be alternated with open-ended questions to achieve variety and mixed interaction, even in a questionnaire.

5. At the end of the interview or questionnaire, respondents should be given the opportunity to add information they think was overlooked in the interview. People should be told how to return a questionnaire, thanked for their participation, told how the results will be used, and offered the final report of the study.

B. Top 10 Principles on Formulating Particular Questions

1. In a questionnaire (mailed or handed out), at least 70% of the questions need to be closed-ended (yes/no, degree of, scales, etc.). Instructions for completing the questionnaire must be extremely clear (e.g., "check one" versus "check all that apply") since no one is there to clarify things.
2. In a personal interview more open-ended questions can be asked, followed by neutral probes ("Could you tell me more?") to encourage depth of response and a depth of data.
3. Closed-ended questions should have categories that are *mutually exclusive* (e.g., age 10–19, 20–29, 30–39 versus 10–20, 20–30, 30–40, where there is overlap).
4. Categories should also be totally exclusive (e.g., "excellent, very good, good, fair, poor" versus just "excellent, very good, good" as categories). The response patterns should be balanced (e.g., positive elements of the program should be balanced by asking about negative parts of the program).
5. Rating scales that show the degree to which a person feels a particular way are much more valuable and should be used more often than yes/no questions.
6. Make sure each question asks only one question (e.g., do not ask, "Did you attend the groups and the individual counseling sessions?").
A question in which two questions are embedded in one question are referred to as "double-barrel" questions and should be avoided.
7. Questions need to be stated in *clear and simple language* that is free of professional jargon. Terms like "intake" and "access to services" should be replaced by "How did you find out about the program?" and "Was it easy to get here?". Professional terms should only be used if they are well known by the respondents or defined in the questionnaire.
8. Avoid questions asking respondents to rank items in order of importance; instead, have them rate each area on level of importance.
9. Comparative judgment questions (e.g., "Did your problem get better, worse, or stay the same?") are excellent to use in an *ex post facto*

questionnaire in which no baseline data or pre–post data are collected and analyzed.

10. *Pretest, pretest, pretest.* The single most important principle is to try out or pretest your instrument. Questionnaires, personal interviews, or focus groups should be tried out and tested to see if questions and directions are clear and easy to answer. The pretest is the most important part of developing a questionnaire or interview. In the pretest it is best to use people similar to the sample to be studied. Changes in the questionnaire itself and in interviewing procedures can be made on the basis of the pretest.

Sampling: Samples and Populations

A sampling plan is a description of how program participants (or staff) are selected to be interviewed or sent a questionnaire, or to participate in a focus group about the program. Because program evaluation employs a research methodology, the principles of sampling need to be applied in *every* evaluation study. In every program evaluation study, the type of sample needs to be specified. By having a sampling plan of how cases are selected, the study is adhering to the principles of research.

In sampling, a *population* is the larger, more inclusive group of *all* people who have used the program. If a program has 1000 program participants in total, 1000 is the population. A *sample* is a smaller, less inclusive group of people who could be selected to be interviewed for the evaluation study. The *sampling plan* specifies how the sample is to be selected. For example, if a sample of 150 participants was selected from the population of 1000, an evaluator could either go to the case files and choose the last 150 participants to enter the program or randomly select 150 participants from the population list of 1000 participants. Each way of selecting a sample and implementing a sampling plan has its advantages and disadvantages.

Ultimately, the characteristics of the sample of 150 people interviewed should be similar to the characteristics of the total population. The 150 cases would then be *representative* of the 1000 cases in the program. This means that if 40% of the participants are female, about 40% of the sample should be female. If 50% of the population is Latino, then 50% of the sample should be Latino. If it can be safely assumed the sample is similar to the population, then the sample can be said to *reflect* the population or to *generalize* to the population. *Generalizability* means that there are more assurances that the results found in the 150 program participants would be similar to the results if all 1000 program participants were interviewed. *Generalizability* and *representativeness* means that the knowledge obtained from the 150 cases has an impact beyond the sample of those 150 cases to the total population of 1000 cases in the program.

Sampling plans also help to determine if the sample is *biased* in any way. For example, the researcher may inadvertently be selecting cases from all one staff person who is known as the best practitioner. Now, the researcher may select cases that represent the "best cases" or "best practices," however, the sampling plan needs to say how "best cases" were determined and what criteria were used to select them. Likewise, if 1000 questionnaires were mailed out to all program participants and only 50 were returned, the researcher needs to report that this sample probably is not representative and has bias, since such a small number of questionnaires were returned.

Small Programs

Often evaluation studies are conducted on relatively small programs. Usually with small programs a sample does not need to be selected from a population list and the total population of participants can be asked to participate in the study. For example, an evaluation is planned for a psychoeducational program which served 100 relatives of persons with chronic mental illness to teach them about mental illness and how to support their relatives. The population size of the program is 100 cases. If the plan is to interview all 100 cases, there is no need to draw a sample; the study would be using the total population of cases. If only 80 of the 100 cases agreed to interviews, the 80 cases would be the sample used for analysis, but there was no selection of a sample. *Non-response* can greatly affect a study in a small program. If the small population is as small as 30 cases, a response rate of only 50% means only 15 cases in the study responded. For small programs which have small populations, sampling error, or the degree to which the sample in the study does not reflect the population will be discussed at the end of this section.

Large Programs

In large programs, where not everyone can be interviewed or sent a questionnaire, sampling plans are needed to determine how people will be selected for the evaluation study. Sampling procedures will help to ensure that a sample is an unbiased sample, reflects the population of all program participants, is representative of that population, and produces generalizable results.

Non-Probability Samples

Non-probability samples are considered less scientific with fewer assurances that the sample will reflect the larger population of all program participants.

The most general type of non-probability sample is the *convenience sample*. If a researcher just starts selecting participants from the program to be interviewed, this would be a convenience sample. In a convenience sample, the chances are that certain types of cases, participants known well by staff or those who use the program more frequently or are around the program more often, would be selected. Current cases would more likely be selected over cases that were in the program a year ago. A convenience sample is usually a less organized sample or a "sloppy sample." It is unlikely that anyone has organized a population list of all people in the program. Furthermore, no one has probably analyzed the characteristics of participants in the program in terms of gender, ethnicity, and types of services used. When a convenience samples is used, there may be little information about the characteristics of the population of all who attended the program.

The biggest mistake that people learning research methods usually make is thinking that a convenience sample is a random sample. While the process of selection seems random, a convenience sample is not a random sample. A *random sample* is a very orderly sample; a population list is organized and randomness is used in selecting people in an unbiased way from that organized list.

A convenience sample can be useful in formative evaluations in which some initial feedback from people attending the program is sought. However, with a little more planning, a better sample, a *purposive sample* can be obtained. In purposive sampling, the sample is selected on the basis of some criteria. The criteria could be based on purposes of the study. For instance, all participants who attended the program in the last 6 months could be selected. In a formative evaluation of an employee assistance program, the employees seen most frequently could be selected so that the experience of employees who make greater use of the program can be analyzed. Likewise, employees who dropped out or did not continue in the program could be selected to determine why they dropped out and how they experienced program services.

Purposive samples can also be implemented by asking health or social work professionals in the program to report on "best cases" or "best practices." Especially in the early stages of program development, examination of the practices and cases that have proven successful can help determine the types of services that should be provided. Good practices versus bad practices could also be selected to determine how the program might be experienced differently by those who appeared to benefit from the program compared to those who did not think they benefited from the program. The most important thing to remember is that purposive samples most likely do not represent the average person in the program and probably do not reflect the larger population of all cases in the program.

Another way in which purposive sampling is used is when types of cases are selected to try and reflect the characteristics of a population. In the employee assistance program, if 50% of the employees served are faculty members, 50% of the sample selected should be faculty. Or, if 30% of the population is Latino, than 30% of the sample selected should be Latino. The problem here is that there are a limited number of criteria on which cases can be selected, so the sample is not usually reflective of the population in all respects. For example, the sample may be similar to the population in relation to gender and ethnicity but not in relation to age.

Similar to a purposive sample is a *quota sample*, in which a certain number of cases are selected on the basis of some criteria. For example, in a high school counseling program, 50 males and 50 females may be selected, so that the outcomes and males and females can be compared. If it is suspected that the program was experienced differently in terms of ethnicity of the participants, or to make sure that there were no ethnic biases, 25 Latino cases could be compared to 25 non-Latino cases in the evaluation. If it is suspected that the program developed better services as it progressed, 30 cases currently in service could be compared to 30 cases seen in the early stages of the program. Quota samples help ensure that a certain number of cases of different types are selected so that enough cases are available to make comparisons in analyzing differences between different groups.

While non-probability samples such as convenience, purposive, or quota samples probably do not reflect any population of cases, sometimes the purpose is not to reflect a population but to initiate a formative evaluation. With non-probability samples, the good news is that the program is being evaluated and some program participants are being selected to tell what happened to them in the program. Even if it is a select number of cases, the program processes are being examined, program operations are being subjected to scrutiny, and program outcomes are being examined. Participants or professionals are being asked about the program and its effects. Having some evaluation is much better than no program evaluation at all, even if the sample does not reflect the population, the sample is less systematic, and there are less likely reports on the total population of program participants. The goals of program evaluation in terms of knowledge building, accountability, and serving consumers are being achieved, even if the sample has limitations.

Probability Samples

When larger programs are being evaluated and program participants need to be selected, probability-sampling techniques have advantages. These samples are based on mathematical probability theory. Probability samples help reduce bias in selecting a sample and help ensure that the sample reflects the population of all cases in the program. Often the services of a statistical consultant are valuable when selecting probability samples.

Probability sampling procedure are orderly and systematic if followed precisely. Probability sampling is usually employed when a large population list of people who have attended the program exists already or is developed by the program administrators and/or the researcher. Having descriptive data about the population and knowing the characteristics of a population in terms of basic demographic data or data on how they used the program go a long way toward both program planning and evaluation.

In contrast to non-probability techniques, where the sample is merely selected, or selected on the basis of some limited criteria, probability sampling techniques reduce bias in sampling because of the orderliness of the selection procedures used. In some situations, when certain types of cases are needed, then a non-probability may be fine. A probability sample, by contrast, would help ensure that not just the best or worst cases were selected.

In a probability sample, the samples is more likely representative of the population so that, for example, if 70% of the population is female, then 70% of the sample selected would be female; the sampling error, the degree to which the sample does not reflect the population, would be 0%. If the population is 70% female but only 50% of the sample is female, then the sampling error rate is 20%. Two basic types of probability sample will be discussed here: systematic selection and a simple random sample.

Systematic selection is a type of probability sample that is very easy and simple to describe and implement. Non-researchers usually get the concept of systematic selection quite easily. The cases are in a file drawer or the computer and every fifth case might be selected out. In *systematic selection*, the researcher looks at the numbers in the population and selects every Nth case from the population. So if the program has 1000 participants and a sample of 100 program participants are to be selected as the sample and interviewed, the researcher creates a *sampling interval*, which is the number in the population divided by the sample size. A population of 1000 divided by the sample's size of 100 gives a sampling interval of 10. The researcher then selects every 10th case for the population, which gives a sample of 100 using systematic selection.

Generally, systematic selection provides representative samples and samples that are unbiased, compared to other probability techniques such as simple random sampling. This is known by comparing samples using systematic selection with samples using simple random sampling and examining the error rates of each type of sample. The more a researcher knows about the population characteristics, the more the researcher can compare the characteristics of the sample drawn through systematic selection and compute the actual *sampling error*, or the degree to which the sample under- or over-represents the population. For example, if it is known that the population is 70% female and a sample of 100 participants is selected through systematic selection, the characteristics of the sample can be examined to see of the percentage is close to 70%. The percent by which the sample does not reflect the population is the sampling error; thus it can be known exactly how effective systematic selection was in selecting a sample that represents the population.

A problem with systematic selection occurs if there is a "cyclical pattern" in the population list. For example, if cases are assigned evenly to 10 health-care or social work professionals in a program and every 10th case was selected through systematic selection, then only the cases from one social worker would be in the sample. If only one worker's cases are represented in the sample, the service evaluated is for only one worker and does not represent the range of all the social workers' practice.

Systematic selection is appealing because of the seeming simplicity in selecting the sample. Everyone can visualize a population of all cases in a large file drawer. Simply count the files and they add up to 500 cases. Then, to get a sample of 100, divide 100 into 500 to get a sampling interval of 5. Select every fifth case and a sample of 100 cases is selected through systematic selection.

However, this seeming simplicity can be associated with sloppiness. What if all the cases in the population are not in the file drawer or the computer listing? What if different types of cases are in some other place? Often, too, the fact that cases are just there to be selected means someone has not taken the time to find out or develop a report on the population and the characteristics of that population to compare to the sample actually drawn. This makes it impossible to report on the degree to which the sample did not reflect the population. Thus, systematic selection should be viewed with some suspicion, to make sure that this sloppiness does not occur. Simple random samples, by contrast, generally have less of this sloppiness.

Simple Random Samples

A simple random sample is the most common type of probability sample and the basis for all probability samples. In a *simple random sample*, cases are selected randomly from a complete and accurate population list of all program participants or all participants within the last year or for a certain time period. To select a simple random sample of 250 cases out of a population list of 1000 cases, the following steps would be followed:

1. Create a population list of 1000 cases either in hard copy or on a computer.
2. Obtain a table of random numbers from the appendix of a statistics textbook.
3. Pick a random starting point and list the random numbers as they appear, one after another. For example, a list of random numbers would look like this:

   45752
   34800
   28314

   As a random starting point, the last three numbers from the first row, 752, 800, and 314, could be selected. Case 752 would be the first case selected, moving down to case 800 as the second case, and case 314 as the third case, proceeding down the list of random numbers. Since most computer programs can generate random samples, steps 2 and 3 can be bypassed by having the computer generate a random sample of 250 cases.
4. Keep selecting numbers until a sample of 250 cases is chosen.

A random sample is a very orderly sample in which the population list is arranged in an orderly fashion. In a simple random sample, every case had an equal probability of being included in the sample at every point a case was selected. Selection depends on the next number in a table of random numbers. So after case 752 is chosen, any case can be chosen if it is the next number on the list of random numbers. In systematic selection, once the fifth case is chosen from the list, cases numbered 1 through 4 can no longer be chosen since they were bypassed; the next case chosen would be case 10 if every fifth case was being selected.

Bias and Errors in Sampling

Bias and errors in samples can come from *(1)* the lack of an all-inclusive population list, *(2)* program attrition, and *(3)* non-response or no participation in the study.

Bias and errors can come from the lack of an all-inclusive population list. Probability samples and random samples are based on the assumption that all cases or program participants are listed in the all-inclusive population list. In non-probability samples, where cases are selected for convenience or because they satisfy some criteria (e.g., cases that have been in service in the last 2 or 3 months), there may be no population list of all cases that have been in service. In both probability and non-probability samples and for purposes of monitoring a program, it is good to have a population list of all cases. In probability samples, a population list or a larger set of all cases is developed from which the probability sample is drawn. However, as they say in the lottery, "You've got to be in it to win it." The population list must include all cases in the program over a specified time period. If a case is left out there is no possibility it will be included in the sample.

In the real world of programs, case records can often be scattered about the organization on the tops of desks or in desk draws. If there is a computerized file, that's helpful, provided that all cases are included in the file. If the file has data on the characteristics of the population (e.g., age, ethnicity, gender, marital status), that's even better because it will allow the researcher to compare the characteristics of this population with the characteristics of the sample to see if it is representative. However, often the researcher needs to scour the program or organization to create an all-inclusive population list of program participants.

Notice that the creation and monitoring of data on all program participants relies on excellent program planning and monitoring in an organization. For example, if an outside auditing agency from the government or a funding source wants to select case records to review for quality control, they would use that all-inclusive population list in selecting a sample. The more the organization or program knows about the characteristics of all cases, the more they can determine if the characteristics of cases chosen for a government audit are representative of all program cases. The organization needs to make sure that some probability sampling technique is used and that the government agency has selected a large enough group of cases to audit. The size of a sample that is needed will be discussed later in the chapter.

Program attrition or people dropping out of the program can greatly affect the accuracy of both probability and non-probability samples to reflect the program experience. Program directors and administrators should track program participants to show at least how many and which types of participants did not continue in the service. If the program has a dropout rate of 30% in the first month, this needs to be reported. If dropouts are totally ignored and there are no reports on program attrition, a biased sample of those who not only found the program but also continued in the program would be produced. This could represent people who were helped more by the program or who at least felt more hopeful about the program.

The evaluation researcher needs to track the rate of program attrition to see how many participants dropped out. By interviewing some participants who have dropped out the researcher can determine why they left the program. For example, was it the need for child care? Were the hours of service inconvenient? Most programs have at least some attrition and the rate of people leaving the program is important program-planning data. The rate of attrition is just as important as the rate of program uptake in program planning, monitoring, and program development.

Non-response, or people refusing to return a questionnaire, be interviewed, or attend a focus group, affects all samples and studies. In a simple random sample, if case number 309 is drawn from the list of random numbers but the person does not return a questionnaire or refuses to be interviewed, then another case needs to be selected from the population list. This is called "random sampling with replacement." If the non-response or refusal rate is as high as 30% or 40%, the final sample could be quite different from the original sample drawn through random selection. The final sample could have significant sampling error or differences between the sample and the population. This is why both a good researcher and administrator always track the characteristics of the sample in relation to the characteristics of the population to see how representative the sample is and where it falls short. Often those who do participate or respond had more positive experiences in the program, thus the sample can be biased toward participants who were helped more by the program.

Non-response is especially a problem with mailed questionnaires, where non-response can be as high as 60% to 80% can be reported. Questionnaires given to people in the last session of a program to fill out or personal interviews or participation in focus groups may have higher response rates. With the recent need to ensure ethical treatment of people in research, the giving of informed consent, and accountability to institutional review boards, research participation needs to be truly voluntary, and non-participation and non-response rates may be increasing. The principle of voluntary participation needs to be adhered to, even if the sample produced is not reflective of the population because people do not want to participate in the study.

Sample Size: Small Programs and Large Programs

How large does the sample need to be to conduct a quality program evaluation? The answer is different for small programs, where the researcher tries to collect data on the total population, or for large programs in which sample size is based on selecting a probability sample from a population list. In either case, the laws of probability can be used to determine the size of sample in relation to the size of the population. While the following examples can be used as guidelines, often a statistical consultant can help ensure that a proper size sample is selected.

In small programs, where it is possible to try and involve the whole population of program participants in participating in the study, the goal is to get as many program participants in the sample as is possible. For a quality evaluation study, enough cases need to participate in the study so that trends can be established in terms of the experiences of a substantial number of persons. So, in a population of 100 cases, the more cases in the study, the better. Non-response to a questionnaire or non-participation in an interview can affect the ability to obtain data from the total population. The standards from probability or simple random samples from small populations can be used to show how non-response affects small-program populations.

The smaller the program the larger the proportion of program participants that needs to be included in the sample. For example, in a program with a total population of 20 cases, each case presents 5% of the total population. Table 8.1 presents data on a population of 20 program participants. The table reflects a *95% confidence level*, which simply means the results would be expected in 95% of the samples from this population. The principle here is to get as many cases as possible. In the first sample, if 19 out of 20 cases participate in the study, the confidence interval, or sampling error rate, would be only ±5%. For a sample of 17 out of 20, the sampling errors rate rises to ±10%. However, if only 10 out of 20 cases are in the sample, the error rate increases to ±22%. This means that although the population is 50% female, the sample could be as high as 72% female or as low as 28% female. So almost the entire population should be included in a small-program population.

TABLE 8.1. Sample Size for a Population of 20 That Is 50% Female[*]

Sample Size	Sampling Error or Confidence Interval	Percent Female in Sample
19 out of 20	±5%	55% or 45% female
17 out of 20	±10%	60% or 40% female
10 out of 20	±22%	72% or 28% female

[*]At a confidence level of 95%, which means being 95% sure that this is the sampling error.

TABLE 8.2. Sample Size for a Population of 100 That Is 50% Female[*]

Sample Size	Sampling Error or Confidence Interval	Percent Female in Sample
80 out of 100	±5%	55% or 45% female
49 out of 100	±10%	60% or 40% female

[*]At a confidence level of 95%, which means being 95% sure that this is the sampling error.

TABLE 8.3. Sample Size for a Population of 1000 That Is 50% Female[*]

Sample Size	Sampling Error or Confidence Interval	Percent Female in Sample
278 out of 1000	±10%	60% or 40% female
319 out of 1000	±5%	55% or 45% female
516 out of 1000	± 3%	53% or 47% female

[*]At a confidence level of 95%, which means being 95% sure that this is the sampling error.

If a program has a population of 100 cases, not all 100 cases would need to be interviewed. To get an error rate of only ±5%, a sample of 80 out of 100 would be needed (see Table 8.2). However, if 49 out of 100 cases were interviewed, the error rate jumps to ±10%. So probably a sample above 49 is needed.

What would happen in a population of 1000? If 278 people were interviewed, the error rate would be ±10% (see Table 8.3). The sample size should be increased to 319 so that a ±5% error rate can be achieved. However, in large populations there is a point of diminishing returns at which it does not pay to increase sample size. For example, to reduce the error rate from ±5% to ±3%, a sample of 516 would be needed—almost double the size of the sample needed for a ±5% error rate.

To further check out how large a sample is needed in different cases the following Web site can be used: http: //www.researchinfo.com/docs/calculators/samplesize.cfm. As mentioned earlier, the services of a statistical consultant should be used once these general principles are known. Also, these are just general principles, they assume that everyone selected in the sample agrees to be interviewed and that the population list includes all cases. Thus the more that is known about the characteristics of the population studies and the characteristics of the sample, the more concrete information you will have about how much the sample reflects the population.

Summary

1. The research design is the overall plan for the study and includes selecting a type of design or study, deciding on data collection strategies,

constructing the data collection instrument, and selecting a sample of people to participate in the study.

2. Formative designs are useful in process evaluations and program monitoring studies.

3. Surveys are an efficient way to collect data on a large number of program participants. The degree to which surveys have large samples determines their success at establishing external validity.

4. Pre–post studies are effective at studying change in program participants, especially if substantive changes in knowledge, behavior, attitudes, skills, and status (KBASS) are goals of the program.

5. Impact assessment studies are experimental and quasi-experimental studies that attempt to examine cause-and-effect relationships between the program and its outcomes. These studies help establish internal validity, that it was the program and the program alone that caused an outcome.

6. There are a number of threats to internal validity, such as a selection bias, program attrition or experimental mortality, outside events or history, maturation, testing and instrumentation, and Hawthorne and placebo effects. These threats can be viewed as opportunities for growth in improving our thinking about program development and program evaluation.

7. Each data collection strategy, be it questionnaires, personal interviews, telephone interviews, focus groups, direct observation, or use of secondary data, has its advantages and disadvantages.

8. Data collection instruments need to be crafted and formatted well. Professional jargon should be avoided, and double-column formats are preferred for rating scales. "Degree of" questions are preferred to yes/no questions.

9. The most important part of developing a questionnaire is the pretest, when the questions are tried out with program participants or people like the respondents who will be used in the evaluation.

10. Sampling plans help produce unbiased samples and samples that reflect a population.

11. Non-probability samples include convenience, purposive, or quota samples.

12. Probability samples include systematic selection and simple random samples. Because of the sample selection techniques used, these samples are often less biased and more likely to reflect a larger population.

13. Generally, the larger the sample size, the more likely the sample reflects a population; however, in large populations there is a point beyond which it does not make sense to increase sample size.

REFERENCES

Campbell, D.T., & Stanley, J.C. (1966). *Experimental and Quasi-experimental Designs for Research*. Skokie, IL: Rand McNally.

Epstein, I. (2010). *Clinical Data-mining: Integrating Practice and Research*. New York, NY: Oxford University Press.

Kreuger, R.A. & Casey, M.A. (2008). *Focus Group Interviews: A Practical Guide for Applied Research*. Thousand Oaks, CA: Sage Publications.

Weiss, C.H. (1998). *Evaluation: Methods for Studying Programs and Policies*. Englewood Cliffs, NJ: Prentice-Hall.

9

Implementing the Evaluation Study and Analyzing the Data

Implementing the Evaluation Study

Program evaluation proceeds from the planning and designing stage to actually implementing the evaluation by collecting and analyzing the data. Collecting data and analyzing data are exciting processes and occur in all evaluations from needs assessment to process evaluation to program monitoring to goal oriented evaluation to impact assessment, Sometimes when needs assessment or a process evaluation or program monitoring is conducted the evaluation can proceed after a shorter planning process. With goal-oriented evaluation, in which goals need to be operationalized or impact assessment studies conducted, and experimental or quasi-experimental studies need to be mapped out, a longer planning process is needed.

In both formative or more summative types of evaluation studies, once the research design or plan has been mapped out (as discussed in Chapter 8), the research may proceed from the planning to the implementation stage. The questionnaire or data collection strategy and procedures have been developed, and the type of sample and sampling plan have been determined. It is now time to go out and collect the data and use the questionnaire or conduct the personal interviews.

The researcher and research staff implement the study by interviewing consumers and/or staff, mailing questionnaires or sending them out on the internet, conducting focus groups, or obtaining data from case records. These are the essential data for the program evaluation.

A famous movie producer once said that before one films a movie, everything needs to be completely planned and mapped out because once the filming starts, all different contingencies can occur. The same is true in planning a program evaluation study. For instance, in program evaluation, a major problem in implementing a study may be obtaining an adequate response rate and encouraging participation in the study. A good plan would anticipate differing response rates for different modes of data collection. However, one can never be sure until the data collection begins as to how successful the response rate will be. For instance, the researcher may be conducting an evaluation of a senior center and all its programs, but getting seniors to forego their usual activities at the center, their exercise or discussion group, may prove difficult. However, if the plan includes a good way to recruit seniors at the center by having staff members stress the importance of evaluation or by asking people to participate and spend a few moments to be interviewed *after* a group activity, the data collection may go more smoothly. If one procedure for recruiting subjects that was planned is not working, a new one needs to be developed. Plan your work and work your plan.

An excellent data collection effort took place in a mental health agency of housing and support services for persons with chronic mental illness. The climate of the organization was such that the consumers really wanted to participate in an agency where they were respected and valued. The agency also compensated the consumers by paying $25 per interview. The consumers felt good about participating and almost all of the 53 consumers took part in two lengthy interviews lasting for 1 hour each. Also, for persons living on Social Security Disability Insurance, the money really helped the people buy items they could not otherwise afford.

Data collection proceeds by handing out the questionnaires, directly observing the program, conducting personal interviews or focus groups, or collecting data from the program's case records. Questionnaires need to be duplicated, interviewers need to be trained, or the material from case records needs to be organized for data analysis.

As the data collection is implemented, *quality control measures* need to be put into place. As questionnaires are returned, someone needs to check that people are filling them out correctly and that people seem to understand the questions. In personal interviews, if there are a number of open-ended questions, the quality of the qualitative data needs to be ensured by interviewers who ask neutral probes to generate comprehensive answers which will result in creating rich, thick, descriptive data for analysis. For example, comprehensive explanations of what the program meant to the consumer should be encouraged rather than thin statements such as "It helped my personal life." In focus groups and personal interviews where most qualitative data are collected and tape recordings used, the quality of the tape recording needs to be assessed so that a transcriber typing up the interview or focus group session can generate complete interviews or focus group sessions. This means the transcription process should begin immediately as the interviews are being completed and the data starts coming in. Likewise with quantitative data, data should be entered into the computer as it starts coming in.

So the final step in quality control is making sure that enough data are collected and that the data conform to these quality standards. For the structured data from closed-ended questions in questionnaires, the data need to be entered in a database-type format into a statistical package such as SPSS, the *Statistical Package for the Social Sciences*. The transcriptions of qualitative data need to be kept in word-processing documents and kept in a secure place. The qualitative data can be analyzed directly by putting similar quotes under headings that represent themes. For more intense analysis, the data can be transferred into a qualitative data analysis package, such as ATLAS, Nudist, or Ethnograph, which is designed to store the data and analyze the data under themes or categories.

Data Analysis

Once the data are collected and the quality of the data has been examined during the data collection process, the data analysis can begin. It takes great skill to present program evaluation data clearly and succinctly. Data analysis means compiling, aggregating, and summarizing data so that formative or summative findings and implications can be presented. While all the methods described in this book help uncover the mysteries and processes of programs in a holistic sense by generating comprehensive knowledge about programs, the actual process of data analysis is more schizophrenic, or split between quantitative and qualitative methods of data analysis. It is best to think of quantitative and qualitative analysis as two distinct processes. While the two processes will be conducted separately, the final report should be one holistic, comprehensive document that tells the story of the program.

Quantitative data analysis includes a set of rules and procedures and statistical concepts based in the science of statistical theory and statistical concepts. This is how structured data such as yes/no answers, number of years or amount of time in the program, checklists, rating scales, and scales measuring substantive concepts and goals are analyzed. Everything that is not an open-end question or descriptive data in written form gets analyzed using quantitative techniques.

Different data analysis techniques and principles are used for *qualitative data analysis*. Qualitative data come from open-ended questions, from descriptive data gleaned from personal interviews that have been transcribed, from process notes from the observation of programs, and notes from focus groups of consumers, case examples of people who have used the program or minutes of staff or board meetings, etc. Michael Quinn Patton (2006), the premier expert in qualitative program evaluations, has traced the origins of qualitative research, which are quite different from the principles and scientific basis of quantitative research. Both traditions are quite acceptable in program evaluation. Recent developments in qualitative program evaluations are quite exciting.

Since the body of data collected from the evaluation is extensive and comprehensive at this point, a plan for data analysis is essential. Key evaluative questions need to be answered first; summaries of the data, conclusions, and implications in relation to the program will be the ultimate product of that plan.

Quantitative Data Analysis

Once all the structured data or responses to closed-ended questions are collected, quantitative data analysis can begin. All the structured data from questionnaires are entered into the computer in SPSS (or another statistical package) or in a database program that will be structured so that it can be read into SPSS easily. Thus knowledge of SPSS formats and procedures is essential (See Yockey, 2007 or other similar guides to SPSS). Every case and every questionnaire are entered. Once the data are entered, the first step is to look at the responses to all the questions. In a statistical package such as SPSS, a frequencies routine can add up all the responses and compute percentages of how many people liked or did not like the program, how many rated the program as excellent, very good, good, fair or poor. A *frequency distribution* is an adding-up of all the responses to see the trends in the data.

Running all the data can also help determine if any of the data were entered incorrectly and maintain control of the quality of the data. For example, data are usually entered as codes, e.g., 5 = excellent, 4 = very good, 3 = good, 2 = fair, 1 = poor; in this code scheme, a code of 6 should not be possible and would be an incorrect entry.

By examining frequency distributions we can get a sense of the overall thrust of the findings in terms of demographics and who attended the program, how often they attended, and what was thought to be the impact of attending

TABLE 9.1. Change in the Problems of Employees

	Number	%
Become much better	36	28
Become a little better	55	42
Not much change	26	20
Become a little worse	13	10
Become much worse	0	0
Total	130	100

the program. In quantitative analysis, the key findings are often uncovered in the first runs of the data analysis.

Frequency distributions are underused in reporting evaluation reports. Simple frequency distributions often contain simple, yet compelling data. The overall findings of the number of people who liked the program and their ratings of the program are crucial in reporting on *all* the evaluation data. As an example, in a university employee assistance program, employees who used the service were asked, "Has there been any change in the problems you requested help with?". The frequency distribution of responses to this question is presented in Table 9.1.

In addition to a table, the presentation of data analyses would be accompanied by paragraphs like the following:

> Employees were asked if they thought there was a change in the problem that brought them to the employee assistance program for service (Table 9.1). Most thought their problem had become better. So, in all, 70% reported improvement. The modal response was for 42% (55) who thought the problem had become a little better. Twenty-eight percent (36) thought the problem had become much better. Meanwhile, 20% (26) responded that there was "not much change" in the problem, and 10% (13) said the problem had become a little worse.

In this type of categorical data, a percent is the major statistic used. A percent is a very important statistic because a finding that "42% of the employees thought their problem had become a little better" without a percentage figure would be cumbersome. It would have to read, "55 out of 130 employees thought their problem had become a little better." With categorical data, the mode is the measure of central tendency. The *mode* is defined as the most frequent response to the question. The *modal category* is where the highest percent of responses fell. Forty-two percent of the employees thought their problems had "become a little better," so this is the *modal category*. It helps place focus on the major response and is the only measure of central tendency that can be used with categorical data.

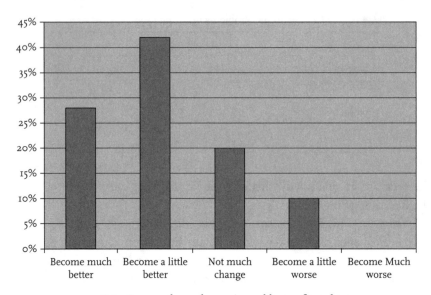

FIGURE 9.1. Bar graph on change in problems of employees.

The presentation of simple frequency distributions can be enhanced by the use of graphs. The simple bar graph in Figure 9.1 shows clearly that most employees thought their problem had become a little better, some thought it got a lot better, a lower percentage said "not much change," and "became a little worse," and no one said the problem had "become much worse." A pie chart is another simple representation of frequency distributions.

When data are numerical, such as number of years or months in the program, or a score on a scale such as an efficacy scale or a self-esteem scale, additional measures of central tendency other then just the mode—the median and the mean—can be used. In the employee assistance program, for employees who used the program, the number of years that the employee worked at the university was important as it showed how much commitment the workforce has to the university. For this type of numerical data the median and mean can be used. The frequency distribution in Figure 9.2 shows the data, but without measures of central tendency the data are difficult to interpret. Notice that the mode was 1 year at the university, as 12 employees had worked for 1 year; however, 10 employees had worked 3 years at the university, and the distribution comes close to bimodal, with two modes. If the data were grouped the mode would show a clearer trend; for example, 30 employees had from 1 to 3 years of employment. This shows that a mode is better for grouped data when one age category stands out.

Frequency Distribution – Years Employed at the University

		Frequency	Percent	Valid Percent	Cumulative Percent
Valid	1.00	12	9.2	9.2	9.2
	2.00	8	6.2	6.2	15.4
	3.00	10	7.7	7.7	23.1
	4.00	6	4.6	4.6	27.7
	5.00	4	3.1	3.1	30.8
	6.00	9	6.9	6.9	37.7
	7.00	10	7.7	7.7	45.4
	8.00	6	4.6	4.6	50.0
	9.00	7	5.4	5.4	55.4
	10.00	3	2.3	2.3	57.7
	11.00	4	3.1	3.1	60.8
	12.00	3	2.3	2.3	63.1
	13.00	2	1.5	1.5	64.6
	14.00	5	3.8	3.8	68.5
	15.00	7	5.4	5.4	73.8
	16.00	4	3.1	3.1	76.9
	17.00	3	2.3	2.3	79.2
	18.00	2	1.5	1.5	80.8
	19.00	1	.8	.8	81.5
	20.00	6	4.6	4.6	86.2
	21.00	3	2.3	2.3	88.5
	22.00	1	.8	.8	89.2
	23.00	2	1.5	1.5	90.8
	24.00	4	3.1	3.1	93.8
	25.00	2	1.5	1.5	95.4
	28.00	1	.8	.8	96.2
	30.00	2	1.5	1.5	97.7
	35.00	3	2.3	2.3	100.0
	Total	130	100.0	100.0	

Statistics – Years Employed at the University

N	Valid	130
	Missing	0
Mean		10.8308
Median		8.5000
Mode		1.00
Std. Deviation		8.32121
Range		34.00
Minimum		1.00
Maximum		35.00
Sum		1408.00

FIGURE 9.2. Frequency distribution and statistics—years employed at the university.

The *median* is the value for the middle case, where 50% of the sample is above and 50% is below. The median or middle case had 8.5 years experience (see statistics Figure 9.2). The *mean* is the average, or arithmetic average. To obtain the mean, all the years of employment are added up, for example, 1 year each would be added up for the first 12 people and 2 years would be added for 8 people, then 3 years for 10 employees, etc., until the total number of years that people were employed is added up. In Figure 9.2, (in the statistics box) the value of "sum" is all the years of employment added up, or 1408 years. Then 1408 (years) is divided by the number of employees, 130, to get the average years of employment. The mean number of years of employment is 10.83.

Both the median and the mean are useful measures of central tendency. The mean is affected more by very high or very low scores. If there are some very high scores, there is a skewed distribution, which greatly affects the mean but not the median. So the mean here is 10.8 years, and the median is only 8.5 years. The mean is higher because of employees who had 27, 30, and 35 years employed. Looking at the *histogram* (Figure 9.3), which is a graph for numerical data, most of the employees have worked from 1 to 10 years at the university, so the median is a better representation of the usual employee. Reporting the mean of 10.8 helps indicate that there was a group of employees who were employed a much larger number of years. So both the median and the mean, and the histogram, tell a lot about the data. However, the median of 8.5 is more like the typical case for these data. For the same reason, in analyzing income, the median is usually used because it reflects the typical case, as the mean is skewed upward by the relatively fewer people making very high incomes. In the

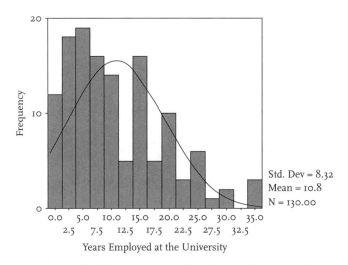

FIGURE 9.3. Histogram—years employed at the university.

histogram shown in Figure 9.3, notice that the tail of the distribution slopes to the right, meaning it is skewed to the right by the employees who had many years at the university and helped make the mean of 10.8 higher than the median of 8.5.

For numerical data too, in addition to the average or typical case, the way in which cases vary or differ from the average is important. There are a number of measures of dispersion that are usually used. The first and the simplest is the *range*, which is the difference between the highest and lowest values. Some employees were at the university for only 1 year and some were there 35 years, so the range is 34 years, quite large. Saying that the years of employment ranged from 1 year to 35 years is a good descriptive way to put it. This creates a picture of an employee recently hired and one who has been at the institution for a long time. The large dispersion in years of employment is also supported by the standard deviation. The standard deviation indicates how far the typical case deviates from the mean score. Here the standard deviation is 8.32 years; a standard deviation of 3 years or 5 years would indicate less dispersion.

Cross-Tabulation

After the frequency distributions are examined, relationships between variables that will answer evaluation questions are examined. These can be key questions to be answered in the evaluation. For example, in the employee assistance program, change in the employee's problem was examined to determine which types of university employee benefited most from the program. Cross-tabulation is the most common form of analysis in which the relationship between two nominal or categorical variables is examined.

Table 9.2 presents the relationship between change in employee problem and the employee's position at the university. The horizontal rows are for the

TABLE 9.2. Change in Problems of Employee by Job Title

	Faculty		Administrators		Secretarial Staff		
	N	%	N	%	N	%	Total
Become much better	24	39	10	27	2	6	36
Become a little better	30	49	19	51	6	19	55
No change or worse	7	12	8	22	24	75	39
Total	61	100	37	100	32	100	130

$\chi^2 = 43.34$, df = 4, $p < .001$.

dependent, or outcome variable of change in problem. The vertical columns show the independent variable of the employee's job title. Column percents that add up to 100% are used, which makes it easy to report the findings. They would read something like this:

> In examining the association between change in problem and job title, there seems to be an association (Table 9.2). While 39% of faculty members said that their problem had become much better, and 27% of administrators said their problems had become much better, only 6% of the secretarial staff said their problem had become much better. Forty-nine percent of faculty and 51% of administrators thought the problem had become a little better, and only 19% of secretaries thought their problem had become a little better. Most revealingly, 75% of the secretaries said there was no change or the problem had become worse, whereas only 12% of faculty and 22% of administrators said their problem did not change or became worse.

A graphical representation, presented in Figure 9.4, sometimes makes the analysis easier to understand. The last column represented in each grouping is the secretarial staff, who have a larger percentage in the "no change or worse" category, and smaller percentages in the categories "become a little better" and "become much better."

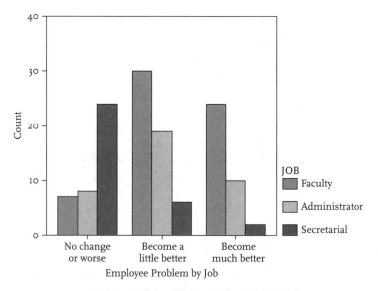

FIGURE 9.4. Graph of change in problem by job.

Statistical Significance

In the previous cross-tabulation there was a very clear trend that secretarial employees did not think their problem had gotten better. The data give a descriptive sense of the association between these two variables. What if the trend is less clear? Is there a relationship between two variables? The researcher, or the researcher with pressure from the stakeholders in an evaluation, could be saying there is a relationship, but it could be based purely on the values that a relationship *should* exist or the desire that a relationship exist. Fortunately, there are statistics available to help determine if a relationship exists. Some relatively objective tests can tell us whether or not there is a "statistically significant" relationship between the two variables.

Royse, D., Thyer, B.A., Padgett, D.K., and Logan, T.K. (2001, p. 345) have some pretty strong words for researchers not using a statistical test of significance:

> The argument for using statistical procedures in analyzing data is that data coupled with the appropriate research designs provides objective evidence that the program was successful or not successful— information not dependent upon the evaluator's [or other stakeholders'] whims or judgment. Avoiding the use of statistical procedures when they are needed not only is amateurish but also suggests incompetence.

There are a variety of statistical tests to be used in different situations. These tests are based on mathematical probability theory. Technically, tests of statistical significance are used to infer whether or not a relationship that exists in the study sample would exist in a larger population of cases. These tests are used as a "relatively" objective standard.

In this situation, where there are two variables that are nominal or categorical, the most commonly used statistic is the chi-square (χ^2) statistic. The chi-square test is like most other statistics tests in that it starts at 0 if there is absolutely no association and goes above 0 as associations exist. The formula to compute chi-square is based on how far the association found in the study differs from what would be expected if no relationship existed between the two variables.

In Table 9.2, the chi-square value was 43.34, which is quite large. The chi-square value by itself does not mean that much on its own. To see if it is significant, a chi-square distribution of typical chi-square values is examined. These charts are usually in the appendices of statistics textbooks; however, they can come right out of the computer (via the SPSS statistical software) along

TABLE 9.3. Probability Distribution of Chi-Square

Degrees of Freedom	Probability Levels				
	.10	.05	.02	.01	.001
1	2.70	3.85	5.41	6.64	10.83
2	4.60	5.99	7.82	9.21	13.82
3	6.25	7.81	9.83	11.34	16.27
4	7.78	9.94	11.67	3.28	18.46

with the cross-tabulation and chi-square analysis. Parts of the chi-square probability distribution are reproduced in Table 9.3.

The *probability level* indicates whether or not there is a statistically significant result. This is a very important number to learn about because most statistics have probability levels and probability distributions. The lower the p, or probability level, the more likely there is a statistically significant result. For statistical significance, $p < .05$ is the generally agreed-upon level of significance, although $p < .01$ and $p < .001$ show that there is an even greater association or relationship.

To find the probability level for this chi-square analysis, one more piece of information is needed, the degrees of freedom. Since the chi-square test measures the data from cross-tabulations in tables, the size of the table needs to be taken into account. For example, in Table 9.2 there are three sets of columns, for faculty, administrators, and secretaries. If a fourth column, custodial staff, were in the table there would be more possibilities for difference because there was another row and more cells in the table. The degree of freedom in chi-square analysis takes this into account.

The degrees of freedom (df) can be computed with this easy formula:

$$df = (r - 1)(c - 1)$$

where r is the number of rows and c is the number of columns. In Table 9.2, there were three rows ("become much better," "become a little better," and "no change or worse") and three columns ("faculty," "administrators," and "secretarial staff"). So df = $(3 - 1) \times (3 - 1)$, or $2 \times 2 = 4$ degrees of freedom for this table. The last row in the above probability distribution of chi-square shows df of 4 (see Table 9.3).

If the chi-square value computed for your data is larger than the chi-square value in the table, then the data are significant at that level. Since the chi-square value from the cross-tabulation table was 43.34 and it is larger than 7.78, $p < .10$; since it is larger than 9.94, $p < .05$, so the result is statistically significant at the .05 level.

However, the result is even stronger than this. Chi-square is >11.67 ($p < .02$), >13.28 ($p < .01$), and >18.46 (where $p < .001$).

So the final result, as it appears in Table 9.2, is chi-square $= 43.34$, df $= 4$, $p < .001$; or it can be written χ^2 (4) $= 43.34$, $p < .001$, with the degrees of freedom in parentheses. This means that there is only one chance out of 1000 that this could have happened just by change. In other words, there was not a chance relationship but a real relationship, a statistically significant relationship. Doing this analysis showed how much of a relationship there was between an employee thinking their problem got better and the type of employee. However, knowing that an association is significant does not provide information on what the descriptive association is. In this analysis, faculty and administrators thought there was improvement, and secretaries did not.

A new first sentence can now be added to the write-up on this finding:

> There was a statistically significant relationship between employees thinking that their problem had improved and their job title (χ^2 (4) = 43.34, $p < .001$; Table 9.2). While 39% of faculty said that their problem had become much better, and 27% of administrators said their problems had become much better, only 6% of the secretaries served said their problem had become much better. Forty-nine percent of faculty and 51% of administrators thought the problem had become a little better, and only 19% of secretaries thought their problem had become a little better. Most revealingly, 75% of the secretaries said there was no change or the problem became worse, while only 12% of faculty and 22% of administrators said their problem did not change or became worse.

The first sentence gives assurances of statistical significance. Note that chi-square analysis did not show what the trend was, so the descriptive data indicating that secretarial staff did not think their problems improved need to be stated. But now a statistically significant result can be reported.

Once a trend is reported, the evaluation needs to help the reader interpret the trend. What does it mean that secretarial staff reported less progress in resolving their problems? Did they have more serious problems? Did they not engage the counseling and other services the way that faculty and administrators did? Other variables in the study, such as the problem that brought them in for service, their experience with the service, or number of service contacts, also need to be analyzed in relation to whether the employees felt the problem was resolved. Then, in a multivariate analysis, the problem that they sought help for in the program and their use of the service could be controlled for while looking at the relationship between problem resolution and job title to see if that relationship holds up, regardless of type of problem or service contacts and service use. Additionally, the qualitative data of comments of secretaries about the program can help determine why their program experiences were less successful.

While the data here were statistically significant, it needs to be determined what the practical significance of this finding would be. Certainly as an implication, the program planners would be concerned about secretarial staff and how they were using the service, to promote more successful outcomes. Statistical significance does not replace practical significance. In fact, even findings that show *some* difference but are not statistically significant may have promise for showing what may work in the long run or which aspects of the program were on the right track in program development.

Comparing Mean Scores: t-Test and One-Way ANOVA (F Ratio)

In relation to the knowledge, behaviors, attitudes, skills, and status (KBASS) model of substantive program goals, introduced in Chapter 6, measures of program goals that are taken at an interval level because standardized tests were used to measure goals would allow the researcher to use *t*-tests and one-way analysis of variance (ANOVA) to test differences in the mean scores related to goals. This is very common in program evaluation; for example, any training or educational program might have standardized measures and look at differences in outcome variables.

As an example, Kilmnick (2006) studied pre- and post-changes in heterosexist attitudes in community college students attending a Family Life and Human Sexuality course. One group of classes had an openly gay instructor and another group of classes had traditional teaching where the instructor's sexual orientation was not discussed. The attitudes of those who had the openly gay instructor improved dramatically in contrast to those with the traditional instruction. In Whittemore's study of the Everybody Needs a Proxy Campaign (Chapter 7 and the end of this chapter), the design could have included a pretest before the session and a posttest at the end to determine concretely if the campaign increased people's knowledge of the health-care proxy. In a program to increase women's knowledge about breast cancer, pretests and posttests can be administered to determine if knowledge was increased and which particular types of knowledge increased.

Cottrell (2002) designed a program to increase the knowledge and attitudes of students in a Jewish high school concerning genetic diseases that affect Jewish populations and genetic screening. The study used a pre–post design to evaluate educational sessions about genetic carrier screening for the Ashkenazi

Jewish population. By providing information about carrier screening during their high school years, it was thought that this population of students would have the opportunity to select the personally appropriate screening method. For example, Tay Sachs carrier screening for Jews of Ashkenazi (Eastern European) descent first became available in the 1970s through an enzyme test. This was one of the first available carrier screening tests, and the experiences with carrier screening helped shape medical opinions on carrier screening.

While the educational sessions were fairly straightforward in the initial training, such training could test out different forms of delivering the educational sessions. For example, one training orientation could be didactic and use a lecture approach, with all the terms and knowledge being imparted in a classroom lecture environment. Another approach could be experiential, using medical professionals and people who have been tested or affected by the diseases to talk about their experiences, along with some didactic teaching. The rationale would be that in the experiential group, people's experiences would motivate the students to learn more about carrier testing. A score on a standardized test of knowledge about genetic testing for Jewish populations could be computed for the two different groups, and a t-test could be used to see which group scored higher on the knowledge test. If the test scores had 25 items, the number of correct items out of 25 would be measured. The mean test score at the end of training could be computed.

If there is one categorical variable with two categories and one continuous, interval-level variable such as a standardized knowledge test, as there is in this case, an independent sample t-test would be used. The measurement on the knowledge test is interval level because the "interval" between one score and another is known, since it means one more correct answer on an item. Number of service contacts, number of months in service, actual age, and scores on reliable tested scales would also be interval level measures.

The t-test tells whether or not there is a significant difference in the mean scores—in this instance, did the didactic teaching or the experiential teaching produce the highest knowledge scores? Like many of statistical tests, the t value starts at 0 if there is absolutely no difference between the didactic and experiential groups, and the t goes up as differences are recorded between the two group mean scores. If there is absolutely no difference between the mean scores, t would be 0.00 and the result would not be statistically significant. In fact, the p level would be $p = 1.00$, meaning there is the highest probability the differences (there were no differences) were just by chance, not real differences.

TABLE 9.4. Knowledge of Genetics and Genetic Testing by Type of Teaching

	Mean Score	Standard Deviation	t-Test	p Level
Didactic teaching (n = 30)	19.0	2.40	3.85	p < .001
Experiential teaching (n = 30)	16.8	2.08		

The results of the t-test analysis for the educational program might be written up like this (see also Table 9.4):

There was a statistically significant relationship found between the type of sessions and the students' score at the end of the sessions (t (58) = 3.85, p < .001). Students who had the didactic teaching averaged 19.0 out of 25 correct answers at completion and those who had experiential teaching had an average of only 16.8 questions correct after the sessions.

Note that the 58 in parentheses is the degrees of freedom for the t test; as in chi-square analysis, there are different probability distributions in different situations. In chi-square analysis the degrees of freedom was based on the number of rows and columns in the table. In the t-test, the degrees of freedom which represent the different probability distributions, are based on the total number of cases minus 2 or df = (n − 2). In this instance, 60 − 2 = 58 is the degrees of freedom. The larger the sample, the more the t distribution is normally distributed and a smaller mean difference is more likely to be statistically significant. With a smaller sample, a larger difference in the mean scores would be needed.

In the second semester of the program a third intervention could be added. Teachers might report that what worked best was the presentation and study of case material related to different types of genetic testing, along with genetic-counseling professionals coming in to talk about testing issues and diseases that affect Jewish populations. This could be a hybrid model consisting of didactic and experiential teaching. There would now be three interventions to assess—didactic teaching, experiential teaching, and the review of case material. In addition to examining knowledge gain, the program was aimed toward improving attitudes of the students toward genetic testing. A standardized scale measuring attitudes toward genetic testing could be used. The scale score could range from 0, for the most negative attitudes toward genetic testing, to 30, for the most positive attitudes toward genetic testing.

When there is one variable divided into three groups or categories and there is one interval variable where the differences in the means scores can be analyzed, a one-way ANOVA is used to test the educational approaches.

TABLE 9.5. Attitudes about Genetic Testing by Type of Teaching

	Mean Score	Standard Deviation	F Ratio	p Level
Didactic teaching	18.8	1.84	40.78	$p < .001$
(n = 30)				
Experiential teaching	19.6	2.08		
(n = 30)				
Review of case material	24.8			
(n = 30)				

The analysis follows pretty much from the *t*-test on the basis of differences in the mean scores of the three groups. Instead of a *t*-test, an F ratio measures the difference in the mean scores. F starts at 0.00 if there were no differences between the three mean scores and goes up from there. If there was no differences in the mean scores, F = 0.00, and the result would not be statistically significant. In fact, the *p* level would be *p* = 1.00, meaning there is the highest probability that any differences found (there were no differences) could have come about by chance.

If a one-way ANOVA were run to test out the three models, the results might be written up like this (see also Table 9.5):

> There was a statistically significant relationship found between the type of session and the students' score at the end of the sessions (F (2/87) = 40.87, *p* < .001). Students who were in the sessions with review of case material had more positive attitudes at the end of the sessions (M = 24.8) than those who had didactic teaching (M = 18.8) or those in the experiential-teaching group (M = 19.6). Both of these groups had much less positive attitudes toward genetic testing.

Note that 2/87 is the degrees of freedom in the F ratio. In the F formula which computes the F score, there are degrees of freedom in the numerator of *k* – 1, where *k* is the number of categories or groups, here 3 – 1 = 2. The degrees of freedom for the denominator is *n* – *k*; here *n* is 90, so 90 – 3 = 87. So the F ratio takes both the number of groups or categories and the total number of cases into account in the probability distribution. Again, the larger the sample, the more the *t* distribution is normally distributed and a smaller mean difference is more likely to be statistically significant. With a smaller sample, a larger difference in the mean scores would be needed.

Measurement of Change Pretest to Posttest: Paired Sample t-Test

While a look at data based only on questionnaires handed out after educational or group sessions *(ex post facto)* tells us something the consumer's knowledge at the end of the sessions, it does not say anything about the knowledge and attitude *change* that took place in the consumers or the students. Although at the end of the sessions the group of students who had didactic education had higher knowledge scores than those of students who had experiential teaching, those in the didactic group might have had higher scores *before* the educational sessions. A standard or independent sample *t*-test does not take change into account.

However, a paired sample *t*-test looks at the pre-score of each group in relation to the posttest of each group. The paired sample *t*-test is based on the differences in mean scores from pre- to posttest in each group. The bigger the change from pretest to posttest, the larger the *t*-value and the more likely it is that there is a statistically significant change. If the pretest mean score is exactly the same as the posttest mean score, *t* would be 0.00 and the *p* score would be 1.00, no difference at all; 100% of the time this would be a distribution that could have occurred by chance. There is no real difference in the two mean scores.

To examine changes in knowledge from pretest to posttest, paired sample *t*-tests could be examined for each type of educational intervention. A paired sample *t*-test might produce the following results, written up like this (see also Table 9.6):

> In comparing change in the mean scores with a paired sample *t*-test, it was found that students who were in groups using either didactic teaching or the review of case material showed increases in students' knowledge. The group given experiential teaching did not show a significant increase in knowledge. In the group with didactic teaching the pretest mean score on knowledge was 15.8 and it increased significantly to 19.0 on the posttest (t (29) = -10.01, $p < .001$). In the group that used review of case material the knowledge score increased from 16.7 on the pretest to 21.1 on the posttest, which was a significant increase (t (29) = -15.01, $p < .001$). The experiential teaching group had no gain in knowledge, from 16.6 on the pretest to 16.7 on the posttest (t (29) = -1.03, $p = .16$). So it seems that both didactic teaching and review of case material were effective at increasing students' knowledge of genetic testing issues facing the Jewish community.

Note that the *t* values are negative in this analysis. A negative *t* value is just as important as a positive one. It simply means that the second mean score, in this case the posttest knowledge score, was higher than the pretest score. The amount of the *t* value still reflects the differences in the mean scores. Note, too, that a one-tailed *p* level was used; whenever the direction of the difference is predicted, a one-tailed *p* level is used. Here it was predicted that the posttest mean scores would be higher, so a one-tailed test was used and a negative *t*-value was predicted.

TABLE 9.6. Paired Sample t-Tests: Pre–Post Changes in Knowledge by Type of Teaching

	Pretest Mean Score	Posttest Mean Score	t-Test	p Level
Didactic teaching (n = 30)	15.8	19.0	−10.01	p < .001
Experiential teaching (n = 30)	16.6	16.7	−1.03	p = .16 (n.s.)
Review of case material (n = 30)	16.7	21.1	−15.01	p < .001

p level for one-tailed test. n.s. = not significant.

The degrees of freedom are based on sample size—in this case, the number in the sample minus 1, or $n - 1$: which in this case is 30 − 1, or 29. One can then look up the probability distribution with 29 degrees of freedom to see if the t-value is statistically significant.

Measuring Change With Categorical or Nominal Data

When there is pre–post data with categorical data or nominal-level data with two categories in each categorical variable, a statistic using principles similar to those of chi-square analysis is used. The McNemar statistic is used in situations where people went from having low scores in the pretest to high scores in the posttest; high or low categories of change are measured rather than changes in mean scores. Also, in looking at change in one question, a McNemar statistic could be used. The McNemar statistic is used to look at the proportion of people who went from an incorrect answer on the pretest to the correct answer on the posttest. In small samples, rather then the chi-square distribution, the binomial distribution is used as the statistic to give an exact p or probability level to determine statistical significance.

In the educational program on genetic testing for high school students, one knowledge question could be examined: "Is it physically harmful to be a carrier of

TABLE 9.7. Pretest-to-Posttest Changes in Knowledge for Didactic Teaching Group

"It is physically harmful to be a carrier of Tay Sachs disease."

Posttest	Pretest	
	Yes	No
Yes	4 (13%)	0 (0%)
No	9 (30%)	17 (57%)

p < .01, binominal distribution used.

Tay Sachs disease?", where the categories are yes/no. The correct answer would be "no." This question would be asked on both the pretest and the posttest.

A McNemar analysis would indicate the amount of change in a categorical variable with two categories. If a McNemar analysis were conducted, the following is how the data of Table 9.7 would be written up for the group receiving didactic teaching:

> Students were given the statement "It is physically harmful to be a carrier of Tay Sachs disease." The pretest and posttest results on responses to this statement were compared, and there was a statistically significant increase in knowledge from pretest to posttest in the didactic teaching group ($p < .01$). Of the total sample, 30%, or 9 students thought it was physically harmful to be a carrier of the disease on the pretest, but they learned the correct answer, that it is not harmful by the posttest. Thirteen percent, or only 4 students gave the incorrect answer on both the pretest and the posttest. They thought being a carrier was physically harmful on both the pretest and on the posttest. Fifty-seven percent of the sample, or 17 students knew that being a Tay Sachs carrier was not physically harmful on the pretest. They also had the correct answer on the posttest.

Another McNemar analysis could be conducted on the group for which experiential learning was used (see Table 9.8). The write-up for these data would look like this:

> There was no statistically significant increase in knowledge from pretest to posttest in the experiential group ($p = .25$). Of the total sample, only 3 students, or 10% thought it was physically harmful to be a carrier of the disease on the pretest, but they learned the correct answer, that it is not harmful by the posttest. Forty-seven percent, or 14 students thought it was physically harmful to be a carrier on the pretest; they also had this incorrect answer on the posttest. Forty-three percent of the sample, or 13 students knew that being a Tay Sachs carrier was not physically harmful on the pretest and had the correct answer on the posttest. Thus the experiential group did not show gains in knowledge on this question.

Since so many evaluations examine changes from the beginning of training or education programs to the end of training or educational programs, the paired sample t-test and the McNemar statistic are very valuable statistical tools in evaluation. They are especially useful in tracking changes in knowledge, behavior, attitudes, skills, and status (KBASS), as discussed in Chapter 6.

TABLE 9.8. Pretest-to-Posttest Changes in Knowledge for Experiential
            Teaching Group

"It is physically harmful to be a carrier of Tay Sachs disease."

	Pretest	
Posttest	Yes	No
Yes	14 (47%)	0 (0%)
No	3 (10%)	13 (43%)

$p = .25$, binominal distribution used.

Some beginning quantitative statistics were presented here for two case examples, a university employee assistance program and an education program about genetic testing. While this is a start, the following authors should be consulted for further details on statistical analysis: Abu-Bader (2006); Munro (2004); and Weinbach and Grinnell (2006).

Qualitative Data Analysis

Most evaluations have at least some qualitative data to be analyzed, so most evaluations will use the methods of qualitative data analysis. The extent of qualitative data analysis can go from merely analyzing one open-ended question, to analyzing 15 open-ended questions, to conducting a major qualitative study with personal interviews with all open-ended questions. If the evaluation uses mostly qualitative data, the major data analysis will be done with qualitative data analysis techniques. When evaluation studies have a significant amount of both qualitative and quantitative data they are called "mixed-methods" studies. Mixed-methods methodologies are now very popular.

Qualitative data to be analyzed and aggregated usually come from the following sources:

- Open-ended questions from a survey
- Data from qualitative interviews
- Qualitative data from a focus group
- Comprehensive notes from direct observations of interventions of social situations
- Process recordings or typed recordings from social interventions or interactions
- Other types of descriptive data such as the minutes of planning meetings, board meetings etc.

Qualitative data is a very exciting, dynamic, and rewarding type of data to analyze. The data are more naturalistic and holistic, providing the person's total program experiences. The purpose of a qualitative evaluation is to present the in-depth experiences and insights of those involved in the program. Qualitative evaluation can provide rich, descriptive data of how the program operates and what it does. Peoples' quotes and descriptions of program experiences are presented in their own words in qualitative evaluations. Staff, administrators', and consumers' thoughts about their program experiences take center stage.

The depth of response as well as responses "in their own words" constitute a mode of implementing participatory models of empowerment evaluation and consumer empowerment. Qualitative research can present the consumer's or patient's perspective, not just the professional's perspective. Furthermore, the professionals' perspectives can also be presented in an in-depth manner, reflecting some of the complexities of practice. Qualitative evaluations are especially useful in providing new insights about the program and can help in suggesting the possible causal connections between the program process and program outcomes and effects.

The traditions of qualitative research come from ethnographic methods used by anthropologists, from phenomenological philosophical traditions, and from sociological "grounded theory" traditions (Strauss, et al., 2007). The process is inductive and proceeds from the data to establishing themes and patterns in the data.

> Conjectures and speculations should not . . . be derived simply from the theoretical predispositions of the evaluator. The cardinal principle of qualitative analysis is that causal and theoretical statements be clearly emergent from and grounded in field observation. The theory emerges from the data it is not imposed on the data. (Patton, 1987, p. 158)

In qualitative analysis, trends in the descriptive data are reported, and the descriptive data must indicate the presence of the trend or theme. Rich descriptive data are needed in this analysis. The richer the descriptions, the better the study and the more likely the researcher can show that trends and themes in the data that have been analyzed. If the researcher states that a trend exists, the researcher must show the quotes supporting the theme or trend in the data; "show me the data" is a primary requirement of qualitative data analysis. The findings need to be based on data, not merely on the researchers' or the stakeholders' own values and perspectives.

Qualitative data analysis can be especially useful in needs assessment, program monitoring, and process evaluations, where rich descriptive data on need or beginning program interventions and program activities are sought. Rich qualitative data can provide the details of the program and the program's beginning successes or failures. Use of qualitative data helps guard against the black-box phenomenon, when limited data is provided on the program and how it operates. Much of qualitative evaluation research involves "pure description of the [need for] the program" and "the experiences of people in the program" (Patton, 1987, p. 147).

There has been an inherent bias in how people view research: qualitative methods are looked at as "subjective" and quantitative methods are thought to be "objective." In quantitative methods, there do seem to be relatively objective standards of statistical tests to assess the data. There are defined levels of statistical significance, be it $p < .05$, $p < .01$, or $p < .001$. These levels of statistical significance are based on mathematical and statistical theory and indicate whether or not there are relationships or associations between variables. Nevertheless, to view qualitative methods as subjective has been called unfair because "subjective means to be biased, unreliable, and irrational" (Patton, 2002, p. 574).

While the process of qualitative data analysis might be influenced more by values, such as the researcher's own values, the principles of qualitative research help to ensure that the findings are in the data, and that the researcher does not generalize beyond the data; it is not a matter of subjectivity or objectivity. These are different forms of data that help show what the program was like and what kinds of outcomes it achieved. Some basic principles of qualitative data analysis are presented here. Basically, the qualitative researcher needs to show that there are trends and themes in the data that come from the data and are not imposed by the researcher or other outside forces such as some of the stakeholders.

The Process of Qualitative Data Analysis

Unlike quantitative research, where computing percents and statistics can begin only after all the data are collected, the process of qualitative data analysis can begin as the data are being collected. The unique and artistic process of qualitative data analysis can begin by following the five steps outlined below.

1. Assemble the qualitative data.

   If a few open-ended questions in a structured questionnaire are being analyzed, all the qualitative responses should be transcribed into a word-processing file. For example, to analyze one open-ended question such as, "What do you think about the program?", the researcher or a research assistant opens up a word-processing program and puts this question at the top of the page. Then the researcher reads through the question-naires and writes each person's response, each of which has an ID number (e.g., Case 1, Case 2, Case 3, etc.).

With more substantial qualitative data, for example, a qualitative study with 40 personal interviews that were tape recorded, a secretary skilled in transcription would have to transcribe the interviews into word-processing files. The interviews for each case, all the files, should be in the computer for eventual analysis.

2. Read through the descriptive data or the transcribed interviews and start making notes on possible trends and themes in the data.

This step can start as an informal process, when the research analyst gets "in tune" with the data and makes notes about the current trends, themes, and categories, and notes potential themes. This process is often referred to as "open coding," the codes being the categories and themes found in the data. If qualitative data analysis software is used, the software has rules about how to mark the categories or themes. Otherwise, in the word processor, the researcher writes in the trend or theme that the quote represents next to the quote. Through this process, the researcher can decide which quotes or observations fit together. If the quotes support a specific theme there is *convergence*, that is, the quotes converge around that theme. This is also referred to as "content analysis," or analyzing the content of the data for patterns and themes. For the question "What do you think about the program?", categories such as *positive, negative,* and *neutral* things that consumers had to say about the program might be beginning trends.

If there is a more substantial amount of qualitative data, for example, if the research involves 40 personal interviews with con-sumers that were tape recorded and transcribed by a secretary into word-processing files, all the files should be on the computer. These files could then be transferred into a qualitative software package such as ATLAS or Ethnograph. Software programs have the facility to mark quotes so that they can be retrieved and linked together and printed out in a report similar to the ones at the end of this chapter. However, it is still amazing how much of the same tasks can be done by a simple word processor following the steps described here.

3. Generate as many descriptive categories, themes, and trends as possible, starting with categories and themes developed in your evaluation plan, and start moving similar quotes together under the trend represented.

The researcher reads through the data and makes notes about possible themes and about themes that repeat themselves. This major type of qualitative analysis, *inductive analysis*, proceeds for quotes and cases to categories, patterns, and theories. This brings order to the qualitative data; without order or a classification system, there is chaos (Patton, 1987, p. 149). The aim is to develop themes without any prior assumptions of what the researcher or other parties wanted to discover when the evaluation was begun.

As an example, in order to examine trends in one open-ended question, "What do you think about the program?", the analysis could begin with simple descriptive categories such as *(1) positive* things people had to say about the program; *(2) negative* things people had to say about the program; and *(3) neutral* things that were neither clearly positive or negative. Quotes that support the theme of positive things should be cut and pasted together. Quotes that show negative themes should also be moved together under the category "negative." And quotes that are neither positive nor negative can be grouped together under the neutral theme.

4. Reread the data and refine the categories on the basis of new themes or subthemes discovered in the data.

The new themes and subthemes indicate there is some *divergence* or difference from the original codes and themes, or refinement of those initial themes. For example, in examining patterns in responses to the question "What do you think about the program?", the general trends were positive, negative, or neutral. Within the positive category, subthemes might emerge; for example, a number of the quotes might relate to the professionalism of the staff and their caring attitude, or other quotes might relate to the services that were provided. Within the positive statements about the services, specific services such as job placement or counseling services might be subcategories. Under the negative category, subthemes might be quotes expressing complaints about the limited hours of service, quotes related to difficulty finding the program, or quotes about services that the program did not provide.

5. Examine the trends, and introduce the themes in the text by stating them in double-spaced text. Link the quotes, single-spaced and indented, to the new themes and subthemes.

The quotes that were cut and pasted and organized under each theme and subtheme will be presented in the research report. Simple statements introduce the quotes, for example: "Twenty out of 40 consumers were very positive about the program overall. A number of people mentioned the services that were provided, such as the job placement service and day care." Then the specific statements that consumers made about the job placement, day care, and other services are listed together, single-spaced and indented.

It is critical to show the actual quotes that support the positive, negative, and neutral themes that the researcher claims exist, since without the quotes there is no data, only conjecture. This is the concept of *key linkage*, or the degree to which it is clear that a quote or piece of descriptive data supports a particular trend so that most people would agree a quote or piece of data represents a particular trend. Further trends, themes, and subthemes develop as the analysis proceeds. The trends can often represent typologies or pre-theory and can assist in the later development of theory.

Example of Qualitative Data Analysis in an Evaluation of a Supported Housing Program for People With Mental Illness

These five steps or stages were used in research on a housing program for persons with mental illness. A mixed-methods study employing both qualitative and qualitative data was conducted evaluating a supported housing program for people with serious mental illness who had graduated from more intensive housing called "supportive" housing to the most independent form of housing, "supported" housing (Fabricant & Smith, 1997).

The residents were asked an extensive set of questions in a personal interview. Among other things, residents were asked about the program activities they engaged in. They were also asked how they felt about the supported housing where they lived and how it compared to other mental health housing where they had been. Two qualitative interviews were conducted with each resident. The interviews were tape-recorded and transcribed into word-processing files for each respondent. Their thick, rich descriptions of participation in the program were indispensable to showing what the program meant to these consumers. Such rich, pure descriptions of the nature of the program can never be underestimated as a valuable contribution of qualitative research in validating programs that need to be accountable through evaluation.

After the interviews were conducted the five-step process unfolded.

1. Assemble the qualitative data. After the interviews had been transcribed and tape-recorded, the data from the interviews were placed in word-processing files on the computer.

2. Read through the descriptive data or transcribed interviews and start making notes on possible trends and themes in the data. The researcher then read through the transcriptions, looking for residents' responses to questions about program activities they had participated in and about their perception of the housing and how it compared to their experience of previous housing programs. Initial themes were noted as the data were read. The *inductive analysis* from the quotes has begun, and categories and initial themes have emerged from the data.

3. Generate as many descriptive categories, themes, and trends as possible, starting with the themes developed in your evaluation plan. Start moving quotes together under the trends reported. Positive experiences from program activities were one theme from the data. There was *convergence* on the theme of positive program experiences and quality of the housing provided.

4. Reread the data and refine the categories on the basis of new themes and subthemes discovered in the data. Within the positive experiences, quotes reflected the value of these activities in achieving outcomes such as reducing social isolation. When analyzing data on the value of specific program activities such as the socials and trips, some quotes explicitly expressed the value of these program activities in preventing isolation. There was some *divergence* within participants' positive program experiences in relation to different program activities and preventing social isolation. This was a subtheme in the data that diverged from the overall positive theme of positive program activities.

5. Examine the trends and introduce the themes in the text by stating them in double-spaced text. Link the quotes to the themes by placing the quotes in single-spaced, indented text under the theme to which it refers. The researcher wrote up double-spaced introductions to the themes and put the single-spaced, indented quotes under the themes to which they refer. The quotes seemed to fit the trends that established

key linkage between the themes and the quotes. This constitutes the end product presented in the next section.

Presentation of Qualitative Data

Overall, the residents presented their positive experiences with the program activities they engaged in. All program activities, such as Friday night socials, Sunday brunches, weekend trips, and exercise classes, which were conducted at the program offices in the housing complex, were valued. Many of the program activities might not have been affordable if the program had not provided them.

> I've come to the socials, every social. Sometimes I'm tired or just finished working, but I come anyway. I love it. We socialize; we eat; we put the music on and we dance. I see the children and it's nice for me because I don't have any children and I like to be around kids. It makes me feel happy. . . . You get to see everybody you don't see all the time, but who you know for many years. I come here for Sunday brunch all the time. I don't come for the food. I have food at home. I just want to get out of my apartment to talk. We sometimes have guest speakers.
>
> Oh, we go on trips sometimes. The staff will rent a van and take at least 12 of us. A lot of the trips are during the summer. They take us to a lot places we probably couldn't go to otherwise. A lot of us just don't have the money to pay for the carfare, so we go together, a bunch of us as a group. It's more fun that way. We went to the Bronx Zoo; we went to the beach a few times, to the pool, to barbecue. We went to see the tree at Rockefeller Center last week. We all went out to a restaurant afterwards.

The program activities residents engaged in seemed to have effects such as preventing social isolation, getting residents to open up and interact with the others, and helping them create a better sense of self.

> I've already come to look forward to the socials. Not necessarily for the food, although I make potato salad and everybody loves it. Get compliments all the time. No, I like coming because of the people. I thought I was open but sometimes I'm not. But here it's just so easy, so comfortable. I see old faces whether I have conversations or not. Just to see everybody and know other people around me. And I have my part. I wash the dishes. I don't know why! It's just part of me that is supposed to be like coming to these parties every Friday.

I have people here who understand me, whom I can talk to. That was a breakthrough for me, than I could extend myself to other people. After coming here, I'm willing to try to communicate with people. That's something in the past I just couldn't do.

It [the program] makes me feel like somebody. This place has helped me get a sense of myself. There are no limits to what I can do. But now I know I don't have to do it alone. There are those days when I come home and I just need to get out, so I come over here for some socializing. Just to talk to someone. I'm a part of their lives. I just pick up the phone and I talk to them and they become friends. So sometimes, you just want to talk to them and see how they're doing, like family.

Overall Satisfaction with Housing—Peaceful and Quiet

Residents were also asked about their perception of their supported housing program. One evaluative question was, "How did residents feel about their housing?". The overall thrust of the residents' evaluation of their housing in this supported housing program was very positive. "Safe," "peaceful," and "quiet" were the words describing residents' housing and the neighborhood where this supported housing program was located. Furthermore, the peaceful atmosphere seemed to help reduce stress and get people refreshed for the next day.

It's just so safe and peaceful here compared to where I lived before. It's peaceful and quiet, the way I like it . . . . There are no stresses, no arguments, no issues, no problems. It's just wonderful. So I can recuperate and get renewed for the next day.

Having a neighborhood that was peaceful and less chaotic and had less crime was valued. A neighborhood with more crime seemed to effect a feeling of uneasiness, insecurity, and being frightened.

It's so peaceful and quiet. You don't have sirens all the time. You just don't have the same kind of criminal element here. My other neighborhood, it was a good neighborhood but you could feel the uneasiness there. You just didn't feel secure. No peace of mind, always frightened.

Having one's own apartment was another value of this supported housing program. Less stress and aggravation and having down time to deal with life's stresses were mentioned as consequences of having one's own apartment.

> There is less stress because I have my own place. There is no aggravation to come home to. My apartment is a place I come to get away from stress. Especially if you're dealing with something that's difficult.

Having one's own apartment was connected with allowing a person to think better, having less chaotic thoughts, and allowing reflection and peaceful thinking.

> Having your own apartment allows you to think better. My thoughts are less chaotic. Having my own place allows me to reflect on things.

The residents' quotes might help generate or support a theoretical model that the quality of housing and independent housing can lead to reduced stress and possibly a reduction of symptoms of mental illness. To support this model residents mentioned the peacefulness of having your own apartment, being in a better neighborhood, and being more secure in the neighborhood.

The residents were also asked about their previous housing, where they often shared an apartment with another person in the mental health system. The overall findings indicated that residents did not like sharing an apartment. Within the general theme of dislike for sharing an apartment, there were some individual themes. "Invading your space" was one expression about sharing an apartment with two other residents.

> The previous program was supportive living and I shared a room with that nut. I shared an apartment with two other people. One guy had his own room. I shared with another guy. Then you had people coming in every day invading your space. They were a pain in the neck.

Residents also felt under attack or in a very tenuous living situation in their previous housing. Most importantly, residents thought that there was not enough supervision by the mental health system; residents reported that "they told me there was nothing they could do . . . when I most needed the help."

> Well, I had one roommate attack me over a 3-month period. They didn't move me out or really calm it down. They left me in that situation for 3 months. I could have been killed.
>
> My roommate was freaking out. I was left alone with her. I called them and they actually told me there was nothing they could do. I was alone in the apartment with her and they told me there was nothing they could do! That was crazy to me when I most need the help.

Sharing an apartment with another person with serious symptoms could have affected the resident to the point where they would "tune everything out."

We never clicked. Never. I always kept my distance. We were all on different levels. Some people were sicker than others. It didn't matter how much you told people you wanted to make contact, they were just out on Mars, out to lunch. Sometimes you just have to leave people alone, go about your business and try to do the best you can under the circumstances. That's what I did. I tuned everything out to a point.

The negative aspects of sharing an apartment sometimes lasted over a long period of time and were often downright abusive.

So being exposed to that for 4 years, constant, in the middle of the night, you don't know when a roommate is going to be barging in and doing something. It was too much. I had a roommate who constantly flushed my medication down the toilet. And the other one became romantically obsessed with me so I had to barricade my door. I can't live like that.

The problems of sharing an apartment included roommates "invading your space" and abusive behavior by roommates. Flushing medication down the toilet and possible sexual abuse were experiences that residents had. What made their living situations worse was the lack of supervision by professionals in the mental health system, even when the residents tried to get help at a vulnerable time in their lives. Ironically, the shared housing was experienced in supportive housing, which was supposed to provide more supervision and services for persons with mental illness. There was no doubt that this had a profound impact on the residents and sometimes led to defense mechanisms such as "tuning everything out."

Indigenous Themes and Typologies

Where do the themes or trends in qualitative analysis come from? Sometimes the trends or themes that are constructed are based on the respondents' own words and their views of their own experiences, called "indigenous themes or concepts" (Patton, 2002, p. 454). *Indigenous themes* come directly from the respondents' own words. These are the phrases and terms that people use to describe their world and to try and understand their experiences. Most importantly, these indigenous phrases are richly descriptive and usually stay in everyone's active memory. By highlighting these themes in the introductions to the quotes and in the analysis, the researcher directs the reader's attention to what the quote means in terms of the program.

In the housing program, residents described their housing as "safe," "peaceful," "quiet," and "wonderful." These are great terms to describe their housing and what their apartment means to them. They are also great terms for administrators, practitioners, and especially policy makers to hear about housing being provided to anyone, let alone persons with mental illness. If program administrators were asked about the housing, they would probably say, "We provide quality housing for people with mental illness." By contrast, the words "safe," "peaceful," "quiet," "wonderful" are richly descriptive and show how residents really feel about the housing and what it means to them. They also imply what residents said about their previous housing, that it often was not in the best neighborhoods and it involved sharing an apartment with someone who was intrusive in their lives.

Another example of indigenous themes comes from qualitative research in which career drug users were asked to provide examples of the types of theft they used to support their habits. "Boosting" was a general term the respondents used for stealing; usually it referred to stealing high-priced items from department stores. "Boosting" may be a more acceptable and less judgmental term than "stealing" or saying that "you stole" something. "Cattle rustling" was another form of theft: a person would go into a supermarket and conceal high-priced meats in their overcoat. This was usually followed by putting the meat in the trunk of a car and stopping on a local street to sell the stolen meat. Again, "cattle rustling" implies a more acceptable form of behavior than "stealing meat." Using the respondents' own words is strongly descriptive and is a major advantage in using indigenous concepts. These indigenous themes can also be used to produce an *indigenous typology* of different types of theft, in which types of theft are placed on a continuum based on the seriousness of the theft or the street value of the stolen goods, or other factors. The categories and themes are called "indigenous typologies" when they are used in a pre-theory or theoretical conceptual scheme that can in turn be used to eventually represent all cases on a type of continuum (Patton, 2002, p. 457). Typologies also contribute to the development of theory.

Another example of an indigenous theme in the supported housing program for persons with chronic mental illness comes from the residents reporting on the program activities they engaged in. When the Friday night socials were mentioned, the statement "I don't come (just) for the food" can be used to show that residents recognized the value of increased socialization. This indigenous theme could be used as a heading for all the quotes about increased socialization through program activities. Eventually the theme could be used to represent a typology of socialization or no socialization, for residents who recognized the program's role in promoting socialization and those who did not.

There were a number of indigenous themes that residents used when the respondents were asked about the housing. These themes were related to the effects of the housing rather then the housing itself. The indigenous themes were as follows: "My thoughts are less chaotic," "I can recuperate and get renewed for the next day, " and "I have less stress." These were all personal and psychological effects that they thought were connected to the housing. These indigenous themes could be developed into an indigenous typology as a pre-theory is developed on the effects of quality housing on the personal lives of persons with mental illness.

In terms of the negative effects of sharing an apartment in the previous supportive housing program, the following indigenous themes were noted: "Invading your space," "barging in," "my roommate was freaking out," "became romantically obsessed with me," and "He attacked me . . . I could have been killed." These descriptive phrases all give a clear, rich description of what people experienced in their previous mental health housing. The terms themselves can be used in the introduction to the quotes to highlight their experiences before the current program. But the themes could also be the beginning of an indigenous typology developed from the respondents' own words. "Invading your space" and "barging in" constitute one level of disruption from sharing an apartment. More serious levels of intrusiveness to the point of physical abuse are "my roommate was freaking out," "became romantically obsessed with me," and "He attacked me . . . I could have been killed." The beginning indigenous typology could be used to develop a theory of seriousness of the levels of negative effects that sharing an apartment with another resident could bring, from lack of privacy and personal disruptions to forms of emotional and physical abuse.

Example of Using Indigenous Terms and Typologies
from the World of Art

Typologies are related to theory development. Another example of using qualitative data to create typologies that relate to theory and of using quotes from respondents to create theory or pre-theory comes from the artist Marcel Duchamp's description of his art on the taped tour of the Museum of Modern Art.

> In 1913, I had the happy idea to fasten a bicycle wheel to a kitchen stool and watch it turn. It was around that time that the word Readymade came to my mind to designate this form of manifestation. A point that I very much want to establish is that the choice of these Readymades was never dictated by an asthetic delectation. The choice was based on

visual indifference. A total absence of good or bad taste. In fact, a complete anesthesia.

Duchamp's own words can be used to develop initial theories of his art. First, he has coined the term "Readymade" to describe a piece of art that juxtaposes ordinary objects in a certain way. This can be a beginning definition of this new art form. "No asthetic delectation" is another concept that might distinguish this type of art, as is "visual indifference" Finally, there is a "complete anesthesia" in relation to this type of art. Theory about Readymades could be advanced by qualitative interviews with artists doing this type of work to see how they come to juxtapose ordinary, everyday objects and to determine if "no asthetic delectation," "visual indifference," and "complete anesthesia" are essential characteristics of this form of art in every case. In this way, the theory of Readymades can be advanced. In fact, the typology of Readymades might specify levels of detachment from lowest to highest, from "no asthetic delectation" to "visual indifference" to "complete anesthesia." On the other hand, Duchamp could just be clowning around.

Analyst-Constructed Themes and Typologies

In contrast to indigenous themes, *analyst-constructed themes or concepts*, called "sensitizing concepts" by Patton (2002, p. 456), are themes created by the research analyst on the basis of trends he or she sees in the data. Again, the data need to support the theme or concept; there needs to be *key linkage*. When the theme comes from the researcher analyst rather than the respondents' own words, the theme or concept is an analyst-constructed theme. The themes the researcher uses may come from the program or program concepts, the purpose of the program, or program processes (e.g., outreach, services, intervention by a professional) or from questions asked of respondents (e.g., "Did the program help you obtain employment?"). Analyst-constructed themes could also come from social science or behavioral science theory, the literature on certain types of programs or program interventions, professional issues in a certain field of practice, or the research analyst's own professional background and orientation.

An example of an analyst-constructed theme from the supported housing program analysis is when the researcher indentified the "lack of supervision" of consumers in the mental health system when they shared an apartment with another person with chronic mental illness and no one monitored their room-mates' behaviors. Although no resident said that there was a "lack of supervision" of the residents, the researcher identified this as a major theme or concept and many quotes pointed to deficiencies in the system in not protecting mental health consumers from their roommates in supportive housing programs. While the residents did acknowledge how the mental health system placed them at risk, they did not emphasize the professional issues of neglect of the consumer and the lack of case management oversight that violated professional ethics.

Analyst-constructed themes may also be developed into *analyst-constructed typologies* as the themes are used to place people on a continuum. An example of a generic analyst-constructed typology from an example in the literature (Patton, 2002, p. 475) is how consumers experience and use a program. Some descriptions of consumer involvement with a program might represent a low level of involvement, merely "showing up at the program." Others get involved and "experience the program," and still others have a more profound experience and are "immersed in the program." Different consumers can be charted by level of their program involvement, which can be a major part of the analysis.

Coaxial Coding

At a second level of analysis, consumers can be charted on a process–outcome matrix (Patton, 2002, p. 474) showing, depending on the consumer's level of involvement, their different outcomes. If program process is one axis to be examined and another axis is the consumer outcome, program participants can be charted on a matrix. Since respondent ID numbers are on each of the quotes, the researcher can take the case numbers for those who "just showed up" and look back on their interview transcripts to see what outcomes they experienced from the program. The same could be done for cases representing consumers who "experienced" the program to see if they experienced different outcomes. In this way, this cross-classification is analogous to cross-tabulation and analyzing relationships between variables in quantitative research. By putting case ID numbers on quotes it is possible to see if certain cases with one trend also have another trend, and this could become the process–outcome matrix. This coding of different types of process and outcomes is also referred to as "coaxial coding," or the cross-classification of one typology, process, with another typology, outcomes. One might expect that cases that just "showed up" had significantly poorer outcomes than those of people who "experienced" the program or were immersed in the program. But perhaps there were participants who only needed to show up and get basic services and had a good program outcome.

Use of Metaphors to Create Typologies

The initial themes in qualitative analysis help create typologies or conceptualizations at the pre-theory phase of theory development. Two types of themes and typologies have been described, indigenous themes and typologies, using the respondents' own words, and analyst-constructed themes and typologies, using the research analyst's words to represent the themes found in the data.

A third type of typology or theme could be constructed on the basis of metaphor or an exaggerated comparison. For example, in a qualitative study on the authority of surgeons in the operating room (Fisher & Peterson, 1993), most nurses reported that the surgeon had unquestioned authority in the operating room. Projecting from the data in this study, a number of metaphors could be used for the physician's behavior in relating to the nurses.

One metaphor could be "the Pope," a surgeon who had total authority and felt as though he was infallible in his attitude toward the nurses and other staff in the operating room. No one would ever question his authority or his behavior. Another type of doctor might be "the good father." Staff could not question his authority in the operating room, but he would behave in a caring and supportive way to his staff much like the father in a large family. Such metaphors are quite descriptive and help present the type of case being analyzed.

Patton (2002, pp. 468–469) has used telling metaphors to describe teacher roles in dealing with high school dropouts. One metaphor used to create a typology was "the ostrich," a teacher who ignored the situation, hoping someone else would do something about the dropouts. Another metaphor was "the traffic cop," who just kept students moving through the system. Another metaphor was "the old-fashioned school master," who wanted to use traditional practices in punishing dropouts for their behavior. Use of these different descriptive metaphors can help in the development of pre-theory conceptualizations in an integrated way to show different types of classifications. Again, the data need to fit the metaphor. The researcher should not chose a certain metaphor and try to make the data fit to it.

Intensive Case Analysis by Case Rather than by Theme

The usual type of qualitative data analysis is by theme or category, finding trends and themes in the data. However, sometimes analysis by case can be a very useful type of analysis. In this analysis, information-rich cases are usually selected. These cases can be especially revealing and the case be presented from beginning to end, presenting a holistic view of the consumer and how he or she experienced the program. Some of the cases selected may be success cases, or best cases or practices, and others may be cases that failed, or the worst cases or practices. Such cases can give an extensive description of what happened to individuals in the program. They might be used to look at individual consumers' experiences from beginning to end—from when they first learned about the program, how they used program services, to their positive and negative experiences and their personal outcomes. Such cases might reveal critical incidents in the way service is being delivered and in achieving certain outcomes in individual cases.

One example of the use of by-case analysis is an evaluation of on outreach program to a population of seniors (Finkelstein, 2004). The program was designed to support the seniors and allow them to remain in their own homes, feeling safe and secure. The total package of services included social work services, in-home nursing services, socialization activities at a senior center, a telephone reassurance program, and transportation and escort services. Individual interviews were conducted with 20 seniors who had used program services. Each of the seniors gave high ratings to the services in a closed-ended, rating scale and had positive open-ended comments to make about each of the services. The themes in each of these service areas were analyzed; however, this did not tell the complete story of the effect all these individual services on each person's life. By linking together the positive comments that each senior made about the services they received, a by-case analysis was achieved, and it could be determined how the total service package affected each person.

The following statements are an example of linking together the seniors' comments about all the services they received. The comments were overall very positive but also indicated implementation issues with some of the services, such as the telephone reassurance service, the car service, and the socialization program. The comments also represent *needs assessment* in spelling out some of the other programs the seniors would have liked.

> I like the nurse very much. She is gentle and spends a lot of time with you . . . . I participate in events on a regular basis . . . . I would love to attend exercise programs and outings. I like the art lectures, but would also like lectures from physicians and doctors about different diseases . . . . I like to sit with the members just to talk . . . . I don't like to be interrupted by the telephone contact when I am doing something, otherwise I don't mind.

> The program is very important for me. The nursing service is wonderful . . . . I liked the transportation service when it was done

with the vans. Car service forgets to pick me up. Even so, I still like the transportation . . . . I like the sociability of the program. I like the luncheons, events, and lectures . . . . The only social activity I have is the program except when my children come to see me . . . . I like when the nurse discusses health issues once a month. I don't like the schmooze and coffee cake. I am not a cake eater. I want something more stimulating. I have somebody to talk to and I made friends through the program. I think it's interesting to have a lecture and I would like exercise programs but I have to be sitting in a chair.

I wish I could find people to play bridge 'cause you need four people to play. I like it when the program goes out to lunch. I like the newsletter and I do read the calendar of events.

Nurse was delightful . . . . When you reach 84 and you can do things it is the biggest present an elderly person can have . . . . I don't need the telephone contact but it is okay . . . . The staff is helpful and respectful . . . . I don't attend the program events because I don't socialize. If it is only with old people it is very depressing. I want to be with a variety of people. I wish the program would have a mix with younger people. I like to do volunteer work, but not with the elderly. When I look in the mirror I see an older person so I do not want to see other old people . . . . I find the luncheons boring cause I need to be stimulated; lectures about different topics would be good.

I like the newsletter and the calendar. I like the art lectures. I do not need anything more. I am very happy with the program . . . . The most important thing for me is to know that someone is available if I need help. Belonging to the program makes me feel secure.

This type of intensive case analysis is not done enough in program evaluation. Intensive case analysis clearly shows the overall effect on each person and the positive and negative comments about the services. The degree to which the quantitative ratings of the individual services (e.g., excellent, very good, good, fair, poor) coincide with the qualitative comments represents *method triangulation* and shows reliability in the findings (see section "Reliability and Validation in Qualitative Data Analysis"). The qualitative comments can explain the ratings and show why the service was rated high or low. The qualitative comments provide more depth in exactly what each senior found useful in the service and their feelings about receiving a needed service and how it helped their lives.

From a program-strengths perspective, sometimes individual cases can show some of the benefits that individual participants received from the program. For example, in a study to provide home care services to parents caring for developmentally disabled children, in a number of cases the relationship between the home care providers and the disabled children was one of the real benefits of the services, as the following qualitative passages from two cases suggest.

> He bathes Angel, he dresses him, he talks to him. Sometimes I can stay in my room and hear them laughing together. He meets the school bus and keeps him upstairs in the afternoon . . . . He entertains him. He tells him stories.

> She gets along well with Maria. She talks to Maria a lot and she listens. They got along fine from the start. Maria gets all the attention that she wanted and so she is happy. In fact, all the kids call the homemaker "Grandma."

Likewise, some cases had particular implementation issues, such as the turnover in home care workers. One parent in particular had five home attendants in 4 months.

> The first home attendant was nice but somewhat irresponsible, she didn't come back after she received her first check. The second home attendant was also young and was in school. It seems that she was only working until she got her grant and when it came through she quit. The third home attendant was also a student. She left after the school found her a better job—something to do with the computer. The fourth home attendant was the best one so far. She was always volunteering to do this or that. Then she left. She got a job working in a factory. I just got a new home attendant today. She is somewhat older so we'll have to see how it works out.

The lack of quality home care and the irresponsible behavior of some home attendants found in some cases graphically showed some of the limits of the program.

> The first homemaker used to fall asleep on the job. I could not trust her with Sandra because of that. One day I left her there with Sandra and she fell asleep. Sandra ate some of the paint that was falling off the wall and got sick. She even got some of it in her eyes. I had to take her to the doctor. She was sick for 4 days as a result of eating the paint. She [the home attendant] can't supervise the child if she is sleeping.

The first home attendant was not appropriate to work with Carlos—she was too young and was not responsible. He got out of the apartment one day when I left them alone because she didn't lock the door like I told her.

Reliability and Validation in Qualitative Data Analysis

In quantitative research, an instrument that has tested and sometimes proven previous reliability and validity can be used. Reliability and validity can then also be tested with the sample in the evaluation study and sometimes improved. In qualitative data analysis, reliability and validation mostly take place *after* the data have been collected. There are a number of procedures to test reliability and validation in qualitative research:

1. Using two researchers to analyze the data
2. Reaching a saturation point
3. Negative cases
4. Rival explanations
5. Triangulation

1. Using Two Researchers to Analyze the Data

To improve the consistency or reliability of the analysis process, the same qualitative data can be analyzed by two researchers to see if they come up with the same trends and themes. More often than not, what results is a clarification of the trends. The two analysts would do an independent analysis to see if they come up with the same themes. If similar themes are found, then the themes of typologies have some reproducibility. Reliability can also be increased by asking about the reactions of others to the themes produced. Other stakeholders such as practitioners or administrators could be consulted to get their opinion of the initial themes and if they are linked or supported by the data. Using more than one research analyst is also called "triangulation with multiple analysts." The idea is that two or more persons independently analyze the same qualitative data and compare their findings (Patton, 2002, p. 560). Sometimes the consumers whose quotes are being analyzed are engaged in the coding or interpretation of the data. This is referred to as "member checking" (Oktay, 2002, p. 783). The consumer could provide an analysis or richer understanding of what they said and the reasons for their statements. This can be a great consumer empowerment strategy in qualitative analysis if the funding is there to implement it. The costs can be as high or higher than conducting more interviews, but it helps establish whether or not the researcher's interpretation of the data is correct.

2. Reaching a Saturation Point

Qualitative analysis includes creating categories or themes from the data to the *saturation point*, or to the point where it seems that all the themes and types have been accounted for. By analyzing additional cases, the researcher would find the same themes popping up, rather than new themes. The larger the sample size and the more cases analyzed, the greater the possibility that a saturation point will be reached in the analysis. When the same trends and themes keep reappearing and being repeated in the analysis, the saturation point may have been reached, although determining when the saturation point is reached can be somewhat subjective. Certainly, in analyzing 50 cases you would be closer to reaching a saturation point than analyzing 30 cases.

3. Negative Cases

Use of negative cases is a method for establishing validation of the findings. Negative cases are cases that differ from the major themes or findings. For example, in the mental health evaluation, most people in the sample had positive program experiences; use of negative cases would mean searching for cases where there were program experiences counter to the major trends in the analysis. Were there any cases that were different from those that had positive program experiences with program activities and the housing? Negative cases do not have to be negative in a heuristic sense, they are just cases that turned out differently—for instance, where residents did not value the program activities or where they found fault with the housing they had. The researcher would actually search for negative cases in which program activities were not valued or cases in which residents did not like their housing. The researcher would describe this search for negative cases in the evaluation report, even if no negative cases are found. However, the search for negative cases needs to be reported, as this increases the validity of findings.

For the finding of residents not liking the sharing of an apartment, negative cases would be those in which the respondents did like sharing an apartment when they were in supportive housing. For example, they might have received support from their roommate, rather than the anxiety or abuse found in the majority of cases.

4. Rival Explanations

One way to validate findings is to consider rival explanations or other possibilities for why things turned out the way they did. This means considering possible alternative explanations for why things turned out the way they did. In the study of housing for people with chronic mental health problems, if qualitative data showed residents liking the housing program, and if the residents' quotes about housing also mentioned a reduction in mental health symptoms, one possible explanation might be that the peaceful, safe housing helped reduce symptoms. However, rival explanations need to be considered: the residents could be experiencing reduced symptoms at this time in their lives because of stabilization of their medication and helpful support services, rather then just the quality of their housing. The researcher needs to see if data exist to support these rival explanations by determining if the residents' medication had changed or if they were being given increased supportive services that could have helped stabilize the residents' mental health symptoms.

In another example, analysis of a senior program, the qualitative data may seem to show that positive experiences of seniors in the program were mostly due to the in-home nursing care they received. Here the researcher would search for other cases where the positive experiences did not result only from the in-home nursing care. These could be rival explanations—the senior liked the program because of the social work services or the activity groups that were offered. The data on the social work services and the activity groups would then need to be examined as rival or alternative explanations for the seniors' high ratings of the program. As Patton (2002, p. 553) has stated, the researcher looks for the best possible fit between the data and the analysis that was conducted.

5. Triangulation

One of the broadest forms of achieving reliability and validity in qualitative research is through *triangulation,* a process whereby the researcher guards against the accusation that a study's findings are simply an artifact of a single method, data source, or a single investigator's bias (Patton, 2002, p. 556). In the mental-health housing program evaluated earlier in this chapter, themes of positive effects of participation in program activities and high-quality housing were found in the initial analysis of cases. The presentation can be balanced, or "triangulated," with quantitative data of the percent of all cases in the study that experienced these positive effects and with other quantitative data that reaffirm the value of program activities and the housing such as residents' rating of certain program activities as "excellent, very good, good, fair or poor." The qualitative data are compared to the quantitative data to see if there is *method triangulation*; the qualitative conclusion is examined from the quantitative lens to see if the results or findings are similar (see "Example of Data Triangulation," below). In all, 37 residents were interviewed for this study, so it is important to document how many of the cases had these positive experiences expressed in their quotes. If their quantitative ratings about the housing are also very high and supported by the qualiatative data, there is method triangulation.

Also, the qualitative finding that the housing was peaceful and quiet, created less stress and clearer thinking, and allowed residents to get refreshed may be supported by the quantitative data showing a reduction of symptoms of mental illness compared to those when residents first came to the housing program. The fact that some quantitative data did document a reduction in mental health symptoms from the previous housing program lent triangulation to the finding, in that these qualitative quotes about their peaceful and safe housing which relaxed them were supported by some quantitative measure of symptom reduction. While correlation between qualitative findings and quantitative findings might seem easy to achieve, often quantitative findings do not support and may even contradict the qualitative findings.

Another form of *method triangulation* is where the results of different methods of data collection are compared to see if similar findings are produced. For example, data from qualitative interviews with program participants should be similar to findings produced in a focus group in which participants discuss their program experiences. Or interview data can be compared with data from direct observations of the program or with written program documents. As Patton points out (2002, p. 556), rather than always thinking that triangulation *must* show similar findings, it is just as important to find inconsistencies that will help add to the richness of the data and the interpretation explaining why things are operating the way they are.

Likewise, there can be *triangulation of different data sources* by comparing data from different sources to see if the same findings appear. Triangulation of different data sources can also be accomplished by including the perspectives of different stakeholders in the program. For example, consumer interviews can be compared with interviews of practitioners to see if the same findings are achieved. Most likely, their perspectives will be different, but having the two perspectives adds validity to the evaluation findings. In the housing study, consumer perspectives on the program could be supplemented by staff interviews to see if staff members have similar perceptions to the consumers. This is triangulation based on different data sources.

As mentioned earlier, having two researchers analyze the data and search for themes can add to the reliability of the analysis. This practice is known as *analyst* or *analytic triangulation*. Staff members or consumers could also participate in this process. If they were not involved in the actual coding or discovery of themes they could nonetheless hear and respond to a presentation of the themes, thus helping with analytic triangulation. When respondents (consumers or staff) are involved in the process of analyzing or reviewing the data this is called *member checking*, which adds great depth to interpretation of the data and the validity of the findings.

Also, the themes and patterns found in the data could be presented to other professional and community audiences for review and comment so that they could add their perspectives and interpretations to the findings. Such audience review has been called *"reflexive triangulation"* (Patton, 2002, p. 561).

One last type of triangulation is *theory triangulation*, in which the data and findings are viewed from the perspective of two or more theories. For example, the data from the housing program for people with mental illness could be viewed using environmental theory, in that the environment affects the person. Or psychological theories could be used to address how a person's psychological state could affect their view of the housing. By examining the data from the perspective of each theory, the interpretations of the finding are enriched and rival explanations can be considered.

Example of Data Triangulation—Quantitative and Qualitative Data from Evaluation of the Everybody Needs a Proxy Campaign

NIKE WHITTEMORE, M.A.

GRADUATE OF THE MASTER'S PROGRAM IN HEALTH ADVOCACY,

SARAH LAWRENCE COLLEGE

One way to enrich both quantitative and qualitative findings is through data triangulation, through which we determine how much the findings from quantitative data are supported by the findings of the qualitative data. The value of triangulation can be seen in the following example from the Everybody Needs a Proxy Campaign which was described in Chapter 7.

Two questions that volunteers were asked in the Everybody Needs a Proxy Campaign concerned their perception of the consumers'sknowledge of the New York health-care proxy before and after contact with the proxy campaign. As shown in Table 9.9, four (50%) of the respondents perceived consumers to have "no knowledge" and three (37.5%) of the respondents thought consumers had "very little knowledge" of the proxy prior to the intervention. Only one respondent thought consumers had "some knowledge" (12.5%), and no respondents thought consumers had "a great deal of knowledge" (0%).

TABLE 9.9. Quantitative Data Analysis: Perceived Consumer Knowledge of Proxy before Intervention

	Number	%
No knowledge (1)	4	50
Very little knowledge (2)	3	37.5
Some knowledge (3)	1	12.5
A great deal of knowledge (4)	0	0
Total	8	100

These findings were supported by data triangulation—qualitative descriptions of the respondents' experiences with consumers. All eight volunteers had something to say about the lack of consumer knowledge, citing that some consumers did not know what the proxy was. Some consumers thought it was a "Dr. Kevorkian" type of thing, and some were reluctant altogether to talk about issues related to dying:

People are not very knowledgeable about the proxy.

Most people don't know how important it is in New York State.

Most people have no idea. In fact, when I asked one woman, who was a janitor in the building where I was volunteering, if she had a proxy, she said yes, she had health insurance. When I explained to her what a proxy was, she said she hadn't realized she needed one and took one.

If they have any knowledge, it's usually misguided. For example, I have to educate them that they don't need a lawyer to fill it out, that it's different from a living will, and that they don't have to fill out the optional box.

I would say that 25% know there's a form out there; another 25% have the living will and proxy jumbled; and the other 50% have no idea.

People don't know what a proxy is. They have the impression that it's a "right to die" document and only used for people who want to die. They don't understand it's about choices, about the opportunity to choose life support, too.

One woman said I was going to go to hell because I was promoting death. Like a Dr. Kevorkian type of thing. Obviously, she had the wrong impression.

In general, the American public is anti-death. They don't want to talk about it. That's why it's important to market it as a *living* will.

Example of Data Triangulation—Quantitative and Qualitative Data from Evaluation of the Everybody Needs a Proxy Campaign (Continued)

TABLE 9.10. Quantitative Data Analysis: Perceived Consumer Knowledge of Proxy After Intervention

	Number	%
No knowledge (1)	0	0
Very little knowledge (2)	0	0
Some knowledge (3)	1	12.5
A great deal of knowledge (4)	7	87.5
Total	8	100

As shown in Table 9.10, seven (87.5%) of the respondents perceived consumers to have "a great deal of knowledge" about the proxy *after* interfacing with the campaign. Only one respondent perceived consumers as having "some knowledge" (12.5%), and no respondents perceived consumers as having "no knowledge" (0%) or "very little knowledge" (0 %) after the intervention.

These findings were supported by data triangulation—qualitative descriptions of the respondents' experiences with consumers. There were, however, only two positive comments for knowledge after the program showing there was less reliability for this finding:

> They are clearer about what it is, how to fill it out, and why it's important.
>
> Afterwards, yes, people have much more knowledge about the proxy.

In this instance, the other qualitative responses helped modify the quantitative data. The volunteers admitted that their pre- and posttest answers about consumers' knowledge of the New York health-care proxy was based primarily on consumers who listened to a presentation or with whom the volunteer could speak to in depth, and not those who simply took a proxy in passing. Volunteers used terms such as "don't know" when contemplating whether the campaign increased the knowledge of those in the latter category:

> The approach is important. I think people have a great deal of knowledge after sitting down to listen to what the proxy is all about and asking questions. However, those who just take a proxy in a rush, I have no idea if their knowledge increases.

In a big meeting/presentation, people's knowledge absolutely increases. In a festival venue, I don't know.

Based on the questions from the audience at the Lion's Club meeting, they're going to remember the information. The people on the sidewalk, I don't know.

Campaign volunteers were asked to rate their own knowledge of the New York health-care proxy before and after the Everybody Needs a Proxy training. As shown in Table 9.11, four (50%) of the respondents rated themselves as having "a great deal of knowledge" about the proxy *before* the campaign's training and the other four (50%) rated themselves as having "some knowledge." This indicates that the campaign was, in fact, successful in recruiting volunteers with some prior knowledge of the health-care proxy. No respondents rated themselves as having "no knowledge" (0%) or "very little knowledge" (0%) before the training.

These findings were supported by data triangulation—qualitative descriptions respondents gave about their pre-training knowledge of the proxy:

My knowledge of the proxy before the training was pretty good.

I am a graduate of the Health Advocacy program and a nurse, so I had a lot of prior knowledge of the proxy before the training.

Not only do I work in health care, I had already gone through another training with a different program about advance directives, so I had a great deal of knowledge prior to the training.

As shown in Table 9.12, all eight (100%) of the respondents rated themselves as having "a great deal of knowledge" about the proxy *after* the campaign's training. This indicates that the volunteers' depth of knowledge increased, especially in relation to legal issues (as noted in their qualitative responses). No respondents rated themselves as having "some knowledge" (0%), "very little knowledge" (0%), or "no knowledge" (0%) after the training.

TABLE 9.11. Quantitative Data Analysis: Volunteers' Knowledge of Proxy Before Training

	Number	%
No knowledge (1)	0	0
Very little knowledge (2)	0	0
Some knowledge (3)	4	50
A great deal of knowledge (4)	4	50
Total	8	100

*Example of Data Triangulation—Quantitative and Qualitative Data
from Evaluation of the Everybody Needs a Proxy
Campaign (Continued)*

TABLE 9.12. Quantitative Data Analysis: Volunteers' Knowledge of
Proxy After Training

	Number	%
No knowledge (1)	0	0
Very little knowledge (2)	0	0
Some knowledge (3)	0	0
A great deal of knowledge (4)	8	100
Total	8	100

These findings were supported by data triangulation—qualitative descriptions respondents gave about their post-training knowledge of the proxy:

I definitely had more depth of knowledge after the training.

I feel that I am very knowledgeable now.

I knew a great deal before the training, but the legal stuff helped a lot, as well as the opportunity to ask questions. I also really liked that video.

I learned a little more in the training because the original training I had gone through with a different program hadn't been given by a lawyer.

I'm now very comfortable with the material.

THE VALUE OF TRIANGULATION

Clearly, balancing the quantitative data with the qualitative data through data triangulation enhanced the validity of both types of data. Qualitative data helped tell the story of why people selected one particular category on a rating scale. For example, explicit details about the consumers' lack of knowledge about a health-care proxy were provided in the qualitative data. Also, the qualitative data provided details that helped modify the quantitative findings about perceived consumer knowledge after the intervention, as volunteers talked about the improved effectiveness of group presentations over that of handing out proxies in open forums (such as street fairs).

Summary

1. Evaluations should be implemented by collecting the data and staying as close to the research design and plan as possible. Once the data start being collected, the processes of quantitative and qualitative data analysis can begin.

2. It is incorrect to think that quantitative methods are objective and qualitative methods are subjective. They are different forms of data, and each has its principles and standards of analysis.

3. Structured data are analyzed through the techniques of quantitative data analysis.

4. Analysis of frequency distributions on the basic data (ratings of the program services, consumer characteristics, etc.) often uncovers novel information about the program even before relationships between variables in bivariate and multivariate data analyses are attempted.

5. Tests of statistical significance are relatively objective standards that show whether a relationship exists between two or more variables; if the p level is $<.05$, an association or relationship is considered statistically significant. A higher test statistic such as the chi-square or t-test will produce a lower p level, meaning the relationship might be a real, not a chance, relationship.

6. When two variables are categorical, cross-tabulation and chi-square analysis can be used especially insofar as program inputs and processes are related to outcome.

7. A t-test and one-way analysis of variance (ANOVA) can be used when one variable, such as an outcome variable, is interval level and the other variable, such as the type of intervention, is a categorical variable.

8. Change data can be analyzed with the help of a paired sample t-test for changes in the mean scores of outcome variables, or the McNemar test for changes in categorical variables.

9. The techniques of qualitative data analysis are used to analyze data from open-ended questions in a survey or personal interview, qualitative data from focus groups, comprehensive notes from observations, process records, minutes of meetings, and other types of descriptive, nonstructured data.

10. Qualitative data constitute a dynamic, naturalistic, and holistic type of data. Rich, descriptive data describe the in-depth experiences of both consumers and staff in their own words.

11. Qualitative data analysis is especially useful for consumer empowerment, empowerment evaluation, and a strengths-based orientation to evaluation.

12. The process of qualitative data analysis begins with assembling the data, reading through the data, generating descriptive categories or themes, looking for new themes and categories, and reporting the themes with the supporting quotes presented directly under the themes.

13. Themes based on the respondents' own words are indigenous themes or concepts. Themes that the research analyst creates on the basis of the program, professional practice issues, or the researcher's own perspective are analyst-constructed themes or concepts.

14. Use of metaphors is another way to develop themes that people do not usually forget.

15. Coaxial coding is a way to look at one theme in a case by means of another theme. For example, the evaluator could chart on one axis the cases that were most intensely involved in the process of the program and chart their outcomes on another axis to see what an intensive program experience produces.

16. In addition to analysis "by theme," intensive description of particular cases, presenting all the ways in which the program has affected the consumer throughout the experience, can be a useful way to focus the analysis.

17. Methods to obtain reliability and validation in qualitative analysis include using a number of analysts or coders, negative cases, rival explanations, reaching a saturation point, and triangulation of methods and data sources.

REFERENCES

Abu-Bader, S.H. (2006). *Using Statistical Methods in Social Work Practice: A Complete SPSS Guide.* Chicago: Lyceum Books.

Cottrell, P.J. (2002). Knowledge and attitudes of modern Orthodox Jewish high school students toward carrier screening. Unpublished Masters Thesis, Sarah Lawrence College, Bronxville, NY.

Fabricant, M., & Smith, M.J. (1997, January). A case study of the supported housing program (mimeo).

Finkelstein, M. (2004). Evaluation of a Comprehensive Senior Outreach Program. Sarah Lawrence College, Bronxville, NY.

Fisher, B.J., & Peterson, C. (1993). She won't be dancing much anyway: A study of surgeons, surgical nurses, and elderly patients. *Qualitative Health Research* 3:165–184.

Kilmnick, D. (2006). Heterosexist attitudes: Changes following contact with an openly gay instructor. Ph.D. dissertation, The City University of New York.

Munro, B.H. (2004). *Statistics for Health Care*, 5th edition. Philadelphia: Lippincott Williams and Wilkins.

Oktay, J.S. (2002) Standards for qualitative research with exemplars. In Roberts, A.R., & Greene, G.J. (eds.) *Social Workers' Desk Reference.* New York: Oxford University Press.

Patton, M.Q. (1987) *How to Use Qualitative Methods in Evaluation.* Thousand Oaks, CA: Sage Publications.

Patton, M.Q. (2002) *Qualitative Research and Evaluation Methods,* 3rd edition. Thousand Oaks, CA: Sage Publications.

Royse, D., Thyer, B.A., Padgett, D.K., & Logan, T.K. (2001) *Program Evaluation: An Introduction.* Belmont, CA: Wadsworth/Thomson Learning.

Strauss, A.C., Strauss, A.L., & Corbin, J. (2007) *Basics of Qualitative Research: Techniques and Procedures for Developing Grounded Theory,* 3rd edition. Thousand Oaks, CA: Sage Publications.

Weinbach, R.W.& Grinnell, R.M. (2006) *Statistics for Social Workers,* 7th edition. Needham Heights, MA: Allyn and Bacon

Yockey, D.Y. (2007) *SPSS Demystified: A Step by Step Guide to Successful Data Analysis.* Upper Saddle River, NJ: Prentice Hall

10

Writing the Report and Implementing the Findings

Writing the Research Report

Once the evaluation study has been completed and the data have been collected and analyzed, the findings need to be communicated in a number of ways. Communication of evaluation findings is multifaceted. The final evaluation report will need to be written and the evaluator or evaluation team needs to report back to stakeholders and feed back results into the ongoing planning and development of the program. The evaluation report should be comprehensive, providing an introduction and a description of the program, presentation of the programmatic and policy issues, the evaluation research design and plan, a description of implementation of the study and the data collection, analysis of the data, a summary of findings and their implications, and the action that needs to be taken in light of the findings. The plan for how the results will become feedback for improving or changing the program is most important. Above all, a final report needs to be written that is readable, understandable, and clear enough so that all parties involved understand what the program is, how it was evaluated, and what the results were and what changes should be made in the program.

An outline for a complete evaluation report should look something like this:

1. Overview Summary or Executive Summary or Summary of Major Findings

   Often it is good to have an overview of the study and the study findings. This allows someone to read the report and know the key findings and perspectives.

2. Program Description (or Need for the Program in Needs Assessment Studies)

   Description of the need for the program—policy issues, etc.
   Review of literature on related programs
   Description of program history and philosophy
   Description of program services
   Program theory (articulated or implied theory, implausible or plausible)
   Setting of the program
   Description of interventive methods
   Characteristics of consumers being served
   Characteristics of program staff
   Cost and funding

3. Program Goals and Objectives (or Need in a Needs Assessment Study)

   Define the program goals and objectives to be studied
   Define the program operations in a monitoring study

4. Research Plan or Research Design

   Research design or type of study (experimental, survey, qualitative study)
   Data collection procedures (survey, personal interview, focus group, observation, or the form used in taking data from case records, etc.)
   Data collection instrument
   Sampling plan – probability or non-probability and type of each

5. Analysis of the Data

   Quantitative and qualitative data analysis

6. Summary of Findings

7. Implications and Recommendations and Results for Feedback

A summary overview, a summary of findings, or an executive summary is now becoming an essential part of the written report. The summary gives the reader the gist of the evaluation without reading the whole report. Weiss notes (1998, p. 297) that the executive summary is important because the reality is that most people will only read this summary. She advises that the summary include the most important findings, concretely and specifically. Most important, the summary needs to explain the evidence that supports the conclusions without having the reader get lost in the technical details. The implications of the study for this program, for the field in general, and for larger policy issues should be presented in the summary.

If the researcher has been following the principles and procedures in program evaluation outlined in this book, sections 2 through 4 of the outline, the program description, the program goals and objectives, the research plan or design, and the analysis of the data will already have been written. Only parts 1 (Summary of Findings-Overview), 6 (Summary of Findings), and 7 (Implications and Recommendations) need to be written at the very end. Having parts of the report written beforehand can greatly allay the anxiety of all involved as the evaluation nears completion.

Reporting to the Stakeholders in Evaluation

In addition to writing a final report, there need to be meetings and the personal communication of findings by the researcher. Communicating findings should be a continuation of the participatory process with all the stakeholders involved. As discussed in Chapter 3, participatory evaluation, empowerment evaluation, and consumer empowerment are very important in this last step, so that everyone gets their say about the findings.

In the last stage of data analysis, other stakeholders may have been involved in analyzing qualitative findings through participation in discovering trends and coding themes. Other stakeholders are not usually involved in the more technical analysis of quantitative data. So this could be the first major interaction with stakeholders since the planning of the research. There should be meetings with the stakeholders, such as administrators, staff, consumers, and funding sources, and meetings with the community at large to discuss the findings and indicate the next steps for the program and its development. The researcher has an ethical commitment to see that the study is living up to its commitment to these participatory processes and the equal involvement of all stakeholders. This is no easy task, with so many parties involved, and often researchers are not paid for their time in communicating findings.

Dissemination of findings to the immediate stakeholders is the most important task at hand. Then comes dissemination to programs and professionals in the field of practice, and then policy and program changes warranted locally and nationally. Weiss (1998, pp. 305–306) notes that certain characteristics will help ensure the utilization of findings. If potential users of the knowledge in the research were included from the beginning of the study, the process of inclusion should be more successful at the end of the study. Also, communication between the researchers and practitioners should be a two-way street, with sustained interaction over time. So the more the original planning and implementation of the study used participatory processes, the more there should be utilization of those findings. This is one of the main points of empowerment evaluation.

In addition to participatory trends, a strengths perspective can be used in relation to the findings. There should be an appreciation of the strengths of the program as it currently exists and the professionals who are involved in delivering the services. The strengths of the consumers and their life situations and the strengths in the community and community members where the program delivers the service should also be acknowledged. Everyone's strengths need to be taken into account in a significant way. The researcher and the study need to carry out the strengths perspective, viewing the program and the people involved in it with a positive frame of reference and attitude.

A good method for initiating these processes is to hold meetings with all the stakeholders to discuss drafts of the final report, so that revisions can reflect people's comments about the program and about the report. In the report, recommendations are made for the program's present and future directions. The results can be fed back into the program and address implications for this program and those more generally for programs similar to this program, locally and nationally.

While implementing participatory evaluation, empowerment evaluation, consumer empowerment, and a strengths perspective can seem over-whelming, it can help to maintain this perspective and keep all the stake-holders in mind. There are many parties at the table with whom to share the final results:

1. The administrators in the organization where the study was conducted
2. The staff in that organization
3. The consumers served in the program
4. The funding sources (federal, state, or local governments, private foundations)
5. Local community groups representing the consumers and their families

Since the researcher has a primary responsibility to the organization sponsoring the evaluation study that is most likely paying for the evalua-tion, the researcher has an ethical responsibility to finish the study and take the interests of the organization into account. Both the organization sponsoring the evaluation and the organizations that funded the study will most likely be actively participating in assessing the findings of the study. So the researcher needs to give special attention to groups who might be left out in the process—primarily the consumers who used the program, the community where the program was located, and the staff who delivered the service.

Reconsidering the Politics of Evaluation at the Conclusion of the Evaluation

As discussed in Chapter 1, evaluation is part of an unfolding political process. The evaluator needs to read the political climate so that people will "hear" the study findings and consider implementing the study findings. Everyone has a perspective on the program. Everyone has a stake in the program, and everyone has a stake in the results of the evaluation.

The political process of negotiation is involved in all evaluations throughout the process, but especially at the conclusion of the study. The researcher needs to assess the audience and report the findings in a way that makes change possible. An open and thorough discussion of research results means that the opinions of the different parties will be taken into account in a rewarding and thoughtful process. If there are irreconcilable differences in relation to the findings, part of the report might include an alternate-views section where those feelings are stated. Sometimes it is hard to reach consensus on how a report should be presented. The aim is to iron out any differences of opinion.

The author was involved in one evaluation study where there was failure to achieve consensus about the research report early on in a draft report of the findings. The conflict escalated to the point that the following memo was written from the agency program department to the researcher that carried out the study:

> It is most regrettable to note the presentation of the project experience is fraught with omissions, inaccurate information and distortions since this pioneering program has a great deal to offer . . . . The staff and I feel an ethical and professional obligation to comment on these crucial factors since a gross injustice to the program, to the clients, the staff and the agency will be committed . . . . Please note we are not evaluating or reviewing the manuscript, but rather bringing your attention to matters of public record . . . . We will present as objective an account as is possible. We cannot emphasize enough the urgency for an honest report of this program.

Clearly, more needed to be done here to reach consensus on a report or at least to offer the professional practitioners who felt this way a form in the report to report their alternative views. After this memo, many meetings were attended by administrators, program staff, and the researchers to iron out those differences that could be changed. Of course, the basic data presenting the program and program outcomes could not be altered, but some of the issues raised by staff could be presented as they raised some methodological and ethical issues that were valid. For example, in the preface to the study report, the researcher identified only some staff members and implied that some staff, who were named in the report, were more valuable than other staff members. Identifying individual staff by name in a report is clearly against the principles of confidentiality described in the ethics section of Chapter 1.

Feedback of Results and Positive Examples

The feedback of results and presentation of findings do not have to be as negative as the above example. There are many evaluations in which the reports are accepted and findings applauded by researchers, staff, consumers, administrator, funding sources, and the community where the program provides service.

One example of how findings were presented in the evaluation of the supported housing program for the mentally ill comes from some of the qualitative data on program activities analyzed in the last chapter. The following paragraphs, which reflect some of the qualitative data presented in Chapter 9, were taken from the Overview and Summary of Findings section in the beginning of the evaluation report:

> The program had an array of program activities and events. These included Friday night social gatherings, holiday celebrations, guest speakers, brunches, and trips. These social events were a pathway to social interaction and the prevention of social isolation.
>
> ... The combination of engaged staff, responsive services, and program activities effected increasingly tighter bonds between the residents and the program. Other residents were frequently described as family members and the depth of these connections was an important contribution of the program. The program deepened the social network of program participants.
>
> "Method triangulation" was achieved as the above findings from the qualitative data were confirmed in quantitative data from the study. The quantitative data showed that the residents in the program showed fewer mental health symptoms, stronger social networks, and less hospitalization and they had better, more secure housing.

A quantitative measure on positive social networks showed
statistically significant increases since being in the program and
negative social interactions decreased when the resident came into the
program. (Fabricant & Smith, 1997, pp. iii–iv)

In the educational program for Orthodox high school students to increase
their knowledge of genetic diseases among Jewish populations and have them
consider genetic testing, the research findings showed mixed results. The
findings were important for educational programs in genetic testing and
were generally accepted by all parties. In the presentation of the findings, the
program clearly showed some positive effects.

The hypothesis that there would be an increase in knowledge after the
educational session was proven. Knowledge scores increased from
46% to 87% from the pretest to the posttest.
   The hypothesis that students would more likely want earlier
genetic testing after the educational session was not demonstrated by
the study . . . . because so many of the sample were pro screening
before the educational session.
   . . . The hypothesis that the presentation would result in more
communication was demonstrated specifically in an increased
willingness to communicate carrier-testing results to a boyfriend or a
girlfriend. Students were significantly more likely to report that they
would tell their boyfriend or girlfriend about carrier screening results
on the posttest.
   [Most importantly, the study went on to report implications.] . . .
This study yielded valuable information about methods of outreach in
the Orthodox community. There is a common perception that
Orthodox institutions are not very open to educating their members
about genetics and carrier screening. . . . Organizations involved in
outreach to educate about genetics are rarely able to get permission to
make presentations at Orthodox Jewish institutions . . . . It does appear
to be easier to get permission to do an outreach program in an
Orthodox institution if one is a member of the Orthodox community.
(Cottrell, 2002, pp. 23–25)

In the study of the use of home care for parents with developmentally
disabled children, a summary of findings showed the potential aid that such
service could provide for this important population of consumers and had
important implications for helping these parents.

> In-home services were found to be highly effective for these parents. The home care workers made the contribution expected of them. They provided direct care in the home and related to the children well. The home care workers relieved the parents by performing household tasks such as cleaning, doing laundry, bathing the child, etc. In-home help also freed parents up to seek jobs, complete their educations, catch up on household chores, spend time with their children, and sometimes simply rest. (Smith, Caro, & McKaig, 1987, p. 1)

In addition to these findings, the implications of the findings for larger programs providing home care to parents caring for children with developmental disabilities were highlighted in the report. There were also recommendations for future programs to use home care workers with more expertise and more training to provide service to this special population.

> Many families had gone through a number of home care workers before they settled on one who was satisfactory. The descriptions of the care needs of the families made it clear that home care workers are needed who are not only responsible but who have knowledge of the specific needs of these children and who know how to interact with them in a caring way. The assignment of an untrained worker meant that parents often had to spend a great deal of time training the worker. If the home care worker is not skilled and responsible, the worker makes little, if any, contribution. The experiences of parents point to a need for better screening, training, and supervision of these workers. (Smith et al., 1987, p. 5)

Taking the Study Beyond the Program

Evaluation involves more than simply using appropriate research procedures. It is a purposeful activity, *undertaken to affect the development of policy,* to shape the design of social interventions, and to improve the management of social programs. *In the broadest sense of politics, evaluation is a political activity.*

—P. Rossi, M. Lipsey, & H. Freeman, *Evaluation: A Systematic Approach* (2004), p. 370 (italics mine)

An important strategy for the local program administrators, staff, consumers, and researchers is to bring the study and its implications beyond the study into the program and policy context and field of practice. Weiss (1998, p. 309) mentions presenting the study to interest groups in the field of practice. For example, in the mental health housing program evaluation presented in Chapter 9, those involved should make sure that the study gets recognized by advocates in the mental health field, such as national organizations that support services to the mentally ill, local and national groups representing social work and health professionals in the mental health field and local and national groups representing relatives, friends, and supporters of persons with mental illness. The home care study of families caring for the developmentally disabled should enlist the support of advocacy groups for the developmentally disabled, such as the Association for the Help of Retarded Children (AHRC), and parent advocacy groups for developmentally disabled children. The educational program for Orthodox Jewish high school students might report findings back to the Orthodox community and groups that support awareness of genetic diseases affecting Jewish groups. The program might also communicate the findings to the American Society for Genetic Counselors, and other health-care and health-care provider groups wanting more data on how different demographic groups understand and use the new information on genetics.

Weiss has discussed the importance of "policy networks" (1998, p. 309), which are informal groups that are in continuing contact about a substantive field. These could be people from federal and state agencies, legislatures, the media, universities, research organizations, and interest groups. Through these networks evaluation findings can be integrated into ongoing policy debates at the local, state, national, and international levels and be disseminated far beyond the local program level.

Summary

1. Evaluation findings need to be communicated in a final report and in meetings and forums with stakeholders and stakeholder groups.
2. The outline for the final report included in this chapter should assist in writing the final report.
3. Much of the final report can be started and written as the evaluation proceeds before all the data are collected.
4. Findings also need to be reported at meetings with stakeholders to continue participatory processes such as empowerment evaluation and consumer empowerment. As stakeholder concerns are taken into account, a richer report and process will occur.
5. Findings should be viewed within a strengths perspective in relation to the consumers served, their community, and the program intervention itself.

6. The evaluator needs to assess the political climate and environment in presenting results that can effect real changes in the program as results are fed back into the program.
7. In addition to changes in the local program, the researcher should communicate findings to the larger local, state, and national audience of policymakers, professionals, and consumer advocacy groups in the particular field of practice.

REFERENCES

Cottrell, P.J. (2002). Knowledge and attitudes of modern Orthodox Jewish high school students toward carrier screening. Masters Thesis, Sarah Lawrence College, Bronxville, NY.

Fabricant, M., & Smith, M.J. (1997, January). A case study of the supported housing program (mimeo).

Rossi, P.H., Lipsey, M.W., & Freeman, H.E. (2004). *Evaluation: A Systematic Approach.* Thousand Oaks, CA: Sage Publications.

Smith, M.J., Caro, F.G., & McKaig, K. (1987). *Caring for the Developmentally Disabled Child at Home: The Experiences of Low Income Families.* New York: Community Service Society.

Weiss, C.H. (1998). *Evaluation: Methods for Studying Programs and Policies.* Englewood Cliffs, NJ: Prentice Hall.

Appendix

University Employee Assistance Program: Client Satisfaction Questionnaire

The Employee Assistance Program would like to know how we have served you. Please take 10 minutes to tell us about your experience with the service by answering the following questions.

Note that this information is completely confidential. Do not put your name on this questionnaire. Also notice that we did not ask you any identifying information such as the department where you work, your position at the University, or any information such as age, marital status, etc.

When you have completed the questionnaire, simply place it in the enclosed stamped envelope and put it in a mailbox.

Your candid responses to the following questions will help us improve services to you and to your fellow employees at the University.

Thank you.

1. Which of the following best describe the kind of situation or problem for which you sought help at the Employee Assistance Program? (Check as many as apply.)

   __ trouble getting along with a spouse or someone with whom you share a close personal relationship
   __ trouble with a child in your family

___ trouble getting along with another family member, relative, or friend
___ stress from a change in living circumstances
___ trouble carrying out responsibilities at home
___ trouble carrying out responsibilities at work
___ physical or health problems
___ financial problems
___ trouble getting along with someone at work (e.g., co-worker or supervisor)
___ general irritability at work
___ trouble dealing with feelings or emotions
___ drinking or drug problems
___ other; please describe: _____

2. Was the problem that brought you to the Employee Assistance Program negatively affecting your experience at work in any of the following ways? (Check all that apply.)

   A. less satisfaction from my job

   Yes___ No____ Somewhat____

   B. reduced ability to concentrate at work

   Yes___ No____ Somewhat____

   C. more absences or lateness

   Yes___ No____ Somewhat____

   D. not doing my work as well as I usually do

   Yes___ No____ Somewhat____

   E. trouble getting along with others at work

   Yes___ No____ Somewhat____

3. Did anyone suggest that you go to the Employee Assistance Program?

   ___ No
   ___ Yes, a co-worker
   ___ Yes, my supervisor
   ___ Yes, someone else, e.g. family member, personal friend; please list their relationship to you (not their actual name)

4. In your opinion, did the Employee Assistance Program respond to your particular problem quickly?

   ___ Yes
   ___ No

__ Somewhat

If no please explain:

5. What would you say the EAP staff person did for you?

6. How frequently did you usually meet with the EAP staff person?

   __ once a week

   __ about every other week

   __ about once a month

   __ less frequently than once a month

7. Were you satisfied with how often the EAP staff person met with you?

   __ Yes

   __ No, would have like less frequent contacts

   __ No, would have liked more frequent contacts

8. How helpful would you say the EAP staff were to you?

   __ extremely helpful

   __ somewhat helpful

   __ not particularly helpful

9. Specifically, what did the EAP staff person do for you that was helpful or not helpful?

10. How do you feel your situation or problem has changed since you first contacted the EAP?

    __ become much better

    __ become a little better

    __ not much change

    __ become a little worse

    __ become much worse

       Why do you say this?

11. In. general, what do you think of the service that you received from the Employee Assistance Program?

    __ very satisfied

    __ satisfied

    __ neither satisfied nor dissatisfied

    __ dissatisfied

    __ very dissatisfied

12. Did the Employee Assistance Program make you feel better about yourself in any way?

    Yes __ No __ Somewhat ___

13. Did the Employee Assistance Program make a difference in your personal life?

    Yes __ No __ Somewhat ___

14. Did the Employee Assistance Program make a difference in your work on the job?

    Yes __ No __ Somewhat ___

15. If you encountered a problem in the future, would you consider returning to the Employee Assistance Program?

    Yes __ No __ Not Sure ___

16. If a friend asked, would you recommend the Employee Assistance Program?

    Yes __ No __ Not Sure ___

In the space below, please make any comments about the service that was provided to you by the Employee Assistance Program or make any suggestions you may have about new ways we might help you or others at the University.

Thank You. We appreciate your help. Now simply place the questionnaire in the stamped envelope and mail it back to us.

Glossary

ANALYST-CONSTRUCTED THEMES or CONCEPTS. Themes created by the research analyst that are based on patterns and themes identified in the qualitative data.

ARTICULATED PROGRAM THEORY. When a particular theory or rationale for an intervention and program methods is used in the program design.

BLACK-BOX or UNKNOWN-BOX PHENOMENON. Occurs when evaluators produce evaluation designs that allocate most resources to documenting the achievement of program goals and objectives and few resources to the program description, interventive methods, and how the program was delivered. Impact assessment studies and experimental designs are often susceptible to the black-box phenomenon, since resources are allocated to measure specific outcomes and the service delivery is often measured as either having service or not having service.

COAXIAL CODING. Identifying cases by their location on two axes or themes, across classification; for example, identifying cases by where they fit on an one axis of program process and another axis of program outcomes.

CHI-SQUARE TEST. Measures an association between two categorical variables.

CHRONBACH'S ALPHA. Considered the gold standard of reliability coefficients, based on average correlations of all the combinations of split-half reliability coefficients. The alpha needs to achieve a score of .80 or above to indicate reliability.

CONCURRENT VALIDITY. Empirical validity can be concurrent if we measure the concept and external criterion at the same time. For example, we measure stress in a caregiver and at the same time measure caregiving responsibilities to test whether the amount of responsibilities is related stress.

CONSTRUCT VALIDITY. Determining whether or not a measure reflects the theory behind the concept. A theory or theories from the literature are reviewed to see if all aspects of the theory have been represented in the measure.

CONSUMER EMPOWERMENT. Increasing the status and power of consumers, clients, and patients so that they can influence their own fate. In program evaluation, consumer empowerment means involving consumers in the planning, implementation, and evaluation of programs and having consumers actively comment on the services they receive.

CONTENT VALIDITY. Determining whether items that are usually related to the concept are left out—for example, whether an item such as "I feel stressed," which we usually think of as measuring stress, is left out of the scale.

CONVENIENCE SAMPLE. Type of non-probability sample in which cases are selected without much attention to how or why they were selected.

CONVERGENCE. The degree to which the qualitative data relate to a specific theme rather than to other themes or subthemes.

COST–BENEFIT ANALYSIS. Analysis in which costs of a program, measured in dollar amounts, are compared to outcomes, which are also translated into their monetary value. For example, the cost of an employee assistance program would be compared according to outcomes such as money saved by fewer employee absences from work.

COST-EFFECTIVENESS ANALYSIS. Cost analysis in which costs in dollar amounts are compared to program outcomes measured in conceptual, non-monetary units. For example, a conceptual outcome such as reduced stress would be measured on a stress scale as a measure of effectiveness.

COST MINIMIZATION ANALYSIS. Analysis of costs or cost–cost of different types of programs and interventive techniques in relation to achieving program outcomes.

COST UTLITY ANALYSIS. Cost analysis emphasizing the value of achieving an outcome for a consumer, a group, or society as a whole.

DEPENDENT VARIABLES. Variables studied as effects or consequences of another variable. In program evaluation, dependent variables are usually the outcomes or program goals.

DISTAL EFFECTS. Ultimate, longer-range effects and goals that have a broader policy context, for example, increasing quality of life, preventing hospitalization, reducing delinquency, or increasing student scores on standardized tests.

DIVERGENCE. Themes and categories that are different from the original themes identified in the qualitative analysis and call for new categories to be created.

DOSAGE. The amount of intervention given to consumers in a program. Dosage can be measured in terms of intensity (e.g., number of contacts per month) and duration (6 months, 1 year, etc.).

DOUBLE-COLUMN FORMAT. An efficient rating-scale format in which statements are listed along the extreme left column and the ratings of "strongly agree" to "strongly disagree," "always to never," etc. are listed in the remainder of the columns.

EMPIRICAL or CRITERION VALIDITY. Determining whether the measure of a concept correlates to some external criterion. For example, a measure of caregiver stress in caring for an aging parent should be correlated with the elderly person's ability to perform the activities of daily living.

EMPOWERMENT EVALUATION. An approach to evaluation that emphasizes the involvement of all program stakeholders, including administrators, staff, consumers, program funders, and government bodies, in a collaborative and participatory process of planning and implementing evaluation activities.

EQUIVALENCE OF GROUPS. The ideal in experimental research, where groups are similar in all respects except that one group received treatment or groups received different forms of treatment.

EVALUABILITY ASSESSMENT. A method for examining the state of a program's development to determine whether the program can be evaluated. Evaluability assessment studies employ a wide variety of methods, such as a review of program documents and interviews with administrators, staff, and consumers, to determine if program processes and goals are clearly stated.

EVIDENCE-BASED PRACTICE (EBP). Narrowly defined as medical, health, social work, or human services practice in which the interventions and practice methods employed are those that have been established as effective, primarily through randomized control experimental studies. More broadly, EBP is "a process involving creating an answerable question based on a client or organizational need, locating the best available evidence to answer the question, evaluating the quality of the evidence as well as its applicability, applying the evidence, and evaluating the effectiveness and efficiency of the solution" (Institute for the Advancement of Social Work Research, 2008. "Evidence-based practice: A brief from the Institute for the Advancement of Social Work Research," p. 1).

EXPERIMENTAL DESIGNS. Research designs in which some people are randomly assigned to the program or other forms of the intervention or to a control group with no intervention. These designs usually have quantitative outcome measures and consumers or clients are studied before and after the program, with the hope that those who attended a particular type of the program will achieve better outcomes or better "net effects" than those who attended less desirable forms of the program or "no program."

EXPERIMENTAL MORTALITY. People in an experiment who drop out between the pretest and the posttest, which may make the groups different at the end of the study.

EXTERNAL VALIDITY. Degree to which the findings generalize to larger populations of program participants or to programs in different settings.

FACE VALIDITY. An initial type of validity in which items selected are judged to see if they appear to be related to the concept.

FOCUS GROUP. A specially selected group of about 6 to 12 people who, in needs assessment studies, may represent potential consumers, planners, experts, or program practitioners. Usually they have had a similar experience, such as attending a particular program. Group members are asked a series of open-ended questions about community and consumers needs, and the types of programs that might meet those needs. Usually descriptive data are recorded and a qualitative analysis of themes is conducted.

FORMATIVE STUDIES. More exploratory studies conducted on a program, for example, process evaluations or monitoring studies that focus more on program process and implementation than on outcomes.

GENERALIZABILITY. When the sample reflects the population and the findings have broader implications for all cases in the program and for the generalizability of the knowledge produced.

GOAL- or OUTCOME-ORIENTED EVALUATIONS. Evaluation studies and surveys that assess the degree to which program objectives and goals are being met. Program outcomes can be studied through a survey after consumers have received the service or by pre–post evaluations documenting changes in knowledge, attitude, behavior, skill, or client status such as gaining employment, reducing symptoms, or improved quality of life.

HAWTHORNE EFFECT. A psychological effect in which subjects show change because they are being studied or observed.

HISTORY or "OUTSIDE EVENTS." Factors outside the program that can cause a change in program participants. Significant outside events should be measured in an evaluation study.

IMPACT ASSESSMENT STUDIES. More formal experimental and quasi-experimental research designs used to determine that the program interventions were the main factors that caused the program outcome or effect.

IMPLAUSIBLE PROGRAM THEORY. When articulated or implied program theory lacks a program logic, that is, it does not seem sensible that a particular intervention could cause an intended effect or outcome.

IMPLIED PROGRAM THEORY. Theory that is not explicitly part of the program design, but is implied in the program logic and interventive methods designed to produce certain results or outcomes.

INDEPENDENT VARIABLES. Variables that are studied as possible causes of the dependent variables. There are two major types of independent variables in program evaluation: the program inputs or the program itself, and the clients or consumers served and their characteristics.

INDIGENOUS THEMES or CONCEPTS. Themes defined in qualitative research by using the respondents' own words and language reflecting their views.

INDUCTIVE ANALYSIS. Proceeding from specific qualitative data, quotes, and cases to themes or concepts that relate to typologies, pre-theory, and building theory from the ground up.

INSTRUMENTATION, TESTING, or MEASUREMENT EFFECT. Tests with less proven reliability when there is instability of measurement. Thus, changes in outcome could be caused by the measurement process, not necessarily by the program or treatment.

INTERNAL VALIDITY. The degree to which the program and the program alone caused the program outcome or effect.

INTER-RATER or INTER-OBSERVER RELIABILITY. Establishing reliability by having two or more raters or observers make judgments about the same observation or case record. A kappa coefficient is used to establish the percent of overall agreement. A high kappa indicates reliability or agreement.

ITEM-TO-ITEM CORRELATION. If two items are measuring the same concept there needs to be a high correlation between a person's score on the two items. This is a type of reliability.

ITEM-TO-TOTAL CORRELATION. If one item on a scale is measuring a concept, there should be a high positive correlation between a person's score on one item and their total score on the scale excluding that one item. This is a type of reliability.

KBASS MODEL. The development and analysis of program goals in relation to changes in knowledge, behavior, attitudes, skills, and status.

KEY LINKAGE. The degree to which a researcher can show that the theme identified exists in the qualitative data so that most people would agree that the data support the trend or theme.

LIKERT SCALE. A summated rating scale using "strongly agree" to "strongly disagree" categories to measure some major outcomes such as attitudes or psychological constructs.

MANAGEMENT INFORMATION SYSTEM (MIS) or CLIENT INFORMATION SYSTEM (CIS). Computerized records that include the characteristics of people in the program and possibly the services they are receiving.

MATURATION. A change that occurs in subjects over time just because of the passage of time, rather than as a result of attending a program.

McNEMAR TEST. A statistic used to study change from the pretest to the posttest when the data are categorical and split into two categories.

METAPHOR. Use of an exaggerated comparison to represent a theme or ideal type of case in qualitative analysis.

MISSION STATEMENT. General statement about the overall focus and intent of the program or the organization where the program is located. Although mission statements are sometimes very vague, they can be helpful in the development of program goals.

MIXED-METHODS STUDY. Study that employs both qualitative methods and quantitative methods to a significant degree.

NEEDS ASSESSMENT. A systematic appraisal, using a variety of research methods to address the nature and scope of a social or health problem that a program might ultimately address.

NEEDS ASSESSMENT STUDIES. Evaluation studies that focus on the processes of program planning and program development. The studies usually employ a variety of research methods and answer questions of whether there is a need for the program and address the types and incidence of that need and the resources or services that might meet those needs.

NEGATIVE CASES. Cases that a qualitative researcher seeks out that went against the main theme or finding first identified by the researcher.

NON-PROBABILITY SAMPLE. More informal samples used in formative evaluations in which there are fewer assurances that the sample will reflect the population.

ONE-WAY ANALYSIS OF VARIANCE (ANOVA). Statistical measure of comparison of mean scores between three or more groups.

OPEN CODING. The initial themes, trends, and categories that the researcher identifies when beginning the analysis and reading through the qualitative data while remaining open to the possibilities.

PAIRED SAMPLE t-TEST. A statistical measure used to study changes between the mean scores on the pretest and the posttest.

PARALLEL FORMS RELIABILITY. Using two different scales or questions measuring the same variables or concepts at different parts in the questionnaire. If both variables or concepts are measuring the same thing, there should be a high positive correlation between them.

PLACEBO EFFECT. The strong psychological impact of program participants thinking they are receiving a correct treatment.

POPULATION. A larger, more inclusive list of people or cases who have used the program.

PRACTICE GOALS. The goals of service for individual clients or consumers that, if they apply to a large number of cases, can also be program goals.

PREDICTIVE VALIDITY. Empirical validity can be predictive if the external criterion is measured after the concept is measured—for example, if caregiver stress is correlated with or predicts a person's decrease in social activities 3 months after the stress is experienced.

PRE–POST STUDY. Studies that measure change before and after participation in the program. Data on a pre-measure and a post-measure are collected, known as the pretest and posttest. For example, major changes in outcome measures of a program, such as knowledge, behaviors, attitudes, skills, or status (KBASS), can be collected before and after the program to see how successful the program was in imparting knowledge or skills to participants, and changing their attitudes, behavior, and status.

PRETEST. In data collection, the process of trying out a questionnaire to see if the questions are clear and that it measures major variables well. Pretesting the instrument should not be confused with the pretest, in which a measurement is taken before the program in pre–post studies or experimental designs.

PROBABILITY SAMPLES. Samples for which the principles of probability are used, to give more assurance that the sample will reflect the population.

PROCESS OBJECTIVES. Objectives that describe the intervention or the means of achieving the program outcomes, for example, "to provide 10 support group sessions to caregivers in which they discuss caregiver stress."

PROCESS EVALUATION. An evaluation study that describes the program model and program activities, determines how the program is being implemented, and assesses initial program goals. Process evaluations are usually characterized by qualitative data about the program process and activities and by more informal types of data collection. For example, a researcher conducting a process evaluation might observe the program in operation and conduct personal interviews with some direct-service staff, administrators, or consumers. The focus of the interview would be to gain thorough descriptions of how the program is being experienced by staff and by program participants.

PROGRAM. A strategy or intervention planned and conducted on a group of people to achieve some desirable consequence or outcome.

PROGRAM ATTRITION. The number and characteristics of people who drop out of the program. A quality evaluation should report on program attrition or dropouts as well as on the people who continued in the program.

PROGRAM EVALUATION. The use of research methods to assess the planning, implementation, and outcomes of social, health, and educational programs.

PROGRAM FIDELITY. The degree to which a program is true to the original program plan or deviates from that plan.

PROGRAM GOALS. The broad outcomes the program hopes to achieve that will need to be measured in an evaluation.

PROGRAM INPUTS. A major type of independent variable that includes the program, program theory, program philosophy, practice methods, types of services, number of service contacts, overall intensity and duration of services, outreach or recruitment methods used, and types of staff in the program.

PROGRAM LOGIC. The sequence of events and interventive techniques that will achieve the program outcomes.

PROGRAM MONITORING. Assessment of the program and program operations that helps to determine factors such as whether the program was implemented as planned, which members of the target population are using the program, whether program outreach seems successful, and the types of initial program successes and failures. In monitoring often structured, quantitative data are used. They can include data from the program's client or management information system, which contains computerized data about the program participants and the services they are receiving.

PROGRAM OBJECTIVES. More concrete and specific program outcomes that may have a time frame of achievement. Program objectives are usually specified in logic models describing the program.

PROGRAM PROCESS MONITORING. A term used by Rossi, Lipsey, and Freeman (*Evaluation: A Systematic Approach*, 2004, p. 171) to acknowledge that both program monitoring and process evaluations are frequently combined in formative program evaluation studies.

PROXIMAL EFFECTS. Short-term goals or immediate changes in consumers as a result of the program. Short-term goals are similar to process objectives.

PURPOSIVE SAMPLE. Sample for which cases are selected on the basis of some criteria that are relevant for the study, for example, a certain type of case (those who attended 5 or more sessions or all cases in the program in the last 90 days). Sometimes referred to as a "purposeful" sample.

QUALITATIVE RESEARCH. The collection and use of less-structured forms of data, in which descriptive trends in the data are analyzed. Qualitative data generate rich, descriptive, in-depth knowledge about a program. For example, program participants are interviewed in person and asked, "What things did you like about the program?" The interviewer asks them to explain their responses, and this results in in-depth, descriptive, qualitative data. The researcher then uses qualitative analysis techniques to examine and report on the trends, for instance, what was it that they liked about the program?

QUANTITATIVE RESEARCH. The collection and use of structured data that can be used in statistical, quantitative data analysis. For example, a researcher asks participants to "rate the program, 10 being the best it could be and 0 the worst." The researcher finds that the average rating is 9.5, meaning that almost everyone rated it the best it could be. Or, the researcher asks a structured question:

"How would you rate the program?

___ excellent (5) ___ very good (4) ___ good (3) ___ fair (2) ___ poor (1)"
The researcher then might find that 75% rated the program as "excellent." Further analysis might show that on a 4-point scale in which 4 was "excellent" and 1 was "poor," consumers who attended group A had an average rating of 4.80 (near excellent), whereas in group B the average rating was 3.90 (close to very good).

QUASI-EXPERIMENTAL DESIGNS. A type of experimental design in which consumers or clients are not randomly assigned to different forms of service. In quasi-experimental designs, consumers receiving different forms of the service may be matched on demographic and other characteristics to help ensure that groups receiving different forms of service or no service are similar, or the researcher may simply study different forms of service, knowing that the groups may not be totally equivalent.

QUOTA SAMPLE. Sample in which a certain a number of cases of different types are selected so that there are enough cases to make some comparisons, for example, 50 males and 50 females.

RELIABILITY. The clarity and consistency of the whole measurement process and parts of that process including questions asked and scales in which a number of items are used to represent a concept.

REPRESENTATIVENESS. When the characteristics of the sample reflect the characteristics of the population.

RIVAL EXPLANATIONS. When the researcher searches for alternate reasons for the findings turning out the way they did in addition to the reasons originally specified by the researcher. This adds validity to the qualitative research findings.

SAMPLE. Cases selected for study from the population list.

SAMPLING ERROR. The degree to which the sample does not reflect the population on a particular characteristic.

SAMPLING PLAN. The steps in the way that cases will be selected for study and the type of sample that will be used.

SATURATION POINT. The point at which it looks like the research has exhausted all the themes, subthemes, and categories in the data, since the same trends and themes keep reappearing in the qualitative analysis.

SECONDARY or AVAILABLE DATA. Data such as case records or program documents collected, not originally intended as evaluation data, which can be used in the evaluation study.

SELECTION BIAS. The way in which people are selected for a program by program staff or the way in which they choose a program or type of treatment that might make groups of participants dissimilar or non-equivalent. Random selection may prevent a selection bias.

SIMPLE RANDOM SAMPLE. A probability sample in which cases are selected from a population list on the basis of random numbers or random selection.

SPLIT-HALF RELIABILITY. Reliability of a scale in which the scale is randomly split into two subscales. If the two scales are measuring the same concept, they should have a high positive correlation. Split-half reliability coefficients use the Spearman-Brown formula.

STAKEHOLDERS. All parties that have an interest in the development of a particular program including administrators, staff, consumers, funding sources, regulative and government bodies, the community, and the public at large.

STRENGTHS PERSPECTIVE. A framework used in both practice and program evaluation which emphasizes the positive aspects and assets of people, communities, and programs.

SURVEY. Study of a group of cases where mostly structured, quantitative data is collected.

SYSTEMATIC SELECTION. A probability sample in which every Nth (e.g., 5th or 10th) case is selected in an orderly manner from a population list.

TARGET POPULATION. The potential consumers, clients, or patients who are thought to benefit most from the program.

TEST–RETEST RELIABILITY. Testing the reliability of a measure or questionnaire by administering the same questions to the same sample or population at two different points in time. High positive correlations indicate high reliability.

TRIANGULATION. A process whereby the researcher tests findings to guard against the accusation that the findings only come from one method, one data source, one researcher, or one theory. Each finding could then by tested by multiple (quantitative versus qualitative) methods, multiple data sources, multiple research analysts, or multiple theories or by exposing the findings to multiple audiences.

t-TEST. A statistical measure of association between two mean scores.

UNANTICIPATED CONSEQUENCES. When both positive and negative effects of a program that were not planned as outcomes are uncovered during the evaluation study. Unanticipated consequences of a program can be found by using qualitative methods, asking open-ended questions about possible program effects, or directly observing the program in operation. The more sketching out and development of possible goals of a program in planning the evaluation study, the fewer unanticipated consequences will be found when the evaluation is completed.

UNIVARIATE ANALYSIS. The first quantitative analysis to be conducted, which includes frequency distributions and percents, tables and charts, and measures of central tendency and dispersion.

VALIDITY. The adequate measurement of a concept you wish to measure. Validity entails how well a concept is being measured, such as quality of care, stress, depression, or health efficacy.

Index